U0591725

共同繁荣与和平发展的新解读

付　敬　著

焦　钰　陈俊宇　译

▼

"一带一路"深化中欧伙伴关系
各国发展战略重新定位
欧亚合作更紧密

SPM

南方出版传媒

广东人民出版社

·广州·

图书在版编目（CIP）数据

共同繁荣与和平发展的新解读 ＝ A New Code for Common Peace and Prosperity ／ 付敬著；焦钰，陈俊宇译. —广州：广东人民出版社，2019.7

ISBN 978-7-218-13077-4

Ⅰ.①共⋯　Ⅱ.①付⋯②焦⋯③陈⋯　Ⅲ.①"一带一路"－国际合作－研究－中国、欧洲　Ⅳ.①F125.55

中国版本图书馆CIP数据核字（2018）第164617号

GONGTONG FANRONG YU HEPING FAZHAN DE XINJIEDU
共同繁荣与和平发展的新解读

付　敬　著

焦　钰　陈俊宇　译

出 版 人：肖风华

责任编辑：卢雪华　李　钦
英语编辑：黄洁华　李丽珊
责任技编：周　杰　吴彦斌
装帧设计：友间文化　六宇文化

出版发行：广东人民出版社
地　　址：广州市海珠区新港西路204号2号楼（邮政编码：510300）
电　　话：（020）85716809（总编室）
传　　真：（020）85716872
网　　址：http://www.gdpph.com
印　　刷：广州市浩诚印刷有限公司
开　　本：889mm×1194mm 1/32
印　　张：14.5　插　页：4　字　数：350千
版　　次：2019年7月第1版
印　　次：2019年7月第1次印刷
定　　价：128.00元（全二册）

如发现印装质量问题，影响阅读，请与出版社（020-85716849）联系调换。
售书热线：（020）85716826

前　言

　　全球化（Globalization）这样的表达虽是近事，但自张骞（前164—前114）出使西域以来，我们的祖先从海上或陆路探险，在亚洲、欧洲和非洲探索贸易路线，他们可以被称为催生全球化萌芽的第一代先驱。

　　后来欧洲人，如马可·波罗（Marco Polo，1254—1324）、克里斯托弗·哥伦布（Cristoforo Colombo，1451—1506）和费迪南德·麦哲伦（Fernando de Magallanes，1480—1521）取得了冒险史上的突破性进步，而他们的国家通过使用积极或消极的手段，改变了世界发展的历史。

　　葡萄牙、西班牙、荷兰、英国、法国、德国和美国都在这个过程中聚集国力，乃至成为世界霸主。二战之后，欧洲和美国一起加快着全球化的步伐。

　　在过去四十年里，来自欧美和亚洲的跨国公司不断扩大国际贸易和对外投资，加速了全球经济增长，而中国在这个过程中通过对内改革和对外开放，飞速发展经济和推动社会发展，创造中国奇迹，提升了全球经济影响力。自21世纪初以来，特别是2008—2009年金融危机以来，世界也得益于中国持续高速的经济增长，中国对世界经济的年贡献率保持在百分之三十左右。

　　如何持续保持这样的全球贡献，如何充分挖掘近14亿人口的市场潜力，是习近平主席在2013年下半年提出的"一带一路"倡议的切入点，答案在于消除中国与亚欧大陆各国之间的各种障碍，增进互联互通，使得亚欧大陆的国家在各个方面进一步缩小距离。

长期以来，我一直在与人探讨这个话题。抓住2017年5月中国举办"一带一路"国际合作高峰论坛的机会，我在3—5月间前往十多个欧洲国家，尽可能多地与政治家、商业领袖和学者交谈，听取他们的高见。

在过去的十年中，中国和世界处在急剧变动中。身为记者，我既感到悲伤，也感到振奋。四川地震、从利比亚撤离中国公民、布鲁塞尔恐怖袭击、气候变化和金融危机，这些新闻让我担心；而奔波于欧洲国家，挖掘他们对于"一带一路"倡议的深入探索丰富了我作为一名记者的职业经历。

在采访中，我很快产生了将欧洲国家对接"一带一路"倡议的可喜进展和他们的隐忧记录下来的想法，而广东人民出版社社长肖风华先生很快接受了我的写书申请。

在编辑黄洁华和李丽珊的大力帮助下，这本书的撰写进展顺利。他们于2017年10月在法兰克福书展安排了新书发布会。南方出版传媒股份有限公司总经理杜传贵先生，德国席勒研究院院长黑尔佳·策普·拉鲁旭（Helga Zepp-LaRouche）女士，比中经贸委员会主席博纳德·德维特（Bernard Dewit）先生和肖风华先生都在我主持的关于"一带一路"倡议和中欧关系的对话中发表了热情洋溢的讲话，我衷心感谢他们。

我也衷心感谢我的人生和职业导师、密友亚历克斯·科比（Alex Kirby）。这位来自英国广播公司的资深记者与我相识多年，在2017年夏天帮助我润色了书中的语言，纠正了文字错误，提高了该书的质量，他的投入极大地增加了文章的可读性。再次感谢亚历克斯，我欠你一杯啤酒。

我还要感谢中国日报社总编辑周树春先生、编委会其他成员和我的同事们的长期支持和帮助，他们让我2017年上半年密集的出差成为可能。当然，还要感谢我的实习生郑锦强、张兆卿、王科举等，他们帮助我安排采访，在我写这本书的过程中也提供了很多帮助。同时我特别感谢陈俊宇和焦钰，他们不畏艰辛，将我的英文版书稿翻译成中文。

当然，写作对于家庭和闲暇时间来说意味着很多的牺牲，我必须要感谢多年来妻儿的理解和帮助。

这本书肯定不是完美的，我为任何错误负责。

付敬，完稿于2017年年底

目录 ·········

1
·······

01

"一带一路"倡议促"不协调"欧盟走向复苏

在 2013 年 9 月，当习近平首次作为中国国家主席在俄罗斯圣彼得堡二十国集团峰会上亮相时，他的团队非常具有前瞻性，中国的二十国集团峰会代表团在各国领导人召开会议之前第一个召开新闻发布会，积极主动地阐述了中国的想法和主张。这种积极进取的外交动作之后，习近平主席旋即便在哈萨克斯坦首都阿斯塔纳的演讲中提出"新丝绸之路经济带"倡议。我当时在俄罗斯的二十国集团峰会的现场；而在这个倡议提出之后，我很快便意识到"丝绸之路经济带"具有的重大意义：我认为它会在接下来的数年里主导中国新领导集体的外交棋局。

习近平在 2012 年末举行的中国共产党第十八次全国代表大会上被选举为党的最高领导人，之后在 2013 年年初，他开始担任中国国家主席。他在阿斯塔纳的一所大学的演讲中提出"丝绸之路经济带"倡议后，在 10 月访问印度尼西亚时提出了建设"21 世纪海上丝绸之路"的计划。本着让中国更加开放，与世界联系更加紧密的考虑，该倡议恰好回应了西方近年来持续地对北京能够分担更多国际责任的呼唤。2008—2009 年的金融危机以后，这些西方国家的需求开始变得更加迫切；而近距离观察欧洲在之后几年是如何回应中国的"一带一路"倡议非常有意义。

2017 年上半年从希腊到瑞士，我在探寻西方国家是如何回应习近平主席在 2013 年前提出的"一带一路"倡议的旅程中发现了许多新思想。在那几个月中我与将近百名政客、官员、思想者、律师和商人耐心地交谈，在港口、机场、工厂和建筑工地中挖掘故事，这使得次次旅程引人深思。

虽然自"一带一路"倡议发布之初我就密切关注其发展，但我的这些采访仍然丰富了我对于该倡议的理解和认知。和意大利前总理罗马诺·普罗迪（Romano Prodi）的交谈很好地总结了我的发现，他称中国的"一带一路"倡议是世纪性的、可以影响近半数世界人口的项目。他说欧洲国家正在互相竞争去寻找与中国"一带一路"倡议合作的机会。他已经敦促意大利政府不要在这次竞争中落后。

实际上，在现今世界的一些地区地缘政治逐渐恶化的背景之下，并且在从美国和欧洲起源的金融次贷危机和主权债务危机的消极影响仍在持续的情况下，这个倡议是中国给出的重建世界和平与繁荣的明确信号。

在2012—2017年里，"一带一路"倡议起到最大的作用就是作为帮助其他国家在地理位置和地缘政治上重新定位自身优势和独特性的催化剂，将亚洲、欧洲和非洲纳入到一个大的全球供应链上或者经济走廊上。许多国家已经重燃它们的热情，并且找到勇气去推出它们的长期国家发展战略。比方说，希腊决心成为区域性船运、能源和交通中心，匈牙利和捷克已经表示他们想要成为区域性航空、物流和金融的中心，塞尔维亚致力于成为巴尔干地区的门户。这些治国理政战略上的变化无疑是振奋人心的，因为这样的远大目标和战略的实施不仅会加快发展本国经济、创造更多就业机会、促进提高当地生活水平，还会成为弥合欧洲区域差异的有力工具。

许多人说西欧相比于中东欧国家至今没有对"一带一路"倡议表现出同等的热情，而且西欧国家也没有清楚表明为了更好地落实"一带一路"而实施的国家战略是什么。但是我认为这些是不值得担心的。随着时间的推移,这些国家会找到更多机会追上其他国家紧随"一带一路"的脚步。

意大利此前在和中国的中兴通讯合作一个总值 10 亿美元的项目,项目是为了推动意大利本国的通信基础设施建设,为意大利进入 5G 时代做准备。这就意味着只要双方都决心去寻找合作机会,即使与发达国家经济体,中国也可以找到促进互联互通的机会。瑞士作为观察员参与到中国与 16 个中东欧国家合作框架中,这是一个范例,为三方合作创造了很好的条件。

大部分欧洲发达国家都是亚洲基础设施投资银行的成员国,并且,通过"一带一路"倡议,他们会寻找到更多合作机会。总之,"一带一路"倡议的实质,其实不仅仅是中国资本、技术、人力、观念和思想的输出,同时也包括国外的资本、技术、人力资源流入到中国;并且该倡议还鼓励中国和发达国家开展第三方务实合作,这更需要耐心。一些欧洲国家需要结构性的改革,但它们的法律体系很是复杂,这就使得它们在投资时需要再三考虑。

西方国家常说,罗马非一日之功建成的,改变需要时间。在对中国通信巨头中兴通讯意大利分公司的采访中,他们的口号"时不待我"同样振聋发聩。为了广泛传递"一带一路"倡议,具有耐心和灵活性对取得共识和促进共同行动具有重要意义。

走上逐步接受之路

"一带一路"倡议刚提出的时候，我可能是第一批去探究中国的"一带一路"倡议和欧盟投资计划对接的人。在 2014 年年末写的专栏中，我就发出了这样的感慨：即使离取得成效还有很长的路要走，但我仍为"一带一路"已经成为两大经济体的主要外交政策感到开心，即使共识的达成离实现还很远。

下面就是我 2014 年年末发表在《中国日报》上的评论：

西方长期以来一直呼吁中国承担更多国际责任。自 2008—2009 年金融危机爆发后，这样的声音愈演愈烈。然而，正当北京开始积极为世界输送更多机遇时，其他几个大国却又表现得有些"无动于衷"。

最近一次插曲发生在 11 月二十国集团峰会。在澳大利亚布里斯班，欧委会主席容克首次作为欧盟机构领导人与中国国家主席习近平会面。

就在二十国集团峰会召开前几天，亚太经合组织领导人非正式会议在北京闭幕。习近平主席的"一带一路"构想当仁不让成为本轮 APEC 峰会的焦点。再观欧洲，"投资与就业"位列欧盟新掌门的任期内十大重任之首。

习近平主席的"一带一路"与容克的"刺激投资"可谓天造地设般契合。这般"合拍"，当然也引得中欧各界对两位最高领导人的初次对话一阵热盼。

可结果却让人不免失望。肩负招商引资大任的容克，在与习近平主席进行首次历史性会面时，对万众瞩目的"丝路"战略只字未提。汇聚欧盟大小事务新闻资讯的欧委会官方网站，就连两人的双边会晤都未曾公布。回想2014年3月习近平主席访欧期间，欧盟还满心欢喜欲与中国一道在各合作领域大展拳脚。虽说当时为上任主席巴罗佐掌权时代，但欧盟对外关系政策具有延续性，绝不会因巴罗佐的离去而人走茶凉。

说回习近平主席的"丝绸之路"构想，2013年9月出访哈萨克斯坦，习近平主席在其首都阿斯塔纳的纳扎尔巴耶夫大学发表演讲时，首次提出"丝路"理念。此后一年多，中国不断致力于将此构想付诸实际。在国内，各省市都受邀向此横跨欧亚大计贡献宝贵意见。

2014年10月，中国国务院总理李克强在米兰出席亚欧首脑会议期间，也向其他50位国家元首再次隆重介绍了"丝路"提议。11月初召开的APEC峰会上，习近平主席更召开专题会议讨论"丝路"，会议期间也确立了亚洲基础设施投资银行及丝绸之路基金。"丝路"构想实为中国由资本、技术吸收大国转向投资输出国推波助澜。

虽说"丝路"仍处初期构想阶段，但此理念毋庸置疑是习近平、李克强领导下中国对外关系的一大重要政策导向。自习近平主席上任后，除了最新的丝绸之路经济走廊、海上丝绸之路提议，中国已执行了一系列极具突破性的改革以及大规模反腐倡廉举措。

"丝路"构想将直接影响沿途亚欧大陆的30亿人口，在全球范围已引起广泛关注。更有学者拿当年美国为振兴欧洲战后经济而实行的"马歇尔计划"与中国的新"丝绸之路"作比较。对此，北京表态中国没有美国二战后那般的全球野心。习近平主席此前发表演讲时，也明确指出中国"丝路"旨在建设基础设施的同时，推动国际贸易增长，促进资本、人力资源流动，以及深化人文交流。

古代"丝路"一路西伸直入意大利。容克接棒巴罗佐时，也恰巧正逢意大利担任轮值主席国。历史存在偶然性，也具有一定必然性。中国"丝路"概念到了欧洲，并没有想象中那般"受待见"。而事实上，全面深化欧洲一体化、加强欧盟单一市场建设，容克为欧盟勾勒的蓝图与习近平主席的"丝路"方案亦有异曲同工之处，两者政策的核心都在于"流动"二字。

游走在第三次坠入经济衰退的悬崖边，为解救欧洲经济窘况，容克欧委会近日宣布了欧盟未来三年向市场注入 3150 亿欧元投资的刺激增长方案。容克的提振计划却被批为"缺乏新意"。的确，眼下要实现经济突围，欧洲需要的恰恰是类似习近平主席"丝绸之路"这样存在无限遐想空间的新主意。

有人说，欧洲近年"家事繁忙"，无力关心"外面的世界"。此话着实难以服众，中国同样面临国内巨大结构性改革压力，不也眼观六路？急待结构性调整这样的理由，并不能成为欧洲制度陈旧、发展缺少"创意"的合理借口。

在 2014 年，2008 年金融危机之后的第六个年头，欧盟仍处于进入第三个经济低迷期的边缘，这说明欧盟应该开始仔细思考原因了。正当欧洲加紧长期的结构化改革之时，中国的"一带一路"倡议会给欧盟注入新鲜活力，尽管欧洲决心继续长期的结构化改革。在21世纪之初，中国决定通过实施西部大开发战略去深化改革开放；现今，当你重新审视欧盟和它的28个成员国，你会有种似曾相识的感觉，东欧、中欧和南欧落后于西欧和北欧。

东方，香港与上海的成功案例，倒是给一些欧洲人提了醒。比如说，占居重要地理位置，希腊雅典是否也能摇身一变成为地中海地区的航运金融中心？

可惜比起其他一些经济大国在基建领域的踌躇满志，欧盟实在是没有多少雄心壮志。欧盟境内高铁不足7000公里，规划中也只是2030年延伸至15000公里。要知道，欧洲可是高铁的"鼻祖"，早在20世纪80年代就建有高铁。反观中国，高铁时代启动六七年，如今中国境内高铁已覆盖13000公里，2020年更将达到30000公里。

要提振经济，欧盟何不参照下中国的新兴主意。若能建成连接北京、布鲁塞尔、巴黎、伦敦的高铁，必将令沿路地区受益匪浅。

这些计划不是水中月镜中花，其实是完全可行的。北京和莫斯科已经开始实施通过高速铁路联通彼此的计划，而且莫斯科离中东欧也不是很远，然而，相对于它的成员国来说，欧盟对于在拓宽和中国的关系方面是相对保守的，欧盟在结束中国和欧盟关于投资协定谈判之前，甚至不想要开启中欧之间关于自由贸易协定的谈判，这与欧盟积极与美国和其他国家开启该谈判形成了鲜明的对比。然而在2015年的两次会议上，欧盟会有不只一个和中国进行谈判对话的机会。中国的西向发展战略很可能会和欧洲的东向战略协同，继而欧盟会对北京的新丝绸之路项目做一些积极贡献。

绿色和数字"一带一路"

上面的文字帮助我在 2015 年获得中国新闻奖一等奖。而我很高兴在欧洲工作的这段时间有幸与几位学者丰富了"一带一路"概念。

2016 年 3 月 17 日在巴黎，《中国日报》和法国诺欧商学院（NEOMA Business School）一起举办了一场研讨会，在会上，绿色"一带一路"的想法成型。5 个月之后，习近平主席在主持一次关于该倡议的会议时也开始使用绿色"一带一路"的概念。而早些时候，在我和诺欧商学院商务孔子学院院长张海晏教授讨论时，我们决定将这个话题作为在巴黎举行的中国新丝绸之路会议的主题，在会上，欧洲的商业代表和学术代表表达了对"一带一路"倡议的信心，相信中国会提供绿色的工业技术，使得"一带一路"沿线国家能够互联互通。

这一绿色概念被在场包括孔子学院的代表，来自中国银行、中国汽车制造商比亚迪、中国通信巨头华为和法国电力巨头 EDF 的中欧商业代表们热烈讨论。张教授在会上说从 2013 年"一带一路"倡议发布以后，亚欧之间对于经济和工业合作有了逐渐增加的兴趣；但是关于环境问题的可行性和结果的担忧也被表达出来了，环境问题一直被认为是实施"一带一路"倡议的关键因素，尤其在全球对于气候变化的忧虑逐渐加深的大环境之下。"这是我们要联合《中国日报》一起组织这个活动的原因，但是从我们的讨论可以看出中国正极力推进绿色合作，正在和新丝绸之路上的国家实现绿色共同发展。"张教授说。

我同时也在思考"一带一路"倡议是在我们处于的数字时代的大环境之下实施的。中国手机用户从 2017 年 10 月开始在中国大陆境内漫游不需要再支付漫游费用，欧盟成员国用户从 2017 年 6 月中旬开始也可以享受这种在欧盟境内免除漫游费的福利。许多人说这个由中国移动、中国联通和中国电信发起的变革是受智能手机用户更喜欢用社交媒体和亲朋好友沟通交流这一转变影响的，比如说，在中国有超过 8 亿的用户使用微信这个社交软件来发送信息、买票、订餐、预订酒店甚至叫的士，也有许多用户更倾向于使用 WhatsApp 或者 Skype，这也说明了移动手机服务端的竞争从未消退过。

尽管欧洲人比中国人在社交媒体上花费的时间普遍更少，但在某种程度上有些相似的原因导致欧盟的通信运营商取消欧盟境内的漫游费用，欧盟也一直在思考建立单一的数字化市场，这一举措是欧盟委员会工作的首要议程。取消漫游费用是移动通信服务商作出的决定性的举措，这一举措将 28 个成员国各自相对分裂的通信市场整合到一起，当然这一举措也同样面临诸多重大挑战。

欧盟和中国的运营商们现在可以考虑其他的更加重大的变革，因为他们有巨大的消费者市场。中国和欧盟为达成投资协定正在进行艰难磋商，希望这些磋商者同样可以讨论由中欧的通信公司主导的更深层次的市场合作和相互渗透。现在中欧的通信公司都取消了境内的漫游费用，他们同样应该考虑为那些常在中欧之间出差往来的人们取消国际漫游费用。这一变革为中欧开拓数字化市场提供了更大的潜能，尽管说服双方的通信巨头实现这个变革是很难的，但是这些努力会是值得的。从长远来看，这些通信运营商没有理由在国际漫游上高收费，中欧单一的数字化市场一旦成型，其带来的效益是巨大的，因为这一变革会减少沟通阻碍并且帮助促进投资流动。

因为中国主导的"一带一路"倡议是致力于拉近亚、欧、非三大洲的关系，以免除漫游费为依托的中欧单一数字化市场的形成对于如何开拓更大的市场会起到很好的示范作用。在 2018 年，旅游已成为中欧联系的纽带。未来，双方可能会进一步讨论取消在两地旅游的移动手机用户漫游费用的可能性，因为这有利于帮助促进两地的旅游业蓬勃发展。

不断累积的认同度

"一带一路"倡议作为中国外交的指导框架，中国将其视作实现和平与发展的重要倡议，这一倡议的内涵会通过与欧洲的合作而得以扩展，在北京的"一带一路"国际合作高峰论坛上，许多欧盟成员国表达了助推"一带一路"的热切期待。

希腊总理阿莱克斯·齐普拉斯（Alexis Tsipras）说，这一倡议着重体现了富有远见性的中欧间的甚至和世界其他地方的连接、合作和对话。匈牙利的总理欧尔班·维克托（Orbán Viktor）同样也是出席该论坛的欧洲领袖之一，他说过去的国际化和全球化模式已经过时，"中国已经迎头赶上了西方"。他将"一带一路"倡议视作"改革的另一个方向，尤其是建立在相互接受的基础上的"，欧尔班还说布达佩斯—贝尔格莱德350公里长的铁路线的现代化改造是中国、塞尔维亚和他的国家之间签订的"最赞"的协定。

通过参与该倡议，这些参与国不仅可以从基础设施建设上受益，同时也可以与国际供应链相连。尽管已经启动了脱欧谈判，但是现在仍是欧盟成员国的英国，同样坚决支持这一提案。英国财政大臣菲利普·哈蒙德（Philip Hammond）说，英国位于"一带一路"的西部终点，是"天然的合作伙伴"，并且英国在近几百年一直是开放的国际贸易体系的强烈支持者。他说英国可以给"一带一路"沿线国家基础设施建设提供资金或者其他必要的支持。

在这方面英国已经是先行者。

当2013年中国提出建设亚洲基础设施投资银行的时候，英国是不顾美国的阻碍第一个站出来回应的西方国家。现今，包括最新加入的希腊，几乎半数欧盟国家都相继加入了这个新生的多边投资银行；甚至欧洲投资银行也与亚投行签订了谅解备忘录，而亚投行自2016年年初成立后已经有超过90个成员加入。

尽管成员国和企业积极响应，但欧盟并未表现出明显的积极性。欧盟委员会副主席于尔基·卡泰宁（Jyrki Katainen）在北京论坛发表讲话时说，"一带一路"的一端是中国，另一端是欧洲。

但他仍然有所犹豫。他继续说："以正确的方式来增加跨境投资可以带来巨大的增长潜力，对我们所有人都有好处。"卡泰宁重申了在中国已经发表的倡议书中提到的公开、透明和可持续性的原则，这些原则是中国早在2015年年初发布的"一带一路"倡议白皮书中强调的内容。专家和中国观察员一直在敦促欧盟发表与其成员国立场一致的意见。欧洲学院（the College of Europe）欧中研究中心研究员邓肯·傅立门（Duncan Freeman）说："欧盟成员国和企业界的意见将是实施'一带一路'的核心，这个项目的成功将建立在共同商业利益的基础之上。"

他补充说，2017年5月举行的北京论坛已经表明，"一带一路"思路已经在全球范围内产生了重要影响，欧盟应该给予高度重视。他还表示，论坛对"一带一路"如何落实以及如何影响中国与其他合作伙伴之间的关系给出了更为详尽的细节。傅立门说："中欧关于'一带一路'的共识将是中欧作为伙伴成功实施该倡议的关键。"

而欧盟委员会前主席、意大利前总理普罗迪指出，在探索与"一带一路"倡议的协作关系方面，"欧洲国家之间的竞争"是令人鼓舞的。但令他感到遗憾的是欧盟层面缺乏合作。"倡议引起了学界和商界的兴趣，但你必须知道这是一个经济和政治项目。"欧盟的政治大师普罗迪说。普罗迪称这是一个世纪项目，可以为全球一半人口提供更好的生计。他说："（在这个项目上）我们必须花费在政治合作上需要的所有耐心。"

尽管如此，时任中国驻欧盟大使杨燕怡对中欧两个合作伙伴之间的协同合作表示满意。她说："公平地说，中欧在实现共同增长、发展和互联互通方面有很多共同点，在'一带一路'倡议方面也是如此，并且迄今为止取得了傲人的成绩。"

习近平主席在2014年初访问欧盟总部时，双方就开始探讨这个问题。当李克强总理2015年在布鲁塞尔与欧洲领导人举行峰会时，双方就支持"一带一路"倡议和3150亿欧元"欧洲投资计划"之间的协同发展达成一致。在成员国层面，中国和数个欧洲国家签署了政府间合作协议，启动了"一带一路"工作组机制，共同推进"一带一路"倡议。

中国启动了与欧洲一些国家的双向铁路货运服务，其中包括中英之间的第一条直通货运路线，它于2017年初投入运营。杨大使说："中国和欧洲国家之间在铁路、港口、机场、电力、运输和物流等领域的双边或三边合作也势头强劲。"

杨大使说，展望未来，中国和欧盟应该继续致力于自由贸易和经济开放，以规则为基础，同时建立透明、公平的国际贸易制度和秩序。她还表示，时间会证明，那些认为"一带一路"就是中国开拓新市场，会对欧洲的未来带来挑战甚至是威胁的说法是错误的、毫无根据的。

实际上，习近平主席提出"一带一路"倡议已有几年，我经常接触的许多中国和欧洲的学者对此进行了研究，位于比利时的欧洲学院欧中研究中心的教授门镜就是其中之一。她在完成关于"一带一路"倡议在2016年会如何影响中国与欧盟的关系的访谈之后，发现欧洲领导人已经意识到这一计划的双赢性，"一带一路"能够使亚欧大陆关系更加密切。"他们的回答总体上是积极的，他们已经认识到习近平主席的提议的重要性。"在 2016 年 10 月与我一起谈话时，她在风景如画的中世纪小镇布鲁日的学院办公室里这样说道。这是由她的团队的三名同事完成的一次调查，从 2016 年 6 月开始密集采访了约 40 位商界人士、智库专家和欧洲官员。

除了进行面对面的访谈，他们还发放了问卷，得到了欧洲排名前二十的智库的答复，这些智库曾经发表过关于中国建设"丝绸之路经济带"和"21 世纪海上丝绸之路"的论文。习近平主席在 2013 年 9 月和 10 月访问中亚和东南亚时提出的这两个想法，实质上，"带"包括原古丝绸之路上的中亚、西亚、中东和欧洲的国家。但北京方面表示，这个倡议没有界定边界，所有有兴趣的国家都可以互相磋商交流。

门镜说，许多欧洲人已经知道这一提议，而且中国和联合国已经就此签署了谅解备忘录。"当我和他们交谈的时候，没有人认为这是一个具有战略性威胁的项目，他们都相信这将是一个互利的好想法。"针对中国主导的提案可能对世界其他国家造成威胁这一说法，门镜这样回应。经过几年的努力，以及中国对落实"一带一路"的大力推动，门镜总结道："这种误解已经消失了。"

2014 年 4 月 1 日，习近平主席提出"一带一路"倡议近 6 个月后，他作为中国国家主席在第一次西欧之行的最后一站访问了欧洲学院，当天，习近平主席对于在欧洲学院建立欧中研究中心表示赞同。他说，双方需要建立和平、增长、改革和文明的伙伴关系，门镜于 2008 年加入该学院并担任欧中关系研究的教授。

作为研究中心的主任，门镜说下一阶段的重点会放在从"一带一路"倡议带来的机遇中受益。过去几年，中国已经与多个国家签署了跟国家经济和社会发展计划相关的协议，其中一些是欧洲国家，如波兰、捷克和希腊。2015 年 6 月，中国与欧盟签署了"一带一路"协议和欧洲 3150 亿欧元投资计划的协同发展协议，这个协议在经过几年运作后，其规模会随着时间的推移而扩大。

双方在通过探索大型项目协同发展来促进贸易和投资流动方面达成了共识，中国是欧盟之外第一个加入投资计划的国家，但是双方在技术层面上还没有达成共识。"据说，欧盟方面从机制上是欢迎中国投资的，但是他们不愿意公开在会上讨论这个倡议，这样的话，北京方面是不会同意的，"门镜说，"所以进入详细谈判环节仍然存在诸多不确定性。"

门镜还表示，南欧、东欧和中欧比西欧对"一带一路"更感兴趣，他们认为"一带一路"的路线不包括欧洲西部。实际上，习近平主席是从几百年前延伸到意大利的古代丝绸之路中汲取的这一理念。

门镜说："布鲁塞尔和雅典是完全不同的。"在谈到她在希腊比雷埃夫斯港的采访经历时，她表示"欣喜"，中国远洋海运集团已经在那里开展了主要业务。几年前中国远洋海运集团租用了集装箱码头，2016 年中远集团收购了比雷埃夫斯港务局 67% 的股份。"中远集团进入后，几乎没有人从港务局离开，当时我在那里采访时，办公楼里我几乎没有见到中国人。"门镜说。

"希腊人民对于保住了工作感到高兴，他们为中远集团在比雷埃夫斯的实力折服。"1000 多名希腊人在这个集装箱码头工作，甚至在希腊债务危机最困难的时候也保住了他们的工作。门镜说："希腊人希望在中远的帮助下复兴已经转移到世界其他地方的修船业。" 其实，更为雄心勃勃的计划是将海运与铁路连接起来，这会帮助比雷埃夫斯成为地中海最大的集装箱转运港口之一，同时它也会成为通往中欧和东欧的门户。"这更具挑战性，需要欧洲不同国家之间的深度协作。" 门镜说。她去希腊的实地考察帮助她更好地理解了中国的"一带一路" 带来的实质性利益。

"首先，欧洲人最急需的就是工作。" 作为研究欧盟与中国关系的教授，门镜说。从习近平主席提出倡议之后，她自己也经历了一个学习曲线。从 2014 年开始，她被邀请在中欧两方的各种研讨会上发言。

她已经开始组织研讨会去发掘双方的观点，探讨如何进一步深化这个概念。近年来她把大部分的研究精力集中在这个话题上，她说学术活动已经帮助欧洲人更好地理解了这个倡议。

中国浦东干部学院"一带一路" 与长江经济带研究中心主任毛新雅于 2016 年年初赴欧洲学院做访问学者，并启动了关于习近平主席的"一带一路"倡议对于中欧关系有何影响的研究项目。除了访谈和调查之外，他们的团队还研究了土耳其在实施中欧大型项目的协同发展中能够起到的作用。

2016 年年底，他们在欧洲议会举行了由欧洲议会对华关系代表团团长乔·莱恩（Jo Leinen） 主持的研究成果研讨会。"一带一路"倡议已成为中国加深与世界各国联系的平台，门镜表示，她的研究中心将在这些领域上下更多的功夫。"'一带一路'及其对中欧关系的影响将是我们未来几年的研究重点。我们希望在未来以更创新的方式进行研究，并且能够取得更多的研究成果。"

02

丝绸之路推动西方文明的
摇篮希腊复兴

自古以来欧洲的国家都有优越的地理位置和独特的发展优势。举例来说，世界上没有一个大陆板块像欧洲大陆这样拥有稳定的自然结构以及宜人的气候条件（除了意大利和希腊之外整个欧洲大陆至今都没有受到大的地震危害）。此外，希腊拥有它自己独特的魅力，这个约1100万人口（2017年），仅为北京市人口二分之一的国家却是中国学生了解欧洲历史的第一课。

但是近些年历史性的光环已经开始褪去。2010年10月我第一次访问雅典，那时正值欧洲债务危机开始席卷希腊以及欧洲其他国家。从那时开始，我有幸获得很多机会和这个经济资产当时位列世界前十的国家的很多政府官员、学术精英、商业领袖甚至是出租车司机以及大街上的失业者交谈。实际上，希腊早已是处于世界经济发展中上游水平的国家：它的人均GDP和人类发展指数排名远高于中国。但是它天文数字的债务打乱了它的经济周期，政府无法继续维持养老金、医疗保险的支出，甚至连公务员工资也都无法支付，更不用说投资基础设施的扩建了。

中国人常说聪明的人往往来自于广大的人民群众，两位希腊受访者告诉了我他们普通希腊人希望将希腊救出于水深火热的富有远见、殷切以及清晰的想法。他们所分享的振奋人心的想法时至今日依然萦绕在我的心头：希腊，这个西方文明的摇篮，一定会和改革开放以来中国取得举世瞩目的经济成就一样，迎来自己的经济复兴。

"一带一路"倡议由中国国家主席习近平于2013年提出的，显而易见，两位希腊受访者并没有明确地说出他们对此倡议的具体想法。但是他们受访时所阐明的观点实质上和"一带一路"提议大致相同：希腊必须大胆地尝试和创新，通过将他们的人民、企业与广大的亚欧大陆、非洲大陆地区的经济联系起来，实现属于自己的繁荣与和平。

2011年年底，我有幸遇见了我在希腊的第一位受访者克里斯托·弗拉霍斯（Christos Vlachos），一位高大的希腊中年人，他和很多希腊精英阶层人士一样在英国出色地完成他们的学业后回到自己国家工作。作为总部位于雅典的咨询公司Silky Finance的经营合伙人，同时也是一位受雇于许多家大型公司的独立经济顾问（其工作主要帮助公司重建和融资），弗拉霍斯已经从我在希腊的受访者变成了我在希腊的好朋友。我每次拜访希腊时都会和他见面，他总会热情地招待我，有次我甚至还在一个很传统的雅典街区拜访了他慈祥的母亲，他母亲带着我们去了一家他们经常一起去的当地小有名气的餐厅共进晚餐。时至今日我都还能记得餐厅的老板开心地和我合照的场景。弗拉霍斯说等他到中国拜访我的时候一定也要受到同样的待遇，但是我至今还没有机会在中国的土地上尽地主之谊。

回到2011年的冬天，当希腊人还在经济衰退的伤痛中挣扎时，弗拉霍斯仍鼓舞他的同胞，他相信他的同胞仍然拥有许多历史、经济、文化、社会和地理位置等优势去赢得一个更好的未来，他相信只要政治领袖们愿意，总会有办法去改变现状，还有就是这个国家迫切需要政治上的统一，特别是在政府接连换任的情况下。

弗拉霍斯说领导人需要展示带领人民走出困难的决心、勇气和决断力，在晚饭期间他以一种让我震惊的语气告诉我："希腊人需要被政治领导人的短期措施和远见卓识所激励。"他说，比如，希腊人会思考从中国拉来投资去建造连通希腊北部从首都雅典到第二大城市塞萨洛尼基的高速铁路，他认为这个对希腊来说不可想象的 500 公里高铁项目可能会给希腊带来翻天覆地的变化。

几年前，选择乘坐高铁往返于城市间的出行方式已经在中国日益流行起来，弗拉霍斯在这些年花了大量时间去关注中国高铁的发展，亲眼见证了不断迭代提高的中国高速铁路速度，十分迫切地希望能将中国这个奇迹般的项目引进到希腊。弗拉霍斯在 2011 年接受采访时提道："我们花费了大量的时间去让我们的政府摆脱以往的保守举措从而接受这项提议，我们不应该一次又一次地让人民对政府感到失望。"

2014 年 6 月在希腊对一个经验丰富的希腊船东的采访也让我印象深刻，他认为雅典应该像香港那样成为全球的海运和金融中心。他的远见如此激励人心让我记忆犹新。作为一名经验丰富的行业领导者，生于 1942 年的乔治·格拉特斯（George Gratsos）作为希腊船运协会的主席已经航行去过世界上许多繁荣的港口，他坚信中国是希腊发展的榜样。

在他距希腊议会仅一街之隔的办公室中采访，其间，他低下声音告诉我："希腊毗邻南欧、东欧和中欧，它发达的铁路网络使得港口成为绝佳的商品分配中心，希腊高层应该进一步深入地和主要港口的运营者们进行合作，最好从远东地区开始。中远集团（中国航运巨头）的运营已经取得了成功，我们支持它在比雷埃夫斯的扩张。"

他还补充道："如果双方都愿意去促成雅典成为国际航运和

商业中心，雅典是有能力成为下一个香港的。" 我在写关于希腊这个和瑞士、比利时、瑞典人口差不多的国家的文章时常常会引用以上这句话。

40年以前，当中国处于改革开放的初期，香港也曾是当时还是小渔村的深圳的发展榜样，此去经年，深圳已经成为了成功的典范，从小渔村成长为人口规模和希腊相当的特大城市，现在深圳被视为中国发展北京周边的雄安新区的典范。可以确定的是，雅典作为亚欧非的关口具有得天独厚的地理位置，但是这一地理位置能否被开发的关键在于希腊领导人能否将这一机会转化为行动，还有就是欧盟是否支持他们这一行动。如果事情进展顺利，希腊人民有一天会享受和香港、深圳人民一样的发展水平，他们的生活水平甚至可能超过瑞士和荷兰的生活水平。

"一带一路" 与希腊的腾飞

希腊是在讨论如何实施"一带一路"的国家中已经设计了基础设施建设蓝图的国家之一。

通常，当中国或者其他亚洲国家通过海运出口到西欧、中欧或者东欧时，集装箱巨轮从印度洋、地中海穿过，到达西欧的港口之后再卸货。

船运可能在抵达目的地之前仍需要花费更多的时间在货车或者火车上，再运到中东欧。近些年，节省时间和成本的其他运输方式也初具规模。希腊港口比雷埃夫斯充分利用被中远集团接管后基础设施条件提高的优势，使得集装箱可以在那里登陆之后直接通过（马其顿）斯科普里—（塞尔维亚）贝尔格莱德铁路线运送至匈牙利的布达佩斯。这条海路运输路线在经过沿线国家的准许之后是可行的，但是它的运输速度相对较慢，因为铁路需要现代化改造，并且有时铁路会在到达马其顿时被难民阻断。

从比雷埃夫斯到货船的终点的这段铁路只是 2013 年由习近平主席提出的，通过建设基础设施、促进贸易投资，从而更好地连接亚欧非的"一带一路"倡议中的很小的一部分。希腊政府已经清楚地意识到这个倡议会怎样帮助他们实现他们成为区域性港口，巴尔干地区、地中海地区和北非的能源和经济中心，更重要的是，这会帮助希腊吸引到更多中国在基础设施方面的投资，一条连接布达佩斯和贝尔格莱德的高速铁路项目已经在进行中，并且希腊对这样的项目很是青睐。

这种发展前景让希腊总理阿莱克斯·齐普拉斯在 2017 年 5 月在北京举行的"一带一路"国际合作高峰论坛上这样总结道，希腊在"一带一路"中起到重要作用。作为西方文明的发祥地的领导人，齐普拉斯参照历史这样说，一千五百多年前拜占庭帝国的查士丁尼大帝派基督教徒去东方探索丝绸制作的奥秘，"之后经过许多冒险，他们将蚕茧藏在他们的包裹之下返回到现在的色雷斯，那是第一次将丝绸引入欧洲。"

但是齐普拉斯指出，如果丝绸之路在今天被重新讲述，世界不仅仅会回忆起一段强权、宗教、民族和商业利益方面的相互合作、竞争的历史，更会了解到历史进程中人民的沟通和交流。据齐普拉斯说:"我们不仅仅会看到丝绸之路是如何从上而下发展的,同样也在自下而上地构建着,中国和希腊人民的商业和文化交流可以追溯到千年以前。"

尽管中国和希腊已经开展了双边贸易、合作和旅游交往,用勤奋努力给予对方灵感,但在齐普拉斯看来,两国之间的经济、文化、教育、研究交流和旅游的真正的高速发展仅仅是近些年的事情,特别是随着多边战略合作关系的确立和"一带一路"倡议的发展。

齐普拉斯,一个从不戴领带的领导人,说,"一带一路"倡议是建立在发展基础设施和互联互通项目的基础上的,它能够使欧洲、亚洲和世界其他地方联系得更加紧密,但是如果"一带一路"倡议只是一系列的项目,那么"一带一路"的愿景将很难被实现,它也不会成为21世纪一条焕发勃勃生机的新的丝绸之路。"一带一路"提供给我们一个推进人们相互沟通的平台,我相信我们会充分利用这个平台。齐普拉斯说:"总体来说,我坚信'一带一路'需要强大的以人为主题的项目来实现其愿景,就像我们的工程师说的那样,愿景需要深厚的基础,这样它才能得到自下而上的支持。"

齐普拉斯支持私有化的政策来之不易,近些年来,在欧洲的经济困境依然持续的情况下,极左和极右的政治党派在欧洲的成功阻碍了洲际之间的一体化融合。

在2014年欧盟议会的选举上,反对欧洲一体化的极右党派获得了比预期更多的席位。2015年1月26日在希腊,极左的党派——左翼联盟赢得了选举,接下来第二天仅40岁的领导人齐普拉斯宣誓任职这个债务缠身国家的总理。

极右党派势力的得势催生了当时的许多辩论，尤其是在英国脱欧（在 2016 年公民投票选出）的背景下应该如何在欧洲实施一体化的问题上。左翼联盟党派也不是反对欧盟的成员国形式和欧元区，实际上他们支持取消现行的紧缩政策，希望和债权国家重新协商如何支付 2400 亿欧元的天价债务。在他赢得选举之前，齐普拉斯说他的首要任务就是重建这个国家随着养老金和工资的减少、工作机会和外来投资的减少而丢失的国家尊严。

当齐普拉斯竞选成功时，很多雅典人民都在怀疑他能否兑现他的诺言，还有言论说齐普拉斯的成功竞选会引起政治动荡和市场的剧烈浮动。是齐普拉斯的倡议有错吗？对于一个深陷经济低潮期的国家，紧缩的措施通常不是合适的政策选择，从另一方面来说，以基础设施建设为主要特征的凯恩斯主义经济学是理想的政策措施。但是希腊的情况不同寻常，因为它还有不能被欧盟财政规则所接受的巨额的财政贷款，这就意味着希腊不可能通过大量举债来维持自己国家的发展，这是齐普拉斯必须面对的困境。既然将债务一笔勾销是不可能的，他就要开始和债权国家见面商讨延长支付期限。

将所有债务还清可以为国家重拾尊严，齐普拉斯和他的团队投入了很多精力和时间与布鲁塞尔、国际货币基金组织协商如何就债务问题达成一致意见；另外一件重要的事情就是恢复这个国家的社会和经济活力。国家尊严同样也和社会生产力相关，但是这些都说起来容易做起来难。为实现这些目标，对希腊来说最重要的就是吸引资金建立新工厂、提高国有资产使用效率。之前的政府也发布过大范围的资产私有化的计划，包括售卖国家最大的港口比雷埃夫斯，对此中远集团表示了购买兴趣，但是当齐普拉斯竞选成功之后，新政府终止这一售卖，因为齐普拉斯的党派反对私有化和外来投资。这在当前国际形势下是行得通的吗？

那时，在我的专栏文章中，我希望齐普拉斯三思他需要做的妥协，这能够保证希腊人民在较为宽松的紧缩政策和恢复经济活力中间进行选择。我坚信希腊有很多途径可以重获国际竞争力，但是希腊需要一条没有政治不确定性的路来刺激经济发展，希腊人民和投资者都讨厌政治不确定性。

回望过去，总理齐普拉斯已经向他的党派作出了妥协，尤其在保持中国对希腊的投资方面。习近平主席在齐普拉斯 2017 年 5 月访华时表示，两国应该在基础设施建设、能源和通信领域深化合作，并且认同希腊是中国新的"一带一路"倡议的重要组成部分。习近平主席还说，现在中国和希腊的传统友谊、合作将继续迸发新的活力。

希腊在"一带一路"倡议中的积极参与也体现在希腊成为中国主导的亚洲基础设施投资银行的成员之一，入股这个新的多边财政融资平台。在希腊总理和其他 27 个国家元首参加的"一带一路"国际合作高峰论坛之前，那时，希腊跟随许多欧盟国家的步伐最终赢得亚投行的会员资格。

实际上，希腊的行动相对较迟，它在亚投行正式运作的 6 个月之后才开始申请加入。而早在 2015 年 3 月，以英国为代表的西欧国家势力就不顾美国的反对积极申请成为亚投行的创始国。希腊政府相信这个决定是政府宏观政策的一部分，致力于为高回报的投资计划减少金融风险，深入与国际投资组织的协作发展。

由帕纳约蒂斯·罗米里奥提斯（Panagiotis Roumeliotis）教授作为希腊方的主要协商代表，仅仅在正式递交加入亚投行申请10个月之后，希腊就取得了会员资格。据之前的报道，亚投行将会投资希腊公司在中东、中国和亚洲其他地区的项目，同样也会资助其他亚洲公司在希腊的投资项目，希腊入股1000万欧元（近1100万美元）。

希腊总统普罗科比斯·帕夫洛普洛斯（Prokopis Pavlopoulos）也是习近平主席提出的"一带一路"倡议的忠实拥护者。引用他在2017年年初说的话，希腊作为欧盟成员国极大地促进中国和欧盟之间的合作，所以希腊拥护每一个让欧亚更紧密的倡议。

希腊总统强调海上丝绸之路的重要性，鉴于比雷埃夫斯是通过苏伊士运河进入欧洲的第一个关口，他说中远集团在比雷埃夫斯的投资是中国和希腊友好互利合作的典范，那充分证明了比雷埃夫斯是在地缘战略上连接亚洲和欧洲的极其重要的关口。

希腊总统帕夫洛普洛斯谈到希腊在和中国的战略合作的框架之下"全心全意支持'一带一路'倡议"，并且希腊已经准备好与中国进行资源合作。由于两国是两个最古老的文明的继承者，中国和希腊一直欣赏、支持对方，在各个方面发展合作。

实际上，在政治层面上，中国和希腊领导人近些年已经进行了密切交流，为在各方面深化合作奠定了基础。习近平主席在2014年去巴西访问的途中在希腊的罗德岛刻意作了短暂的停留，在那里会见了时任希腊总理安东尼斯·萨马拉斯（Antonis Samaras）。在希腊领导人访华、在北京与习近平主席见面之前，习近平主席在 2015 年 9 月在纽约会见了希腊总理齐普拉斯。希腊前总理萨马拉斯与李克强总理在 2014 年访问希腊时举行了会面，李克强总理 2016 年在北京会见了齐普拉斯。在多次的会面中，契合双方发展蓝图的深化的、战略性的合作被提上日程，所有的希腊领导人也在极力吸引中国的投资，并且欣赏中国对深陷债务危机的希腊进行扩大投资的勇气，尤其是在其他投资者纷纷撤出的情况下。

在 2017 年 3 月和我的一场采访中，中国驻希腊大使邹肖力曾经在大使馆说过一段非常有名的话：希腊的政治党派虽然在很多问题上有异见，但在"一带一路"倡议上达成了一致。希腊前任总理萨马拉斯在 2017 年年中访华，在访问期间，萨马拉斯获得了中国总理李克强的高度赞赏，感谢他带领希腊政府对"一带一路"倡议的支持。李克强总理 2015 年访问希腊时，萨马拉斯告诉李克强总理说他们是真朋友，因为他们在给对方分享观点时都在看着对方的眼睛。

与希腊共渡难关

当萨马拉斯在 2012 年当选为总理时，希腊正处于破产的边缘、失控的债务违约、被要求离开欧元区和外交崩盘的窘境中。2014 年年中，萨马拉斯在接受我的书面采访时这样写道，当中国在一众国家中坚持站在希腊这边与希腊一起共渡难关时，仿佛所有的困难都"远去"了。"我难以形容我是多么感激，多么感谢"，萨马拉斯这样写给我。

萨马拉斯说，在现今世界中，希腊紧邻苏伊士运河和地中海，最有条件成为中欧和东欧市场与远东和中东进行国际贸易的欧洲门户。但是这要求投资各种基础设施建设，比如说主要港口、高速公路和铁路，希腊已经在比雷埃夫斯有了很好的开始，现在有诸多朝不同方向拓展的计划。

造船业和海洋工业是代表共同利益的另一个方面，毕竟全球15%的海上贸易是由希腊船东所完成的，同样，旅游也是已经深化合作并具有巨大潜力的领域，"希腊是中国人在欧洲旅游的第一站"，萨马拉斯这样说道，"并且希腊文明对于那些欣赏超越时间的文化的人们来说有着极大的吸引力，可能中国人民更能欣赏在这方面希腊所能提供的独一无二的文化瑰宝，因为他们自己也为自己国家的文明而感到骄傲，毕竟'希腊'在汉语中的字面意思是'其他文明'"。

"你看，文化不是'过去的事情'，这是一个动态的现象，它定义了今天的人们，并在国家间产生了强烈的精神纽带。"但萨马拉斯说，我们正在逐步建立的经济关系中存在着强大的商业元素，希腊是"地中海饮食"的精华，许多希腊农产品，尤其是生鲜、加工和制造的产品，从特级初榨橄榄油、羊乳酪芝士到优质葡萄酒和各种草药产品都可以引入中国市场。

对于他来说，双方正在一些共同关心的领域，包括具体的投资计划、贸易协定和合作扩大，取得实质性的进展，并建立起了一种有着巨大前景的坚实关系。在萨马拉斯在任时期，他表示私有化项目由于结构上的僵化而在开始时进展缓慢，但其势头正劲，在比雷埃夫斯已经有了一个重大"突破"，正是中远集团 2016 年的开拓性投资取得了如此巨大的成功。"因此，我们现在正在此基础上进一步扩大，我相信，中远投资只是中国在开辟'欧洲走廊'的过程中战略性地参与希腊基础设施项目的开始，希腊一些成熟的私有化计划是接下来的具体步骤的候选方案，包括铁路项目甚至机场枢纽。"萨马拉斯强烈认为，中欧之间的商业关系纽带这个"大局"实际上应该通过开放、降低贸易壁垒的方式来重塑，而不应该封闭或提出新的壁垒，当然这些都应以互惠互利为基础。

"请注意我描述我们共同战略前景的用词：就国际贸易而言，是中国和欧洲之间'门户'；就投资和长期经济关系而言，是'欧洲走廊'；就聚到一起相互理解而言，是两个最古老、最有影响的文明之间的'文化窗口'。"

"我们越了解彼此，我们就越了解自己。我们对过去的认识和讨论越多，对未来的启发就越多。"柏拉图、亚里士多德和修昔底德不仅是希腊文化遗产的创始人之一，他们更是西方文明不可分割的一部分。萨马拉斯说："我相信孔子、老子和孙子也是世界文化遗产的组成部分。我们越了解彼此，就越发现惊人的相似之处，而且我们越来越意识到这些中希两国独特的历史经验是相辅相成的，其潜力也是无穷的。"在这种情况下，他建议双方不应该把两块"宝藏"分开，应该一起开启一场充满活力的文化"连锁反应"。

萨马拉斯说："让我们把两份'宝藏'放在一起，创造一个群聚效应。"比如说，希腊语和中文是世界上最古老的仍在使用中的语言，它们以前所未有的规模在发展壮大。来想想积淀在这两种语言中的经历千年的所有文化财富。因此，他说他会从期望和鼓励更多的希腊人在未来的几年中学习汉语开始，中国人和希腊人都是快速学习者。"我很惊讶一些中国人能流利地说希腊语，我听说我们也已经有一些中文流利的希腊人了……似乎我们可以做更多的事情来增进理解，所以，让我们从做一件真正大胆的事开始：通过消除我们之间的语言障碍……"萨马拉斯说。

萨马拉斯支持并倡导中国和希腊之间的文化交流；作为一个爱好收藏古代文明瑰宝的人，资深的希腊图书管理员齐普格洛（Tsimpoglou）非常清楚具有悠久历史的中国的重要性。

齐普格洛是位于雅典的希腊国家图书馆的馆长，希腊国家图书馆坐落在一座可追溯到1832年的宏伟建筑内，载有以各种语言记载的有关希腊文明的丰富的文化典籍。齐普格洛的办公室墙上挂满了希腊的经典之作，他说，本着文化交流的精神，他为中国读者提供了一些阅读建议，但这些建议看起来可能是从希腊古老文化守护者这里得到的一种非常规的传统。

他说："我以为他们之前读过希腊经典，所以我建议他们多阅读一下希腊的现代杰作。"齐普格洛列举了现代著名希腊诗人康斯坦丁·卡瓦菲（Constantine P. Cavafy，1863—1933）的一系列作品，他从个人经验和自己深刻而广泛的历史知识，尤其是希腊时代的知识中提炼了他的主题。

齐普格洛说："诗人总是用自己的人生经验来表达内心的挣扎、命运和困境，这就是我想要推荐的。"他还推荐了作家、诗人和哲学家尼科斯·卡赞扎基斯（Nikos Kazantzakis, 1883—1957）的作品。

齐普格洛说，他认为希腊文明的一大贡献是通过借词给其他文化，包括"逻辑、困境、经济、生态和危机"等广泛使用的词汇，丰富了全球的表达。

虽然他还没有机会访问中国，但是齐普格洛愿意到中国进行访问。他尊重延续千年的中华文明，对他而言，中华文明代表着人类通过"努力和活力"所取得的重大成就，"也就是说，我们的文明在中国悠久的历史面前只是一个婴儿"。

像萨马拉斯，他提出交换我们各自语言的经典作品，他说他希望用他的中国经典作品的希腊文译著来交换在中国的希腊文学瑰宝的中文译著。他说："我们有一些中文的希腊经典作品，但我们需要在图书馆增加更多这样的作品。"

齐普格洛长期从事图书馆学方面的工作，在 2014 年担任新职务之前，齐普格洛曾在收藏了大量的研究论文和其他文献的希腊国家文献中心工作了 16 年，之后担任塞浦路斯大学图书馆馆长长达 14 年。

他说他喜欢拓展自己的视野。他的爱好是旅行和摄影。"这样，当你仔细看照片的时候，你好像可以在曾经生活过的地方再活一遍。"齐普格洛说他对希腊经历的经济危机有点担心，但是他强烈地相信希腊的未来，因为希腊是"欧洲地域和文化"的大门，也是孕育了西方文明的哲学家与思想家的地方。

"所以如果有人想要了解欧洲的文明、文化、心态甚至人民，他或她必须转向了解古希腊哲学家们。"他说。齐普格洛将他的图书馆比作他的国家。希腊国家图书馆，被他称为希腊思想的一面镜子，在 1999 年 9 月发生的一场强烈的地震中被部分毁坏了。他指着办公室的角落和天花板说，有关部门刚刚用混凝土填补墙上的裂缝来稳固房顶，"这和希腊的情况非常相似"。

他解释说，希腊多年来用借来的钱保持繁荣昌盛，部分用于所谓的过度的公共福利计划，福利计划也随着几年前的债务危机的到来结束了，就像当年的那场地震一样。他说："接下来我们会努力保持国家稳定，而不是修复或重建国家的结构体系。……我们仍然生活在一个需要彻底改变的危险体系中。我们必须承认，希腊现在就像我们的图书馆一样。"

他补充说，虽然越来越多的人转向阅读和学习知识，以充实自己，让他们更有机会找到工作，但从美国、希腊到欧洲其他国家的政府都已经削减了对公共图书馆的开支，但希腊人现在需要通过守护自己国家的文明来寻找克服危机的方法，并帮助他们展现改变和改革的勇气。

他说："这是我们的希望，这也是我们对未来的展望。"他说，希腊面临的不仅是困难，而且是一个困境。这是齐普格洛经常使用的一个希腊词语。"我们如何在改变的同时维护我们自己的文明是目前我们面临的困境之一。"

希腊人不仅遭受了经济危机，而且也遭受了价值危机，这个国家需要清楚自己的首要任务是什么和需要为地球作出什么贡献。他说，希腊人应该采取行动来决定自己的命运以改善自己的生活，正如古希腊哲理所表达的，"我对希腊的未来持非常乐观的态度，作为人类，我们自己必须乐观"，他说："否则，我们还留在山洞里。我们会渡过危机，但我不知道是在两年、三年还是五年之后。"

他认为，希腊需要更加自律、更加遵守法律。至于欧洲，其使命之一就是维持和平，因为这个大陆在过去的一个世纪中遭受了两次世界大战的重创。他说："这是欧洲必须面对的挑战。中国是一个历史悠久，人口众多，幅员辽阔，资源丰富的国家。"他补充说："如果中国不能实现和平发展，其他国家也不可能做到。"

希腊总统和总理对"一带一路"倡议的深刻理解已经传递给希腊各级官员，希腊政府经济发展部副部长比齐奥拉斯（Pitsiorlas）在前往北京参加 2017 年 5 月举行的"一带一路"国际合作高峰论坛时表示，5 月双方正在签署一项三年行动计划，计划内容是关于持续吸引对希腊的投资，从而实现"一带一路"倡议与希腊发展战略的协同发展。比齐奥拉斯从论坛回来后还表示，希腊在中国的投资计划中占有重要的份额，这也是"一带一路"倡议的一部分，其中运输、电信和能源是两国合作的三大主要方向。

在中国和希腊双方签署的三年行动计划文件中，双方都说明了中国"一带一路"倡议是如何与希腊政府在该地区的战略完美契合的，比齐奥拉斯说："我认为这一倡议与希腊发展战略的协同发展将为双边合作揭开新的篇章。"尽管中国在希腊的投资总量与德国、法国和英国相比仍然是小规模的，但是比齐奥拉斯表示相信中国投资的发展前景，特别是在中远集团前几年取得了傲人业绩之后，"两国在困难时期通过扩大投资和提供紧急救助资金深化了双方的友谊。"

作为回报，2011 年希腊帮助中国从利比亚撤出数千名工人，将他们送到克里特岛，然后送他们乘飞机返回中国。

比齐奥拉斯还赞扬中远集团深入参与比雷埃夫斯港的发展建设，为其他中国的潜在投资者提供了鼓舞人心的榜样。该副部长表示，中国房地产产业的跨国公司万达，电商巨头阿里巴巴和重量级能源企业神华集团此前与希腊已经有了密切的投资合作，希腊准备为中国投资者提供更多吸引力，让他们落实自己的投资计划。"比雷埃夫斯港正在成为地中海地区交通运输的核心，这说明希腊可以在亚洲和欧洲之间架起一座桥梁，"比齐奥拉斯这样说，"作为鼓励中国投资者的一个开放的姿态，希腊机场和海港、餐馆和景点很快就会出现许多中文标志。"

中国驻希腊大使邹肖力透露，中国对希腊在"一带一路"倡议中的支持和积极参与表示高度赞赏，他相信希腊不仅能走出债务危机，而且还将通过实施区域战略为实现区域内部的和平与稳定而发挥更重要的作用。2017 年 3 月，邹大使在位于雅典的中国驻希腊使馆与我进行了长达一个小时的谈话。"这不仅符合希腊的利益，而且也符合中国和欧盟的利益。中国和希腊的合作对中欧合作以及对世界上不同区域之间的合作也具有重要而深远的意义。"邹大使说。他自己也意识到，许多中国投资者纷纷涌向希腊寻找机会，特别是 2016 年开始，他不仅接待了企业，还接待了市级和省级的领导，他们看中希腊作为中欧门户的天然优势，对在希腊寻找机会表现出了浓厚的兴趣。

邹大使对中远比雷埃夫斯项目所产生的"龙头"效应的趋势（即吸引了更多来自中国的投资者）表示了肯定，他说这是迄今为止在希腊乃至欧洲最成功的基础设施合作项目。他说："这大大提高了中国企业投资希腊的兴趣和信心。" 双方在谈的项目涉及的覆盖面很广，包括造船、船舶修理、港口、机场、电力、电信、金融、保险、旅游、房地产乃至能源等。他收到了两家来自上海的公司在希腊竞标的标书。邹大使说："这是振奋人心的，我们希望更多的中国投资者能来。"

但邹大使说，双方应该深化教育合作，以期进一步为投资、贸易、旅游和文化交流提供便利和支持。与其他欧洲国家相比，没有多少中国学生前往希腊，据统计，在雅典的大学中，中国学生人数不会超过 20 人，而在布鲁塞尔的大学中，中国学生的人数已经超过 3000 人，更不用说伦敦、巴黎和柏林的人数了。"我认为我们应该提供更多的激励机制来鼓励学生前来希腊学习。"邹大使说。

旅游业是双方在"一带一路"倡议的框架之下探索机遇的另一个领域。希腊旅游部部长艾兰妮·龚朵拉（Elena Kountoura）已经深入参与了这项工作，在迈向政治生涯之前，龚朵拉曾于 1989 年和 1998 年两次访问中国，当时她是一名在巴黎和雅典的时尚界工作的国际知名的模特，她回忆说，当时在中国推广时尚概念的时候，记得北京的道路很宽阔。1989 年的时候她看到的是自行车道；1998 年，当她第二次去北京时，她看到遍地都是汽车。

希腊这位模特出身的优雅的旅游部部长在 2017 年 3 月的一次讲话中表示，5 月和 6 月她一直忙于准备赴中国的宣传旅行，她说这是总理齐普拉斯中国之行的热身和后续活动。龚朵拉坐在位于雅典市中心、与历史悠久的希腊议会大楼很近的办公室里，谈她去中国的旅行，观察到这个国家几十年来的迅速变化。这引发了她深刻的思考。龚朵拉说："现在我对第三次去中国感到兴奋不已。"

她说她的使命是吸引更多的中国游客到希腊旅游。她自信地说："我准备欢迎中国不断壮大的中产阶级带着中国悠久的文明来访希腊。"她预计，北京和雅典之间的直飞航班会有助于吸引更多的中国游客。据悉，中国航空将于2017年重新启动北京—雅典的直飞航班，这趟航班也会在德国慕尼黑市停留。龚朵拉承诺，她的部门将努力帮助中国游客轻松地从希腊大使馆获得签证。她表示，2016年中国有超过十万人向希腊驻华使馆申请了旅游签证，并且有更多的游客通过其他欧洲国家来到希腊。

对深陷债务危机的希腊来说，旅游业是该国低迷的经济中唯一增长的部门，希腊政府的目标是将入境游客从2016年的2800万增加到3000万。龚朵拉说，中国对希腊来说是个不断增长的市场，希腊的旅游业为其经济产出和创造就业贡献了大约五分之一产值。据统计，2016年中国游客达到20万人次，而希腊决心到2021年将每年游客数量提高到100万人次。"如果我们有更多的直飞航班，对中国游客来说会更容易、更方便地来到希腊，我欢迎更多中国人的到来，我希望2017年中国游客的人数将达到50万人。"她说，希腊正在推广365天旅游目的地的概念，扩大其岛屿旅游，包括文化、冒险运动、自然。针对中国游客的发展趋势，她认为，当中国人到希腊旅游的时候，他们的停留时间肯定会超过六天，但是如果他们也要去另一个国家游玩的话，这就要看情况。

"据我们所知，当中国人进行这种国际长途旅行时，他们希望在欧洲看到尽可能多的东西。他们在希腊游玩的同时，也希望去其他国家旅行，而且通常他们会停留一个多星期。"她说。她还表示，中国游客是"消费好手"，他们的平均消费水平超过欧洲人。"因为中国、美国或澳大利亚的游客来到海外，他们的平均消费比欧洲人要多，这是肯定的，"她补充说，"许多年轻的中国夫妇在希腊的岛屿上结婚或者度蜜月，这在过去的两年里变得非常受欢迎。"

她说："我们仍然想要开发这种产品，以确保游客在希腊旅行期间度过美好的时光。"但她指出，希腊不仅仅有岛屿，希腊已经于2017年4月26日至27日在亚历山德鲁波利斯举办了第一届西方丝绸之路国际研讨会，她说，"希腊支持'一带一路'倡议，希腊的旅游业可以为中国领导的这个倡议作出贡献，特别是通过推广文化旅游这方面。"

除在政界之外，关于希腊"一带一路"倡议的讨论也在学术界掀起了热潮。超越对于中国、希腊两国的双边意义，一些学者已经在思考在（2017年）5月份北京举行的论坛结束之后，如何建立一个新的区域合作机制。

在众多学者当中，雅典经济与商业大学副校长迪米特里斯·布兰托尼斯（Dimitris Bourantonis）表示，"一带一路"倡议实质上是提倡建立区域合作，至关重要的是建立一个平台讨论如何以可持续的方式实现这一目标。布兰托尼斯说，（2017年）5月份在北京举行的"一带一路"论坛只是一个开始，并且这种形式的论坛应该制度化，"如果二十国集团峰会避免讨论具有重大意义的地区性问题，如果这个新生的论坛能够讨论与人民生活和地区发展密切相关的问题，那么我认为这个论坛值得继续下去。"他说，论坛可以从 2017 年开始在不同的国家举行。"当然，为什么不考虑在北京建立一个永久的'一带一路'论坛呢？"教授说，"'一带一路'论坛作为全球治理的新手段是可以被接受的"。

我所见到的意见领袖甚至敦促希腊政党对国家战略采取一致立场，确保战略实施进程不因政治反对党而中断，令人振奋的是，在谈到"一带一路"框架下与中国的合作时，执政党领导人及反对党都在同一个层面上发表一致的论调。2017 年 3 月，我与希腊前总理、新民主党名誉主席康斯坦丁·米佐塔基斯（Konstantinos Mitsotakis）的儿子基里亚科斯·米佐塔基斯（Kyriakos Mitsotakis）进行了非正式谈话；自 2016 年 1 月起，年轻的米佐塔基斯是新民主党和反对党的领导人。在雅典新民主党总部的谈话期间，尽管希腊反对党领导人拒绝透露他对"一带一路"倡议的看法，但他的幕僚们高度评价了这一倡议，说"一带一路"倡议会有助于振兴希腊经济。这些确实都是非常令人振奋的信息：希腊人已经准备好向已持续十年之久的危机管理阶段说再见，并且讨论如何转向下一步的可持续发展。

希腊是一个人口 1100 万的国家，在欧洲，有很多与希腊人口数量相当的国家已达到更高的发展水平。希腊与比利时、荷兰和德国有相似之处，拥有天然港口来发展物流业，也拥有通往欧洲内陆的经济走廊。比较而言，希腊拥有比处于内陆的瑞士更多的地理优势，但后者已成为世界上最富有的创新国家之一。所以无论如何，希腊有很大的机会成为欧洲大国。为了释放这种力量，在希腊人民之间进一步形成长期和有远见的发展共识是关键。与此同时，欧盟应该支持希腊开发这种潜力、成为欧洲新的经济引擎，而不是只监管对其的救助和私有化计划、担心它对其他海洋国家造成不良影响。

案例：中远集团创造的希腊奇迹

大约 30 年前，傅承求已经成为中国航运巨头中远集团的资深船长，后来被派驻意大利建立跨国分公司。自 2008 年以来，在中远集团拿到比雷埃夫斯港口两个码头 35 年的租赁权后，也就是说希腊允许将码头租借给中国公司之后，傅先生一直管理着比雷埃夫斯港两个集装箱码头。

这是一个巨大的成功：在集装箱装卸能力方面，比雷埃夫斯已经从 2010 年的第 93 位在 2016 年一跃成为全球排名第 38 位的最繁忙的港口。在希腊债务危机中，1200 多名港口工人因比雷埃夫斯港的卓越发展避免失业。

凭借如此令人信服的信誉，在中远集团 2016 年 8 月以 2.85 亿欧元的价格购买了这个先导的私有化项目 51% 的股权之后，年过 60 的傅先生掌管了 35 平方公里的比雷埃夫斯港务局。在五年内，中远拥有比雷埃夫斯港口管理局 67% 的股份，总支出达到 3.685 亿欧元。

"责任明显如山重。"已经白发的傅先生坚定地说。他现在是有近 90 年历史的比雷埃夫斯港口管理局的首席执行官。

他坐在游轮形的比雷埃夫斯港口管理局大楼的教室大小的办公室的沙发区，看着窗外的渡轮和其他船只穿梭，他说他的团队花了近半年的时间努力去认识"新家庭的每处细节"，包括其财务报表、客户关系和员工的真实工作情况。傅先生承认，现在让他头痛的是如何提高"老龄化的希腊国有企业"的效率，在比雷埃夫斯港口管理局的 1200 多名工作人员中，平均年龄是 51.5 岁。

而且，他继续说，比雷埃夫斯港口管理局只需要大约 700 名工作人员来维持运行，如何处理冗余工作人员也是一个挑战。"但是底线是，我们不会为了提高效率解雇任何一名工作人员。"傅先生回忆说。在 20 世纪 80 年代和 90 年代中国实施国有企业改革后，他的一些亲戚朋友都有下岗后很难找到新饭碗的记忆。

"当年中国为求职者提供了很多机会，但现在希腊和欧洲的情况是不同的。"他说。欧洲许多国家的平均失业率仍然高达两位数，每两名年轻希腊人中就有一人失业。

傅先生说，比雷埃夫斯港口管理局的业务范围从集装箱装卸到货运、邮轮运营、汽车码头、修船到港口经济区。他已经把比雷埃夫斯港口管理局分支机构的数量从 94 个减少到了 23 个。"我几周前完成了这个任务，我们必须提高管理效率。"傅先生说。他的名字已经被列入港务局管理层历史沿革表上，这个列表就挂在他办公室旁边的会议室的墙上。

初步数据显示，傅先生的团队是很有能力的。其财务报告显示，2016 年的收入为 1.385 亿欧元，而 2015 年为 9990 万欧元；2016 年税前利润达到 1100 万欧元，比 2015 年增长 13%。此外，

2016 年员工成本下降了 220 万欧元（下降比例为 4.3%）；行政开支也大幅减少了 550 万欧元（下降比例为 20.2%）。傅先生说："我很高兴看到我们的收入在上升，成本在下降。"

傅先生说，他的公司将在未来几年投资 1.9 亿欧元用于扩大港口业务，另外从欧盟获得的 1.3 亿欧元将主要用于深海游轮码头投资。

他说他的公司还将在造船和船舶修理、国际游轮和汽车码头等方面扩大投资和业务，改善 1 号集装箱码头的基础设施。他相信，随着中欧经济关系的进一步密切，港口在不同的经营活动中拥有着光明的前景。

一项研究显示，中远集团对比雷埃夫斯的投资将使希腊国内生产总值增长 0.8%，预计在 2016 年至 2025 年之间将新增 31000 个就业岗位。傅先生却很谦逊，他说："我不想作出这样的估计，我所相信的就是采取行动，让未来的结果来证明。"他不愿意预测对比雷埃夫斯的投资将为希腊带来多少工作机会。

近几年来，我曾在负债累累的希腊与傅先生进行过三次谈话，对于大多数企业来说，单纯的生存已经是一个艰巨的挑战，但傅先生成为了一个极其罕见的成功榜样。

距离雅典市中心大约半小时的车程的比雷埃夫斯的集装箱码头比以往任何时候都繁忙，大型起重机和拖拉机在不停地运转，码头工人在不停地工作。当我于 2012 年在他的港口办公室遇见他时，中远集团比雷埃夫斯集装箱码头公司的总经理傅承求说，在欧洲经济危机的环境下，他的公司已经取得了破纪录的成功。"在集装箱装卸业务方面，我们不仅生存了下来，而且还打破了纪录，"傅先生说，"但是这样的成功来之不易。"

2010 年 6 月，中远集团在激烈的全球竞争中签下合同后，开始经营比雷埃夫斯的 2 号码头，并重建 3 号码头。中远集团签署了 35 年的租约，每年向希腊政府支付 1 亿欧元。当时由于美国的金融危机，全球经济一直处于衰退之中，欧洲主权债务危机刚刚在希腊开始。但是经过两年的运营，中远经营比雷埃夫斯的业绩数据似乎表现出逆势回升。

在执掌中远意大利子公司之前，傅先生曾是一艘货船的船长，他为公司在比雷埃夫斯头几年的发展伟绩感到骄傲。尽管仅用了四个月的时间就使这个之前一直亏损的港口扭亏为盈，但傅先生说，挑战是巨大的。

他接手公司后不久，希腊港口工人就开始罢工，有等待进港的 5 公里长的集装箱卡车，以及在炎热的烈日下等待的驾驶员的愤怒投诉。在许多集装箱的数据丢失导致船期延误之后，船东们也抱怨纷纷。"最重要的是开始工作。"傅先生回忆说。他主动与卡车司机和港口工人进行谈判，承诺尽快解决问题。

傅先生的管理团队，有七名中国成员，与希腊方面的管理层进行了密切的合作，同意为重返工作岗位的港口工人涨薪；傅先生还要求集装箱数据要计算机化。"一开始，我们度过了好多个不眠之夜来应对这些挑战。"

起初希腊工人担心中远会用有经验的中国工人取代他们，但只有七名中国人在港口工作，中远在希腊创造了大约 1000 个工作岗位。"我们没有把中国工人带来，而是把中国的高效率带来这个港口。"

尽管希腊如此深陷债务危机，傅先生仍然认为比雷埃夫斯是通往欧洲的航运的重要门户。"港口的地理优势和我们提供的优质服务帮助比雷埃夫斯港在危机时期实现快速发展。"

中远的成功赢得了希腊政府和当地员工的尊重。许多希腊官员说，热烈欢迎中国投资者，并希望其他中国公司能够跟随中远成功的脚步。

傅先生表示，在声誉逐渐提升的情况下，中远集团正处于参与希腊计划的 22 家国有企业私有化的优势地位。

他表示，公司正在进行一项针对参与希腊政府提出的各种私有化项目的深入可行性研究。2012 年的选举结果宣布后，新的联合政府上台，可能会帮助中远集团参与这些私有化项目作出决定，他补充说道。

希腊当局已经对中远集团和其他中国公司的进一步投资国有资产的私有化的一系列项目表现出兴趣，投资价值预计将达到500 亿欧元。由于在海外的成功，傅先生经常受邀与中国公司的高管对话，传授经验、分享教训。

他说有四个要素确保他连续取得成功。首先，安全是港口经理人的"绝对优先考量"。其次，工人必须高效工作，以确保船舶靠离的时间准点。傅先生说他根据"中国的速度和经验"培训希腊工人后，他的港口将是欧洲效率最高的港口之一。再次，装卸集装箱的成本需要保持在合理的水平。最后，服务和与船东的沟通必须做到及时、友好。"如果你能做好这四个方面的工作，客户就会来找你。"傅先生说。

中国一直在鼓励企业到海外投资，但傅先生提醒说："应该要谨慎行事。"他建议中国投资者应该在自己以往有经验的行业领域进行投资。"只有这样才有赚钱的机会。"

我在 2014 年采访傅先生的时候发现，如果告诉出租车司机你要去比雷埃夫斯，他立刻就知道去的是距离希腊首都市中心仅十多公里远的比雷埃夫斯的集装箱码头。

在不到五年的时间里，中国航运、物流、造船和船舶维修在这里就成了成功的代名词。

在相对较短的时间内，比雷埃夫斯集装箱码头已经获得了每月装卸约 200 艘货轮的能力，而该公司 2009 年开始运营之时仅达到 40 ~ 50 艘。

除了装卸能力增加了约四倍之外，它还创造了约 1200 个就业岗位，这还不包括航运业产业链带来的无数的间接就业机会。

所有这一切都是在希腊最糟糕的经济环境的背景下实现的。

无可置疑，中远集团的成功得到了政界和商界领袖的一致好评，李克强总理也在 2014 年 6 月 20 日访问了该码头。虽然增长势头强劲，但中远子公司经理傅先生在对过去五年工作的评估中仍然保持清醒冷静。

坐在港口中远主办公室的办公桌前，身后挂着中国、希腊和欧盟的旗帜。显然，傅先生是一个高标准的人。"我们在比雷埃夫斯的业务已经变得稳定和成熟，但我认为它还不能被贴上成功的标签。"他坚持说。他反而关注于他所描述的有关各方的共赢局面。

傅先生说，比雷埃夫斯已经提供了一个将货物运送到中欧、东欧、南欧和北非的很好的门户。对于仍在苦苦挣扎的希腊政府而言，比雷埃夫斯代表了一个可以带来稳定收入的国际业务，将来可以基于此建造经济特区，这样的经济特区进而可以用来落户中国的装配工厂，这些计划已经在制定中了。

2014 年年初，希腊私有化机构 HRADF 提名中远集团及其他四家公司为合格投标者，将持有比雷埃夫斯港 67% 的股份。除中远集团外，美国最大的港口运营商——美国海运码头运营商（Ports America Holding Inc）和其他来自世界各地的领先运营商，包括来自英国和荷兰的运营商也都名列其中。

竞标者很快被邀请提交详细的最终尽职调查，希腊政府在年底前作出决定。"我们正在积极准备招标文件，以提升我们在比雷埃夫斯的战略性表现，如果成功，这将确保在这里取得更多的双赢的成果。"傅先生并没有详细阐述。港口项目是希腊政府的几十个私有化计划之一，希腊政府试图通过出售国家基础设施，包括铁路、能源设施、公用事业公共设施和房地产来平衡其财务账簿。如果中远集团成功投标中标，那么这将是继五年前签署了第一个经营并升级国有比雷埃夫斯港两个码头的 35 年合约之后，该公司的又一重大的里程碑。

傅先生说："我们正在努力把比雷埃夫斯港变成一个地区性枢纽，这可以创造更多的就业机会，并且帮助恢复当地的经济，但显然，我们的长期计划是建立在我们最终中标的基础上的。"

比雷埃夫斯是地中海最大的港口之一，也是欧洲十大集装箱港口之一，拥有超过 1500 名员工，每年为超过 24000 艘船舶提供各种服务。根据《国际集装箱化》杂志的报道，2011 年和 2012 年这是世界上增长最快的集装箱港口，是世界排名前 100

的集装箱港口。2016 年，在按集装箱数量排名的世界排名前 100
位的集装箱港口中，上海排名第一，鹿特丹则在欧洲领先。

就中远集团而言，其计划将使比雷埃夫斯成为地中海的重要
枢纽，并成为包括黑海地区在内的中欧、东欧和东南欧的主要分
装中心。

傅先生说，他的团队有能力吸引到像惠普、华为、中兴和三
星这样的大型零售出口商，把比雷埃夫斯港作为他们主要的区域
分销中心。他已经有计划将海运码头与航空和铁路连接起来，为
客户提供更加灵活的选择，同时拓展码头的综合能力。

傅先生说："特别是我们的海铁系统已经改变了传统的历史
航运模式，这标志着一个真正的重大转变。"

2014 年 4 月下旬，第一列集装箱列车从比雷埃夫斯出发，两
天后抵达匈牙利西北部的杰尔。2017 年，有 7 个集装箱列车服务
在希腊与中东欧国家之间运行。按照惯例，来自远东的货物停靠
在鹿特丹、汉堡或安特卫普，然后再通过公路或铁路运送到中欧
或东欧。"但是我们的海铁战略会将传统运输周期缩短 7 ~ 10 天，"
傅先生说，"这意味着给我们的顾客节省了巨大的成本。"

曾帮助公司重组、融资的独立财务顾问、Silky Finance 的执
行合伙人弗拉霍斯说，在欧盟、国际货币基金组织和欧洲中央银
行的帮助下，希腊政府已经成功地恢复了部分的秩序。尽管企业
环境好转，但希腊经济的全面复苏"还需要做很多事情"。

他说："我们的政治家没有像以前那样花钱，而且外国对希
腊的看法也有所改观。"他补充说，计划中的私有化项目对国家
的经济复苏至关重要。他说，中远参与比雷埃夫斯的管理为进一

步私有化可能带来的好处提供了借鉴。

"中远集团的成功在于把一个发展缓慢的、亏损的港口转变成了一个业务骤然繁忙的码头。比雷埃夫斯的成功案例可以通过私有化计划在其他行业进行复制。"弗拉霍斯说。希腊人和中国人可以相互理解,因为他们都有相似的价值观,比如在招待、商业心态和家庭方面。"我们总理对中国的重要性的理解远远超过他的前任。"他表示特别欢迎中国国有企业参与希腊的基础设施建设和金融行业。

希腊企业联合会主席塞奥佐罗斯·费萨斯(Theodoros Fessas)说,有鲜明的迹象表明,希腊的商业环境正在改善,海外投资者开始再次看到该国提供的投资机会,鉴于其在欧元区和欧盟的成员国位置。另一个主要因素是,目前几乎所有的希腊资产的价格都很有吸引力,一旦经济复苏,价格就会上升,投资者也会获得回报。费萨斯预测,中国很快将成为世界上最大的经济体,而且希腊是一个完美的进出口中心,这个进出口中心可以将中国与欧洲其他市场连接起来。"中国进入欧洲需要一个关键的多功能中转中心,希腊可以成为最强有力的选择之一。"他指出,中国投资者一定会关注希腊港口和机场的投资机会。费萨斯说,他预计希腊的领导人会鼓励更多来自中国的跨国公司来投资并在雅典设立其欧洲总部。

希腊航运联合会总裁乔治·格拉特斯(George Gratsos)也是中远投资比雷埃夫斯的坚定支持者。他说:"我们非常高兴中远的投资在不断增长,并且运转良好。"他补充说,李克强总理2016年的访问突出了两国之间长期"持续了很多年,很多年"

的友谊。他说，希腊毗邻南欧、东欧和中欧的优越地理位置以及其强大的铁路网络使得比雷埃夫斯港成为理想的货物配送中心，他敦促希腊有关当局与主要的港口运营商进一步合作，尤其是远东的港口运营商。

"中远的业务取得了巨大的成功，我们支持其在比雷埃夫斯扩大业务。"他指出，将希腊作为通往欧洲的门户有利于中国和中国制造的产品，因为中国出口商通过该港口可以避免缴纳欧盟进口关税。"如果双方都有推动雅典成为全球航运和商业中心的共同愿景，那么雅典有能力成为下一个香港。"

除此之外，希腊的集装箱码头工人明确表明，面对高达两位数失业率的希腊政府向中远集团出租这两个码头是很正确的事情。39 岁的 Melissis Dimitrios 及其同事 40 岁的 John Stamatelopo 在 2009 年年底中远集团开始管理码头后，负责港口集装箱卸货。他们每周工作五天，每月赚大约 1200～1300 欧元，按希腊收入标准来说已经处于较高水平。"现在工作条件相当好，我们很高兴，许多希腊人都很羡慕我们，他们也想在这里工作。"Stamatelopo 站在一艘高层货船旁边说。装载集装箱后，每天两次的火车、卡车和小货船会将货物运到欧洲的其他地方。"我希望更多的人能来，这对我们是有好处的。"他高兴地说。

他的愿望是可以实现的。除了随着港口业务扩大而增加的就业机会外，傅先生还承诺，到 2018 年，比雷埃夫斯的集装箱码头将处理 500 万标箱（20 英尺标准集装箱）。傅先生认真而冷静地说："到那时它将进入世界 30 大集装箱港口的序列。"而且从长远来看，傅先生的公司已经表现出将集装箱装卸能力提升到

1000 万标箱的决心，这将在港口业务的全产业链上创造更多的就业机会。傅先生指着办公桌上他可爱的孙女的照片，说："艰苦的工作之后，她才是幸福的源泉。每当我看到这张照片，我都很高兴。"傅先生微笑着说："我对待港口和我们的希腊人民就像对待大家庭一样。"

希腊航运协会的执行官安德烈亚斯·波塔米亚诺斯（Andreas Potamianos）在谈到中国政府对希腊的投资支持及其推动希腊经济复苏的巨大潜力时，他看起来似乎比他 79 岁的年纪要年轻。

波塔米亚诺斯，年近八旬，充满热情，曾长期领导希腊知名家族航运企业之一的 Epirotiki Lines，他为自己准备了一份中国投资的重点名单，波塔米亚诺斯的名单包括铁路建设、港口管理和旅游，位列他的名单榜首的是中国投资兴建大型游轮，来满足不断增长的中产阶级假期旅游市场。希腊客轮船东联合会名誉主席波塔米亚诺斯说："现在是中国开始发展邮轮业务和投资来满足市场需求的好时机。"

他表示，他看到与中国合作建造具有新一代先进设计和节能系统的游轮的巨大潜力。

波塔米亚诺斯的公司经营七艘由自己家族建造的游轮，他说，他的部下正在与中国公司进行谈判，他们希望在李克强总理 2014 年的访问期间获得一些突破性的进展。

毫无疑问，作为希腊中国友好协会主席，他相信需要通过将希腊有竞争力的航运业与中国的发展联系在一起，来加强双边关系。波塔米亚诺斯说："我只想说中国应该加快增加希腊市场占有率的步伐。"他的家族企业对货运和客运都有浓厚的兴趣。

波塔米亚诺斯在办公室里，面对着希腊最大的比雷埃夫斯客运码头指出了他的家族建造的第一艘船的模型，该船于1850年下水运行。

他表示，中国拥有具有能力建造游轮的造船厂，而且有很大的市场潜力。波塔米亚诺斯说："我们在船舶建造和船员培训方面都有专长，可以与我们的中国朋友分享。"他曾经在1998年到2003年在职时，向时任国务院总理朱镕基提议建立一个航运联盟，但在那时，中国还有其他的发展重点。

现在情况不同了。他说，中国是第一批建造大型游轮的亚洲国家之一，尽管中国在大型货船建造方面取得了长足的进步，但市场中仍然以欧美企业为主。在亚洲，日本和韩国已经开始与其他国家一起建造游轮，现在亚洲的游轮业务正在快速增长。

随着中国人均GDP超过8000美元，中国政府不断鼓励游轮业的发展。国际上的经验表明，当人均国内生产总值达到5000美元时，游轮行业已经有成熟的条件可以增长；人均GDP达到10000美元是发展这种娱乐休闲行业的黄金时代的前奏。中国政府预计，到2020年之前，游轮行业将为国家经济贡献约500亿美元。在美国，这个行业目前每年创造约400亿美元的价值，雇用35万工人。波塔米亚诺斯说："所以你可以看到中国发展游轮业的巨大潜力。"波塔米亚诺斯说，除了联合开发游轮外，希腊人对中国扩大在希腊的业务感到满意，因为中国专注于做生意。"但一些其他国家不是这样，他们希望在希腊占主导地位，这是我们不能接受的。"他说。

他说："中国和希腊有着悠久的友谊和思想共识，和中国做生意，我们没有这种被统治的恐惧。"

希腊的经济形势也使得该国渴望建立伙伴关系。波塔米亚诺斯说："从心理上来说，希腊人感觉情况正在好转，但现实情况是希腊做得非常糟糕，电视上有许多承诺，但具体的实施却让经济很难摆脱危机，许多希腊人已经变得贫穷，自杀人数上升，许多公司倒闭。"希腊人已经感觉到与欧盟的距离在不断增加，虽然他们没有退出欧盟，但是欧洲人对保护希腊人没有提供多少帮助。他说："在这个背景下，越来越多的希腊人把目光转向了中国。"

希腊希望中国成为其最大的贸易伙伴，中国目前是希腊第17大出口国和第5大进口国。

波塔米亚诺斯表示，希腊人希望看到中远集团这家中国大型国有企业除了在比雷埃夫斯的集装箱码头扩建之外，参与更多关于比雷埃夫斯港口管理的私有化计划。

他说："每个人都在谈论中远，因为它给我们带来了工作和希望。"

他说："当然，我们也期待中国投资改善雅典和布达佩斯之间的客运铁路。"他补充说，这将为希腊带来更多的就业机会和游客。他说："最重要的是，我们期待越来越多的中国游客到希腊来旅游。"

为鼓励旅游，波塔米亚诺斯说，他希望希腊政府能够使得来希腊旅游更加便捷，并且启动从中国主要城市飞到雅典的直飞航班。他补充说："我们还需要设计量身定做的旅游套餐来吸引中国人。"尽管他年近80，但是波塔米亚诺斯对商业和生活的热情并没有减弱，他的业余生活仍旧活跃，参加滑雪和周末的徒步。

他从上午九点工作到晚上七点，他希望为增进中希两国关系付出的努力能够取得成果。"我在中希两国之间建立商业桥梁方面花了很多时间。"

许多人希望波塔米亚诺斯的努力能够得到回报，尽管与大多数欧洲国家相比希腊近年来已经抢占了很多世界新闻头条，但是大多数的报道只涉及三个主题：与债权国旷日持久的救助谈判，频繁的选举以及国家的私有化进程。

从我 2010 年到欧洲开始，这些事情耗费了我不少精力。当时的情况就是面对严重的主权危机和金融紧缩计划可能导致的财政破产，希腊是否能够维持发展下去。在英国启动脱欧的谈判之后，虽然希腊经济依然脆弱，但希腊退欧基本上不再是威胁了，可是一些当地人对紧缩性的改革仍然不满，其他人仍然会担心结构性改革。数据显示，希腊已经经历了多年的衰退，对于这个国家来说，进入一个新的经济周期还是很困难的，主要是因为这个国家惨淡的商业环境没能激发全球投资者的信心。

然而，在 2017 年年初的采访中，最令我印象深刻的是，许多希腊人都在关注 Vlachos 顾问和老牌航运领导人 Gratsos，讨论将希腊定位为区域航运、物流甚至能源中心的国家战略。这一国家战略考虑到希腊南邻地中海，北接东欧和中欧。

他们讨论的主要内容是希腊战略与中国的"一带一路"倡议相一致，两者都是关于增进连接性、货物流通以及其他生产力要素。

03

"一带一路"倡议为中捷
两国传统友谊续写新篇章

最近和朋友聊天时脑袋里突然蹦出一个想法：希腊、捷克共和国两国领导人正在通过和中国政府的紧密合作，尤其是将中国提出的"一带一路"的倡议与自己国家的发展战略相匹配，从而来缩小自己同西欧发达国家之间的差距，改变他们国家的命运。我在 2016—2017 年访问捷克时的发现更加证明了我之前的这个猜想。我甚至可以假设，可能现在全世界范围内没有一个国家领导人像捷克总统米洛什·泽曼（Miloš Zeman）一样如此迫切地希望同中国建立紧张繁忙的合作关系。

2017 年 7 月 18 日，在捷克举办中捷商业洽谈会和"一带一路"国际合作高峰论坛后，泽曼总统在他位于首都布拉格的雄伟壮丽的总统城堡里宴请来自中国和捷克的近 1500 名商界人士、专家、政府官员。这是继 2017 年 5 月在北京举行"一带一路"国际合作高峰论坛后，在海外举办的规模最大的一次相关主题的活动。作为东道主，泽曼总统在讲话中说道他对欧洲和中国的各位参会者们对中国领导人提出的"一带一路"倡议表现出的积极性和责任感印象十分深刻。

中国有句古话："众人拾柴火焰高。" 自从习近平主席提出要更好地连接亚洲、欧洲、非洲大陆，中国明确指出这项倡议是一个资源共享、多方合作的新平台。泽曼总统在理解和实施这项倡议时用自己的实际行动，为其他国家领导人树立了一个非凡的榜样，表现出了自己卓越的政治智慧。除了 7 月份在总统城堡宴请中捷两国工商界精英外，泽曼总统还在之前的 3 个月里，在他的总统办公室分别会见了两国年轻的足球运动员、飞行学员、媒体代表，并送上了亲切的问候和热情的款待。此外他还在 5 月份飞去中国出席了"一带一路"国际合作高峰论坛。

博胡斯拉夫·索博特卡（Bohuslav Sobotka）总理通过支持捷克在"一带一路"倡议中作为核心角色来加强中西欧之间合作的举动表明了他在加强合作领域的平等政治策略。索博特卡还讲道，捷克作为一个中欧地区的核心内陆国家，希望通过自身的发展战略以及响应中方的"一带一路"倡议，发展成为一个像西欧的伦敦、巴黎、法兰克福那样的地区性金融和航空枢纽。很明显，捷克共和国现在是欧洲大陆上经济发展最快的国家，已经在初期阶段获得了一定的经济增长。索博特卡7月份在布拉格举办的论坛上说道，他长达十五分钟的演讲无法穷尽已经开始实施和计划开始实施的中捷合作项目。

例如，中国的几家金融机构已经在捷克首都建立了分支机构，前往捷克的游客也从2012年的5万人次增长到2017年的50万人次。同时布拉格与中国北京、上海、成都的直飞航线也已经开通，与此同时布拉格直飞深圳、昆明的航线建设也在加快实施中，可能没有第二个国家会在人口只有1000万的一个国家开通5条直飞航线。当捷克首都布拉格和以经济繁荣著称的中国浙江省义乌市的物流链建立成功后，2017年7月19日浙江省开始在捷克境内寻求建设物流园区，初期计划占地1平方公里。这个项目预计同时会给捷克创造3000个新的工作岗位。

所有这些令人振奋的商业计划和人们之间的信息互换交流表明，泽曼的政治智慧已经得到了应有的反馈。当然，这种势头只会增加，因为双方刚刚打开了表达自己愿景和目标的第一页。习近平主席称"一带一路"倡议是需要持续不断努力的世纪项目。

捷克总统泽曼在过去几年中曾六次约见习近平主席，泽曼赞赏地回应道"一带一路"是一个"全球梦想"，有着如此远见，把布拉格变成地区性金融中心和航空枢纽不仅符合两国的利益，也有助于缩小欧洲地区之间的经济差距，这也应该是欧盟的首要议题，而且，他希望中国和捷克成功结合发展战略的经验可以被其他国家复制。

如果是这样，泽曼的政治智慧将会产生溢出效应。这样的效应就体现在捷克共和国中部的波希米亚地区代表和中国西南部的四川省的代表坐在布拉格旧城区的中心地带一座古老建筑的一层。在四川的省会成都，他们也正在联合开设推广中心。在布拉格的推广中心充满了捷克语的宣传材料，其中有来自四川的熊猫纪念品、当地茶叶、长虹电视等特产。这座大楼的顶层是泽曼总统顾问扬·科胡特（Jan Kohout）建立的布拉格新丝绸之路研究所（New Silk Road Institute Prague），该研究所旨在推进习近平主席提出的"一带一路"倡议的发展，作为一个把这个区域和四川省联系到一起的总设计师，科胡特说他有很好的理由把这些推广中心和他的研究所放在一起。"这是一个创新性的政府推广中心和智囊团的混合体，在4月份，一方面我们需要深入思考如何结合'一带一路'倡议，另一方面我们要推动具体的项目实施。"

刚刚从四川省会成都回来的前外交部部长科胡特说，他已经去四川二十多次。现在他正在为说服该省政府在他的国家建立工业园做努力，甚至想要引进大熊猫。此前，四川电视机制造商长虹已经扩大了在捷克的投资，成都和布拉格之间的直飞航班已经启动。"我理解的是两国之间已经建立了一条政治高速公路，我们需要通过扩大在各个领域的合作来提高这条公路的使用频率。"科胡特说。

他所说的政治高速公路是近年来形成的紧密的战略伙伴关系，两国间高层访问频繁。2017 年 5 月，科胡特陪同泽曼出席"一带一路"国际合作高峰论坛，这是泽曼在其总统任期内第三次访问中国。那天我还遇见了中国驻捷克大使马克卿。她赞同科胡特的观点，中捷高层政治交往的频率空前高涨。"三年内，习近平主席和泽曼总统已经在不同场合进行了六次会晤，泽曼在现在的总统任期内将对中国进行第三次访问，这表明了我们最高政治领导层的密切关系，我们需要继续发展这一势头。"

习近平主席在 2016 年 3 月对捷克共和国进行了历史性的国事访问。将近一年之后，马大使表示，捷克共和国承认中国的重要性，表明了两国准备将两国关系提升到战略伙伴关系的行动，因为捷克只与包括美国和俄罗斯在内的 6 个国家有这样的关系。

2015 年 11 月，中捷两国签署了共同推进"一带一路"建设的谅解备忘录，这是中国同中欧国家签署的第一份这样的文件。到了 2016 年 11 月，双方将谅解备忘录变成了"一带一路"倡议工作方案。马大使说，在捷克共和国，对于通过在对方的大型项目中实现协同发展，来推动务实合作，以实施中国"一带一路"倡议的支持力度是巨大的。马大使在官邸说："习近平主席去年访问捷克后，他们的反应更为积极。"

科胡特说："捷克共和国对这一倡议的支持力度显而易见，现在对我们来说，最重要的是通过将平台制度化并且设计合适的项目来丰富该倡议的内涵。我想谈的另一点是，'一带一路'倡议应该是一个双向的平台。"他表示，双方还应该帮助捷克共和国和欧洲其他国家的投资者在中国寻找更多的投资机会。

为了实现捷克共和国提出的将布拉格作为中国在中东欧的金融中心的建议，捷克的中央银行最近批准了中国工商银行的营业执照。马大使表示，中国在捷克的投资数量已经飙升，2016 年就吸引到了 11 亿美元。"与我们在全国的投资相比，中国的投资数额不是很大，但是它已经从低位开始发展起来了。在 2014 年之前，中国在捷克的总投资还不到 3 亿美元。"她说 2016 年捷克共和国的中国游客数量为 35 万，同比增长 22%，2017 年第一季度的中国游客数量同比增长达到 50%。

马大使说，在帮助捷克实现成为区域性金融和航空枢纽的远大目标的同时，中国也正在努力加强与捷克在工业和先进制造业领域的合作。"除了基础设施和其他投资外，我们还应该通过加强与捷克的合作来提高中国在工业竞争中的竞争力。在这方面，捷克是一个很好的合作伙伴，因为这个国家紧紧跟随着德国的步伐。"

事实上，2016 年习近平主席访问捷克共和国时，我与政治家、商人、作家、体育教练甚至路人在街边的交流都表明了捷克共和国是中国"一带一路"倡议的"新天地"。我的兴奋来源于捷克人已经准备好配合中国的"一带一路"倡议发展，加上捷克人有一长串让已经参与进来的中国人保持参与度的想法，捷克已经准备好把这些想法变成现实。

这样一个积极主动的态度，是在习近平主席提出要把亚欧非三大洲紧密连接起来、基础设施更完善、贸易和金融手段更丰富、人才流动更顺畅、文化交流更丰富的倡议的三年之后形成的。捷克共和国正在成为与英国、法国、巴基斯坦、俄罗斯、印度尼西亚、希腊和其他国家一样的"一带一路"倡议的主要亮点之一。北京的立场十分明确：这个倡议是为了世界的繁荣发展和消除贫困而提供的，但是参与者应该提供具体的想法来丰富它。简而言之，这是中国的倡议，却是世界的机会，捷克共和国已经很好地理解了这个概念。

习近平主席的"一带一路"倡议实际上是一个和平项目，不仅仅关于经济利益，而且连接不同国家的人民。捷克总统泽曼在中国问题上的顾问扬·科胡特在 2016 年与我会面时告诉我："习近平主席的'一带一路'倡议是为世界摆脱战争和冲突、实现繁荣发展提供了解决办法。不仅仅是商业合作，也是人与人之间的更紧密的沟通与合作。"称习近平主席为"'一带一路'倡议之父"，曾两次担任捷克共和国外交部部长的科胡特表示，这一倡议是政治性的，但中国没有地缘政治动机。"中国不是推动每个国家加入，中国也不是在施加压力，这是相互的，是由每个国家自己决定的。"

基于他长期与中国领导人、企业界和学术界的交往，为响应不断急剧变化的世界地缘政治、经济发展，科胡特于 2015 年 9月成立了布拉格新丝绸之路研究所。科胡特说，他的研究所首先与习近平主席的提议精神相符合，旨在帮助建立一个能够更好地进行交流的世界，而不是无目的地对抗世界。科胡特说，在"一带一路"倡议框架内，他将为双方领导人和政府创造良好的合作环境，并且给予建设性的建议。他认为，新丝绸之路背后的推动力绝对是两大洲共有的经济利益，这将增加亚欧之间的连通性，如高速铁路、高速公路网、智能海空基础设施、高速数据网络和可持续能源的基础设施。

"但是，这个想法不应该仅仅归结为经济利益，我们不应该低估它在教育、文化、相互理解和意识形态互动等领域的重要性和影响，"科胡特说，"所有这些都是新的大型项目设计的重要组成部分。"

研究所将围绕更具体的领域，特别是为可行的基础设施和物流项目、金融合作和能源技术等方面提出更具体的建议。"我们专注于高速公路、高速列车和基础设施的前景，也关注软项目，这是我们的目标，但现在我们期待着习近平主席的这次访问，这对我们来说是历史性的时刻。"他把他的研究所称为欧洲的先驱者，他说在习近平主席访问期间，双方都希望在"一带一路"倡议上进行更加深入的合作。

科鲁特说，泽曼总统是捷中关系的大力支持者和推动者，坚决支持"一带一路"倡议。他说："捷克政府和企业也对这一倡议表示了强烈的支持，所以这些都是令人振奋的。"因此，我们可以开始在基础设施、贸易和金融方面实施更多重点项目。

中国已经制订了大规模的互联互通建设计划，这是"一带一路"倡议的核心内容。捷克共和国是一个内陆国家，总人口只有北京的一半，这个想法是完成连接多瑙河、奥得河和易北河的"水廊"，因为捷克共和国是 28 个欧盟成员国中不能直接接触到海的成员国，也无法接触到黑海、波罗的海和北海，捷克人热衷于寻求中国的帮助来实现这一梦想。

当然，由于许多欧洲国家都用"门户"这个词来形容自己的地理优势，捷克共和国也愿意同中国合作，把布拉格变成航空和金融中心。捷克共和国已经与四川省合作建设了一个高新技术产业区，还有开始投资捷克的媒体、足球俱乐部和娱乐场所。捷克政界高层人士透露，他们已意识到与中国接轨的发展战略的重要性。除了这些经营理念，捷克共和国已经动员了大量的资源来进行思想工作的协调，政府已经专门成立了工作小组来处理中国的事务，其中有六位副部长在职，该小组直接向总理和总统汇报工作。与此同时，专门从事"一带一路"倡议研究的智囊团也已经成立，他们为高层决策者提供建议和意见，所有这些举措都非常新颖和令人振奋。

他们甚至想到将思想联系在一起。我待在捷克的最后一天，我和一位多产的捷克中年翻译家李素（Zuzana Li）进行了一次午餐采访，她指出，中捷合作不仅涉及商业和贸易。她曾把十本当代中国的小说和诗歌翻译成捷克语，她甚至开始为捷克的中学教师提供在线资料来介绍中国文学，她说这是看中国的另一个窗口。这让我想起著名作家鲁迅的一句话：世界上本没有路，走的人多了，也便成了路。对"一带一路"倡议来说，它亟需世界人民的主张和积极贡献，我们希望捷克方面能够积极主动地将中国的倡议变成自己的国家工作议程，这是走上共同繁荣发展道路的过程，在这个存在地区冲突、战争、恐怖主义和经济动荡的世界中，我们迫切需要这样一条发展道路。

资深政治家的敏锐嗅觉

在2016年和2017年，我有机会与捷克思想家和政治家深入交流。我没有看到他们在任何其他国家进行过集体的、积极的分享以及对话记者，这是我职业生涯中最快乐的时光之一。我在2016年年初习近平主席访问捷克共和国前不久，见到了捷克共和国前总统瓦茨拉夫·克劳斯（Vaclav Klaus）。他说，习近平主席的访问是"具有历史意义以及遵循理性发展的"，表明双方是如何认真对待双方的发展战略关系的。他说，中国应该觉得与像捷克这样的欧洲国家发展如此明确的伙伴关系是符合自己的战略利益的，他从2003年到2013年一直担任捷克共和国总统，也担任了较长时间的总理，他自己退休后在布拉格成立了全球事务研究所。

克劳斯多次访华，他认为现在开始和中国合作是合乎逻辑的。1993年，捷克和斯洛伐克独立，克劳斯说，捷克共和国首先与邻国建立良好的关系是自然的，但是这种只关注邻国的外交已经持续很长时间了，当时与欧洲国家的贸易额达到总量的近80%。"习近平主席的这次访问是这种情况的合理发展，我本人和中国的关系很好。"克劳斯说。

他说："现在我们也应该与中国保持更密切的联系。"他补充说，捷克共和国非常认真地对待习近平主席的访问。克劳斯说："当习近平主席决定访问时，我们发现中国在认识捷克在中欧关系框架中的作用也是非常严肃的。我们很高兴习近平主席没有去英国、法国或者德国，而来了捷克，他来到了欧洲的中心地带。"克劳斯说，中东欧国家曾经和中国有着类似的政治制度，与其他欧洲国家相比，他们更容易了解中国。

作为高级经济学家，克劳斯对中国经济前景持乐观态度，谈到欧美经常讨论中国经济的放缓，他说："我是这个话题的第一个反对者。如果中国的经济增长率在 6% 到 8% 之间摇摆不定就认为是经济放缓，那么你们长期增长率几乎为零的大陆（欧洲）又是什么呢？"他知道中国面临诸多挑战，但辩论的重点不应该是增长率本身。他说："辩论应该是关于中国能否给我们带来正的增长，我的答案是肯定的。"

捷克前总理鲁斯诺克（Rusnok）从来没有访问过中国，但他脑子里却有着许多中国城市和企业的名字。当习近平主席 2016 年 3 月 28 日至 30 日乘飞机前往捷克进行国事访问时，鲁斯诺克表示，他的国家应该跟随欧洲同侪的脚步，加强和深化"各个方面"的合作。"在许多方面，双方的关系在过去的几十年里并不像过去几年那么好，我们许多同侪已经走在我们的前面，我们还有很长的路要走。"在习近平主席访问之后不久，他开始担任捷克共和国中央银行行长。对于这次访问，他认为应该是对捷克共和国最高层次和最重要的访问，这确实证明了双边关系处于有史以来最好的时期。

鲁斯诺克说："我相信这将促进我们在各方面的合作关系。"他补充说，双方的关系将从商业向文化、健康、教育、科研、交通和科学合作的方向深化。鲁斯诺克坐在布拉格中央银行的办公室里说，这非常棒，因为迄今还有未开发的潜力来进一步加强合作，但是匈牙利、波兰和德国、法国、英国等西欧大国已经与中国建立了战略合作伙伴关系，他说："所以我们似乎赶上了近十年来我们一直错过的事情，我很敬佩总统和总理在过去两三年取得的进展。"

鲁斯诺克表示，这些变化背后的原因是捷克政治内部的自然发展，大部分政治代表已经意识到，他们的国家曾经错过了与中国建立关系并获得更多中国市场的机会，我们过去的确犯了一些错误，我很高兴现在我们有一些务实的方式和中国进行合作。他说："我们跟上了欧盟的合作伙伴的步伐，他们与中国的合作也早了几年。"

当被问及捷克是否应该考虑加入亚洲基础设施投资银行时，他表示他的国家应该像许多欧盟国家那样做。"所以我应该说我们没有理由不成为亚投行的一分子，因为我相信，如果我们加入亚投行，促使我们的商业公司去竞标亚投行资助，以争取由这家银行资助的项目是可能的。"鲁斯诺克说。同时他表示，亚洲显然是发展潜力很大的地区。"所以我认为我们不应该错过这个机会，捷克政府应该考虑抓住这个机会加入亚投行，"鲁斯诺克说，"但是，我不确定在习近平主席访问期间是否会讨论这个问题。"说到合作，鲁斯诺克说，由于捷克处于连接东亚和欧洲的门户位置，双方都应该把交通作为合作重点。他说："布拉格机场仍然有客运和货运的潜力。"

鲁斯诺克说，除了其他的航班，成都和布拉格之间的直飞航班是非常重要的，因为他相信成都是一个欧洲人前往东南亚或是南亚理想的转机机场。鲁斯诺克说："与北京和上海相比，成都机场对我们来说是一个有趣的地方。"例如，每年有 30 多万捷克人在泰国旅游，但是只有 20% 的人使用从成都中转的路线，这将提高经济上的可行性。而且货运的前景也是令人振奋的，因为许多亚洲投资者已经在捷克共和国的制造业和工业领域展开业务，这些领域非常具有竞争力。他说："他们需要从中国运输电子零件，所以空运货物也很重要。"

2005 年，帕鲁贝克（Paroubek）任捷克总理时，他很有远见地飞到北京，与时任中国国务院总理温家宝举行会谈，加强捷克与中国的业务关系。至少中国的电视制造企业长虹已经在捷克成立了一家新工厂，这是他帮助实现的成功合作的一部分。2006 年 9 月在他卸任后，捷克政要主要关注内政，到目前为止，长虹在欧盟内部的贸易额仍占了其总贸易额的最大比例。在过去的两三年里，捷克再次努力深化与中国的经贸关系。

生于 1952 年的帕鲁贝克，在 2016 年与我谈话时说："在十年前，我与中国领导层谈考虑我们的战略伙伴关系，我对这一改变感到非常高兴。"他说，他感谢双方领导人的"勇气和远见"，考虑把双方关系提升到战略高度，习近平主席的访问给双边关系带来了巨大的积极影响。帕鲁贝克表示，习近平主席是一位"有远见、认真踏实"的全球政治家，他非常了解中国人最需要的东西。"习近平主席为打击腐败，维持中国经济高速发展作出了巨大努力，这已经给我留下了深刻的印象。"

同样让他印象深刻的是习近平主席的远见卓识，他带领中国积极主动地走向世界，为推动中国走向世界舞台作出贡献。他说："中国为世界作出的贡献是显而易见的。"捷克愿意与中国合作，特别是在促进双边贸易方面，但现在这个内陆国家的贸易伙伴还是在欧洲。他认为，捷克的工业竞争力非常强大，其产品质量可以与德国相媲美，而德国在贸易关系方面远远超过捷克。"我们与德国生产的产品质量相同，但价格偏低，所以我们需要加强对中国的出口。"帕鲁贝克说。

同时他说，捷克应该更加努力地与中国的"一带一路"倡议协同发展。他承认，捷克没有成为亚洲基础设施投资银行的创始成员，这是一个错误。他说："我希望我们能够在这方面做些事情赶上来。"帕鲁贝克还表示，除了与亚投行有可能进行合作之外，如果双方考虑在捷克高速铁路建设以及改善物流和货运方面进行合作，这将是很有意义的。帕鲁贝克说，两国应该超越正常的商业合作，试图探索音乐、绘画和电影的机会，丰富两国人民的思想。帕鲁贝克说，这次访问对中国加强与中东欧国家的关系是至关重要的。"这是习近平就任国家主席后首次来到中欧、东欧地区，我相信这次访问对于促进中国与中东欧国家的关系非常重要。"

他还认为，习近平主席将为2014年访问欧盟传递一个信号。他说，推动北京与布鲁塞尔的关系是非常重要的，但在一些领域，布鲁塞尔会受到华盛顿的影响。帕鲁贝克说："我们可以看到欧盟缺乏独立性，因为它的一些政策，比如难民、乌克兰危机和与俄罗斯的关系，都会受到美国的影响。"欧盟应该承认中国的市场经济地位，承认中国为全球的经济作出的贡献，承认中国在过去几十年对欧洲发展的贡献。帕鲁贝克说："西方人应该非常了解这一点，并认识到这一点，但由于某种原因，美国对欧盟的影响仍在。"

2014年年初，习近平在2013年3月当选中国国家主席之后，先后访问了四个西欧国家和欧盟总部，进行了首次欧洲之行。他还参加了2014年3月在海牙举行的世界核安全峰会，并于2016年年初访问了捷克共和国，然后飞往华盛顿参加世界核安全峰会。

在中国和之前承诺成为最好的西方合作伙伴的英国之间，中英战略伙伴关系的黄金十年在中国国家主席习近平于2015年10月对英国进行国事访问后揭开了序幕。习近平主席还参加了2015年年底举行的巴黎气候变化峰会，帮助达成遏制温室气体排放的全球协议。综观习近平主席所有"具有里程碑意义"的欧洲之行，其他中国领导人近三年来也多次访问欧盟国家，欧洲国家也增加了来中国访问的频率。所有这些高层政治和外交行动都伴随着令人振奋的、多元化的商业合作和人文交流。

尽管如此，欧洲朋友也曾多次向我提出疑问：北京和布鲁塞尔下定决心建立战略伙伴关系，但北京正在深化与成员国之间的关系，同时加强与中东欧国家的合作。这是为什么？基本上这是一个错误的命题，中国坚持欧洲一体化的原则，坚持让所有主权国家参与进来。在实践层面上，在2014年结束访问时，习近平主席明确表示，决心建立"和平、增长、改革、文明"的伙伴关系。基于欧盟及其成员国的现实，这四个词同时适用于欧盟国家和欧盟的目标和竞争力。

所以我对这个问题的回答是一个口号：找到能够奏效的任何方式积累中欧关系正能量。这意味着如果中国一直朝着实现这一目标的方向努力，就应该鼓励各级的联系和参与。因此，要问北京应该和谁合作，特别是在欧洲正面临经济增长、恐怖主义、移民和一体化进程等各种挑战的时候，这是毫无意义的，中国倡导的积极、务实的欧洲政策才是欧洲急需的。

北京不仅提出了方案和想法。政界人士、商界领袖甚至普通人（游客或送子女到欧洲接受更好教育的人）都已经采取了行动。尽管双边贸易活动受到了全球经济放缓的影响，但双向投资依然活跃，中国投资者仍将欧洲作为公司兼并收购扩张的首选目的地。

欧盟成员国显然很欢迎中国的做法，其目的是在经济上寻求更多的双赢机会，增进人民之间的相互理解，共同承担更多的全球责任。例如，英国承诺要成为中国在西方最好的朋友，而布拉格决定把两国关系扩大到战略层面。

令人鼓舞的是，许多欧洲国家加入了北京的"一带一路"倡议，以加强基础设施、贸易和人员流动的联系合作。多达20个欧洲国家作为创始成员加入了北京发起的亚洲基础设施投资银行。回顾前十年、二十年，近两年来中欧领导人所做的这些决定应该被视为是历史性的、战略性的、有意义的。

总而言之，世界现在还缺乏使得地球更加和平繁荣的统领性的思想。中国人已经提出了，欧洲人也回应了中国，尽管部分西方列强反对，或者至少有些犹豫。这应该被视为近几年来中欧伙伴关系的最大成就。但这只是真正的战略合作伙伴关系的开始。

在谈到2016年习近平主席访问时，捷克共和国议会副议长沃伊捷赫·菲利普（Vojtech Filip）表示，已经认识到这个欧洲国家在帮助推动中欧关系、建立多极世界的作用，这是符合捷克共和国的利益的。"我们相信，习近平主席的这次访问是我们可以追溯到 67 年前的两国关系的里程碑事件，我们的目标是建立一个面向 21 世纪的战略伙伴关系，其主题是塑造多极世界。"菲利普在习近平主席访问前接受采访时告诉我。3 月底，习近平主席会见了菲利普等议会和党派领导人。拥有四万二千名成员的捷克议会最大的党派——波西米亚和摩拉维亚共产党的主席菲利普，他在访问中国之前曾与习近平主席会面。

菲利普说，习近平主席是一个有远见卓识的人，对欧洲和世界形势有着深刻的了解，还是一位经验丰富的沟通者。菲利普说："他是一个具有个人魅力的人，我认为 90% 的捷克人都喜欢他，并期待着他的访问。"他还说，他与习近平主席的第一次谈话发生在 2011 年的北京，当时习近平还是中国的副主席。"他有信心，有远见，有很多想法。"对于这次访问，菲利普也把它看作是一个新的起点，因为两国在 20 世纪 50 年代就建立了密切的关系，捷克斯洛伐克（当时的）是世界上第一批承认新中国的国家。他说，这是双边关系的基础，捷克总统泽曼在 20 世纪 90 年代以后，特别是担任总理期间时，就开始促进双方保持更加密切的联系。

而现在，泽曼在 2013 年当选总统后，双方加紧了建立更密切关系的步伐。"显然，总统和总理都与中国的关系更加紧密，在过去三年里，捷克和中国的重要领导人之间进行了重要的会晤和访问，这对我们来说很重要。"菲利普说。他表示，双方的战略伙伴关系将面向 21 世纪，其中多极世界是关键，中国和欧盟是这个多极世界的重要组成部分，捷克对中国深化与欧盟的关系表示强烈的支持。现在很明显，中国在世界上发挥了负责任的、积极的作用，习近平主席的"一带一路"倡议被看作是中国为世界和平提供"经济基础"的解决方案。他说，习近平主席访问捷克共和国是在二战结束七十年后发生的。菲利普说："思考全球大国如何为世界和平作出贡献是有意义的，中国已经树立了建设性的榜样。"

捷克共和国前国防部部长雅罗斯拉夫·特夫迪克（Jaroslav Tvrdik）也表示，从政治信仰到家庭联系，捷克总统泽曼和捷克总理博胡斯拉夫·索博特卡（Bohuslav Sobotka）长期把中国视为"战略伙伴"。特夫迪克说："他们有详细的、优先级别高的议程来处理他们与中国的关系，我相信他们已经投入了大量的精力。"

现在他担任捷克最高领导层的特别顾问，负责协调习近平主席访问捷克的各方面的安排。泽曼曾于 1999 年访华，时任捷克总理，而后曾在其担任捷克共和国总统期间两次访问中国，他数次与习近平主席会面。特夫迪克说："他是中捷关系的长期支持者，这是一个长期的愿景。"他从政生涯的早期阶段就投入了大量的个人热情和爱心来发展捷克与中国的关系，他的政策是始终一致的。

索博特卡总理和他的父亲都曾在 2015 年访问中国，他的目的是加强捷克与中国的关系，然后邀请习近平主席提前访问他的国家（原定于 2017 年年中）。为了庆祝自己 70 岁生日，索博特卡的父亲于 9 月底从布拉格飞往北京，重温他在大约二十年前作为工程师在中国工作时所留下的回忆。特夫迪克说："这也是特别的，因为总理为他的父亲及其在 2000 年一起共事的同事买了飞机票作为父亲的生日礼物。"

索博特卡总理的父亲和同事在中国天津工作了三年，他在中国的经历很可能影响了索博特卡总理对这个新兴大国的看法。据特夫迪克说，索博特卡总理的父亲愉快地接受了儿子的礼物，不过有两个额外的要求。首先，他需要一名翻译陪同；第二，他需要一个中国阅兵式的 T 恤，庆祝于 2015 年 9 月 3 日举行的中国人民抗日战争暨世界反法西斯战争胜利 70 周年纪念活动。"最后，总理的父亲在 2015 年 9 月访问中国的整个过程中都穿着这件 T 恤，"特夫迪克说，"那时他也 70 岁了。"

索博特卡总理开始与中国进行"家庭联系"，2015 年 11 月底访华时，他也带去了他的孩子们。在孩子们出发之前，孩子们的祖父给了他们一个去中国参观游览的教程。当索博特卡总理与习近平主席结束会谈时，他们曾有个轻松的时刻。习近平主席说，他对捷克共和国有深刻的印象。"因为我年轻的时候，父亲在离开捷克回家的时候给我买了一双皮鞋，那是我生命中第一双皮鞋。"

时任中国国务院副总理习仲勋曾于 1959 年访问了捷克斯洛伐克，索博特卡总理还与习近平主席分享了他的家人在中国的故事。特夫迪克引用索博特卡总理的话说："我为我父亲在中国工作而感到骄傲，我在延续这份友谊。"索博特卡于 2007 年首次访问中国，并在总理任期内成立了中国事务工作组。

人心相通

在 2016 年 3 月 28—30 日访问捷克共和国期间，习近平主席和捷克总统泽曼进行了密集的政治会晤，与青年足球和冰球运动员进行了热烈的交流，签署了合作文件，还一起参观了老布拉格的斯特拉霍夫图书馆。在博物馆馆长介绍了中捷交流 300 ~ 500 年历史的馆藏后，两位国家元首走上了阳台，一边啜饮着他们的告别啤酒，一边俯瞰布拉格。

习近平主席离开布拉格前往华盛顿参加核安全峰会后的不久，我也有机会参观了这座宏伟的图书馆，这个图书馆由哲学馆和神学馆组成，其中哲学馆收藏了《论语》的捷克语版本和早期全面介绍中国的典籍；神学馆则由灰泥和绘画装饰。关于中国的书籍，有些是原稿，大部分是由几百年前的传教士回到捷克时撰写的。

负责为习近平主席准备物品的图书馆馆藏负责人简·帕雷兹（Jan Parez）说，习近平主席对捷克社会和文化有着深刻的理解和尊重。感谢帕雷兹，我有幸参观了现在向游客开放的两个大厅，享受了布拉格的全景，并沉浸在捷克总统和中国主席喝告别啤酒的地方的美丽风景中。

习近平主席说，看到如此丰富的艺术和文化宝藏是一种难得的经历。其他一些报道此次访问的记者称这是世界上最美丽的图书馆。这是一个知识和美的灯塔，传达了强烈的信息。两位国家领导人都是偏爱历史和文明类书籍的阅读者，悠久的历史和丰富的文化遗产是捷克人民的宝贵财富，中国有着 5000 多年历史的古老文明，习近平主席在访问期间突出强调了建立战略伙伴关系之后两国相互学习、扩大文化交流的巨大潜力。两位领导人都知道，加强民间交流和文化交流是为两国关系发展奠定坚实基础的关键。

习近平主席访问捷克共和国期间，提倡文化的相互尊重，但是他的访问不仅限于经济和文化交流。习近平主席在中国宣布"十三五"（2016—2020）规划后不久访问了捷克。到 2020 年计划完成时，中国人均 GDP 有望达到 12000 美元，成为一个相对高收入的国家。

鉴于这些事实，可以说习近平主席对斯特拉霍夫图书馆的访问也体现了他给有需要的人提供足够的公共物品的承诺，这是拥有丰富经验的欧洲可以给中国提供建议的领域，例如，欧洲已经使用一个小孩在家读书的数量这一指标来衡量一个地区的人们的生活条件。

中国要建立更多的图书馆，让贫困家庭的孩子能够获得更多的书籍，因为这些书籍可以帮助他们摆脱贫困。按照欧洲的标准，图书馆、博物馆、剧院、体育中心和游泳池都应该被优先考虑，以促进中国的经济发展，提高人们的收入和生活水平。

当泽曼总统于 2014 年年底在中国人民大学发表演讲时，他收到了一份特别的礼物：中国著名作家阎连科的小说《四书》的捷克语版。这是作为大学教授的阎连科花了二十年时间构思，两年时间写作的一部关于 20 世纪五六十年代中国发展的作品，该作品获得了 2014 年的国际卡夫卡文学奖。

来自捷克共和国的李素是翻译苏童、刘震云等中国作家作品的译者。李素回顾了泽曼接受的礼物，她说，中国与欧洲国家之间的富有成果的交流也很大程度上依赖于建立在普通人心灵上的信任。"文学和电影是达到这个目标的理想工具。" 在泽曼去北京出席"一带一路"的国际合作高峰论坛之前，李素在布拉格热闹的咖啡吧告诉我。李素说，她希望把这个信息传达给参加论坛的人士，即使在数字化转型的时代，也应该大力支持文学翻译，弥合文化理解上的差距。

从 20 世纪 90 年代开始学习中文的李素说："电影现在占了上风，但文学在弥合相互理解的鸿沟方面也是必不可少的。" 她十年前在北京大学修读中国文学博士学位，她热爱文献中所描述的中国人的日常生活的爱情、艰辛、绝望、悲伤和成功。这位勤劳的中年捷克语译者将中文翻译成捷克语，她过着非常简单的生活：她每周花六天时间在布拉格安静的书房里进行翻译工作；她每天工作六个小时，如果有截稿日期，她甚至会在星期天加班，而且她每天的工作时间甚至会更长。她在闲暇时间会阅读中国书籍和观看中国电影，来丰富她对中国社会和文化的理解。当然，她补充说："当我疲于翻译时，大概会花等量的时间进行阅读；有时候，理解各种作家的叙事风格是很难的。"

但是她说了解那些普通中国人的生活，他们如何养家糊口，他们的命运发生怎样的变化，是最令人愉快的事情。由于她的勤奋努力，她每年至少翻译两本中国现当代文学的书籍。"这是我的爱，我很幸运，因为不是每个人都能过上这么平静的生活，"李素说，"如果我不做翻译工作，我无法想象我还能做什么，我确实认为我们的交流会超越商业，着重于文化和文学交流上。"

沉浸在中国相关书籍中的这种专心致志的生活，李素用自己的方式去体会这个国家近年来的进步，这也体现在一批优秀作家的诞生之中，这些作家的杰出作品有可能赢得诺贝尔文学奖。"作家莫言获得诺贝尔奖对中国来说无疑是一个巨大的成功，"李素说，"但是我觉得有很多中国作家应该获此殊荣。"在中国获得博士学位之前，李素的学术和阅读经验囊括了欧美文学。"所以我认为，中国作家已经出版了很多高质量的作品，就像其他国家的作家一样。"

她的结论是从行动中得出的。20 世纪 90 年代，她发现很难找到捷克语的中国小说和故事，她也不明白为什么，因为她在中国学习了一年，知道这是一个文学丰富的国家。她联系了一家出版商，试图填补这个空白，但是由于出版商对中国一无所知，最后她失败了。后来，她遇到了一位 Verzone 出版社的人，他曾经去过中国并且爱上了它。她回忆说："他感到很遗憾的是，很少中文书籍被翻译成捷克语，我相信更多的捷克语读者会感受到阅读这些故事和情节的喜悦。"

最近翻译的作品是《炸裂志》，这本书也是由阎连科撰写的，其主题是他的家乡，河南省中部的一个村庄，如何在中国取得经济奇迹的四十年中改变的。李素说，她翻译的《四书》和《炸裂志》也将帮助她的读者了解中国过去几十年发展的轨迹。另外一本书是由著名作家刘震云创作的《我不是潘金莲》。在翻译过程中，李素对刘震云的写作风格印象深刻，她认为这种写作风格非常幽默，读者也很容易阅读。"刘震云以诙谐幽默的方式描述了中国人的日常生活，这也是捷克出版商对这本书感兴趣的原因，所以我认为这也是捷克读者看中国人生活的好方法。"

因其翻译中国现当代文学的娴熟技巧，她得到了孔子学院总部的资助。2016 年 8 月，她在文学翻译方面的不懈努力获得了中国政府的表彰，刘延东副总理接见了全世界 19 位杰出的汉学家。刘于"一带一路"倡议，她说："我认为这是一个庞大的事业，需要多年的耐心和细致的工作。我相信，我正在帮助捷克人通过翻译过来的中国畅销书来认识中国普通人的日常生活，这为发展'一带一路'奠定了基础，这是至关重要的、必不可少的、有效的。"

除了文学交流以外，中国和捷克共同启动了由中国国家外国专家局和捷克科技联（CAST）实施的新一轮人员交流与合作协议。捷克科技联主席贾罗米尔·沃尔夫（Jaromir Volf）在接受采访时说，习近平主席 2016 年初访捷是在捷克总统和总理访华之后进行的，他相信习近平主席的历史性访问会让中捷双边关系更加深远、广泛。沃尔夫表示，这次访问是"两国之间最重要的政治事件"，捷克科技联是由 67 个技术和工业协会组成的独立法人实体，有近 10 万名成员，是捷克政府与技术人员沟通的重要渠道。"我们拥有如此庞大的数据库，我们愿意与中国政府合作，挑选出中国需要的专家。"沃尔夫说。

沃尔夫曾三次访华，现在已成为首位在新的合作框架下工作的捷克专家："我开始频繁地往来于中捷之间，为双方找到专家。"沃尔夫是一名工程师，他于 2016 年年底在山东省工作，他已经签署了一份为期五年的合同。他说："我非常高兴能够成为两国交流的桥梁的建设者，加深彼此的合作。"他说，他每次接待中国代表团时，他们都表现出对捷克专家的极大兴趣，对农业和技术领域充满热情。他相信两国在这些领域应该有巨大的协同发展的潜力。捷克在种植小麦、玉米等方面具有竞争力，他说："中国也已经表现出对这些领域的兴趣。"

作为一个先进的工业国家，捷克在机械技术、自动化、建筑、机器人技术和电子方面也有很强的竞争力。沃尔夫说："如果中国提出合作需求，我们愿意在这些领域与中国进行合作。"他补充说，中国现在的科技竞争十分激烈，上海、香港、北京等地都拥有先进的大学。他说："这些城市的科学技术水平非常高，我们可以进行高科技的双向交流。"

中捷两国体育交流也是一个重点。冰球教练斯拉沃米尔·莱纳（Slavomir Lener）依然记得二十年前他在中国的东北在零下30 ~ 40摄氏度寒冷天气里训练中国运动员，这被他称为"疯狂而伟大"的经历。之前他从来没有体验过如此严寒的低温。在那之后他没有再访问过中国。他在2016年年初告诉我，当一群年轻的种子选手接受他的训练为2022年冬季奥运会的比赛做准备时，他感到非常兴奋，因为2022年冬奥会将在北京和河北张家口举行。

"我们已经开始了第一阶段的准备，训练他们成为中国国家队在2022年冬奥会上的核心力量。"曾经于1995年在中国国家队执教了大约六个月的莱纳说。他在捷克冰球协会接受采访时说，二十名年轻中国球员于2016年3月24日在布拉格开始了为期八天的训练。莱纳是训练营的主教练，负责制定训练时间表、安排最好的教练训练球员们，并为年轻球员们组织三场比赛。"这是与中国冰球球员的第一次接触，我们会根据这次培训后的效果来判断合作是否会继续。"这些都发生在习近平主席对捷克进行的为期40个小时的国事访问之前。在此次访问之前，身为一名足球迷的习近平主席还主持了 2022 年冬奥会筹备工作的会议。

在泽曼总统（2016 年 9 月）和索博特卡总理（11 月）访问中国时，他们都与中国领导人谈到了体育合作。

2015 年末，当中国奥委会原主席刘鹏访问布拉格时，他表示非常愿意在筹备 2022 年冬奥会阶段向捷克学习冬季体育活动和赛事组织的经验。"我发现可以从捷克的冬季运动中学到很多东西。"刘鹏这样说。习近平主席是 67 年以来首次访问捷克的中国国家主席，双方将很有可能借此契机宣布冬季体育运动方面的合作计划。捷克国家奥委会主席吉日·科耶瓦尔（Jiri Kejval）说："在习近平主席访问期间，除了中国的冰球运动员接受训练之外，年轻的足球运动员也将参加比赛。运动和友谊是相关的，我们知道中国不仅要组织冬奥会，还要参与到比赛中来。"

科耶瓦尔说，他的国家准备在六年内帮助中国赶上冰球强国。2015 年，中国在全球男子冰球比赛中排名第 38 位，中国冰球队只有跻身世界前 18 强才能有资格参加 2022 年奥运会。科耶瓦尔相信他的教练们有能力实现这一目标。在 20 世纪 50 年代，捷克教练教过俄罗斯人，现在（2015 年）他们的成绩是世界上最好的。科耶瓦尔说："尽管团体项目比个人项目更难，但我百分之百相信中国一定可以培养出具有极强竞争力的冰球运动员。"

莱纳说，运用他的训练能力，中国已经为胜利做好了准备。他说中国球员非常专注，渴望学习和竞争。他补充说："我们要训练他们打曲棍球的感觉，因为这是一场十人的比赛，而不是一场个人比赛。"他和科耶瓦尔都高度赞扬了中国在体育和赛事组织方面取得的巨大进步，称 2008 年北京奥运会十分壮观。"现在中国开始转向发展冬季运动，这给我们带来了很多合作机会。"科耶瓦尔说。他认为中国也可以在足球方面与捷克合作，因为足球已经成为一项大范围推广的运动。他说，学习是双向的。"我们可以从中国学习排球、乒乓球和其他运动。"

2016 年 3 月，习近平主席访问布拉格时，斯拉维亚国际杯首次亮相，来自两国的几支年轻球队参加了比赛，习近平主席和泽曼总统接见了这些球员。

4 月 21—23 日，中国和欧洲球员来参加 2017 年的比赛时，泽曼接见了来自两国的球队成员，他在 5 月份进行第三次访华时表示："虽然我不是一个足球运动员，但我知道足球比赛充满着乐趣和欢乐，我希望你们能成长为不会被你们的粉丝们遗忘的明星。"他回忆说，他一生只踢过一次足球。他说："但我会为来自中国和捷克的年轻男孩们欢呼。"

电影也是两国沟通交流的媒介。颇受欢迎的浪漫爱情电影《有一个地方只有我们知道》就是几年前在布拉格拍摄的，这个电影是由曾获奖无数的徐静蕾导演并主演的。据中国驻捷克共和国大使马克卿介绍，近年来，由于两国关系的不断加深，这个国家的宏伟建筑和壮丽的自然美景已经被几部中国电影取景。在中国与欧洲国家交织关系的背后隐藏着值得双方共同探索的话题，可以满足数字时代影视剧观众不断增长的需求。题材则从历史到时局交流、战争、爱情、英雄、家庭和食物，取之不尽。

如果他们把更多的故事搬到屏幕上，就会产生连锁效应，因为中国电影和电视剧的需求正在迅速扩大。中国的一个现实就是这个国家的中产阶级正在迅速扩张，几年之内其规模将相当于欧洲的总人口，中产阶级对娱乐和旅游有很大的胃口，当他们对电影印象深刻的时候，他们会考虑去到影视剧拍摄地旅行。2017年，捷克共和国的中国游客数量翻了十倍，达到 50 万人，这就是典型的例子。

此外，对于中国游客中的电影爱好者来说，他们尤其应该参观布拉格市中心的电影海报展览馆，该电影海报馆展出了 1936年至 1961 年的 1200 张原创电影海报。"现在我们正试图吸引越来越多的中国游客，因为许多中国游客纷纷涌入布拉格。"画廊的高级顾问佩特拉·帕罗贝克（Petra Paroubek）说。她表示，习近平主席的访问将使布拉格对中国游客更具吸引力，她相信越来越多的人会来到布拉格。她说："我们相信很多中国游客都是喜欢看这些原创海报的电影影迷。"

帕罗贝克还说，她的团队正在联系旅行社来介绍这个展览馆，与此同时，该团队正在开发中文版海报和网站。据帕罗贝克介绍，这个展览馆汇聚了一批来自好莱坞和欧洲电影黄金时代的独特收藏，参观者可以看到像马龙·白兰度、约翰·韦恩、索菲亚·罗兰、马琳·迪特里奇、阿兰·德隆、让·加宾等人。她说："参观者可以买到海报的副本或有海报式样的 T 恤。"展览馆里的第二次世界大战领袖的蜡像作品，主要是对学生开放的，蜡像全部是在 20 世纪 50 年代和 60 年代以传统工艺手工制作而成的，而不是铸造的。帕罗贝克说："这里展出的所有物品都来自私人的收藏。"

商业机会

当25 岁的廉永平从中国的西南地区搬到捷克开始帮他的公司从零起步建厂时，他觉得这个国家很陌生。在与当地工作人员第一次开会时他对于如何表达自己感到不知所措。

而如今该工厂 2016 年生产的电视机多达 100 万台，著名家用电器品牌长虹负责欧洲业务的总经理廉永平在捷克经过多年的摸爬滚打之后，已经有了再扩张三倍市场的梦想。"我的雄心壮志源于我们的经验，我们发现扩张是迫在眉睫的，是具有可行性和实操性的，"廉永平说，"现在是雄心勃勃的时候了。"

他说他们工厂的电视机销量增长很快，在过去的三年里，增长率平均达到 20%。廉永平说："一旦我们的电视销量超过 100 万，占欧洲市场份额的 3%，那么从我们前十年的经验来看，超过两百万就相对容易了。但关键是如何以一种聪明又统一的方式实现这一目标。"

首先，他的公司决定在工厂旁边建立一个研发中心。同时，也将转向生产冰箱、洗衣机等家用电器。

"这是为我们的欧洲家电生产基地而设计的，我们的目标是提升自己的品牌。"廉永平指着他的公司已经在工厂旁边购买的空地说。其次，他感到有充足的动力去扩大生产链以保护产品的生命周期。他说："我们的目标是建立自己的物流中心，将业务扩展到销售、售后服务和维护，这些都比制造业更有利可图。"

廉永平表示，他的母公司十分支持他对拓展业务链的想法。他说："一旦我们有了自己完整的业务链，我们也可以使用这个平台为其他电子产品提供服务。"他的工厂已经租用了布拉格附近的仓储空间，以此作为实现扩张计划的试点步骤。"再次，我想吸引更多的中国投资者来到捷克，一起在我们工厂所在的宁布尔克建设一个高科技工业区，"廉永平说，"我想分享我的经验和教训，然后我们可以共同为捷克的发展作出贡献。"

目前，宁布尔克和四川省已经开始在廉永平的工厂旁边合作建设高科技工业区。四川省政府已经开始吸引更多的投资者来这个占地约400万平方米的区域。廉永平说："我们十年前从零开始，我相信这个工业园将在未来十年成形。"

他说，习近平主席的这次访问大大提高了双方的政治互信，为企业扩张铺平了道路。同时，廉永平说，习近平主席的这次访问也有助于捷克和欧洲人再次认识到中国制造的产品的竞争力，捷克这个国家的目标是把制造能力提高到一个更高的水平。廉永平说："我们对中国领导层的全球共赢的愿景感到振奋。引入'一带一路'倡议，以更好地连接亚洲、欧洲和非洲国家，从商人的角度来看，这是在为我们创造机会，促进货物流动。"

他说捷克共和国是中国投资者在欧洲扩张的理想地点，因为捷克具有门户优势。尽管处于内陆地区，但捷克可通过公路、铁路和航空运输通往欧洲和世界的其他地方。

同时，廉永平说，捷克人受过良好教育，劳动者工作勤奋，并且工资水平低于西欧。廉永平说："在我看来，这是中国投资者的理想选择。"

但他表示，中国投资者应该足够谦逊，因为大多数欧洲国家在过去的几十年中，在工厂运营和业务扩张方面已经经历了技术、工业和管理"革命"，这给欧洲国家留下了宝贵的财富。廉永平说："我们只能先学习，然后在学习的同时考虑创新，这会是一个可行的选择。"他的工厂已经在组装过程中实现了自动化，管理高度依赖于数字软件应用；与他的资深团队一起，他开发了一个管理软件应用程序，使用大约 500 个关键数据和评判标准实现在一个系统里衡量他的 400 个管理人员和员工的表现。"我只需要关心负责生产、销售、采购和财务的各个经理的表现，如果我需要检查，我只需打开我的手机，看看应用程序中显示的进度，"廉永平说，"如果不能达到目标，我会先收到提醒，然后我会提醒经理们。"但是一般情况下，他很放松。"因为每个人都知道自己的责任，系统会自动提醒他们。"

而捷克技术大学校长彼得·库沃柳卡（Petro Kouvaliuka）说，除了新建项目外，中国和捷克的研究人员还成功地开发了一台时速超过 500 公里的铁路发动机。

在 2016 年 3 月 28 日至 30 日，习近平主席访问捷克前，库沃柳卡宣布了这一成就。这一突破是由他的大学团队与中国大连东北部的专门从事高速发动机研发的中车大连电力牵引研发中心有限公司共同完成的。

库沃柳卡在 2016 年年初接受采访时告诉我："中捷两国的研究人员取得了突破性的成果，时速超过 500 公里的发动机是可行的，它速度快并且具有商业可行性。"库沃柳卡说，他们在连接北京和成都的两千公里铁路上使用这款高速发动机。"之后，他们会尝试在欧洲或美国销售。"

当被问及发动机是否可以在捷克使用时，库沃柳卡说现在是不可能的，因为捷克铁路常被河流、山脉和乡镇阻隔为曲线铁路，捷克列车的最高速度是每小时 160 公里。库沃柳卡说："但也许我们可以建造连接布拉格和距离我们大约 200 公里的第二大城市布尔诺的高速铁路。"

中国已经提出"一带一路"倡议，通过改善基础设施来更好地连接亚欧大陆，一些捷克政界人士表示有兴趣在捷克建设高速铁路，尽管面临着巨大的障碍，如环境影响的评估和公众参与造成的决策缓慢等问题。关于捷克是否应该考虑让中国参与修建高速铁路，前总理鲁斯诺克说，捷克在这方面欠发达，应该有一个长期的考虑，但捷克人知道中国正在帮助其他中东欧国家发展类似的项目。鲁斯诺克说："我们会把中国参与修建铁路作为一种参照项目，既然中国进行得很成功，为什么不进一步进入中欧，进入捷克共和国呢？"

捷克前外交部部长科胡特也表示，他的总统和其他官员一样对中国从天津到北京的高速列车印象深刻。"毫无疑问中国公司在铁路建设方面有绝对的竞争力，"科胡特说，"不仅捷克需要这样的技术，中欧也同样很需要。"他说，中国正在帮助建设布达佩斯和贝尔格莱德之间的高速铁路。捷克和德国将在德国的德累斯顿市和布拉格之间建立一条高速铁路线，从而将旅程时间从 2 小时 15 分钟缩短到 50 分钟。"这是一个小的开始，但是由于环境影响评估和公众参与决策很难实现大的基础设施项目。"科胡特说。但如果中国公司想在欧洲投资这样的项目，他们应该在招标开始的前两三年过来欧洲。科鲁特说："在竞投大标之前，在当地进行投资是非常重要的。"

尽管高速铁路项目还在讨论之中，但布拉格与位于中国浙江的经济蓬勃发展的著名商品输送城市义乌之间的首条货运列车于2017年7月20日从捷克首都首发，货运铁路的开通受到了泽曼总统和索博特卡总理的赞誉，这是习近平主席2013年提出的"一带一路"倡议下的双边合作的又一个重要里程碑。

捷克国家最高领导人在一年一度的中国投资者论坛上讲话时同意签署该项目，那次中国投资者论坛有1500多人参加，时任中共中央政治局常委刘云山也作了主旨发言。义乌官员对捷克的地理位置重要性作出了高度评价，称这个内陆国家可以轻松抵达方圆1000公里范围内的大多数欧洲国家。"捷克共和国有其独特的地理优势，其发达的交通网络几乎覆盖了整个欧洲。"在浙江省省长袁家军和中国驻捷克共和国大使马克卿之前，时任义乌市市长林毅介绍了义乌与捷克共和国之间的合作蓝图。

林毅说，义乌旨在提高和布拉格之间的货运列车的频率，这样中国的出口货物可以很容易地分销到欧洲其他地区。他说："理想情况下，我们希望每天都有从布拉格和义乌两地出发的火车。"第一列火车上载满了来自捷克的80多个水晶制品的集装箱、汽车零部件和啤酒，用了十六天的时间到达目的地义乌。

"与海上运输相比，尽管成本会更高，但运输时间要短得多，"林先生说，"现在越来越多的汽车生产商已经开始使用这种运输方式在中国分销他们的零部件。"在浙江省政府的支持下，林毅说，义乌计划在2017年年底之前开始在捷克共和国建设一个面积约 1 平方公里的物流中心，该项目将为捷克创造约 3000 个就业机会。泽曼总统坚决支持"一带一路"倡议，他预计布拉格与义乌之间的货运列车将有助于促进捷克的农产品出口到中国。自"一带一路"倡议 2013 年启动以来，中欧城市之间的货运列车数以千计，有效地推动了双方经济合作。

为了鼓励中捷两国能够进行更加积极的经济交流，中国智库的专家们一直在传递积极的信息。清华大学教授、中国人民政治协商会议全国委员会委员李稻葵曾表示，中国经济将在 2017 年触底反弹，2018—2019 年的经济增长率将达到 7.0%。

李稻葵说，全球经济的持续复苏、中国经济的成功转型和捷克政府欢迎新投资的热情日益增强，是他"谨慎乐观"地认为未来中国经济增长是呈上升趋势的背后的"三大积极因素"。李先生说："如果我们能够不断妥善地管理国内外的风险，根据我们的研究成果，中国有潜力在几年内保持 7 个百分点以上的增长。"如果李先生对中国经济的预估是准确的，这意味着中国将对 2012 年到 2016 年间的经济低迷阶段说再见，这几年的经济增长率分别达到了 7.9%、7.8%、7.3%、6.9% 和 6.7%。

欧洲国际政治经济研究中心主任弗雷德里克·埃里克森（Fredrik Erixon）也表示，中国的增长全年会保持在一定的水平。埃里克森表示："中国已经认识到需要做的事情是重新平衡经济，开放更多的竞争领域，并且推动服务、创新和技术应用的增长。北京方面已经认识到调节信贷增长，让资本市场更好地配置资金的重要性。如果能够保持更快的经济增长，未来的挑战就是继续实现这些目标。"

位于捷克的国际消费信贷集团捷信集团（Home Credit Group），也是捷克在中国的最大投资者，是试图进一步加大在华投资的先行者。"我们还打算与中国公司建立合作伙伴关系，在其他国家进行投资，这是我们迎合'一带一路'倡议而制定的新战略。"曾在中国担任过首席财务官的现任菲律宾捷信集团首席执行官大卫·米纳（David Minol）说。捷信已经与东莞的中国智能手机制造商 OPPO 电子有限公司建立了合作伙伴关系，他们通过向手机买家提供贷款，共同增加了在越南和菲律宾的业务。

米纳表示，他的公司也正在与其他智能手机生产商，如华为，在第三国进行这种合作。集团最高管理层表示，捷信从位于香港的私募股权公司太盟投资那里"立即"获得了 20 亿元人民币（相当于 2.78 亿欧元），此次合作旨在帮助集团的中国业务最终可以上市。

捷信集团董事长依西·施梅兹（Jiri Smejc）宣布，两家公司于 2017 年 7 月签署合作协议，这使得捷信集团在进入中国长达十年之后能够通过寻求中国股东加快本土化的步伐，预计还需要三到五年的时间才能完成监管机构的批准过程，使得太盟投资成为捷信在中国的股东。

施梅兹表示，他的集团与太盟投资的合作伙伴关系已经显示出对中国金融市场稳定和上升前景的信心，并表示中国的监管机构前几年为激活市场作出了巨大的努力。捷信集团在华业务注册资本达 70 亿元，新增的投资将使得太盟投资成为少数股东。施梅兹说："投资将立即到位。"他表示，经过两年的谈判，我们的伙伴关系已经敲定，长期以来，他的团队一直试图寻找"合格"

的中国合作伙伴和投资者。他表示："这对我们来说是一个非常重大的战略决策，这一决策展示了我们对这个充满活力的市场的信心和承诺。"

亚洲最大的私募股权公司之一太盟投资集团董事长单伟健表示："我们非常高兴与世界上最具创新性的消费金融机构之一的捷信集团建立合作关系。"单先生还表示，他的公司将在中国市场运用自己的知识，来帮助捷信进一步成长，更好地为客户服务，同时双方确立了"最终使捷信在国际认可的股票市场上市"的目标。

根据双方的协议，双方承诺在中国发展健康的消费金融业务，同时认识到这一领域的巨大潜力。捷信表示，与太盟投资的合作将使捷信集团能够与更多的当地合作伙伴就战略合作和投资而展开对话。施梅兹说，中国是捷信集团规模最大、增长最快的市场，总资产达到75亿欧元，2017年年底，活跃用户超过1320万，在全国有17800个销售网点。由于捷信在中国的成功运作，施梅兹说他的公司也是亚洲国家（除印度外）的最大消费金融提供商之一。施梅兹说："但很快，我们也将成为中国最具竞争力的公司之一。"他补充说，他的公司主要为社会底层的人提供小额贷款。

除了企业外，中捷两国银行业监督机构也都表示愿意支持银行和金融公司在"一带一路"倡议下增加在对方市场的参与度，这将有助于推动整个亚欧地区的连通性。双方还决定深化跨境危机管理的合作，防范金融危机的风险。

时任中国银行业监督管理委员会主席的尚福林和时任捷克国

家银行行长的米罗斯拉夫·辛格（Miroslav Singer）在 2016 年年初习近平主席访问时作出了承诺。在把两国关系提升到战略高度的同时，两国决心深化务实行动，实践 2013 年习近平主席提出的"一带一路"倡议。"在加强监管和危机管理合作的同时，我们大力鼓励我们的银行和金融部门主动参与多样化的金融服务，以促进捷克和中国之间的投资和贸易活动。"辛格说，"这个倡议为两国互惠互利经济合作创造了潜力，我们热衷于扩大与中国伙伴的合作。"

尚福林所在的中国银行业监督管理委员会和捷克国家银行签署了谅解备忘录，分享危机管理经验。尚福林补充说，根据习近平主席的提议，中国银监会正在组建亚洲金融合作协会，这个协会将成为"一带一路"沿线国家的银行和金融机构的合作平台。捷克银行协会非常支持这个协会的成立，并愿意成为该协会的成员。"目前，双方合作的巨大潜力已经释放，双方都表现出进一步深化合作的意图，我们准备与捷克国家银行保持更密切的关系。"尚先生说。

尚先生说，捷克是"一带一路"沿线的重要国家，中国支持与捷克的金融合作。2016 年 8 月，中国银行在布拉格成立分行，成为双方企业的金融合作平台。

尚先生表示，中国银监会积极支持在"一带一路"沿线国家设立银行分行和金融公司的分支或子公司。他补充说，截至 2016 年年底，已有 9 家中资银行在"一带一路"沿线 24 个国家设立了 56 家分行，"一带一路"沿线 20 个国家在中国设立了 56 家商业银行的分行。

中捷两国也加强了航空合作。除了航班数量的增加外，还有　批来自四川航空学院的学员在距布拉格车程约　个小时的 FAIR 飞行学校学习以获得他们的飞行证书。

飞行学校校长米哈尔·马尔科维奇（Michal Markovic）说，学生们会在 FAIR 待 14 个月，来完成飞行员培训课程，其中包括近 900 个小时的理论知识和 230 个小时的飞行培训。

马尔科维奇说："最后，学生们应该会获得欧盟飞行执照，这是我们第一次邀请一大批中国学员来学校。"他认为他的项目对于深化中国与中东欧国家人民的交流起到了促进的作用。

04

瑞士与塞尔维亚，
两个对"一带一路"倡议
充满热情的非欧盟成员国

瑞士和塞尔维亚共和国这两个国家都是非欧盟成员国，但它们所处的发展阶段截然不同。然而，它们积极与中国接触，以不同的方式丰富"一带一路"倡议。瑞士是欧洲第一个与中国建立自由贸易伙伴关系的国家。瑞士认为这一倡议将有助于拉近各经济体间的距离，而塞尔维亚则希望通过这一倡议来加强其基础设施建设，实现再工业化，并提高塞尔维亚在该地区的地位。所有的目标都是合情合理，互相兼容的。

中瑞共同的价值观

瑞士在 2017 年 5 月 14 日至 15 日举行的"一带一路"国际合作高峰论坛中发挥了独特的作用。习近平主席在 2017 年 1 月对瑞士进行国事访问期间，在一年一度的达沃斯世界经济论坛上发表讲话时宣布中国将举办"一带一路"国际合作高峰论坛这一具有重要意义的活动。在习近平主席访问期间，时任瑞士联邦主席多丽丝·洛伊特哈德（Doris Leuthard）迅速确认了她将出席高峰论坛。

在习近平主席到访瑞士之前，洛伊特哈德已对加强与中国的合作寄予厚望，并在 1 月接受我的独家专访时谈到她与习近平主席有"同样的价值观"。在习近平主席发表达沃斯论坛讲话后，我在国会大厅里采访洛伊特哈德时，她再一次提到了这一点。在我的采访经历中，从未像这样，一位国家领导人在一周内两次接受我的采访。随和的洛伊特哈德是非常典型的瑞士人，他们的人生辞典中没有"不"这个词。目前为止，在我的记者职业生涯中，瑞士是我最常访问的国家之一。不用说其他采访任务，仅达沃斯论坛我就已经参加了 2011 年至 2018 年八届论坛，虽然在忙碌的季节里总是很难在拥挤的滑雪小镇中找到一张床位，但对我来说每一次都是既具启发性又非常充实的旅程。

在过去十年，瑞士在加深西方国家与中国的伙伴关系方面起着先锋作用。"只有开放和开放经济才能有更好的结果，而且现今全球化是大势所趋，"2017 年 1 月 12 日，洛伊特哈德在瑞士首都伯尔尼接受我的采访时说，"我们要与保护主义做斗争，习近平主席有着相同的价值观和理念。"

在谈到接见习近平主席和他的夫人彭丽媛时，洛伊特哈德表示，习近平主席访问瑞士发出了一个强烈的信号，鼓励全球合作，打击保护主义政策。"我认为很多国家都站在我们这边，他们知道合作比孤立主义和保护主义要好得多。"本着这样的精神，两国宣布升级双边自由贸易协定，这项旧的自贸协定于 2014 年 7 月生效实施，免除了中瑞双向贸易的大部分关税。不过，洛伊特哈德表示，双方已决定对更多产品降低关税，甚至实施零税率，以促进贸易流动。她说："我们发现还有待提升的空间，所以我们决定升级我们的自由贸易伙伴关系。" 她补充说，全球金融市场并不稳定，作为世界第七大金融市场的瑞士也处于同样的境遇。这位瑞士联邦主席说："我很想知道习近平主席针对这些挑战的看法。"

洛伊特哈德有意让日内瓦和苏黎世这两个传统的金融中心进

行竞争，以吸引中国的银行在两个城市扩张业务。她补充说："竞争是一件好事，我们欢迎中国的银行在瑞士投资。金融合作是习近平主席访问期间双方签署的协议的一部分。"她还表示，双方在达成治理环境问题的协议后，将加深在能源领域的合作。她说："我知道中国的污染相当严重，这也是为什么我们想要分享我们在扩大能源和环境领域的合作方面的经验和技术。"举例来说，在中国的一些城市，取暖仍然依靠燃煤，她指出负担得起的替代能源和技术已经存在。她说："这不是成本问题，而是适应变化的问题。"但是洛伊特哈德预测，中国在治理污染和雾霾方面的速度将超过预期。她回忆说，瑞士在工业化进程中有着不好的经验，用了 40~50 年的时间才解决了这个问题。

洛伊特哈德在 2016 年 8 月访华后，于 2017 年初接替约翰·施奈德-阿曼（Johann N. Schneider-Ammann）就任瑞士联邦主席。施奈德-阿曼 2016 年 4 月对中国进行了国事访问，并在与中国国家主席习近平的会谈中就创新战略伙伴关系达成共识。施奈德-阿曼表示这给中瑞双边关系增添了新的方向和活力。施奈德-阿曼访问期间，瑞士成为了中国与中东欧 16 国合作协议的观察员。瑞士政府由七名联邦委员会委员组成，每位委员都享有相同的地位、权利和义务，委员由联邦议会选出，任期四年。联邦委员会的每位委员各自掌管一个联邦政府部门，瑞士联邦主席任期为一年。

中国驻瑞士大使耿文兵说，越来越多的国家对与中国的自由贸易谈判表现出兴趣，这主要是因为瑞士从 2014 年建立的高层次贸易伙伴关系中受益，对华出口稳步增长。瑞士政府的官方数据显示，2016 年 10 月和 11 月，瑞士出口放缓，但对中国的出口量在两个月内仍保持了两位数的同比增长，这在全球贸易萧条的时期非常振奋人心。具体来说，10 月份同比增幅高达 24.1%，11 月份瑞士对华出口同比增长 11.5%。"这样喜人的成果让更多的国家对中国的自由贸易谈判产生兴趣，甚至有些国家向我索要中瑞两国签署的协议文本，"耿大使说，"我相信每一个与中国签订贸易协定的国家都将成为赢家。"

在耿大使看来，中国已经把投资和贸易主导型经济转变为消费和创新主导型经济，这无疑为进口创造了巨大的机会。耿大使说，习近平主席出访瑞士正是发生在全球地缘政治形势复杂多变和贸易投资保护主义抬头的背景下。2016 年 12 月，全球三大经济体欧盟、美国和日本拒绝履行 15 年前中国加入世贸组织时作出的视中国为平等贸易伙伴的承诺。但是，包括瑞士在内的数十个世贸组织成员在 2007 年已经承认了中国的市场经济地位。除了促进贸易伙伴关系方面的努力，耿大使说，瑞士领导人愿意把政治交往提升到一个新的水平。瑞士早在 1950 年就与中国建立了外交关系，是第一个（批）与中国建立外交关系的西方国家。2016 年 4 月，施奈德－阿曼访华期间，双方决定开展新型伙伴关系。

时任瑞士联邦经济、教育和研究部部长的施奈德－阿曼说，瑞士一直"高度关注""一带一路"倡议，因为他的国家是出口主导型、开放型经济，与各国保持紧密的联系正是瑞士的利益所在。施奈德－阿曼在回顾 2016 年其担任联邦主席期间对中国的国事访问时表示，他在与习近平主席会晤时详细了解了这一倡议。施奈德－阿曼在 2017 年年初在伯尔尼的办公室接受我的专访时说："2018 年，新任的洛伊特哈德主席将很快会在北京提出我们瑞士的立场。" 现在，虽然关于这个倡议的讨论在瑞士并不广泛，但是他说政治家、政府和议会已经知晓了这一倡议，新任主席有她的团队、中国专家和联系网络来探讨这一倡议。

尽管当时他还不能提供更多关于瑞士立场的详细信息，但施奈德－阿曼说，瑞士一直是加强与中国坚实的伙伴关系的先行者。这样开创性的关系不仅体现在瑞士是西方第一批承认新中国的国家，向中国出口先进技术，承认中国的市场经济地位，与中国达成自由贸易协定和创新战略伙伴关系，还体现在成为亚洲基础设施投资银行的创始成员国，以及成为中国与中东欧 16 国家合作框架的观察员。施奈德－阿曼回忆说，2016 年 4 月在其对中国进行国事访问期间，特别是在国宴期间，习近平主席慷慨地与他分享了自己的观点。施奈德－阿曼说："现在，我们频繁的政治交往表明我们是如何稳步地推进我们的伙伴关系。我学到了很多，我们也解决了很多实际问题，虽然这是我第一次与习近平主席见面，但令我印象深刻的是，他的政治家精神、真诚，还有与一个欧洲小国交流的诚意。"

施奈德－阿曼还表示，习近平主席也坦言了当前中国所面临的挑战，在访问期间，他发现习近平主席是一个非常非常让人尊敬的人，双方就创新战略伙伴关系进行了非常详尽的交流，中国也将与瑞士的创新战略伙伴关系放在发展议程的优先项的位置。施奈德－阿曼说："我们在这个话题上用了很多时间，习近平主席热衷于了解瑞士的详细政策和实际情况。" 他补充说，现在双方已经举行了推进自由贸易协定的专门会议，双方将每两年定期对协议进行一次审议。

除了政治和经济交流外，双方也在探索教育、旅游乃至体育方面的机遇。施奈德－阿曼还表示，习近平主席对瑞士职业教育体系表现出了浓厚的兴趣。日内瓦大学校长伊夫·弗吕克格尔（Yves Flückiger）说，他的大学已经和清华大学启动了日内瓦—清华计划，该计划已经发展成为一个宏大的有关联合国可持续发展目标的联合教育计划，得到了日内瓦当地基金会的支持。他的大学已经开展了两项日内瓦—清华计划框架下的活动，并开展了与"一带一路"倡议相关的研究和发展。"'一带一路'倡议的宏大目标和规模必将带来许多极具吸引力的研究项目和教育机会，无论是先进工程学还是国际法和跨文化交流的问题，"弗吕克格尔说，"当然，一旦完成这一了不起的基础设施建设，我们可以期待它对整个欧亚大陆的学生交流产生重大影响。"

瑞士首都冰球队 SC Bern 首席执行官马克·卢蒂（Marc Luthi）与中国驻瑞士大使耿文兵会面，并讨论了如何在中国开展冬季运动。"习近平主席 2017 年 1 月份对瑞士的访问和即将在中国举办的冬季奥运会为我们的探索提供了机会，我们已经准备好了。"马克·卢蒂说。习近平主席访问期间，双方领导人就深化冬季体育合作达成共识。瑞士旅游局全球客户总监兼亚太区总监西蒙·博沙特（Simon Bosshart）也表示，在吸引更多中国游客方面，冬季运动已经成为卖点。西蒙·博沙特说："欧洲安全局势恶化和恐怖袭击事件影响了中国游客的数量。但是我们注意到，来自中国的个人游客数量一直在增加，这对我们来说也是一个新趋势。"

中瑞文化纽带

有没有哪个西方国家通过把中国古代的智慧纳入治理体系并应用而获得巨大的成功？瑞士可能已经这样操作了，尽管是以无意识的方式。德国哲学家莱布尼茨（Leibniz，1646—1716）在论述中欧关系时说，双方都有一些可以为对方带来好处的东西。比如瑞士可以从中国古代智慧经典《道德经》传达的诸多思想中获得宝贵的灵感。

自二十世纪九十年代末以来，瑞士汉学家胜雅律（Harro von Senger）计划通过参考据称生活于2500多年前的中国哲学家老子的古代经典来解读瑞士的国家治理方式。

所以胜雅律从那时起就开始精心准备，大量阅读，埋头写作。他的著作《瑞士之道》（*Das Tao der Schweiz*）由六章组成，笔记和参考文献近70页，于2017年5月初在著名的新苏黎世出版社（Publishing House of the Neue Zürcher Zeitung）首次亮相。"瑞士基本实现了老子治理小国家的典范。"任职于设在洛桑的瑞士比较法研究所（Swiss Institute of Comparative Law）的胜雅律在2013年年初接受采访时这样说。

胜雅律坐在家乡艾因西德伦（Einsiedeln）Bären餐厅的一楼，这里距离苏黎世仅一小时车程。他指着窗外的Benedictine修道院，说他在那里接受了八年的中学教育。在此期间，胜雅律已经学习了拉丁语八年，古希腊语六年，法语七年，英语两年，而他的母语是德语。

胜雅律进入苏黎世大学后，开始对汉语表现出浓厚的兴趣，其博士论文是关于中国古代法律史上的销售合同。但很快话题就转到了他书中各章节引用的老子的 80 多句话，他用了 1000 多个参考文献来佐证瑞士的成功与中国古代思想的联系。1.95 米高的胜雅律用流利的汉语说："这是一个成功的国家，成功的背后是老子深刻的思想。"

瑞士当然没有有意识地按照老子的思想行事，但是它的成功可以用老子深刻的思想来诠释。"小国寡民"，这是老子的著作《道德经》第 80 章的一个词。瑞士人口不到 900 万，是老子梦寐以求的国家的大小，胜雅律说。

老子主张柔弱、和缓、谦虚、无为。他说，当一株植物开始长大的时候，它是小而弱的，这是开花的象征；但是当一株植物即将枯萎时，它会变得又大又僵，这是死亡的标志。出生于 1964 年，20 世纪 70 年代在北京大学学习的胜雅律说："我们小而弱。"

"这些对我们来说是好事，因为我们不被其他国家看作是危险的。"另外，胜雅律说，瑞士也实践了另一位著名思想家庄子的思想。庄子与老子生活在同一时代，二者形成了道家的思想精髓。庄子在他的著作中说：人皆知有用之用，而莫知无用之用也。胜雅律说，瑞士能从这些无用的东西中获益。

胜雅律解释说："我们的类似于道家的政策使得瑞士对于任何外国势力都毫无'用处'，而且幸运的是瑞士军队最终取得了巨大的成功。"但他进一步强调，他的国家的"无用"使其成为了诸多国际组织的驻地，为解决争端提供了平台，为全球和平与繁荣作出贡献，这便是"无用"的"有用"。

所有这些都与道家的另一个重要部分相联系，也就是谋略。他说，这个想法在西方语言中没有得到恰当的表达。例如，一位被称作是"美国政府最重要的中国专家之一"的美国学者把"谋略"翻译成"欺骗性战略"，这是非常肤浅的。

因此他创造了英语单词 supra-planning，他说这比西方认为的最高规划的"战略思维"更胜一筹。胜雅律说："有时候，我们需要创造一个词来引起对另一个文明的独特现象的关注。"他说，supra-planning（谋略）是一个基础广泛的但只在中国发展起来的规划艺术。胜雅律用阴阳符号来解释谋略。阳代表法律、法规、习俗和惯例，而阴则是隐藏解决问题的方法，需要智慧和创造力。

胜雅律是一位多产的学者，自 1975—1977 年在北京读书以来，他已经阅读了《人民日报》和《光明日报》等中文报纸。他的著作《谋略》有 15 种语言译本。除了谋略的阴阳特性之外，胜雅律说谋略的另一个特点是长远的思考。

胜雅律说，中国领导层提出了两个百年目标，到 2020 年，中国国内生产总值和城乡居民人均收入比 2010 年翻一番，全面建成小康社会；到本世纪中叶，建成富强民主文明和谐的社会主义现代化国家，实现中华民族的伟大复兴。

关于这两个目标的公开讨论直到 2011 年才在中国广泛起来，但是他在 2008 年以德语出版的《*Moulüe*》一书中已经写到了这点。这是关于这一话题的唯一一本西方著作。他从书包中拿出他在瑞士颇具影响力的德文报纸《Neue Zürcher Zeitung》上发表的一篇文章。这篇文章的发表时间是 1985 年 4 月 19 日。"这是我为 2049 年的目标写的一篇文章。"胜雅律说。他补充说，中国在二十世纪八十年代就已经探讨了这样一个长期目标，旨在成为一个发达国家。

胜雅律说："三十二年前，我知道中国有一个很长远很长远的目标。"胜雅律说，长期目标是谋略的一个主要特征，但是西方的战略思维就不能持续这样长久。通常情况下，西方的战略，比如欧盟于 2000 年 3 月达成的里斯本战略只持续了十年。但是，瑞士是一个例外。他补充道："瑞士也有长远的思考，也就是关于中立的立场。"

瑞士的软实力

就像胜雅律教授提到的，瑞士以其为数百家国际组织的所在地为傲，他们对"一带一路"倡议的态度是有帮助的。设在日内瓦的国际道路运输联盟的秘书长翁贝托·德–普雷托（Umberto de Pretto）说，"一带一路"倡议是一个源自中国的构想，可以作为一套"全球性的宏大计划"，为全世界各个地区的经济稳定和繁荣带来深远的影响。虽然这一倡议是中国政府的构想，主要关系到中国和"一带一路"沿线国家，但是这个宏伟计划是全球性的。他说："这一倡议鼓励采取更加全球化和综合性的方式来实现开放、包容和平衡的区域经济，我相信这一倡议将为全世界各地区带来经济稳定和繁荣的深远利益。"德－普雷托在2017年5月在北京举行的"一带一路"国际合作高峰论坛前夕表示，我们应该提醒世界各国，繁荣与和平是通过加强贸易关系来实现的。这是一条强有力的信息，也是引起中国和国际社会极大兴趣的信息。据他介绍，习近平主席首次提出"一带一路"倡议以来，这一倡议已经在欧洲赢得了广泛认可，许多欧洲人相信这将有助于把新的商业区和内陆国与欧洲和中国的主要市场连接起来。他表示，这一结论是在国际道路运输联盟于2016年11月在布鲁塞尔主办的运输和"一带一路"倡议会议上达成的。国际道路运输联盟在全球公路运输网络中推行标准与安全措施已经有七十年的历史。

德－普雷托说，会议对在"一带一路"倡议下欧洲面临的机遇和挑战进行了专门讨论。德－普雷托说，会议期间，欧洲300名运输业的代表达成广泛共识，该倡议具有增加贸易，刺激经济发展和缩短运输时间的巨大潜力。

德－普雷托还表示，国际道路运输联盟代表国际公路运输业的利益，并且在全球100多个国家拥有成员和组织活动，国际道路运输联盟热衷于推动"一带一路"倡议。德－普雷托说，中国一直在鼓励"一带一路"沿线国家实现经济政策协调，开展更广泛的区域合作。他说，中国已经批准了一个基于全球范围内执行的联合国公约的国际过境制度，允许海关密封的车辆和货物集装箱运往过境国，不设边界检查。德－普雷托说，中国还批准了世界贸易组织的《贸易便利化协定》，表明中国融入了全球运输和贸易规范中来。德－普雷托说："这表明中国已经为通过消除障碍来改善全球互联互通树立了一个良好的榜样。"中国政府已经表达了积极发展国际道路运输、到2020年建设现代化国际道路运输体系的决心和意愿，但德－普雷托也表示，尽管中国与14个国家交界，是世界上邻国最多的国家，但目前中国的公路运输仅占国际商品交付的10%，证明仍有巨大的尚待开发的潜力。他说，中国的国际公路运输业与中国的地理和经济重要性不相称。例如，中国大约有300家公司从事国际公路运输商品过境服务，但是土耳其有2000家，波兰有6000家。

瑞士在软实力方面颇具竞争力。典型的例子是一年一度的世界经济论坛，每年来自世界各地的政界人士、商界领袖、记者和名人聚集在瑞士达沃斯的年度"思想交易会"上。由于论坛的重要性和代表人数众多，据说达沃斯医院的一些病床也"出租"给与会代表们。鉴于这样疯狂的程度，在过去的七届论坛上，我从来没能在达沃斯预订到酒店房间，而是只能在附近的一个城镇住宿，然后每天乘火车一个小时往返于会场。不过，由于论坛所带来的新思想、新趋势、新讨论和新对话，世界经济论坛一直是我的一个必订日程。尽管瑞士是一个人口不多的小国，但它却在经济和商业界占据着显著的位置。现在，达沃斯除了在非洲、中东和世界其他地区召开重要区域性会议之外，还在天津和大连轮流举办姊妹论坛——夏季达沃斯论坛。除此之外，日内瓦还是联合国的第二个总部，有数十家国际组织坐落于此，包括世界贸易组织和世界卫生组织。所有这些都增强了瑞士的软实力。

中国可以通过向瑞士学习来塑造自己的软实力。自习近平主席于 2012 年年底成为中国最高领导人以来，世界发展面临困难，挑战越来越多，他说中国将采取主动的方式来面对和解决所有这些问题。除了中国政治家为解决全球问题不断努力之外，中国还在努力提高智库的能力建设。最近鼓励 25 家学术组织产出高质量的智力成果。所有这些发展表明，中国热衷于在帮助解决全球性问题、使世界更美好方面发挥积极作用。在这方面，瑞士至少为中国提供了参考。中国需要投入精力、时间、耐心和努力，为产生有影响力的思想观点搭建平台。为了使讨论有趣而富有成果，政府、企业、媒体和学界应该发挥各自的作用。例如，企业应履行其社会责任，为建立这样的平台提供财务支持。

世界经济论坛发展了四十多个年头，才达到了今天这样有影响力的地位。中国发展高层论坛、博鳌论坛和夏季达沃斯论坛分别在每年三月、四月和九月举行，但只侧重于中国或区域议程。既然中国领导层的目标是提供更多的全球性解决方案来维护世界的和平与发展，那么中国需要提供更多的平台来产生具有全球影响力的思想。而且中国应该举办更多的全球性和区域性会议。日内瓦和纽约都是北京、上海和其他中国城市效仿的典范。在这方面，上海合作组织秘书处和亚洲基础设施投资银行北京总部以及金砖国家新开发银行上海总部的成立是喜人的发展，因为它们将有助于加强中国的软实力。不过，中国需要作出更大的努力来发挥与其经济实力相匹配的国际角色。

目前，世界面临着全球利益相关者不愿意合作的紧迫挑战，简而言之，全球化面临风险。然而，中国仍然是呼吁重振多极世界、加强全球治理的推动力量。令人鼓舞的是，总部设在日内瓦的世界经济论坛创始人兼执行主席克劳斯·施瓦布（Klaus Schwab）曾邀请习近平主席在对瑞士进行国事访问后于 2017 年 1 月 17 日发表开幕演讲。在结束 2017 年的首次海外访问之前，习近平主席还访问了设在洛桑的国际奥委会总部和设在日内瓦的世界卫生组织总部，并在联合国日内瓦办事处举行高层会议之前发表了讲话。施瓦布的组织自 1979 年开始与中国合作，他高度重视习近平主席参与这次年度盛会，这也是中国领导人第一次出席这一年度盛会。他表示，习近平主席的参与与论坛主题相契合，即积极反应和负责任的领导班子。随着世界向多极化的地缘政治和经济格局过渡，中国现在在经济实力方面与美国旗鼓相当，他希望习近平主席能够表明中国将在全球事务中发挥积极作用。

习近平主席到来之前，施瓦布说："2017 年，我们生活在一个真正意义上的多极世界里，围绕我们共同面对的挑战——全球合作水平的下降有着非常现实的可能性。在这个背景下，我们的主题反映了对那些掌握权力的人通过聆听和理解人民的期望作出积极回应的，并积极大胆地提供和实现可持续和社会包容的未来愿景提出了明确的要求。"他说，最需要积极反应的和负责任的领域包括促进增长，确保全球经济更具可持续性和社会包容性，设计更好的全球合作系统，为第四次工业革命做好准备。

他还说："最后一个领域至关重要，因为技术和创新在减少工作岗位的同时，也通过创造更多的角色和建设更强大的社会来帮助人类。当务之急是立即采取行动，以便我们拥有得当的治理和价值观念，让技术为人类服务，而不是为人类制造挑战。"

施瓦布认为，中国是一个正在崛起的超级大国，我们期望中国作为一个积极反应和负责任的全球领导者发挥日益积极的作用。我们已经看到这正在发生，《联合国气候变化框架公约》第二十一次缔约方会议上中国对支持保护环境起到的催化作用，中国作为国际贸易和投资的拥护者支持发展和基础设施融资，并着手发展和扩大全球数字经济。

施瓦布表示，随着中国越来越以其创新实力而闻名于世，世界预期中国的专业知识在许多关键领域的讨论，无论是基础设施发展、清洁能源还是物联网，都将扮演越来越重要、越来越突出的角色。中国通过亚投行和国家开发银行进行基础设施融资，通过区域全面经济伙伴关系协定和"一带一路"倡议进行的贸易和投资的创新的做法，也都是值得鼓励的。

施瓦布说，他喜欢习近平主席在当年的二十国集团工商峰会上引用的一句有名的中国谚语，"小智治事，大智治制"。对我来说，这完美地阐释了全球治理对于我们国际社会的共同良性发展具有重要意义，反映出中国愿意为更加公平、更加繁荣和更具可持续性的地球作出贡献。

当我问道："显然，在世界齐聚一堂寻求解决方案之前，西方国家在2008—2009年进入了金融和经济危机，你如何评价现状呢？目前，黑天鹅事件一次又一次地发生在七国集团，你怎么看待现在西方面临的'政治危机'？"施瓦布回答说："2016年的政治事件已经很明显地表明，政治领导人与选举出政治领导人的民众之间的信任水平已经遭遇巨大的压力。在当今复杂而相互联系的世界，领导人肩负的责任从未如此之大，现在迫切需要各国领导人共同努力，加强我们的全球体系，重新设想新的国际合作方式。事实上，七国集团的好几个国家面临的最大的挑战是收入的不均衡增加，领导人失去了倾听人们需求的能力。"

我很好奇，瑞士这个小国拥有巨大的竞争力和软实力的原因。施瓦布说，瑞士有很多竞争优势：它是众多世界级创新公司的所在地，拥有优秀的学术研究机构，且与私有部门合作，使新技术商业化；具有高效灵活的劳动力市场和稳定的宏观经济环境。瑞士人口规模小，这成为了瑞士积极鼓励与欧盟和世界其他合作伙伴发展深厚的贸易关系的强大动力，并积极投资发展其最富有的自然资产——瑞士人民，帮助他们培养创业人才。施瓦布说："开放贸易和发展创新、培养创业人才是中瑞两国可以共同努力的方向。"

几乎与施瓦布出生于同一个时期的让－皮埃尔·莱曼（Jean-Pierre Lehmann），以他的全球化研究闻名于世，形成了自己观察中国开放性演进的独特方式。我在 2017 年与他有密集的谈话。那年他七十一岁，他在电脑笔记本上存储了从毛泽东到习近平这些中国政治家的照片，这些照片记录了全球舞台上历史性的时刻。尤其是瑞士洛桑国际管理发展学院（IMD）莱曼教授几乎保留了所有习近平主席与世界各地的领导人握手的照片，现在还在 IMD 和香港大学教授全球事务的他用这些照片来说明中国面对世界其他国家的姿态，并观察被他描述为新的全球混乱秩序中的亚洲。"我必须说，习近平主席握手的所有照片都令人印象深刻，这些信息都展示了一个我们正在谈论的新时代。" 莱曼在四月下旬在洛桑日内瓦湖畔宁静的 IMD 校园办公室接受采访时说。他耐心地介绍这些照片，接着说："显然没有其他领导人在这么短的时间内握了这么多手。这是中国的亮相，是一种姿态，但也是一个象征。"

习近平主席在 2012 年年底成为中国最高领导人，之后的四年半时间里，他曾到访过约 50 个国家，并在北京主持了亚太经合组织峰会、二十国集团峰会和"一带一路"高峰合作论坛。莱曼回忆中国的历史，称习近平主席与世界各国政治家进行积极的会晤是"极好的新闻"，显示了新兴国家与世界其他国家积极往来的决心。这与一些领导人倾向于修建隔离墙并支持孤立主义形成鲜明对比。

尽管莱曼说与唐纳德·特朗普相比他更喜欢贝拉克·奥巴马，但他对奥巴马的关于跨太平洋伙伴关系的中国政策持非常批评的态度，这一政策把中国排除在这个亚太贸易协定之外。但特朗普在入主白宫后宣布美国退出协定。"奥巴马说，我们需要写出没有中国的贸易规则。为什么那么说？为什么不说我们一起写规则？"全球主义者莱曼问道，"这是一个新时代，我们需要调整。"莱曼已经对全球保护主义表示了担忧：世贸组织多哈回合全球贸易谈判由于西方国家和日本拒绝适应新的现实无果而终，特朗普也威胁说要退出《联合国气候变化框架公约》；他认为西欧是非常自满和内向的，尽管中东欧更加开放。为对抗全球性丧失信心，他认为中国对全球化的介入是一场大革命。

莱曼说，习近平主席热情地握手，与全球领导人交谈的过程中习近平主席和中国都在一直思考一个宏大的构想和宏伟的计划，这将把世界各个部分聚集在一起。他认为，"一带一路"倡议是中国组合解决方案里的重要组成部分。但是，这仍然是一个构想，需要与世界各国一起制定不同的战略。"他建议中国不应该避免使用"战略"这个词，因为它基本上是中性的。莱曼说："特朗普的墙是一个糟糕的战略，但增加连通性是一个好的战略。"他说，他总是告诉他的听众们，"一带一路"倡议还处于早期阶段，有一些批评意见是正常的。但是他继续说："这些意见并不意味着任何战略上的意义，尽管这一点是正确的。现在这只是一个构想，战略会跟上。"对于批评这一倡议只符合中国利益的说法，他回应说："世界上没有一个国家会为了对方的利益而做一些事情，而不顾自己的利益。"他补充说，中国已经在构想文件中明确表示，这是一个双赢的倡议。西方一些人也批评这一倡议只是空谈，没有具体的实施。他说："我不认为这是真的。"

当然，现在应该有争辩和讨论，因为这个想法只提出了三四年。莱曼甚至警告说，在未来的五到十年内将构想转化为战略将存在"困难和障碍"。他说："但是我的立场是，'一带一路'倡议应该受到欢迎而不是被抵制。"例如，他说他对美国和日本持"非常批评"的态度，因为他们没有加入亚洲基础设施投资银行创始成员国，亚洲基础设施投资银行现在（2017年）已经发展成为拥有多达80个成员的多边融资工具。

以他参加的2015年在西安举办的"一带一路"媒体合作论坛为例，莱曼说他因看到来自欧亚大陆的伊朗、印度、巴基斯坦、乌克兰、格鲁吉亚的代表而欢欣鼓舞。"但是没有美国人，也没有日本人。这是一个全球性的倡议，你需要做一些事情。"他说。他认为，欧亚大陆和非洲的商业界已经开始接受这个想法。世界必须承认中国建立一个开放、全球和包容的平台的勇气。对中国的怀疑、忧惧和焦虑也随着中国走向全球舞台的中心而越来越多，这是不公平的。在这种情况下，莱曼说，中国还有很多工作要做，以便更好地与世界各国沟通。他表示："中国必须在软实力上下功夫，因此中国人应该更好地宣传这个倡议。"他回忆起自己十八九岁的时候，有一个很大的担心，那就是美国要征服世界，这是当人们拥有新的孩子时很自然的一种担心。他说："但是，你们必须努力安抚，使世界各国以更加成熟的方式去参与。"

莱曼说，中国在文化、经济和技术上可以对世界作出巨大的贡献。他差不多二十年前加入 IMD，并于 2012 年退休，尽管他偶尔还会讲学。他还在香港大学任教，他说亚洲商学院的学生们总是能不断丰富他对于如何看待不断变化的世界的看法。"我喜欢这里的教学环境。春天在这里，鸟儿在外面唱歌。这是让人非常愉悦的。"他在 IMD 办公室说。作为一名法国公民，他于1997 年移居瑞士，长期在法国境外居住，分别在日本、瑞典、英国和美国工作过。在过去的五十年中，莱曼在亚洲工作，并见证了戏剧性的变化在那里发生。尽管他支持讨论西方和中国的价值观，但莱曼却相信共同的世界价值观。他说："但是我认为在许多情况下，我们的价值观是一样的，尽管表达方式有所不同。"莱曼说他教过许多来自中国、亚洲其他地区和世界其他地区的年轻父母。他说，他们想要的是让自己的孩子好好长大、快乐，可以为世界贡献力量。

他承认，有时他会为西方政治家提出价值主题时的口气感到尴尬。他说："就好像我们是纯粹的，美国的全球秩序是温良的，潜在的（台词则是）中国秩序是恶毒的。"

塞尔维亚共和国的繁荣之梦

塞尔维亚共和国是一个拥有 700 万人口的国家，与中国的一些大型地级城市的规模大致相同。2019 年的经济增长预期为 3.5%。根据世界银行的消息，其经济增长预期比平均每年增长约为 2% 的欧盟更为乐观。这部分归功于扩大道路、铁路，城市扩建，高科技园区建设投资等国家级计划，类似于中国部分城市的增长引擎。2017 年 4 月，我第一次到访这个国家，在那里我发现塞尔维亚共和国在塑造竞争力和改善民生方面效仿中国。

中国投资者通过出口资本和专门技术，增加了对该国的投资强度，为当地人创造就业机会。中国驻塞尔维亚共和国大使李满长在贝尔格莱德的大使馆里接受我的专访时说："中国在塞尔维亚共和国正在进行和正在准备中的项目的投资额度约为 100 亿美元。" 在会议室里李满长大使给我展示了已经在塞尔维亚完成的项目的样板。大使馆会议厅展示的模型包括巴士、发电站、桥梁等。李大使说，这些成果都是源于塞尔维亚共和国领导层高度认可中国"一带一路"倡议的重要性，双方于 2015 年签署了谅解备忘录。

李大使援引塞尔维亚领导人的话说，他们一再强调，习近平主席 2013 年提出的"一带一路"倡议将有助于全球经济摆脱

2008—2009 年金融和经济危机以来的经济停滞。"因此，塞尔维亚共和国最高领导人要求他们的国家抓住机会，寻求与'一带一路'倡议的契合点。"李大使说。

塞尔维亚共和国第一副总理兼外交部部长伊维察·达契奇（Ivica Dacic）证实，2017 年 4 月时任总理、现任塞尔维亚共和国总统的亚历山大·武契奇（Aleksandar Vucic）率领该国代表团出席在北京举行的 "一带一路" 国际合作高峰论坛。达契奇在接受采访时告诉我："这说明了塞尔维亚共和国对这一全球性重要倡议的重视程度。"在武契奇访问前，前总统尼科利奇（Nikolic）2017 年年初对中国进行了国事访问，继 2016 年 6 月习近平主席访问塞尔维亚共和国之后，尼科利奇参加了 2015 年的纪念中国人民抗日战争暨世界反法西斯战争胜利 70 周年大会。

外交部部长说，他也期待着塞尔维亚与中国之间直飞航线的开通，同时塞尔维亚特别重视贝尔格莱德—布达佩斯铁路线的现代化，这是中欧之间陆海联络运输网络的开创性项目。"这是本地区发展的大好机会，将带来更多的货物销售及人员流通。"他说。

外交部部长说，塞尔维亚希望与世界保持最密切的联系。"在这方面，我们希望看到与中国在基础设施投资合作方面有更加强劲的势头，使塞尔维亚成为区域交通枢纽。"达契奇说。李大使遵循国家战略，在使馆的客厅展出了双边合作中 "几个第一"。

他说，中国在欧洲建造的第一座桥梁位于塞尔维亚的多瑙河河段。中国在欧洲的第一条高速铁路，连接贝尔格莱德和布达佩斯，其中一部分在塞尔维亚完成，该项目预计在欧盟委员会完成贷款协议审查后的一年内启动。而在欧洲，塞尔维亚共和国是第一个给予中国护照持有人免签证入境停留时间长达 30 天的国家。李大使说，目前中国企业正在塞尔维亚兴建公路和发电机组，中国投资者已经与贝尔格莱德市政府签订了建设环城公路的合同。

中国也正在改善塞尔维亚首都的废水处理设施和供暖网络，另一个投资总额高达 9 亿美元的发电项目也在计划中。在这 100 亿美元的项目中，中国还将帮助塞尔维亚一期建设占地 300 公顷的工业园区。李大使说，在 2015 年签署备忘录后，双方将准备在 2017 年年底之前签署一项协议，为 2018 年破土动工铺平道路。"至少其他巴尔干国家对塞尔维亚表示'嫉妒'，塞尔维亚抓住了加强与中国合作的良好契机，"李大使说，"我认为塞尔维亚已经在这方面起了带头作用，其他欧洲国家可能会效仿。"

考虑到巴尔干当前的政治和经济形势，不难理解参与"一带一路"倡议的重要性，这不仅对塞尔维亚而且对该地区所有国家来说都是如此，设在贝尔格莱德的塞尔维亚国际政治与经济学研究所所长布拉尼斯拉夫·乔尔杰维奇（Branislav Djordjevic）说。他说，虽然他的研究所长期以来对中国抱有兴趣，但两国在 2016 年确立战略伙伴关系之后，兴趣更加浓厚了。现在研究所已经重点着眼于"一带一路"倡议。他说："繁荣带来和平与稳定是一个古老的事实。"

他也表示，中国的"一带一路"倡议有助于塞尔维亚更有资质加入欧盟。"由于每个国家都在寻求加入欧盟成员国，因此它们更容易被吸收为经济和政治稳定的国家，"乔尔杰维奇说，"随着'一带一路'倡议而来的一些必要调整，塞尔维亚本身有可能成为这样一个进程的引擎。"

据李大使介绍，继意大利前总理罗马诺·普罗迪（Romano Prodi）、法国的计 – 皮埃尔·拉法兰（Jean-Pierre Raffarin）、波兰的瓦尔德马·帕夫拉克（Waldemar Pawlak）等欧洲高层次政要之后，塞尔维亚共和国前总统尼科利奇也表示，在他卸任之后，有意为与中国的"一带一路"倡议合作作出贡献。2017 年6 月 1 日起，总理亚历山大·武契奇接任 65 岁的尼科利奇成为塞维利亚共和国总统。"尼科利奇总统考虑在退休后在贝尔格莱德设立'一带一路'倡议办公室。"李大使告诉我。和现年 93岁的美国政治家亨利·基辛格（Henry Kissinger）相仿，尼科利奇把他退休后的工作重点放在促进与中国的关系上，他所关注的范围将覆盖中国与塞尔维亚共和国的各前沿领域，李大使说。

李大使说，尼科利奇在最近访问中国时提出了这个想法，他说中国的"一带一路"倡议对世界各国人民的前途命运具有重要意义。尼科利奇在担任总统期间，提升了塞尔维亚与中国的战略关系，2016 年习近平主席访问塞尔维亚，双方同意把两国关系重塑为中国和其他欧洲国家的榜样。自从习近平主席在 2013 年提出"一带一路"倡议以来，许多欧洲智库都把该倡议纳入到研究议程中。随着越来越多的（如曾担任欧盟委员会主席的普罗迪和法国总理拉法兰等）政治家支持这一倡议，许多智库也在丰富"一带一路"主题研究内容，启动学术项目，组织辩论和对话等。

除了尼科利奇的热情之外，塞尔维亚学者也对在塞尔维亚建立以中国为主题的智库表示出了强烈兴趣，他们视塞尔维亚为巴尔干地区的门户国家。设在贝尔格莱德的塞尔维亚国际政治与经济研究所是一个有 70 多年历史的著名学术机构。该研究所国际合作协调员伊沃娜·拉杰瓦茨（Ivona Ladjevac）表示，中国社会科学院是研究所在中国的重要联络单位，双方在中国和中东欧16国的"16＋1"框架下顺利实施了联合研究计划。

伊沃娜·拉杰瓦茨说："在我们的30名研究人员中，有5人专门进行'一带一路'倡议的研究。"她自己也参与其中，并开始学习中文。

国际政治与经济研究所前所长杜斯科·迪米特里耶维奇（Dusko Dimitrijevic）说，2016年习近平主席访问塞尔维亚期间，国际政治与经济研究所与中国社会科学院组织了一次高层次的丝绸之路论坛。迪米特里耶维奇说："我们打算建立一个联合研究合作中心，以推动16＋1框架下的智库网络。我们希望能够在未来成为我们地区与中国学术合作的协调人。"他说，他们学院在与中国多年的良好合作基础上有了新的想法。

中国与美国、俄罗斯和欧盟并列为塞尔维亚的四大战略重点之一，迪米特里耶维奇说。他说，在过去的七十年里，国际政治与经济研究所与世界各地的200多个研究机构建立了良好的关系。

在谈到迪米特里耶维奇的建议时，李大使说，中国和塞尔维亚都在努力提高交流机制和平台，赶上双边关系发展的良好势头。"这非常令人鼓舞，我认为未来也会推动智库的合作，"李大使说，"如果总统尼科利奇在他退休后牵头成立中国-塞尔维亚合作办公室，我建议智库合作可以作为他工作的一部分。"

贝尔格莱德孔子学院院长拉多萨夫·普西奇（Radosav Pusic）同意这个看法，称塞尔维亚是一个巴尔干小国，并在每一个关键的历史时刻成为一个受害者。"当大国争霸时，小国遭殃。贝尔格莱德在历史上被摧毁了40多次，甚至在20世纪90年代仍遭受了战争的困扰。"普西奇说。而且，虽然战争已经结束，但这个国家经济停滞已经有些年头了，金融危机更加剧了困难局面。许多年轻人正在离开塞尔维亚。但普西奇说，现在对塞尔维亚来说是一个"历史性的时刻"，因为在"一带一路"倡议合作框架下，塞尔维亚与中国的经济和投资活动比以往更加频繁。

著名汉学家普西奇表示："得益于两国政治和战略伙伴关系的牢固，这为其他合作打下了坚实的基础。"他已经撰写或翻译了三十本关于中国古典文学、诗歌和哲学的书籍。"在这种背景下，塞尔维亚的很多人都对'一带一路'倡议表现出了兴趣，"普西奇说，"但是如果十年前提出来的话，这种认可可能不会那么容易。"

普西奇说还需要更多的努力，特别是在文化和宣传方面。"丝绸之路倡议是一个具有巨大历史意义的概念，所以它也提供了另外一个视角来加深我们对中国的了解，"普西奇说，"我会在帮助塞尔维亚了解中国的传统文化方面做更多的事情。"现在普西奇正在全身心地写一本关于中国古代哲学史的书。

复兴一座钢铁厂，挽救失业

二十年来，斯韦特兰娜·拉多萨夫列维奇（Svetlana Radosavljevic），为数不多的塞尔维亚蓝领女工人之一，在该国最大的钢铁厂斯梅代雷沃钢铁厂（Zelezara Smederevo）从事一线工作，她在一座老生产厂房的玻璃壁控制室里监控着钢铁制造。

这个距离贝尔格莱德不到一个小时车程的工厂多年来只能运行两条生产线中的一条。它每个月大约损失 1000 万美元，5000 多名青壮年员工中有很多人无所事事，工作不在状态。长期低下的竞争力迫使它逐渐走向破产的边缘。但是，自从总部设在河北省的中国大型企业河北钢铁集团有限公司以 4600 万欧元收购了这家公司后，这家 105 年历史的钢铁厂被赋予了新的生命。河钢塞尔维亚公司——斯梅代雷沃钢铁厂的新名字——的两条生产线已全速运转，2017 年其产量将达到 200 万吨，达欧盟和塞尔维亚同意的最高限额，钢铁厂结束了七年亏损，在 2016 年年底开始盈利。

重要的是，工人们欣喜地看到，他们所有人的工作都得到了保证，工资也有所提高，比收购前平均高出 8%。"现在更安全，产量更好，我更加专注于工作，因为我不必担心有一天会失业。"拉多萨夫列维奇愉快地说道。她好像已经忽略了热轧生产线，这个在 20 世纪 70 年代由传奇的南斯拉夫领导人约瑟普·布罗兹·铁托（Josip Broz Tito）（1892—1980）引入的生产线。即使是现在，这样的生产线在欧洲也只有三条。拉多萨夫列维奇的控制室距离制成钢板的生产线末端约 50 米。2016 年 6 月访问期间，习近平主席在拉多萨夫列维奇的控制室会见了部分工人和管理团队。

他们回忆说，习近平主席的这次访问给塞尔维亚的这条命脉带来了新的活力和信心。除一线工人外，现任塞尔维亚共和国总统的武契奇也对这样短时间内取得的业绩感到兴奋。"我当时和总理说我们今年的收入目标是 8 亿美元左右，"负责公司管理的河钢塞尔维亚执行董事宋嗣海在最近的一次采访中说，"武契奇马上要求他的助手计算这个数目（这个公司的历史高点的一倍）与该国经济总量的比值。"

宋嗣海，河北母公司高层管理人员，坐在办公室里说，引用武契奇的结论，2017 年河钢塞尔维亚的收入对塞尔维亚国内生产总值的贡献将超过 2 个百分点。"毋庸置疑，这将大大有助于振兴塞尔维亚的经济发展。"宋嗣海自信而响亮地说。此前，武契奇曾表示，中方收购塞尔维亚国有企业将帮助塞尔维亚在 2017 年实现 3.5% ~ 4% 的经济增长率，这将使塞尔维亚接近欧盟标准。当分析他的团队创造的奇迹时，他说这归功于在中国过去几十年的高速工业化和城市化进程中，国内母公司发展起来的强大竞争力和优势。

"通过利用我们的优势，我们已经把塞尔维亚钢铁厂带入到我们的全球运营周期中。"宋嗣海还补充说。他的公司已经成为一家重量级的全球运营商。塞尔维亚的原材料主要依靠进口，而销售到塞尔维亚以外的国家的产品仅占其总销售的五分之一。宋嗣海说："这是一家典型的公司，两端都在生产国之外，所以降低成本是关键。"河钢集团拥有数百万吨的年生产能力，在一些国家的原料采购方面具有决定性的发言权。宋嗣海说："对于我们的塞尔维亚公司，我们依靠全球采购平台来购买原材料，成本要低得多。"

同时，母公司 2014 年拿到了位于瑞士的杜弗克国际贸易控股公司的控股权，现在杜弗克正在帮助探索河钢塞尔维亚工厂节约成本的市场空间。过去，该厂主要将产品销往西欧，然后再销往南斯拉夫和其他巴尔干地区。宋嗣海说："在我们的行业，我们必须要考虑缩短销售半径来降低运输成本。"他举了一个例子：如果产品在塞尔维亚出售，每吨的成本是 1 ~ 2 美元，但是如果它被运到意大利出售，那么平均成本就会飙升到每吨 33 美元。他说，现在南斯拉夫的市场份额最大，约占总销售额的 50% ~ 60%。他们也在探索多瑙河沿岸的目标市场，它主要指德国和保加利亚，尽管欧盟对市场的保护力度很高，但水运则较为便宜。

宋嗣海说："我们甚至在美国找到了机会。"他补充说，2017 年 4 月在美国的销售量将超过 2000 吨。他说，在他们从欧盟市场出发的同时，英国市场也在筹备中。除了母公司提供的销售和采购优惠之外，宋嗣海的团队还专注于控制和提高产品质量，提高环境标准。

2016 年，母公司投资了 1.2 亿美元现金，以确保这个低迷的工厂能够全力运转。宋嗣海说："即使我们在接手后马上开始正式运营，我们还是采取了两条路线，努力寻找未来管理层的漏洞。"而 2017 年他的公司又投入了 1.2 亿美元来升级生产设备。宋嗣海说，在运营中，他还发现了很多降低成本的潜力。例如，现在这个工厂是由天然气驱动的，到目前为止，废热和能源回收再利用技术都还没有被应用。

基本上，工厂的生产能力可以进一步提高。如果生产线配备升级的现代化设备，生产能力将达到 4000 万 ~ 5000 万吨，比目前的水平翻一番。宋嗣海说："但是我们没有提高产能的计划，而是把重点放在安全生产、产品质量和环境标准上。" 从长远来看，他的公司将瞄准高端生产，如汽车行业的钢铁。这也将提高工厂的环境标准。宋嗣海说："几年内我们将努力达到欧洲的环保标准。" 他补充说，中国大部分钢铁企业的竞争力和环保标准现在甚至高于欧洲竞争对手。

他说："所以我非常有信心把河钢塞尔维亚变成欧洲最有实力的钢铁公司。" 联系到中国的"一带一路"倡议，宋嗣海说，在这个大背景下，他的公司的竞争力会有助于促进全球互联互通和生产要素的流动。他回顾说，中国在改革开放初期积极引进资金、技术和人力资源。在他所在的钢铁行业，一些中国公司甚至将欧洲钢铁厂的一部分迁到中国来，以实现这些目标。

"现在到中国了，" 宋嗣海说。"我们依靠强大的竞争力来升级塞尔维亚的命脉公司，我们的目标是为这个国家的再工业化进程作出贡献。" 他补充说："在'一带一路'倡议的背景下，我们为我们的合作伙伴作出积极的贡献，我们希望树立一个好的榜样。"

刷新电影记忆

对 于许多中国人来说，南斯拉夫的电影，如《瓦尔特保卫萨拉热窝》和《桥》等，都深深地留在了他们的脑海中。2015 年，在北京会见塞尔维亚总统尼科利奇和他的代表团时，习近平主席说他会用口哨哼出《桥》的旋律。

在 2016 年 6 月，访问塞尔维亚前夕，他发表在塞尔维亚报纸上的文章中提到，两部电影重新激发了两国人民的爱国热情。"中国国家主席和总理都对这两部电影十分了解。"塞尔维亚共和国文化部部长弗拉丹·武科萨夫列维奇在接受专访时对我说。这次专访就安排在他陪同塞尔维亚总统结束北京之行后不久。由于《桥》的效应，武科萨夫列维奇说，双方已基本达成协议，加强电影方面的合作。"我们有想法刷新人们的观念，基本上这将是一部商业电影，这可能会吸引全世界的电影观众。"武科萨夫列维奇 2017 年 3 月在他位于贝尔格莱德的办公室说。

为了实现这一目标，他说，中国提供了北京出色的电视和电影制片厂，以及非常棒的平面摄影。"我对中国快速发展的经济印象深刻。我在 2016 年第一次访问和 2017 年访问的时候都看到了。塞尔维亚人应该也看到。"武科萨夫列维奇说。

他建议，剧情应该和现代年轻人的故事结合起来，他们如何生活，他们怎么思考，他们如何相爱，他们是如何看待自己周围的这个世界。"但是在这个故事里面，我们应该展示我们文化合作和联系的深层渊源。再加入一些老电影的音乐和场景。"武科萨夫列维奇说。

"但这个故事应该是当代的。我希望这部电影会有很多中国观众、欧洲观众。"他认为，双方有很好的机会制作优秀的电影，但这不是唯一的方式来展现文化潜力，应该有更多的东西。"但是，我们必须努力制作一部好的和漂亮的电影，然后参观国际电影节。"他说。

他相信，中国的电影导演和艺术家们与塞尔维亚同行进行合作的潜力非常大。许多中国的艺术家在全球范围内闻名。"优秀的电影导演赢得了许多国际奖项。所以中国不仅在经济上迈向未来，"他说，"中国也在现当代文化界迈出了重要一步。中国有很多东西要向全世界展示。"他还说，双方领导人一直非常支持在贝尔格莱德建立中国文化中心。相应地，塞尔维亚将在北京建立一个类似的中心。贝尔格莱德中心，将建在 1999 年 5 月遭到北约轰炸的中国驻南斯拉夫大使馆的地方。

回忆起被故意投掷的炸弹，武科萨夫列维奇部长表示将在该地点建造的中心将成为中国文化和商业推广大楼的一部分。它于 2018 年竣工完成。"塞尔维亚将在北京开设当代文化中心，我可以公开表示，这是我们文化合作的历史性的一步。"武科萨夫列维奇说。

05

第五章

匈牙利和波兰在中东欧
领航"一带一路"倡议

每个欧洲国家在吸引外资的时候都有标榜它作为门户优势的习惯。但现实情况是，在中欧和东欧甚至南欧，没有哪个港口可以与鹿特丹、安特卫普和汉堡竞争，没有比法兰克福、巴黎、阿姆斯特丹和伦敦更繁忙的机场。但在中国和中东欧关系愈加紧密之后，它们也有了成为区域性金融和航空中心的雄心。在摆脱2008年金融危机和欧洲债务危机的负面影响过程中，中东欧国家通过挖掘潜力来提高竞争力的决心也越来越大。

他们注意到亚洲经济复兴的模式，特别是中国持续繁荣的秘密。他们开始改善基础设施，雄心勃勃地扩建高速公路、港口和机场，建设高科技园区、吸引外资，而中国可以满足他们的这些需求。

2012年，中国和十六个中东欧国家的领导人在华沙、布加勒斯特、贝尔格莱德、苏州和里加进行了会晤，讨论和实施各个领域的具体计划。到2016年，基础设施建设、能源、教育和金融等领域的已经完成的项目达到50个。在2016年里加峰会上，他们推出了几十项工作计划，而且在2017年布达佩斯峰会上进行了复盘回顾。

中国驻匈牙利大使段杰龙在接受采访时说，2013年习近平主席提出"一带一路"倡议为中国与中东欧国家的合作注入了新的动力。段大使说："在习近平主席的'一带一路'倡议背景下，中国与中欧和东欧国家的合作出现了新的机遇和发展前景。"在他看来，中国在中东欧地区的投资已经开始活跃起来。

段大使表示，2017年年初在匈牙利投资的中国企业已达40家。他说："2016年这个数字大概为30家。"他没有说明具体的投资额，但是告诉我这些业务主要投资于汽车零部件、化学工业和电子产品。他说，连接布达佩斯和贝尔格莱德的铁路项目是具有里程碑意义的铁路项目。

欧盟委员会正在审查项目报告，然后才会开"审查通过"的绿灯。这意味着运抵希腊比雷埃夫斯的集装箱可以在卸货后，直接通过铁路运送到布达佩斯，经由马其顿的斯科普里和塞尔维亚的贝尔格莱德；该合作也涉及亚得里亚海、波罗的海和黑海以及内陆水道的港口合作。

他们知道，亚得里亚海—波罗的海—黑海港口合作将有助于扩大中国—中东欧国家的务实合作范围，有助于"一带一路"倡议与中东欧国家以及欧盟的跨欧运输网络的发展战略的协调发展。

与此同时，波兰、匈牙利和捷克已经从中欧铁路货运服务中受益，该服务从2011年开始启动，已经成为"一带一路"倡议的重要组成部分。据新华社报道，截至2017年3月底，货运列车已累计运营3557辆，服务范围覆盖27个中国城市和11个欧洲国家的28个城市。

在习近平主席提出"一带一路"倡议并且实施了初期项目之后，各国在区域乃至跨大洲的"门户优势"的重要性变得尤为突出。

中国驻捷克大使马克卿说捷克的目标是把自己建成区域性航空和金融中心，波兰领导人已经决定把波兰这个约有四千万人口的国家变成一个地区性的甚至欧洲的中心，而即使是过去一直处于新闻头条和救助谈判困境的国家——希腊也已经制定了参与

"一带一路"倡议的国家战略，计划成为区域性的能源、航运和物流中心。"希腊一直在实施结合'一带一路'倡议的国家发展战略。"驻雅典的中国大使邹肖力说。

为了进一步深化"一带一路"倡议的参与程度，捷克总统泽曼，匈牙利总理欧尔班·维克托和波兰总理希德沃，与其他国家的领导人一起参加了于2017年5月14—15日举办的"一带一路"国际合作高峰论坛。论坛上，中东欧国家的领导人们就如何在基础设施、产业投资、经贸合作、资源能源、金融合作、人文交流、生态建设和海洋产业等方面进行合作提出了意见。

为了进一步发掘机遇，中国社会科学院在布达佩斯成立了中国—中东欧研究院，这家智库专注于中国与中东欧国家间的合作。时任中国社会科学院院长的王伟光说，新研究院的设立是中国智库走向全球的一个里程碑。中国社会科学院欧洲研究所所长黄平，也是中国—中东欧研究所的带头人，他说："这应该是我们在欧洲建立的第一个智库，在推动'一带一路'倡议在欧洲发展的方面将发挥重要作用。"实际上，有着1.23亿人口的中东欧，2012年其16个国家对华贸易额达到500亿美元，相当于中意之间的贸易额。中国在中东欧16国的投资相当于中国对瑞典的投资，而他们在中国的投资甚至不及奥地利一个国家的投资量。

与此同时，中东欧国家在公路铁路建设、港口和电厂扩建等方面的需求很大，渴求来自中国的投资。现在，据中国商务部统计，在全球经济形势不景气的情况下，中国与中东欧双方的贸易额正在适度增长，许多国家的投资额增幅较大。

匈牙利与"一带一路"倡议的协同发展

在最近与来自浙江省青田县，今年 41 岁，居住在布达佩斯的叶小荣见面后，我突然间知道一种新型的唐人街正在兴起。中国的"一带一路"倡议正及时地推动着他实现梦想。在欧洲城镇的许多华人社区里，中国的餐馆、杂货铺、中医诊所甚至旅游景点都在相邻的街道上。这些街道和商店通常是由当地政府为向中国人出租而建造的。

叶小荣在他位于布达佩斯郊外的办公室请我喝中国茶时，以一种清醒冷静却热情的口气说："我喜欢可以讨价还价的市场，我喜欢讲价。"当我们喝茶的时候，他告诉我，和生意伙伴探寻商业机会是他日常生活中不可或缺的一部分。

我知道很多人把浙江省的人民与有商业头脑的犹太人等同起来，当他说话时，他表现出充满勇气、灵活和务实的特质。布达佩斯建材市场创始人叶先生微笑着跳过关于营业额的问题，说道："我可以告诉你，我梦想着把我们周围生活的地方变成一个现代化的唐人街，有数百家批发商店来满足欧洲人的生活需求。"由于长期以来，人们离开家乡到全球各处定居，叶先生的家乡有50 万人，但已经离开中国的人数已经达到了 30 万人，他们中的百分之九十在欧洲做餐馆老板或者店主。

叶先生，这个设计了匈牙利首都的新唐人街的人，与众不同。有些微胖的叶先生给我透露说，他小时候和五个兄弟姐妹在一个不起眼的农村家庭长大，像那些年的许多中国商人一样在

20世纪90年代初退学，他开始的时候与兄弟在家乡卖冰棒，赚取一两分钱他都会很高兴。

当他开始做服装批发生意的时候，他亏本不少，甚至连母亲都劝他放弃生意。经过他软磨硬泡的请求，他母亲借给他1000多元让他重新开始他的生意，在他1999年来到布达佩斯之前，在亲戚的帮助下，他赚得约30万元。叶先生说："我从一开始的亏钱中学到了很多东西。"

像生活在布达佩斯这个通往其他国家的门户的许多中国人一样，叶先生很快就开始在这个棚户区一样的旧的中欧商业中心向匈牙利周边国家批发服装和其他廉价的中国产品。即使商业环境不好，该中心仍然拥有2000名店主，但是叶先生却梦想着有个干净、有序、体面的商业氛围。

2001年，他创办了一家房地产投资公司，开始在废旧土地上建设一个新的唐人街，它距离旧商业中心大约一公里远。2008年新唐人街加快建设，现在，由三条街组成的新唐人街已经驻进服装批发商店、餐馆、超市甚至律师事务所，其中有家中餐馆的菜非常好吃，以至于吸引了香港动作片明星成龙光临。

这些成就还没有使叶先生停下来。三年前，他和他的弟弟又推出了另一个计划，在5～8年内再建造三条街道，用于批发销售建筑材料、墙砖、灯具、供暖和制冷设备以及汽车零部件。"我的目标很明确，至少在这个地区我们必须成为最大的玩家。"叶先生告诉我。

现在，第一条新街已经建成，批发商铺林立两旁，现在已经有40多家商户入驻，其中一半是中国人，一半是匈牙利人。最后他说，这三条街将会容纳 500 个批发商，并将为匈牙利人创造至少 3000 个就业机会。唐人街和叶先生规划的建材商店街距离布达佩斯和其他欧洲国家首都之间的主要铁路线仅有数米之远。中国、塞尔维亚和匈牙利已经同意根据"一带一路"倡议框架对布达佩斯和贝尔格莱德之间的铁路进行升级改造。

叶先生非常肯定，这条铁路线会变得更加繁忙，因为许多货物将通过连接希腊和匈牙利以及欧洲其他地区的海陆物流进行运输，于是他请求布达佩斯铁路局在市场旁边建立一个小型货运站。目前这个问题还在讨论中，而这个货运站将帮助他节省从另一个火车站装货，然后运输至唐人街的成本，每个集装箱节省约 400 欧元。叶先生认为，这将是一个新型的中国商业社区，在一个长的链条上为欧洲人提供服务，为匈牙利人创造就业机会。他还表示，该市场的供应商遍及全球，但是大部分建筑材料仍然来自中国。

他站在铁路旁边告诉我："我们的蓝图现在终于变成现实了，我们的唐人街将成为布达佩斯的一个景点。"他甚至计划为观光游客引入随上随下的嘟嘟车。

叶先生六条街市场的梦想真的是使唐人街的面貌焕然一新。匈牙利人总是说他们是唯一具有东方血统的欧洲人，他们对中国禅宗和功夫文化的经久不衰的热情证明了这一点。

在匈牙利采访期间，除了叶先生的雄心外，1999 年移居匈牙利的少林寺武僧的 32 代传人王德庆在传播中国文化方面也给我留下了深刻的印象，他被任命为匈牙利国家警察学校的教练、特种警察部队的首席教练和总统保镖护送队的教练。

"很多人可能会认为我会教他们中国功夫，"在他于 2003

年成立的位于布达佩斯郊外的国际禅武联盟上，王德庆说，"这并不是事实，特别是在训练总统的护卫队时。"

根据他的经验，"禅"意味着禅宗，"武"意味着武术，他们同等重要。而当他到匈牙利的时候，他的联盟的目标就是要把中国文化与禅宗、武术联合起来传播。王先生说："我主要利用禅宗来培养一直在高压状态下工作的匈牙利狙击手。我已经教会了他们如何保持冷静，他们在超危险和危急的情况下也能保持平静的心态，同时独立工作并且隐蔽起来。"

他在匈牙利多年的努力得到了认可。他曾担任与匈牙利内政部有联系的中匈警察交流协会的执行主席，匈牙利前总理迈杰希·彼得曾邀请他共进晚餐，并感谢他在匈牙利促进中国文化的发展方面所作出的贡献。

王先生说，正是在梅杰西的大力帮助下（在他担任总理的时候），中国传统医学、针灸、功夫甚至汉语开始在匈牙利得到大力推广。"在促进中匈文化交流方面，前总理梅杰西是一位有远见的、受人尊敬的匈牙利领导人。"

除了对警察和保镖护卫队的贡献之外，他还训练了欧洲的禅武教练，现在全世界有大约30个禅武联盟的分支机构，其中大部分在欧洲。据估计，全世界有近20万名练习者在接受中国文化。他说："我认为禅武在匈牙利最受欢迎，一名匈牙利教练告诉我，他已经教了大约1000名学生，这是相当了不起的成就。"

王先生说，所有的学生都被要求保护和推广正宗的少林功夫，正如他在少林寺时自己的师父教给他的一样。其中包括学习传统的礼仪和纪律，培养武德，建立和谐快乐的态度和价值观。

禅武已经设立了九级制度，人们通过考试来确认学生在武术学习中的所得。

尽管他获得了成就和认可，王先生仍然过着简单的生活。他说："如果我没有练功夫，那么我会成为那些被主流价值抛弃的人。"

王先生于 1974 年出生在浙江，小时候非常调皮，所以九岁的时候，他的父母把他送到河南省少林寺附近的一所体育学校。三年后，他和另外 15 人组成了少林寺武术队，成为了一名新手武僧。"起初我很着迷，但我很快发现，饥饿是寺庙最大的担忧之一。"王先生回忆说。18 岁的时候，王先生成了一名真正的武僧，他的法号叫石兴红。

不久他就开始在全世界传播功夫文化。王先生的武术和心智修炼结合的概念，在他到匈牙利定居之前甚至吸引到了西班牙政府的注意力，他曾被邀请到西班牙教导少年犯。

王先生回忆说，他在西班牙教了不到一年，因为他被西班牙方面安置在一个宽敞的古老别墅里。他说："尽管我的训练对青年违法者是有用的，但我习惯了寺庙里的简单生活，这些是接受不了的。"

标志性的 350 公里的布达佩斯 – 贝尔格莱德铁路项目

中国和匈牙利官员都证实，中国参与布达佩斯—贝尔格莱德 350 公里铁路线的现代化改造的进程正在顺利进行，而欧盟委员会正在审查相关的设计和融资安排报告。

中国驻匈牙利大使段杰龙在接受采访时说："双方已经签署了建造合同和融资方案备忘录，我们正在为尽早启动关键项目做努力。"

段大使表示，中国将把铁路建造成为双轨线，匈牙利设计部分已经完成，中匈两国已经形成了投资和实施该项目的共同体。

来自中国方面的建筑公司也准备在塞尔维亚破土动工。据来自塞尔维亚的可靠消息称，欧盟表示可能会"很快"为这个项目开绿灯。匈牙利外长西雅尔多（Szijjarto）也表示，布达佩斯—贝尔格莱德铁路的现代化改造是中国与中东欧国家积极推进合作的"旗舰项目"。

西雅尔多在接受采访时说："这是因为它是创新型合作模式，有利于加强区域连接性的跨境基础设施投资。"

他还表示，该铁路线是作为中欧陆海快线的"一带一路"倡议的核心部分，可能成为连接希腊比雷埃夫斯港和西欧地区的最快、具有最强运输能力的运输路线。他表示，这条铁路线将使许多国家在产业转型中受益。西雅尔多说："与匈牙利类似，沿线国家可以通过工业园区和物流中心连接到中欧陆海快线，带着他们的产品出口到中国。"

他的国家从一开始就对这一举措表示欢迎，认为这是一个吸引投资的独特机会，也是中东欧地区实施的以改善连通性的新融资选择。

西雅尔多说："布达佩斯—贝尔格莱德铁路线是这方面的一

个重要项目。"

他说，中国是匈牙利在 2010 年开展的"向东开放"战略的重点国家，"一带一路"倡议刚好契合了匈牙利的发展蓝图。

欧尔班对北京进行了正式国事访问，除了与李克强总理举行了双边会晤外，欧尔班还得到了习近平主席和最高立法机关官员的接见。欧尔班在北京说，旧的全球化模式已经过时了，"东方已经赶上西方了"。

他认为"一带一路"倡议是"另一个变革方向，尤其是建立在相互接纳的基础上的"，布达佩斯—贝尔格莱德的铁路线现代化改造是"最壮观的"合作。

在参与这个倡议的过程中，三国不仅受益于基础设施的改善，而且也受益于与全球供应链的联系。

在"一带一路"倡议框架下，西雅尔多说，匈牙利作为该地区的金融中心正在发挥越来越重要的作用，以促进人民币的交易。

段大使还表示，实施"一带一路"倡议后，两国的经贸关系日益密切。他表示，中国是匈牙利在欧洲以外的最大贸易伙伴，全球贸易惨淡的环境下，2016 年贸易额超过 88.9 亿美元，同比增长 10.1%。段大使还说 2016 年匈牙利对华的出口额已经刷新了历史纪录，达到 34.6 亿美元，增长 20.5%。优质农产品和食品产品吸引了来自中国的越来越大的需求，其前景尤为乐观。

目前，匈牙利是中国在中东欧国家最大的投资国，累计投资额超过 41 亿美元。段大使说，华为、中兴、中国银行等 40 多家中国企业在匈牙利投资，已经创造了 7400 个就业岗位。

在中国的投资者中，中国领先的电动汽车供应商比亚迪是匈牙利的新人。比亚迪欧洲总经理何一鹏（Isbrand Ho）表示，他们公司将在 2016　2018 年二年内向新工厂投资 2000 万欧元，新工厂距布达佩斯约 50 公里。这家工厂将会创造 300 个就业岗位，绝大多数岗位会提供给当地招聘的具有技术背景的匈牙利人，他们两班倒，每年组装 400 辆电动公交车。

何先生说："这些巴士将出口给欧洲大陆的客户，最初的产品将是电动公交车和客车，但其他产品将很快跟进。"何先生说，"一带一路"倡议旨在打造世界上最大的经济合作平台，许多公司已经签署了沿线项目的合作协议。他说："不仅比亚迪欧洲公司、我们的客户，供应商和其他同行也从这些改善了的联系中受益。"

他表示，比亚迪非常清楚匈牙利在该地区公交车制造方面的优势，匈牙利附近的工厂每年建造数千辆巴士，为前东欧集团供货。何先生说，在匈牙利政府试图重建这个行业的过程中，比亚迪很自豪地站在这个行业的前列，并希望成为帮助匈牙利实施公共交通电气化改造的强有力的合作伙伴。"我们预计，欧洲的电动公交车和工厂数目的增加会提高我们满足客户需求的能力。"何先生说。

波兰和中国：
重新定位与新丝绸之路的伙伴关系

作为世界著名作曲家、钢琴家肖邦（Frederic Chopin，1810—1849）的故乡，波兰在习近平主席访问期间为习近平主席和他的代表团组织了一场肖邦作品音乐会。2016 年，当我采访波兰总统安德烈·杜达（Andrzej Duda）时，他说中国国家主席习近平在不到三个月的时间里第二次来到中东欧地区，这表示习近平主席充分认识到了该地区的发展活力和重要性。"我毫不怀疑习近平主席完全了解这个地区的发展活力，我们正在快速发展，中国也是如此。" 杜达在书面采访中告诉我。

杜达说，他的国家在习近平主席和夫人彭丽媛到塞尔维亚访问后，已经准备好欢迎他们到波兰来。

杜达曾于 2015 年 11 月访问中国，他说："我的第二次的中国之行（相差不到三个月），说明了中东欧对中国的重要性。"回顾在第一次中国之行中留下深刻印象的中国数千年的历史和传统文化，杜达强调，习近平主席认为波兰是一个极具吸引力的市场，是拥有深化经济合作的无限机遇的地方。在其 2015 年 11 月访华期间，中国和波兰签署了"一带一路"合作文件，波兰随后成为亚洲基础设施投资银行的成员国。

杜达表示："我们认为这是寻找资助波兰和中东欧其他国家基础设施项目的新途径。" 波兰领导人表示，波兰必须改进自 2004 年加入欧盟以来一直被忽视的北南轴线，并需要建造更多的高速公路和更多的铁路，这将形成波罗的海和巴尔干半岛之间的纽带。

杜达说："我相信这会给我们所有人带来巨大的推动作用，中国在这方面可以发挥重要的作用。"

杜达说："另一方面，我们也希望波兰公司能够从'一带一路'倡议中获得巨大的收益。" 他补充说，他们拥有丰富的经验和高素质的员工队伍，他确信他们可以与中国企业建立长期的、富有成果的合作关系。

杜达说，他意识到中国在国际舞台上扮演着越来越重要的角色，很多中国公司在国外都名气大增。

他说中国现在最大的挑战是社会不平等和城乡发展不平衡，他知道中国当局为解决这个问题作了多少努力。

杜达说："另一方面，许多欧洲国家最近也面临着同样的问题。"

杜达表示，在他的访问期间中波将签署数十个双边协议，这将是中波两国进一步合作的基础。杜达说："但是我们的关系不应该只停留在经济层面。"

"我相信习近平主席和彭丽媛夫人都会爱上波兰文化、波兰音乐，还有波兰美食。"

正值波兰这个中欧国家积极推动经济外交之时，中国和波兰为"一带一路"倡议和2030年发展战略形成协同效应打下了坚实的基础，中央顶级智库——国务院发展研究中心主任李伟说。

"中国'一带一路'倡议为双方深化经贸关系创造了重要的机遇，波兰的长期发展战略与这一倡议相呼应。波兰2030年的长期战略旨在实现高水平的现代化，2013年，习近平主席提出了'一带一路'倡议，以加强亚洲、欧洲和非洲的连通性。"李先生说。就中波经济关系而言，中国是波兰在亚洲的重要投资国和最大贸易伙伴，而波兰则是中国在中东欧较大的贸易伙伴，也是在中东欧极为重要的投资国。

"现在波兰大大增加了对基础设施建设的投资，这为中国企业带来了巨大的机遇。"他说，历史上被称为欧洲东部的门户的波兰已经成为中国"一带一路"倡议的积极参与者，而在所有连接中国和欧洲国家的铁路货运路线中，其中六条将会途径波兰抵达目的地。

在习近平主席访波期间，中欧各城市之间各条货运路线统一更名为"中欧班列"，"中欧班列"比"海上运输"快10天。

李先生说，这个倡议是中国发展的重中之重，中央和各省、市、自治区已经制定了关于"一带一路"倡议的蓝图。他说，在对外方面，中国已经与蒙古、哈萨克斯坦等30多个国家签署了协议，寻求与对方重大项目的协同发展。2015年，中国和俄罗斯宣布他们找到将"一带一路"倡议和俄罗斯领导的欧亚经济联盟联系起来的方法，目前这个联盟由五个国家组成。中国和欧盟也签署了深化"一带一路"倡议和欧盟投资3150亿欧元计划（被称为"容克计划"）的合作协议。

"在实施'一带一路'倡议的同时，我们在基础设施建设、贸易和工业园区项目方面也取得了很大进展。"

例如，连接莫斯科和喀山的770公里高速铁路，雅加达—万隆高速铁路和中国—老挝铁路正在建设之中，中国通过提供技术解决方案和工程经验在项目中获得了很大收益。

李先生说，中国已经与"一带一路"沿线的许多国家签署了本币互换协议。除了亚洲基础设施投资银行和丝绸之路基金之外，中国还与欧盟、俄罗斯等国家或组织建立了联合金融平台。他说："我们正在设法解决资金紧张的问题。"

李先生还表示，中国已经和46个国家签署了取消入境签证的协议，另有19个国家同意为中国公民签发落地签证。他说："这些措施极大地促进了人员往来、旅游、经济合作和贸易往来。"

中国和波兰在2016年习近平主席访问期间，把战略伙伴关系提升到了"全面水平"。2016年，建立中波战略伙伴关系的五年之后，也是在近年来波兰调整外交政策的背景下，两国关系通过让全球所有参与者而不是西方主要国家参与进来的方式而深化。中国驻波兰大使徐坚说："在过去的几年中，我们的双边关系在各个方面都取得了巨大的进展，双方都认识到了习近平主席访问期间的大丰收。"

曾担任驻罗马尼亚大使的徐大使说，中国与中东欧国家伙伴关系的迅速发展也是习近平主席访问时重新定位中波关系的原因。习近平主席对塞尔维亚进行了为期三天的国事访问后访问了波兰。"我认为我们的关系已经达到了全面战略伙伴关系的水平。"徐大使说。

近年来，特别是在2008年金融危机之后，中东欧国家多年来一直与西方国家紧密合作，现在它们开始调整外交政策，中国的经济活力和市场也成为吸引它们的磁铁。在该地区的16个国家中，波兰、匈牙利等国家成为发展与中国伙伴关系的积极引领者，而其他国家，如捷克共和国，则发誓要追赶上来。

"我相信，习近平主席在三个月内第二次访问中东欧地区，这充分说明了我国如何重视中国与16个国家的关系。中波两国务实合作近年来顺利开展，现在双方都对波兰基础设施项目的合作表现出浓厚的兴趣。"

徐大使说，波兰曾邀请中国参与波兰的机场建设、公路建设和高铁项目，波兰加入了由中国发起的亚洲基础设施投资银行，并积极支持"一带一路"倡议。最近，亚投行行长金立群访问了波兰，该国正在寻求欧盟之外的其他金融资源来资助其基础设施项目。

中国和波兰在习近平主席访问期间签署了针对"一带一路"倡议的新文件，这进一步降低了基础设施合作的难度。

中国的国家和私人投资者都承诺在"一带一路"倡议的框架下向波兰和欧洲其他地区注入新的资本和技术，以促进欧亚间的联系。他们在国务院发展研究中心及其全球合作伙伴组织的为期两天的丝绸之路论坛上宣告了自己的合作承诺，而习近平主席于2016年对塞尔维亚、波兰和乌兹别克斯坦共和国三国进行了国事访问。

"与其他欧洲国家相似，中国和波兰面临着经济重组和可持续发展的挑战，我们热衷于在欧洲投资基础设施、节能、高科技和创新领域的项目。"丝路基金董事长金琦说。丝路基金是一支中长期基金，于2014年年底成立，首期注资100亿美元，习近平主席承诺投资总额为400亿美元。

中国和欧盟正在就建立联合基金进行磋商，将"一带一路"倡议和欧盟的3150亿欧元投资计划联系起来。丝路基金有望成为联合基金的中方创始人之一。"我们决心在中国、欧盟及其成员之间形成巨大的协同效应。"金琦在丝路国际论坛上这样表示。此次论坛是继2014年在伊斯坦布尔和2015年在马德里举行的第三次论坛。

2016年在波兰举行的"丝路国际论坛"着重讨论了欧亚陆路交通运输体系的标准化、融资方式的创新、全球治理与可持续发展以及中欧在区域层面的合作。

中国投资有限公司董事长兼首席执行官丁学东说，当波兰和中东欧其他国家需要资金时，中国投资有限公司也准备好弥补资金缺口。丁先生认为，预计该地区十六个国家未来十年，通过修建道路、高速公路、机场和其他设施来改善基础设施，至少需要一万亿美元。"面对如此巨大的基础设施建设资金需求，政府投资并不能满足需求，这些国家需要更多的资源。"

丁先生说，即使是西欧大国在升级基础设施方面也面临着资金缺口的挑战。他说："所以有效的机制是从政府、政策性贷款工具、投资基金和私营部门汇集资源。"他补充说，波兰和欧洲其他国家是这个国家基金的投资对象。

除了中国投资巨头之外，私人投资者也越来越重视波兰和其他欧洲国家。其中北京神雾环保能源科技有限公司董事长吴道洪说，中国民营企业在高科技领域与欧洲合作伙伴有合作的优势。吴先生说，他甚至带来了三项生物质能和清洁能源专利技术，特别是更清洁使用煤炭的专利技术；但他们与波兰伙伴的谈判仍在继续。吴先生说："我们确信，我们的煤炭技术正在向前推进，波兰和中国都拥有丰富的煤炭储量，如果煤炭的使用能够避免污染，就可以带来巨大的机遇。"

总部位于伦敦的四十八家集团（48 Group Club）俱乐部的主席斯蒂芬·佩里（Stephen Perry）说，"一带一路"倡议是中国对外开放的延续，这一倡议将持续 20 到 50 年，其中一个关键的决定因素将是西方国家的回应。他说，中国希望西方参与，因为西方国家拥有许多关键的先进技术，并且拥有这个项目所需要的资金、管理能力等。佩里说："如果西方国家投入这个项目，我们将获得巨大的回报和增长。"

06

第六章

西欧国家对"一带一路"
倡议的接受程度有所不同

德国、法国、意大利、荷兰、比利时和卢森堡是欧盟最初的 6 个创始国，在英国真正"脱欧"前欧盟仍有 28 个成员国。自习近平主席宣布"一带一路"倡议后，这些国家表现出的接受程度不同；英国率先积极回应，但比利时则失去了成为亚洲基础设施投资银行创始成员国的机会；希腊在推动"一带一路"倡议方面走在前面，意大利则有人主张在这方面赶超希腊；德国认为这一倡议与其国际发展战略一致，而法国的意见领袖则希望新总统能够更加积极主动地与中国互动。而卢森堡也已经和中国中部的郑州通过空中丝绸之路——货运航空进行连通。

事实上，2017 年前七个月，有四个国际场合供全球领导人共商国际议程，即七国集团峰会、二十国集团峰会、达沃斯世界经济论坛和在北京召开的"一带一路"国际合作高峰论坛。在 5 月 14 日至 15 日数百位外宾北京聚会之后，意大利总理真蒂洛尼（Gentiloni）和德国经济和能源部部长布丽吉特·齐普里斯（Brigitte Zypries）成为消除隔阂、实现和平与繁荣这一共识的重要信使。因为真蒂洛尼在北京与世界各国领导人会晤后将主持 5 月 26 日至 27 日在西西里岛的陶尔米纳镇举行的七国集团峰会；在 7 月 7 日至 8 日德国主持的汉堡二十国集团领导人会议上，齐普里斯将代表德国总理安格拉·默克尔（Angela Merkel）出席会议（默克尔由于时间冲突无法参加）。

真蒂洛尼和齐普里斯应该注意到在北京为期两天的论坛上提出的倡议、解决方案和建议。中国提出的"一带一路"倡议实质上是倡导全球要加强协商与合作，实现和平与繁荣，而搞对抗只能引发矛盾。丝绸之路精神的复兴正是七国集团峰会和二十国集团峰会迫切需要的。在 2017 年结束的七国集团会议上，七国集团财长和央行行长未能正式通过坚决反对保护主义的立场，主要是因为美国代表的反对。

二十国集团财长在 2017 年 7 月份的会议上也未达成一致，他们放弃了承诺不采取单边保护措施的做法。然而，不仅仅是美国采取了保护主义的立场。欧盟也对中国钢铁管材出口采取反倾销措施。聚集在北京的领导人发表了一份公报，强调他们达成的共识，即通过更好的基础设施、创新的金融工具和措施鼓励其他生产要素如资本、技术和人力资源流动，通过连接不同的国家、地区和文化来支持深化合作和创造更多机会。

传达这一信息的任务就落在了意大利和德国的肩上。的确，这些会议在一个艰难的时期进行，法国总统埃马纽埃尔·马克龙（Emmanuel Macron）才刚刚开始他的五年任期，特朗普在 2017 年 1 月就职，真蒂洛尼在 2016 年 12 月才开始领导意大利政府，英国首相特雷莎·梅也是一个新面孔。但领导者不应该把时间花在建立"信任的基础"上，这似乎总是他们聚会的核心任务。要取得具体成果，他们必须要果断，必须与保护主义作斗争，共同学习在北京召开的"一带一路"国际合作高峰论坛的"丝绸之路"精神。他们必须确保全球努力应对气候变化的成果。这为在汉堡举行的以互联互通为主题的二十国集团峰会铺平道路。

在很多方面，这个主题已经反映了"一带一路"倡议的一些成果，应该鼓励与会者进行讨论，要实现更大的基础设施互联互通，不仅要通过公路、高速路、铁路和港口而且要通过金融开放和数字化转型。在北京，世界经济论坛创始人克劳斯·施瓦布

（Klaus Schwab）将中国提出的“一带一路”倡议称为促进经济发展和国际合作的典范。他计划通过各种场合将该倡议与他的研究和议程设置联系起来，进一步深化世界经济论坛辩论和讨论的范围。作为正当其时的使者，肩负把世界变得更美好的使命，意大利和德国可以仿效施瓦布，用丝绸之路的和平交流精神指导七国集团和二十国集团的首脑会议。

德国与“一带一路”倡议

基本上，意大利作为七国集团主席国在 5 月底的会议上并没有讨论“一带一路”倡议，而在中国的外交棋盘上，德国和其他欧盟成员国的重要性可以从习近平主席对这些国家访问的频繁程度上得知。事实上，他在参加 2017 年的汉堡二十国集团峰会之前，先抵达柏林对德国进行了一次国事访问。

中国一直高度重视德国。这是习近平主席继 2014 年 3 月的访问后对德国进行的第二次国事访问。2014 年，李克强总理也访问了德国。另外，2017 年习近平主席对德国的访问仅在李克强总理访问德国之后的一个月。

德国同样重视中国，德国总理默克尔在任期间曾多次访华。总理办公室的一位官员说，除中国外，默克尔可能不会如此重视任何一个国家。德国是一个有竞争力的出口和制造大国，因此是中国的理想榜样。中国正在进行市场化改革，其社会福利和市场体系也在广泛讨论中。几十年来，德国在中国市场占有很大的份额。比如大众、奥迪、宝马、奔驰等德国汽车品牌在中国随处可见。

而且由于中国投资者刚刚开始探索高端产品市场，习近平主席可能会与德国领导人探讨如何消除贸易和投资壁垒，进一步推动双边关系，在对方市场扮演更重要的角色。全球化面临着越来越大的挑战，特别是英国脱欧、美国总统特朗普的"重振美国"的内向型政策，但其实这些都是贸易保护主义。特朗普也将美国从全球气候变化协议中拉了出来，而 2015 年几乎所有联合国成员国都欢迎并签署了巴黎协议。

德国一直拥护自由贸易和更密切的全球互联互通，并继续致力于应对气候变化。2017 年 1 月在瑞士达沃斯举行的世界经济论坛上，习近平主席重申了中国对全球化和自由贸易的承诺，得到欧盟领导人和政界人士的一再引用和欢迎。对中国来说，德国不仅是一个市场，也是一个探索欧盟经济的平台。近年来，北京一直在关注中国和欧盟的 19 亿消费者市场。

这正是习近平主席提出"一带一路"倡议的原因之一。德国对该倡议的积极响应带动了其他欧盟国家。例如，中国启动亚洲基础设施投资银行，许多欧盟国家作为创始成员加入，在第三方市场探索更多的机会。

在汉堡二十国集团峰会之后，我对汉堡峰会和华盛顿会议的成果文件进行了比较阅读。第一次举行这类发达国家与新兴经济体领导人会晤还是在金融巨头雷曼兄弟（Lehman Brothers）2008年破产两个月后。这可能是既让人鼓舞又令人担忧的。

很显然，经过德国总理默克尔团队集中的外交努力（她可能是唯一一位参加了 12 届二十国集团峰会的领导人），议程上的议题远远超出了风险管理、金融市场监管、金融流动性担保以及复苏经济增长的紧迫性，这些议题在一开始就引起了热烈讨论。那么国际社会的主要任务就是要通过让中国这样的新兴经济体参与世界经济增长来避免全球市场紊乱，与此同时，国际社会也急需资金来确保金融机构稳定运行。

国际货币基金组织称，从全球经济衰退的深度上来看，2008—2009 全球金融危机是 1929—1933 年大萧条以来最具破坏性的时期，中国贡献了全球经济增长的一半。相应地，中国在既定的国际经济治理中获得了一些应有的话语权：人民币进入全球货币篮子，人民币在双边交易中的使用日益频繁，欧洲央行将之作为储备货币买入。

中国在北京和上海分别成立了亚洲基础设施投资银行和金砖国家银行（新开发银行）等多边融资平台，提出"一带一路"倡议，使全球经济更加强大，更具包容性。由于中国的贡献（如汉堡文件所示），这次为期两天的安保严格的德国港口城市会议的成果得到了极大的拓展，这些成果典型地集中反映在发达国家渴望与发展中经济体对话上。

二十国集团领导人似乎已经就开放经济、自由贸易、能源和可持续发展、数字经济、与非洲的伙伴关系、健康和妇女权力达成了共识，这些共识被浓缩成了 15 页的宣言和若干附件。这给人的印象是，除了气候变化，他们已经都达成了一致。在气候变化问题上，美国通过立即停止贡献于控制全球温度上升来反对其他 19 国。

这些协议是令人欢欣鼓舞的，因为领导人们非常清楚保持全球经济增长稳定、可持续发展和包容的重要意义。与他们在华盛顿二十国集团峰会上所构想的愿景相比，这是一个巨大的飞跃。但是，当 2008—2012 年发生经济危机时，我们发现当今世界正面临着另一场危机——缺乏全球集体领导和国际政治信任。

印度在边界挑衅中国，美国在亚太地区积极展示其军事存在，欧美之间的分歧不断扩大，俄罗斯与西方的关系不融洽。

现在很明显，一些经济较好的经济体的政治意愿正在变弱。有些国家正在转向国内市场保护、地缘政治算计和军事实力展示，而不是设法提供更多的全球公共产品来真正将汉堡共识变为现实。相较而言，现在越来越难在各股力量之间达成妥协。美国，又在使用它的"京都议定书"伎俩，再次通过退出《巴黎气候变化协定》来表明立场。这对国际合作是有损害的，因为所有其他参与者都认为最大的经济体应该是一个值得信赖的合作伙伴，应该执行已经达成一致的协议。

情况令人担忧。如果这种政治信任不能加深，妥协的精神就无法得以维持，二十国集团的共识只会成为纸上的共识，它的实现能力将会被削弱。

西欧和其他国家不同的是，时任德国驻华大使施明贤（Michael Schaefer）表示，欧洲人正在对中国"一带一路"倡议形成"统一态度"，期待这一倡议可以稳定中欧之间的广大地区。他补充说，习近平主席利用双边会议甚至二十国集团平台进一步诠释了这一世纪倡议的意义，这不仅有利于中国，也有利于世界其他地区。施明贤于 2007—2013 年任德国驻华大使，他在柏林接受我的专访时说："与一开始的不情愿相比，欧洲人已经开始形成对'一带一路'倡议的统一态度。我直言不讳地说，我支持这一倡议，而且欧洲需要作出更积极的回应。"

作为柏林宝马基金会的主席，施明贤表示，他不确定"一带一路"倡议是否会在二十国集团峰会上讨论，但他表示，习近平主席至少可以在会见国家领导人时提出这些议题。他认为，中国可以做更多的事情来获得信任，以解释这一重大举措的愿景，这将为那些潜在脆弱地区带来稳定。施明贤表示，现在欧盟已经表现出对这一倡议的浓厚兴趣，自从 2013 年习近平主席提出倡议后，许多德国人已经加深了对这个项目的了解。

施明贤指出，"我认为这是一种为潜在脆弱地区带来活力的聪明的方法"，这一倡议将远远超越中国与欧亚大陆之间象征性的和历史性的联系以及基础设施问题。施明贤说，这个倡议不仅谈到市场的关联，而且也谈到人文的互通，这具有非常大的意义。施明贤说："我认为，欧盟、中亚和中国参与这一倡议，能帮助稳定处于相对脆弱状况的国家，这符合他们的共同利益。从这个意义上讲，这是一个稳定中国和欧洲之间广大地区的项目。"

他表示，通过发展和合作增加人类福祉，对于东欧和中国的近邻乃至中国西北贫困地区都是至关重要的。"这就是为什么欧洲应该更积极地行动。"他说。施明贤还表示，"一带一路"倡议的海上部分非常重要，因为世界需要一个连接非洲、中国和欧洲的海上安全通道，这可以帮助非洲发展。

他补充说，脆弱性不仅对外国企业不利，对有关地区人民的发展也不利。他甚至敦促所有参与"一带一路"倡议的国家都应该有长远的眼光，因为它可能会持续三十到五十年。施明贤说："我们需要明白，这不是一年或者是五年内就能完成的项目，我们需要在未来的三十年或五十年内作出贡献。"

施明贤曾于 2009 年习近平主席访问德国时做陪同工作，他发现习近平主席是一个"非常认真而令人钦佩的人，而且对历史有着浓厚兴趣"。"我们已经讨论了很多事情。"施明贤说。他还说，在他七年驻京大使任职期间，德国总理默克尔曾六次访华，但都不在选举年。施明贤表示，中国是一个独一无二的国家，改革开放在如此短的时间内极其成功地让如此多的人摆脱贫困。现在中国的中产阶级人口达到四亿。他说，习近平主席正在把中国引领向国际社会的中心，无论从历史、人口还是经济影响力方面来看中国都应该得到尊重。

施明贤说，习近平主席很清楚，在 21 世纪只能通过合作才能实现上述目标，而不是采用 20 世纪一些国家使用的霸权方式。施明贤说："在我看来，自从成为中国领导人，习近平主席作了两件令人印象深刻的事情。一件是反腐，另一件是'一带一路'倡议，打造全球合作与互联互通。"

中国驻德国大使史明德也表示，中国国家主席和总理同年访问德国是中德关系中罕见的外交行动，即使在中国的对外关系史上也是非常之罕见。他说："因此这得到了全世界的高度关注。"

史大使把德国视为欧洲的"核心力量"，实力最雄厚，综合实力最强，在全球舞台上有巨大的影响力。"中德两国在发展双边关系，解决地区性和世界性难题，探索发展机遇方面，有着越来越多的共同点。" 史大使说。在各个方面的共识已经帮助德国连续42年成为中国在欧洲最大的贸易伙伴。2016年,取代美国,中国成为德国最大的贸易伙伴。中德之间的贸易往来已经占到了中国与欧盟28个成员国的三分之一,史大使援引德方数据说。"德国对中国市场潜力和经济前景充满信心,中国已经认识到德国高科技产业和管理经验的重要性。"

他补充说,多年来,在对华技术转移方面德国也是欧洲最大方的国家。习近平主席2017年的访问见证了中德建交45周年,史大使高度赞赏说:"我们的关系是历史上最好的时期,这种双边关系已成为中欧伙伴关系的驱动力。"

史大使表示,习近平主席在访问期间将会勾画与德国的双边关系的发展蓝图。"我相信,在习近平主席的访问期间,中德坚实的伙伴关系将会被注入新的动力。" 史大使表示,习近平主席将出席柏林动物园大熊猫馆开馆仪式,并将出席中德青少年足球友谊赛;习近平主席将与德国领导人讨论如何深化"一带一路"框架下的合作,这将是领导人议程上最重要的话题之一。

史大使说,德国已经意识到,这个倡议是一项重要的全球公共产品,而且德国对"一带一路"倡议的态度在过去几年里发生了"巨大的变化"。当中国表达举办"一带一路"国际合作高峰论坛时,默克尔表示,她繁忙的国内议程不允许她出席会议,因此她派出她的代表以此表明德国支持这一倡议。史大使说,德国是对中国的提案表达及时支持的西方国家之一,是中国、印度和俄罗斯之后的第四大股东,并且是设在北京的亚洲基础设施投资银行中最大的非区域性股东。史大使说:"以往发生的许多案例表明，通过参与'一带一路'倡议，中德可以相互合作，在亚洲、非洲和世界其他地区发掘更多的市场潜力。"

丰富多彩的中德关系

习近平主席和德国总理默克尔都是足球迷，在过去的三年里，他们一直在努力扩大两国的足球伙伴关系。习近平主席在2014年年初第一次作为中国国家主席访问德国期间，会见了在德国训练的中国少年足球运动员。而当默克尔在2016年6月和9月访问中国时，她甚至还与习近平主席讨论了如何开展更多的足球合作。

努力已经得到了回报。当刘延东副总理2016年年底访问德国时，双方足球协会和联赛正式达成了深化合作的协议。默克尔会见了中国代表团，并与刘副总理进行了长达一个小时的会谈，在此期间，自然也绕不过足球话题。在国际形势严峻的背景下，在德国和欧盟近年来对中国投资贸易的强硬立场的情况下，两国不断探索双边关系的新领域，此举值得称赞。

中国希望打进世界杯，也希望有一天能举办世界杯，甚至赢得世界杯。虽然还有一段路要走，但这激发了中国寻求帮助的积极性。

中国的目标之一是在学校储备5万名足球教练，到2020年在全国范围内建立1.5万所足球学校。德国多年来通过投资、贸易和出口高科技技术,帮助中国实现经济腾飞。德国队四次夺得世界杯冠军,也是帮助中国实现足球梦的天然合作伙伴。德国很可能有机会培训中国学校的教练,甚至向中国的一些学校输送德国教练。

当然,中国领导人认为,足球的推广远远超出了世界杯的目标。中德之间的足球合作可以带来其他机会。中国拥有5亿球迷,他们中的许多人是德国队球迷。为球迷们提供乐趣和享受的长线商机正在等待中德两国去探索。

在硬件方面,中国计划在2020年前建设7万个足球场,并准备允许私人和外国投资者参与足球发展基金。德国人也可以通过帮助中国实现这些目标来寻得商机。目前,大多数中国人正在努力提高生活质量,愿意在休闲和运动上投入时间和精力;而且父母们也鼓励孩子们进行体育运动。所以中德两国甚至可以在如何通过推广体育运动改善生活质量方面交流想法。

在达成协议的同时,默克尔还开玩笑地表示,她担心德国正在培养德国在足球世界的竞争对手。但德国不应该担心。这个国家有很多优势。基本上,没有全球性的或欧盟的规定限制德国转移足球教练和管理人员到中国。然而,德国将不得不与其他国家竞争。在欧洲范围内,意大利、法国、英国、西班牙、葡萄牙,甚至波兰和捷克都可以与德国争夺跟中国足球合作的机会。而在非洲、南美和亚洲也有这样的竞争对手。各国在努力实现自己的足球目标的同时与中国合作,这样的竞争是很有价值的。

多年来,中年摄影家赵辉一直在山上、街头,甚至庙宇里抓拍中国百姓的笑脸。以"中国故事"为主题,赵辉在美国、欧盟总部等地展出了这些照片，帮助世界通过照片看中国。在过去的两三年里，赵辉和妻子李琛则在做另一件事情。就是希望用镜头留住阳光的外国面孔，然后在中国展出。

赵辉，江苏人，20 世纪 80 年代在美国学习摄影，现已定居北京。他把摄影目标定为意大利人和德国人。德国人经常是一副严肃的面孔，有些人在镜头面前相当害羞，而且很多人不愿意被陌生人拍照。对于长期用镜头展现老百姓快乐微笑的赵辉来说，这是一个挑战。他在布鲁塞尔接受采访时说："你必须拥有一个先进的长焦镜头，而且你只能从远处拍摄，才不会被注意到。"

赵辉和他的妻子李琛现在开车穿越德国，在街上、公路、森林、村庄甚至小岛上发现那些有灵感的瞬间。这是近几年来他们第五次访问德国。赵辉的工作得到了高度的肯定，德国总统弗兰克 - 沃尔特·施泰（Frank-Walter Steinmeier）办公室邀请他在习近平主席访问期间在总统府内拍照。这对夫妇有充分的理由为这种认可而自豪，这是他们通过不懈的努力获得的。每次到德国去拍照时，他们都会把可爱的女儿留在家里，在德国花上三四个星期的时间，驱车约五千公里。

赵辉开玩笑说，他们二万五千公里的德国里程已经等于红军长征的路程。赵辉说："我们已经收获了近 6 万张照片，这对我们来说是非常珍贵的财富。" 此外，赵辉说，这些照片是发现德国人性格的"窗口"，人们可通过这些照片深入地挖掘这个国家的文化和历史。

普通德国人，如邮差、店主和服务员常常成为赵辉的"模特"。当被问到中国人和德国人的笑容有什么不同时，他回答道：

"所有幸福的人都是一样的。" 在成千上万张照片中，赵辉说他喜欢一张德国邮递员的特写，邮递员腰间挂着一圈他邻居们的钥匙。赵辉说，邮递员告诉他这些不是邮箱的钥匙，而是小镇居民家的钥匙。赵辉说："这是一个小社区的信任，简单而深切的信任，这表现了德国人的古朴风貌。"

2017年3月，他受邀为拜仁慕尼黑足球队和多特蒙德足球队的比赛拍摄。"这是我第一次拍摄足球比赛，" 赵辉说，"当然，勇猛和狂奔的时刻应该是典型的德国故事的一部分。" 除了人物照片之外，赵辉说建筑和自然景观也是他选集的一部分。他喜欢他拍摄的汉堡易北爱乐音乐厅（Elbphilharmonie）的照片，汉堡易北爱乐音乐厅于2017年年初开幕，并为二十国集团领导人呈现了一场音乐会。"这是一座德国地标性建筑，有弧形窗户和波浪状的屋顶，顶部则是红砖底座的玻璃结构，" 赵辉说，"在我看来，这是德国现代和传统元素的结合，这是我非常喜欢它的原因。"

2017年是中德建交45周年。德国驻北京大使馆已经同意举办这对夫妇的德国故事摄影展。赵辉的妻子李琛一路陪伴着他，开车载他到每一个他相信他的照相机会拍出极美的照片的地方。李琛说："他全身心地投入，对照片质量有接近疯狂的执着，而且总是渴望完美一拍。"

7月7日和8日，工业化国家和新兴国家领导人聚集在德国的港口城市讨论世界面临的迫切挑战，这些领导人被邀请到汉堡的新地标性音乐厅享受音乐的美妙。汉堡国际海事博物馆主任彼得·塔姆（Peter Tamm）也提出一个历史性的邀请：他的博物馆展出着多达120件记载了十三世纪至十七世纪中国海上丝绸之路历史的藏品；他邀请领导人去参观。

塔姆在这个宁静的港口中心的博物馆里说："各位领导人应该来了解，在这一时期，不同的文化和文明是如何以一种让人赞叹的和平方式进行交流和沟通的。这些展品展现了中国在那个年代取得的令人难以置信的成就。"

6月至9月，这一展览由汉堡国际海事博物馆和广东省博物馆联合展出。这些展品将于2017年晚些时候到罗马展出。海上丝绸之路主题展览位于博物馆的二楼和三楼，展览布置得专业而精致。展览品包括沉船残骸、瓷器、植物、宗教和文化物品。海事博物馆是一座11层的建筑，2008年由他的父亲开馆，塔姆的父亲的终身爱好就是收集海洋模型和文物。塔姆的父亲于2016年12月去世，老人经常说海洋是人类的源泉，人民和国家间的交流与贸易离不开它，中国的海运和贸易史总是让他感到兴奋。

塔姆说："正如我父亲的座右铭说的，我们很激动能举办这个展览，我们很高兴越来越多的博物馆参观者对中国文化和丝绸之路的历史感兴趣。"深耕于船舶经纪、媒体和文化事业多年的塔姆说，这表明了中国文化让德国人和其他欧洲人印象深刻。他说，所有的展品都是珍品，特别是在中国南海沿岸被发现的南海1号和南澳1号沉船的特殊展品给他留下了非常深刻的印象。借助巨大的船只，通过贸易和文化交流的方式，中国和世界其他地区的距离近了。

塔姆说："它们是中国这一历史时期的象征，但在德国却鲜为人知。中世纪的时候，在这些航线上，奢侈品从中国运往中东，再从中东到欧洲。"他说，这次展览有助于诠释中国的

"一带一路"倡议，倡议的目的正是通过合作、贸易和投资实现共同繁荣、相互理解和更加密切的互联互通。塔姆说，每年平均约有 12.5 万名游客参观他的博物馆，但这场以"东西汇流——13 至 17 世纪的海上丝绸之路"为主题的展览却吸引了不少客流。

塔姆并没有提供具体数字，但在 6 月份他博物馆的参观者人数同比增长了 35％。中国文化部部长雒树刚说，展览通过反映文化和商品交流、历史文物和水下考古的多维内容，充分展示了这个时期不同文明在海洋上的共同进步。雒部长说："我相信这次展览将为中德之间加深了解作出贡献。"

中国方案提升比利时竞争力

2015 年，许多西欧国家都申请成为亚投行创始成员国，比利时前首相埃利奥·迪吕波（Elio Di Rupo）在接受我的专访时对涉及北京的两个关键决定表示既兴奋又遗憾。迪吕波说，他很高兴看到中国以这么快的速度把两只大熊猫送到了比利时。2013 年 9 月与李克强总理会晤后的 24 小时内，为期 15 年的大熊猫租借申请获得了批准，在不到一年的时间里，两只大熊猫已经抵达比利时。

2014 年 2 月，两只大熊猫来到了比利时天堂动物园（Pairi Daiza Zoo），比利时国王菲利普（Philippe）和习近平主席于一个月后共同出席了大熊猫园开园仪式。受访时，迪吕波说，"时光飞逝"，大熊猫已经在比利时生活一年了。他补充说，此次活动是两国密切的双边关系的准确写照。

现在，蒙斯市长迪吕波计划在 2015 年通过"欧洲文化之都"项目推广他的这座城市。据欧盟称，"欧洲文化之都"称号每年将颁给欧盟两个成员国的两座城市，以期支持欧洲文化合作。当谈到比利时政府不愿加入亚投行这一吸引了全球 50 多个国家申请的倡议时，迪吕波表示遗憾。迪吕波说他并没有关注银行方面的新的事务，但他对比利时没有申请表示震惊。他说，他会向国家政府和首相查尔斯·米歇尔（Charles Michel）询问，为什么比利时没有跟随其他西欧国家的脚步进行申请。

同一天，我还遇到了法国鲁昂诺欧商学院商务孔子学院院长张海晏老师，他认为，北京在设立亚投行方面所起到的主导作用导致西方一些国家的意见产生分歧，但他相信比利时不是因为与中国的密切关系而保持谨慎。

然而，看得出美国的态度比较谨慎，尽管美国财政部部长雅各布·卢（Jacob Lew）在 2015 年 3 月 31 日截止日期前的最后关头访问了北京，但并没有向亚投行提交申请。美国前国务卿马德琳·奥尔布赖特（Madeleine Albright）日前表示，华盛顿不寻求成员资格的决定是"失算的"。一些比利时人说，他们的国家申请加入亚投行在财务上是不可行的。有人说，比利时政府在协调所有三个地区政府方面很困难。如果说希腊因为在财政上过于紧张而无法申请成为创始成员是可以理解的，那么比利时并不处于相同的境况。在 2011 年欧洲主权债务危机期间比利时银行等欧洲银行被要求提高存款利率，比利时作出了迅速的反应。

我认为比利时不愿申请亚投行成员国是由于双方沟通不畅造成的。当然，比利时不像美国那样试图在许多方面遏制中国。

西方国家在决策过程中可能存在的效率低下，已经饱受专家们诟病。以应对金融危机为例。许多分析人士表示，欧盟各方长期以来的争论导致成员国错过了寻找解决方案和政策增援的机会和窗口，从而延长了危机的持续时间。

我一直在问欧洲人如何改革欧洲的政治制度，改善决策过程，避免政治不稳定，就像发生在希腊的情况那样。许多人耸耸肩，摇摇头。他们没有答案，只有一个简单的答复：这是欧洲。

值得庆幸的是，比利时已经转变了态度。比利时已在2017年3月成为亚投行成员，但并不是创始成员，比利时的很多人都把这视作国家竞争力提高的标志。比利时瓦隆大区外贸与外国投资局局长帕斯卡莱·戴尔科米内特（Pascale Delcomminette）在介绍自己国家的优势时提到，加入亚投行是比利时吸引外资的优势之一。

瓦隆大区的高级官员说，瓦隆大区是比利时三个区之一，人口不到四百万，瓦隆大区将在探索与"一带一路"倡议的契合点上发挥"有益的作用"。"我们是亚投行的成员之一。"她说。比利时具有欧洲门户的地理位置、成熟的市场、开放性等优点。当西欧所有国家效仿英国在2015年年初申请中国提议的亚洲基础设施投资银行的创始成员国资格时，比利时未能及时采取行动，因此比利时未能赶上时代的步伐，比利时最终只能在2017年成为这一新的多边金融工具的成员国。她认为比利时将和中国一道捍卫自由贸易和全球化，即使世界其他地区不再相信自由贸易和国际合作的时候。"中国和欧洲有着共同的目标。" 戴尔科米内特说。

戴尔科米内特表示，瓦隆大区在欧洲最发达的中心的"战略位置"将有助于将"一带一路"倡议的一部分变为现实。戴尔科米内特说，在过去的两年中，许多中国人乘坐包机通过位于瓦隆大区的列日机场来到欧洲旅行；列日机场与上海、广州和香港之间有频繁的货运航班。她还表示，瓦隆大区理想的地理位置使其能够提供与欧洲市场主要门户连接的便捷通道，其多种交通解决方案已经使瓦隆大区成为欧洲的物流中心。戴尔科米内特说："通过航空、火车、海路和水路从中国抵达的货物可以快速分拣并运送到所有欧洲主要城市。瓦隆大区为中国经营者提供了进入到这个发达的欧洲运输网络的大量机会。"

针对一些国家在吸引中国投资方面具有一定的保护性，她引用美国投资战略家基思·菲茨杰拉德（Keith Fitzgerald）在 2012 年接受采访时的话说："一个强大的中国即将到来，我们有两个选择。要么我们在桌旁，要么就在菜单上。"戴尔科米内特还说，比利时是 1958 年欧盟六个创始成员国之一，从一开始它就是欧元区的一部分。她说："最重要的是，我们没有对中国的恐惧。我们相信，欧盟将在促进与中国的双赢合作、捍卫所有成员国和合作伙伴的利益方面发挥主要作用。"

她表示，比利时不惧怕中国投资，"相反，我们欢迎中国投资"，戴尔科米内特说，她的国家有欢迎外国人的悠久传统，他们以比利时是世界上对外国投资最友好的国家之一为傲。她说，比利时考量一个双赢的外国投资关系的方式是确保投资者能够成功地开展业务，并从他们所需要的当地专业知识和激励措施中受益。她表示，中国在瓦隆大区的主要投资是位于新鲁汶的 CBTC（中国—比利时科技园）项目，现在有 22 人在中国投资方——联投欧洲科技投资有限公司（United Investment Europe）旗下为该项目工作。该项目涉及高科技、生物技术、数字化、电子化和绿色环保等领域，于 2016 年 6 月 20 日正式启动，预计将于 2017 年 6 月开始动工。她表示，该项目将于 2025 年完成，会创造共 1300 个就业岗位，合同显示其中 40% 会是中国专家，另外 60% 是当地雇员（780 人）。

戴尔科米内特说，对于中国人来说，创造 780 个当地就业机会并不是什么大不了的事，"但你必须记住，瓦隆大区的人口比中国的人口要少得多。瓦隆大区的 780 个岗位相当于中国的 30 万个岗位（因为人口规模的巨大差异）。这样你就会意识到这项投资有多重要。"

曲大使在 2014 年年底接任大使一职，他对人口只有北京一半的比利时的实力印象深刻。"这是一个小国，但它具有巨大的全球影响力。"曲大使说。中国驻比利时大使馆就坐落在布鲁塞尔郊区郁郁葱葱的林荫大道上，曲大使坐在大使馆装修一新的会客厅中，谈到比利时是欧盟总部、北约总部、许多智库和主要媒体的所在地。在他的身后是中国和比利时的国旗，很典型的使馆布置。

曲大使说："当我们谈论西方世界时，布鲁塞尔应该是位列华盛顿之后的第二个象征。"这指的是国家软实力使得比利时与其他欧洲国家不同。在介绍完背景之后，教授出身的曲星大使详细谈了比利时在研发、外贸、教育和物流等方面的优势。这样一串清单，即使是对一个大国来说，都十分令人印象深刻。

由于中国一直在经济结构调整和对外投资增长的过程中，曲大使一直忙于探索中国和比利时企业的合作机会，他尽可能多地安排了实地考察进他的日程。他穿着一身灰色西装，刚刚从距布鲁塞尔半小时的彩印和医疗保健解决方案的领导品牌爱克发（Agfa）总部回到大使馆。他说："我对其前沿的研究能力印象深刻。"

爱克发同美国柯达和日本富士一起在彩色印刷领域位列全球三甲。曲大使还参观了制药、民用核技术和微电子等领域的公司。每一处都让他觉得了不起。比利时不是一个大市场，"但是"，他强调，比利时是研发的大本营。

利用比利时作为欧盟中心门户的优势地理位置，比利时人倾向于发展国际贸易，重视开拓比利时研究竞争力的市场。另外，比利时拥有便利的交通枢纽，可以轻而易举地通过水、陆、空等方式与巴黎、卢森堡、阿姆斯特丹、法兰克福等欧洲其他城市连接。

曲大使指出，比利时拥有数所世界排名前 200 名的大学。所有这些因素都有助于提升它在贸易和投资方面的活力。曲大使在欧洲生活过很长时间。他 1986 年到 1992 年在巴黎居住，同时在巴黎政治学院获得政治学硕士学位和博士学位。2006 年至 2009年间，他任中国驻法国大使馆公使、副团长。

曲大使说，比利时位于法国、德国、英国和荷兰之间，是拉丁文和日耳曼文化的交汇点,"具有与生俱来的包容性、宽容性和开放性"。它也是最早的工业化国家之一。

他说他现在肩负着帮助深化比利时和中国多个领域双边关系的重大责任。曲星大使是著名教授,于 1995 年至 2006 年期间担任中国外交学院院长助理、副院长,2009 年至 2014 年任中国国际问题研究所所长。他善于组织数据,形成描述双边关系的新的论述。

他说现在中国和比利时的商务人士每 7 个小时经手的贸易量,相当于 45 年前两国建交时一整年的贸易量。事实上,在曲大使提到的诸多显示两国在过去几年所建立的紧密的伙伴关系的因素中,双边贸易可能是两国关系中最令人印象深刻的特征。2015 年两国双边贸易达到了 232 亿美元。"这是我们建交之初贸易量的 1150 倍",他自豪地说,并补充道,过去五年的年增长率为 16%。

他表示,两国的公司比以往任何时候都更具互动性,并且正在向对方的企业投资。例如,自中国吉利接管沃尔沃的根特工厂以来,沃尔沃的根特工厂一直在蓬勃发展。每分钟 5300 名当地雇员能够生产出一辆汽车,一年的生产率创下了 25 万辆汽车的历史新高。凭借如此高的业绩,该公司在全球汽车市场相对低迷的情况下表现良好。

自 1971 年 10 月两国建交以来,双方的伙伴关系取得了长足的进展。"我们关系密切的指标之一就是高级别交流的次数频繁。"曲大使说。

在 2016 年 3 月,在巴黎恐怖袭击后,布鲁塞尔也遭遇恐怖分子在机场和地铁站的爆炸袭击。曲大使说，这些事件曾对比利时的旅游业产生了"负面"的影响，一些旅行社和个人取消他们的出行计划。由于安全问题，游客人数一直在下降。"但是，"曲大使说，"比利时因其持久的优势仍然吸引了许多中国投资者。我们可以看到投资趋势仍然在上升，因为普遍来说投资者在制定战略决策时会有一个更长远的眼光。"他指出，在瞬息万变的环境下，恐怖袭击的危险性难以预测，每个国家都要承受这样的风险。"但是，"他说，"继续社会正常生活是打击恐怖主义的另一种方式。"他说："这不仅仅是比利时。从这个意义上说，恐怖袭击不会阻止投资者。"

连接意大利与中国：丝绸之路

意大利是古老的丝绸之路的欧洲的终点，是丝绸之路让中国和欧洲文明交汇。在寻求与中国提出的"一带一路"倡议——也就是许多欧洲人现在所说的新丝绸之路的协同作用之时，意大利人对凭此契机重振本国经济表现出了深厚的热情。意大利总统塞尔焦·马塔雷拉（Sergio Mattarella）就是其中之一，他早在2014年便承诺意大利将积极响应并参与由习近平主席提出的这一倡议。在2017年2月为期六天的访华期间，他说，鉴于意大利连接亚洲、非洲和欧洲的地缘政治优势，中意两国可以在实施互联互通为主题的这一倡议时"书写历史的新篇章"。

　　新总理保罗·真蒂洛尼（Paolo Gentiloni），在 2016 年 12 月接任马泰奥·伦齐（Matteo Renzi）任总理。真蒂洛尼于 2017 年 5 月 14 至 15 日同 30 名其他国家领导人一起出席了在北京举办的"一带一路"国际合作高峰论坛。真蒂洛尼对中国相当熟悉。早在 2014 年他在伦齐内阁担任外交部部长时就与中方外长有过亲切会谈。

　　2016 年 5 月，真蒂洛尼作为外长，与中国外长王毅达成共识，双方应推进三大战略联盟，即中国"一带一路"倡议和意大利发展战略的对接，"中国制造 2025"和意大利的"工业 4.0"的对接，以及中国"互联网 +"战略与意大利技术创新规划的对接。"意方热切期望可以被中方视为共同建设'一带一路'的重要合作伙伴，并希望更多的意大利企业将有机会参与'一带一路'倡议的相关合作。"援引自真蒂洛尼的一份官方声明。

　　2016 年 11 月，习近平主席在去往南美的途中经停意大利撒丁岛，当时的总理伦齐也在他们的会议上承诺意大利将积极参与"一带一路"倡议建设。"意大利领导人表现出了强烈的合作意愿。马塔雷拉主席也对'一带一路'倡议表现出了充分的信心，总理真蒂洛尼也在许多场合显示出了他对'一带一路'倡议的大力支持。"中国驻意大利大使李瑞宇说。

　　除了意大利领导人对倡议的高度认可，意大利商业机构也对探索这一双赢机会表现出浓厚的兴趣。李大使说："意方组织了很多主题性的宣传活动，将经贸合作推向了新的高度，我参加了许多这样的活动。"最近的一次是由中欧数字协会主席鲁乙己（Luigi Gambardella）组织的。中欧数字协会是一家以商业为导

向的国际组织，总部位于布鲁塞尔。李大使在 2017 年 5 月 3 日
在罗马举行的数字合作研讨会上讲话时说，中国和意大利在工业
和数字化转型过程中都有着巨大的机遇。

意大利人鲁乙己也表示中意两国可以通过提高"一带一路"
沿线数字和电信基础设施建设来探索 5G 时代的第三方合作。他
表示，他将在北京的"一带一路"国际合作高峰论坛上提出一个
数字"一带一路"倡议的构想。李大使说，中国和意大利之间
的贸易量已经超过了 430 亿美元，而截至 2016 年年底中国流向
意大利的投资存量已经超过了 120 亿美元。

"我们中国公司参与了意大利的一些重量级项目。"李大
使补充说。中国和意大利愿意延续他们的合作行动计划。两国
2014—2016 年的三年合作计划已经到期。

中国的电信业巨头中兴通讯是意大利的中国投资者之一，中
兴通讯在 2016 年年底竞标成功一个十亿美元的项目，以提升意
大利的电信基础设施。中兴通讯负责西欧业务的主管胡坤说，其
意大利分公司正忙于聘用当地专业人士加入公司。

"除该项目之外，我们也有可能将赢得意大利其他几个项目
的竞标。因此我们缺乏人手，而且还需要租用更多的办公室。"
胡坤在其位于罗马工业区的意大利办事处如是说。针对这个价值
数十亿美元的项目，中兴通讯将升级意大利的电信基础设施，为
5G 时代做好准备。他说："项目完成后，意大利将成为欧洲电信
基础设施的领跑者。"

而在实施这个项目方面，胡坤说，承包商们也将在未来两年
半的时间为意大利创造多达 2500 个新的工作岗位。他说，中兴

通讯也在扩大意大利智慧城市和研究设施方面的业务。

约翰·胡珀（John Hooper），总部位于伦敦的《经济学家》杂志的资深记者，一直密切关注着意大利如何能够从亚洲的活力中，尤其是中国的发展中获益。

他说，意大利是传统意义上的出口国，经济很容易受到外部因素的影响。而现在，该国需要经济结构改革来进一步释放潜力。"这个国家需要外部需求来发展经济，特别是来自中国的需求，"胡珀说。

他说，设计、奢侈品、旅游和时尚正在吸引中国发展壮大的中产阶级。"但意大利仍然是一个以家族企业和中小企业为主的国家，这使得意大利企业难以适应中国需求以及渗透中国市场，"胡珀说，"我建议让意大利中小企业依地区组成联盟，以参与中国市场，从而在中国这个大市场上占有一席之地。"

欧洲资深政治家普罗迪接受了我的两次独家采访。2017年4月，在罗马，他告诉我，中国的"一带一路"倡议将改变未来几十年世界上一半人的生活，全球领导人应统一决心，把握机会。他称这一倡议是将持续数十年，主要为改善亚洲、欧洲和非洲的互联互通的"百年工程"。

曾任两届意大利总理、一届欧盟委员会主席的普罗迪说，让他印象最深刻的是，这一倡议将改变欠发达国家，特别是亚洲的人们的生活和命运。普罗迪说，实施"一带一路"倡议的第一个也是最明显的成果将是，许多中亚国家将与中国合作发展并完善他们的基础设施。"这不是修建公路铁路，而是改变这些国家人民的日常生活。我期待这一点，因为这将是这些国家的新的一页。"他说。

现在,他很高兴看到,经过三年的宣传推广,欧洲国家一直在与"一带一路"倡议"争取获得协同增效"。普罗迪说:"但这也将是一个艰巨的任务,会长达数十年,最重要的是要获得沿线国家更多的政治意愿和支持。"

但他表示,他对进展颇有信心,因为这个倡议已经通过过去几年中国政府、企业和智库的宣传而被广泛接受。"经过三年的准备,北京'一带一路'国际合作高峰论坛将被视为是开启未来大规模合作的绿灯。"普罗迪这样说道。他一直忙于推广此倡议。

还在天津和北京任教的普罗迪一直往来于中国和意大利之间。普罗迪刚结束为期一周的讲座,从北京回到意大利,他说他在去中国出席论坛之前,见了新任意大利总理真蒂洛尼。普罗迪没有透露他们的谈话要点,只说真蒂洛尼是"一带一路"倡议的坚定支持者。

普罗迪说,"一带一路"倡议是通过陆路和海路来构想和实施的组合。"作为一个欧洲人和意大利人,我应该说,大部分的货物流动仍然经由海上,地中海地区的作用对于实施该倡议至关重要。"普罗迪说。

与意大利处于同一地区的西班牙和希腊的领导人也出席了2017年的北京论坛。普罗迪还表示,该倡议源于历史悠久的丝绸之路的概念,意大利则是丝绸之路的终点,而全球家喻户晓的威尼斯人马可·波罗远在700年前就把中国介绍给欧洲。"所以我建议下一次的峰会应该在威尼斯举行,这具有象征性的意义,意味着习近平主席的倡议在北京论坛之后把过去与未来联系起来。"普罗迪微笑着说。

在准备我的"一带一路"倡议和意大利采访之旅时,我十分渴望见到西罗·波罗·帕多莱基亚(Siro Polo Padolecchia)。他是马可·波罗(1254—1324)唯一在世的后裔,他撰写了《新马可·波罗游记》(*The Travels of Marco Polo*),这本书描述了几个世纪前欧洲人的财富和繁荣。由于他现居摩纳哥,我们没能见面;但是老人帕多莱基亚及时地发给了我长达5页纸的采访问题的回答,富有想法、让人感动并且生动的答案,弥补了我们无法见面的缺憾。

帕多莱基亚和他父辈并没有失去其祖先与中国建立起来的密切联系。他八岁那年去了中国,因为他父亲在那里做生意,他在中国度过了三年的童年时光。因此他在给我的信中写道:"没有什么比把我在中国长期生活时我的中国朋友慷慨地分享给我的知识与这次采访结合起来更合适的了。"

他说我的问题帮助他吸收和改善了童年时期他对中国的模糊概念。帕多莱基亚回忆说,他在抵达中国之前,他一直很好奇,想了解我们星球的另一部分,这个与他出生的地方相距甚远的国家,同时又担心他无法读懂中国,无法理解它的语言、它的文化、它的笑话和它的情绪。但是现在,他的记忆和马可·波罗的回忆一样令人伤感。

对他来说,中国的魅力是人民的善良,是开满可爱的白色木兰和各种鲜花的季节,是漂浮着睡莲、载着小舟缓缓向前的湖泊——那样的不受干扰和快乐。帕多莱基亚甚至告诉我,对他来说,中国已经毫无疑问地成为了一个重要的地方,是他走过的世界上其他 126 个国家中的任何一个都无法与之相提并论的。

多年来他一直致力于促进欧洲与中国之间的沟通，并创立了欧中国际商业咨询委员会，并在多年前扩大了马可·波罗协会（Marco Polo Society）的活动。他特别自豪的是，马可·波罗协会已经开办多年，成为了他的祖先马可·波罗的原则的延续，并且被视为联合国和欧盟主持下不同组织之间的桥梁。当被问及从他第一次到中国以来中国发生的变化时，他说，是人们的态度，无论是在大城市，还是小城市或乡村，你可以在他们的眼中读出一种满足感。

他认为了解中国的最好方法就是到中国去。就像中国有句谚语说的，"百闻不如一见。" 现在，他专注于习近平主席的"一带一路"倡议，他说，"一带一路" 有利于改善中欧互联互通，推动亚欧的发展和贸易，将巩固这个地区的各个国家的稳定和安全。

他认为，非洲和中亚地区的一些庞大的中国项目，有助于增强对中国在国内外开展类似基础设施项目的能力和信心。他引用意大利人和欧洲人的看法说，"一带一路" 倡议是试图实现建设和平与共同繁荣的大外交政策项目。

帕多莱基亚称习近平主席是这个连接亚洲和欧洲和平项目的建筑师，它涵盖了与马可·波罗 13 世纪的轨迹几乎相同的路线。他将该项目置于相当长的历史镜头下：如果说 20 世纪是由美国梦的概念主宰，那么在 21 世纪中国梦的概念将占主导地位，特别是就自由、机会和新中国的正面形象而言。

法国也瞄准合作

法 国资深政治家让－皮埃尔·拉法兰（Jean-Pierre Raffarin）表示，"一带一路"倡议是"向欧洲发出的看向东方的邀请"。他被法国总统马克龙任命为特别代表参加定于 2017 年 5 月 14—15 日在北京举行的"一带一路"国际合作高峰论坛。拉法兰说，马克龙在击败国民阵线玛丽娜·勒庞（Maric Le Pen）赢得法国总统大选后不久就作出了这一决定。拉法兰在出席 5 月论坛前接受我的书面采访时说："事实上，我受习近平主席邀请，将率领法国代表团参加'一带一路'国际合作高峰论坛。"

作为法国总统代表的拉法兰说，他会传达的信息是"一带一路"倡议将通过改善互联互通来维护欧亚大陆的战略和地缘政治的地位。他说："这是邀请欧洲人更多地看向东方。"

"尤其是，我不会低估推动经济增长与宣扬和平这样的信息。"至于法国大选后中法两国的双边关系，他说，马克龙总统将维护与中国深厚的友谊和战略合作伙伴关系。

拉法兰说："在我的国家，自戴高乐将军以来，抛开我们内部各方的政治分歧不说，我们一直对中法关系有着浓厚的兴趣。"他说，鉴于已经建立的共同的信任，双方要优先考虑和平与发展的全球平衡，这是建立在全球多极化和多边主义之上的共同愿景。

同时，他表示，双方应努力加强经济交流，促进文化合作关系。"我相信习近平主席和马克龙总统会同意把创新和研究作为我们合作的核心。"拉法兰说。

他补充说，两国与非洲的关系也可以列入优先议程。他证实，习近平主席和马克龙总统进行了非常积极和富有建设性的电话会谈。据新华社报道，习近平主席祝贺马克龙当选为法国总统，号召双方秉承友好关系，加强战略互信，切实尊重彼此核心利益和重大关切，扩大在各领域的务实合作。马克龙说，他将继续奉行法国对中国的积极、友好政策，坚持一个中国立场，深化两国在外交、贸易和工业领域以及"一带一路"建设框架下的务实合作。拉法兰说："据我所知，他们在电话中已经谈到了很多话题。"

并非只有拉法兰持此观点。早在 2015 年，在李克强总理出访法国和习近平主席年底出席巴黎气候变化大会前，法国就打算成为第一个支持中国提案的西欧国家，建立一个现代丝绸之路。这与华盛顿近期升级针对北京的遏制措施、对任何新想法都持冷漠态度形成了鲜明的对比。法国的支持信号来自 1984 年至 1986 年任总理、时任外交部长的洛朗·法比尤斯（Laurent Fabius）。2015 年 6 月 12 日，他在法国上诺曼底地区委员会组织的关于中国"一带一路"倡议的论坛上发表了精彩的演说。

作为外交部长，他说他刚刚结束了对中国的第十次访问，他访问中国的频率甚至高于访问美国的频率，这表明他的国家对中国的重视。中国驻法国大使翟隽回应说，他嫉妒这位法国人比他去北京的次数还要多。

法比尤斯在演讲中说，在历史和全球背景下，法国没有理由无视中国的崛起，中国一直在"写下世界历史的新篇章"。他说，"一带一路"倡议表明中国正在积极地承担全球责任。

因此，从战略角度来看，法国必须认可和参与新的丝绸之路提案，确保它成为一条"中法之路"，他说："习近平主席开启了中国改革开放的新篇章，法国不能失去支持中国倡议的机会。"他还承认，法国对于中国提供的发展机会没有作出足够的回应。

法比尤斯对"一带一路"倡议的重要性的解读赢得了掌声。中国学者、中国领导人顾问迟福林，赞扬法比尤斯是第一位对习近平主席的倡议进行"清楚、扎实、全面"阐释的外国外交官。

法比尤斯非常认真看待与中国企业的交往，他还用整个上午和午餐时间在论坛上听取了其他发言人的意见。这位外交部长是诺曼底人，诺曼底是一个旅游和商业资源丰富的地区，他表示，该地区将通过抓住中国投资和旅游业指数级增长的机会，从"一带一路"倡议中获益。法国的中国游客数量预计将在未来三年内从两百万增加到五百万，法比尤斯说，"一带一路"倡议的益处可能会超越旅游业。

倡议提出的路线要比两千年前商人们使用的古代丝绸之路要长得多，法比尤斯说，它们的作用远远不只是贸易。自从夏尔·戴高乐与中国领导人有胆识地跨出建立外交关系这一步之后，法国在过去50年发挥了建设性的作用。

07

芬兰和丹麦代表北欧国家
塑造新丝绸纽带

虽然我曾在欧洲出差多次，但在 2017 年 4 月初习近平主席访问芬兰前，我还不曾有机会在芬兰做采访。习近平主席对芬兰的国事访问安排在他出访美国之前。2008 年我到这个发达的国家进行十天媒体巡访，但遗憾的是一场毁灭性的地震发生在我结束芬兰之旅，落地北京后的短短几个小时后。当我在进行这个章节的写作的时候，一场没有那么强大、但仍具破坏性的地震发生在我的家乡四川省。多么让人痛心的巧合。

2017 年，最让我兴奋的是我与芬兰总统和总理分别进行了短暂但面对面的访谈。一次能够采访到一个国家的两位领导人，这是对我的报道和我的职业生涯的一次极大的认可，在我长期驻欧期间，这是一次不寻常的经历。

在与习近平主席会晤之前，芬兰总统绍利·尼尼斯托（Sauli Niinisto）在赫尔辛基总统府接见了我，他早有准备会晤中国国家主席并超越双边关系讨论自由贸易和巴黎气候变化协议。美国总统特朗普上台后不久，这位芬兰总统赞扬了习近平主席"稳定而深刻的"思想。"这是一次短暂的访问，但我们正在尽我们所能，让我们伟大的客人习近平主席及其夫人有宾至如归的感觉。"尼尼斯托用流利的英语告诉我。他充满自信、让人安心。

尼尼斯托说，他准备好了听取习近平主席关于世界动态的看法，并讨论如何将两国双边关系发展到一个新的阶段。回顾四年前，他访问中国期间，尼尼斯托说，他与习近平主席达成一致，将发展一个新型国家间战略伙伴关系。"具体而言，我们看到了什么呢？我们已经看到了很多商务往来以及政治交往方面的发展。"尼尼斯托提及他与习近平主席 2012 年当选中国国家领导人后的首次会晤时说。

尼尼斯托说，他在过去几年的多个场合，已经与习近平主席建立了深厚的个人关系。习近平主席及夫人甚至在尼尼斯托夫妻对中国进行访问、在海南出席博鳌亚洲论坛之际为尼尼斯托的妻子准备了一个生日蛋糕。

尼尼斯托说，双方一直在讨论他们的伙伴关系，并有一致的看法，那就是双方的伙伴关系可以走得更远。当芬兰在 2017 年庆祝独立一百年时，他说，芬兰非常荣幸地邀请习近平主席到芬兰访问，这也显示了对芬兰自 1917 年独立以来的尊重，这对芬兰来说是十分重要的。"因此我们深感感激。"尼尼斯托总统说。

他说，世界在全球范围内存在很多问题，因此领导人之间的关键的联系越来越重要。"现在，习近平主席将从这里继续前往美国。我想整个世界都在注视着这次访问将如何进行。"尼尼斯托说。

尼尼斯托说，在同意我的采访之前，他刚刚在俄罗斯举行的北极论坛上与俄罗斯总统见面，并补充说他欣赏习近平主席 2017 年在达沃斯举行的世界经济论坛上提出的观点，特别是习近平主席针对自由贸易的观点。"他的看法与欧盟和芬兰立场非常相似，都是坚定地支持自由贸易。"尼尼斯托说。他也听了习近平主席谈论维持巴黎气候协定的重要性，这是另一个相似的立场。"这些都是非常重要的问题——我们如何提高在这些领域里的认识是非常重要的。这也是为什么我们迫切希望看到接下来会发生什么的一个因素。"尼尼斯托说。

在中欧关系中，双方在重大问题上有着相同的看法，这也是进一步推进其他问题的良好基础。尼尼斯托说，他的北欧的朋友们对于习近平主席和他在赫尔辛基举行峰会都感到非常好奇。尼尼斯托说："当然，我们将讨论所有的北欧国家如何与中国建立更好的合作关系。"

尼尼斯托总统还表示，双方应该确保商业领域有足够多的合作空间，创新是其内容之一，他还指出清洁技术领域的创新十分重要，因为这在中国城市化繁荣发展的今天是非常必要的。另一方面，他说，中国企业一直有兴趣投资芬兰，现在就有一些企业计划投资可再生能源。

尼尼斯托曾任芬兰足球协会主席，他说足球是他和习近平主席之间的"共同语言"，虽然芬兰不是一个强大的足球国家。"但是，我们在冬季运动方面非常具有竞争力，我认为双方可以加深在这个领域的合作。"尼尼斯托说。

"总而言之，我将邀请习近平主席讨论如何发展我们两国之间的关系。我非常有兴趣听取他对'一带一路'倡议的看法。"尼尼斯托说。

在习近平主席到访之前，我专访了芬兰总理尤哈·西比莱（Juha Sipila），他坚持在采访对话期间不能有他的任何工作人员在身边。只有到了拍照环节他的工作人员才能进来。

和他的总统一样，西比莱承诺，芬兰将和中国一道，倡导自由贸易和全球化，即使在这一理念受到在世界上某些地方的攻击。"自由贸易是非常重要的。"西比莱在习近平主席访问前夕，在他位于赫尔辛基市中心的办公室里谈到。他说，他一直在为这次访问做准备，并期待这次访问中双方能就"很多问题"进行讨论。

在孤立主义和保护主义日益滋长的威胁之下，他回顾说，在最近的一次欧洲理事会会议上，欧洲领导人特别讨论了在瑞士达沃斯世界经济论坛年会上习近平主席的讲话。

西比莱说，尼尼斯托总统将把重点放在与西方的政治和外交事务上，而西比莱本人将重点放在经济问题上。回到习近平主席在达沃斯的讲话，西比莱说，这是令人鼓舞的，因为在美国讨论加强贸易壁垒来保护美国工业的时候中国支持自由贸易。

"对于欧洲和芬兰来说，中美关系保持良好关系、继续自由贸易非常重要，因为这也影响到我们。中美贸易战的前景令人担忧。但是我认为最终常识会占上风。也许会有一些协议的重新谈判。我不知道。但我认为继续自由贸易符合我们的共同利益。"

中国在芬兰的投资正在增加。根据西比莱总理的说法，现在中国企业在芬兰北部的两个项目中各投资了大约一百万欧元，并计划投资两个生物工厂。西比莱说，中国和芬兰将在习近平主席访问之际签署投资协议，但细节尚未最终确定。

旅游业也在不断增长。近年来，来自中国的游客人数翻了一番，因为许多中国人梦想去圣诞老人的故乡。西比莱说，芬兰在大学和创业企业的创新方面有着很好的纪录，可以补充中国的制造能力，尽管他注意到中国在创新方面也有了重大的改进。其他领域的合作可能包括生物燃料、清洁技术、绿色能源、信息通信技术、金属和林业，他补充道。有些欧洲人对中国投资持怀疑态度，但芬兰和欧盟对中国投资不设任何阻碍。"我是自由贸易的朋友，没有任何限制。所以芬兰是自由贸易和投资流动的支持者。"西比莱说。

2017 年的三个月内，习近平主席两次飞赴欧洲。习近平主席 1 月份出席世界经济论坛年会并对瑞士进行国事访问后，在与美国总统特朗普会谈前，于 4 月 4 日抵达芬兰。

当然，这两次欧洲之行包含了大量信息，当今世界充斥着保护主义、民粹主义甚至某些国家对和平构成威胁，中国将如何预期这个世界的发展，中国将发挥什么样的作用。以瑞士和芬兰为平台，传达这样的立场和承诺，体现了中国的信念：包括欧美在内的所有国家，都应该为建设一个繁荣和平的世界履行应有的责任，而不仅仅是观察中国将采取什么行动。

2016 年，中国宣布三步走路线图实现复兴目标。首先，中国的目标是到 2020 年成为一个创新型国家，这意味着其对研发的投入将超过总经济产出的 2.5%，而知识密集型服务业至少应该贡献 20% 的经济产出。

其次，到 2030 年，2.5% 的比例应上升到 2.8%，中国的企业应该转向全球供应链的中上游。中国将成为全球创新的领导者之一。最后，到 2050 年，中国的目标是成为世界科技强国，经济以创新和科技突破为驱动。届时中国将把一些大学和研究机构建设成为世界一流行列的大学和科研机构，科研人才将成为国家战略资源的骨干力量。

这些创新目标将与中国的经济结构调整、脱贫、应对老龄化挑战、改善民生等努力齐头并进。尽管中国近年来在创新能力方面取得了较快的进步，但是中国深切地知道差距仍然很大。根据世界知识产权组织（World Intellectual Property Organization）的年度报告，中国2016年排名第25位，从2012年习近平成为中国领导人时的34位上升了9位。

瑞士在全球创新排名中位居第一，芬兰居世界前五，中国选择了完美的合作伙伴一同努力。瑞士和芬兰在全球创新排名中成绩突出，究其原因，是因为瑞士人和芬兰人是谦虚的、包容的，愿意分享，愿意为知识和技术转移贡献力量，平等竞争，共同成长。这样的开放给两国带来了巨大的好处，两国人口都不到一千万，但是却融入了14亿人口的大市场。

另外，这种合作是互补的，因为这些国家在全球价值链上的位置各不相同。即使在中国提升其地位和竞争力的过程中，开放和全球化仍将有助于双方研究机构和企业的互利互惠。中国的创新政策已经渗透到国家计划的各个方面。例如，中国贫困的贵州省，把瑞士作为实现脱贫目标的标杆，尽管它们的发展水平相去甚远，但贵州省和瑞士有相似的内陆山区地形。贵州省将创新与脱贫结合起来。这样的比较与合作将有助于贵州省了解它的潜力。现在贵州正在为环境保护、基础设施建设、旅游和教育等方面注入资源，努力将贵州改造成中国的瑞士。

在中国和瑞士建立了国家层面的创新伙伴关系的同时，贵州省也已经采取行动来实现他们的目标。同样，中国在实现梦想的路上也有很多东西要从芬兰身上学习。

今年24岁的芬兰小姐雪莉·卡尔维宁（Shirly Karvinen）正在做一些特别的事情。她的父亲是一个典型的芬兰人——谦逊、羞涩，而她的中国母亲则开放和随和。但是她的父母有一个共同的特点：勤劳。

卡尔维宁说，她很幸运，继承了她父母双方的性格。她 14 岁的时候就开始通过电话销售芬兰杂志的方式挣钱。"我 14 岁的时候一个月的收入就有 400 欧元。"卡尔维宁说。卡尔维宁在 2016 年 5 月获得芬兰小姐桂冠。"我认为在我的班级里没有其他人可以这样做。"

所以她说独立是她从父母那里遗传来的另一个优势。

"从我父母那里继承来的基因优势使我比普通芬兰人肤色更深一点，这让我在 2016 年的芬兰小姐大赛中脱颖而出。"身高 170 厘米的卡尔维宁说。典型的芬兰人皮肤较白，在过去几十年里，仅有三位混血小姐荣获年度桂冠。拥有一半中国血统，一半芬兰血统的卡尔维宁说，她因习近平主席在访美前到芬兰进行访问而感到"自豪和荣幸"。

"我很高兴我有一半中国血统，一半芬兰血统，我为有两个祖国感到骄傲，"卡尔维宁说，"我非常期待习近平主席的这次访问，我相信此次访问必将促进双方的理解。"卡尔维宁说，她热衷于推动中国与芬兰之间的交流，这将在极大程度上让双方受益。"我觉得我有两个祖国，特别是现在我长大了。我真心觉得我妈妈来自中国是一件特别的事情。我为我的中国根感到骄傲。"

已经从赫尔辛基大学毕业的卡尔维宁说，她的母亲来自湖北，在非洲与她的父亲相识，她 7 岁的时候全家人搬回到芬兰为她小学入学做准备。回顾在非洲的童年经历，她的父母在不同的国家工作，她说，她会想办法接受一切，她当时太小，还意识不到她要去哪儿。

"我认为这是一件非常好的事情，因为这给了我一个非常国际化的背景。在新的环境中，我非常善于应对新情况。所以我认为，我很小的时候实际上学会了很多。"她高兴地说。当她还是一个小女孩的时候，她的芬兰祖父发现了她的潜力，总是说，当雪莉长大了，她会成为芬兰小姐赛事的获胜者。

"这一切的开始就源自一个儿时的梦想，但后来我长大了，尤其是当我来到赫尔辛基的时候，我意识到，这是我真正想要做的事情，"卡尔维宁说，"我想变得与众不同，我想要向所有人展示，有各种各样的芬兰人，有不同的长相，而且这一直是我的梦想。我决定要去追求我的梦想。"

一边追逐梦想，完成学业，卡尔维宁一边继续她从 14 岁开始的兼职工作。"我不知道我已经作了多少兼职工作，这些兼职工作教会我用自己的两只脚站立，"她说，"所以我认为这对我有很大的好处。我生活在国外，从 14 岁开始工作，所以我很成熟。我知道芬兰小姐不仅仅是一个头衔，更是一种责任和荣誉，更重要的是这是一项工作。"

自 2016 年 5 月以来，卡尔维宁一直担任芬兰小姐，在各种场合推广她的国家。这项工作已于 2017 年 9 月完成，因为 2017年的比赛一直推迟到那个时候。在她所有的活动中，卡尔维宁说她最感兴趣的是主持电视和电台节目。"在芬兰小姐之后，我真的很希望有自己的电视节目，或者在电台工作，或者在国外的某个地方工作。如果有机会做国际化的工作就太好了。"

她说她涉猎了很多电视和广播方面的话题。有一个话题非常贴近她的内心：学校霸凌。"除了有趣的东西，我也一直在非常强烈地反对霸凌。"卡尔维宁说。她回忆小时候，她住在芬兰中部小城镇，因为她看起来和别人不一样，所以有时她会被欺负。

卡尔维宁放低了声音说："所以，现在作为芬兰小姐我一直在强烈地反对霸凌，谈我自己的经验，并试图帮助那些有相同处境的人。"

2016年11月上任的芬兰奥林匹克委员会主席迪莫·力塔卡里奥（Timo Ritakallio）说，芬兰应探索更多的与中国在冬季运动方面合作的可能。中国申办了2022年冬奥会并决心发展冬季运动项目。

"2022年冬季奥运会在中国举办不仅将为中国体育带来新的发展，也会为国际体育大家庭带来新的发展。"力塔卡里奥补充说。习近平主席的访问将使两国在冬季运动领域进行更加密切和深入的合作。

芬兰总统尼尼斯托对国家和国际体育都十分了解，力塔卡里奥说。他认为，尼尼斯托总统和习近平主席还将谈及体育合作，因为习近平主席也是一个足球迷。其中一个例子就是在习近平主席和德国总理默克尔两位热情的足球粉丝的支持下，2016年中德建立了足球合作伙伴关系。"我知道中国越来越重视发展冬季体育运动。中芬两国长期以来有着良好的关系，因此这是芬兰政府应该抓住的一个机会。"力塔卡里奥说。

他说，芬兰是一个在冬季运动方面非常强大的国家，特别是越野滑雪、单板滑雪和冰球。"在这方面我们有世界顶级的教练，我想中国正需要发展这些运动和队伍。与可以为中国提供帮助的世界滑雪运动组织和体育机构保持联系将是一件好事。"
他说。

除了输出教练员和经验，力塔卡里奥说，芬兰在以环保的方
式制作人造雪和人造冰方面也很有优势。"由于气候变化和全球
变暖，即使在芬兰，我们也必须在一些场合依靠人工干预的措
施，来提供足够的雪和冰，以满足这些运动的最低标准。"力塔
卡里奥说。

他说，芬兰清洁技术公司也已为转让专业技术给中国做好了
准备，并补充说芬兰公司 Snow Secure 已经开始了与 2022 年冬
奥会中国奥组委的合作。力塔卡里奥说，冰球运动在芬兰很受欢
迎，小城市冰球馆采用人工冰建造。芬兰还建有小型雪房为滑雪
运动提供人造雪。

"除了奥运会，我们也可以在推广体育运动项目（在非专
业人群中）方面进行合作，正好中国也已经计划要推动非专业
人群参与体育运动。"力塔卡里奥补充说，芬兰商业和体育部门
热衷于发展与中国的合作。由于这是一个志愿的职位，芬兰奥
林匹克委员会主席力塔卡里奥的任期将于 2020 年东京奥运会后
结束。

"这是一个自愿性的工作，我的正职在投资领域。"力塔
卡里奥说。他是赫尔辛基 Ilmarinen 互助养老保险公司的总裁
兼首席执行官。他说，他的公司在中国股票和其他金融产品方
面迄今投资了大约十亿欧元。他说："我经常访问中国，因为
就像大家的普遍反应一样，我觉得中国是未来。中国有最好的
机会。"

丹麦：一个与中国的关系源远流长的国家

丹麦首相拉尔斯·勒克·拉斯穆森（Lars Lokke Rasmussen）喜欢熊猫。在 2017 年 5 月初与中国领导人会晤之前，他专程到四川成都看望了两只大熊猫。像其他欧洲国家一样，这对大熊猫将以租借的形式运往丹麦。

除了对熊猫的喜爱，这个北欧国家还为支持习近平主席提出的"一带一路"倡议作了很好的准备，称"一带一路"倡议是亚洲和欧洲的经济增长和繁荣的"未来发电机"。拉斯穆森在 2017 年 5 月 2 日至 5 日的中国之行前，接受了我的书面采访，许诺丹麦将积极参与"一带一路"倡议，他将会利用此次访问来进一步促进芬兰与中国的关系。"'一带一路'倡议的确是非常有意思的外交政策战略，"拉斯穆森说，"通过贸易和双边合作，进一步把欧洲和亚洲紧紧连接起来，将有希望成为两大洲增长和繁荣的未来发电机。"

习近平主席、李克强总理和时任全国人大常务委员会委员长张德江，与拉斯穆森在访华期间见面或举行会谈，就双边关系和共同关心的问题交换意见。拉斯穆森的这次访问是近期北欧各国与中国之间的高层交往之一。习近平主席在 2017 年 4 月初访问芬兰后不久，挪威首相埃尔娜·索尔贝格（Erna Solberg）对中国进行了访问，以加强双边关系。

拉斯穆森曾于 2009 年至 2011 年担任丹麦首相。他目前的任期是从 2015 年 6 月开始的。拉斯穆森说，"一带一路"倡议有希望为中亚和南亚——东亚与欧洲之间的门户——提供稳定经济和发展。"这对两大经济体之间的贸易是至关重要的。"他补充说。他的国家作为世界上最重要的海运国家之一，在上百年的时间里一直起到两大洲的联结作用。

这次访问安排在 2017 年 5 月 14 日至 15 日在北京举行的备受瞩目的"一带一路"国际合作高峰论坛的前几天。拉斯穆森说，他的国家的代表将出席会议，并将在会议期间"很高兴地"在政治和商业层面作出"积极贡献"。

他说，中国是丹麦在亚洲最大的贸易伙伴，丹麦是第一个与中国签署了全面战略合作伙伴关系的北欧国家。"我们现在将把双边关系提高到一个新的高度，"他说，"我特别高兴的是，我们将在我的访问期间启动我们的第一个'联合工作计划'。"

拉斯穆森透露，该计划包含了 58 个具体的联合合作领域，涵盖了 2020 年前中国与丹麦 80 个国家机构之间的合作方针，他还表示这需要双方机构向深入合作方向迈进。在拉斯穆森访问期间，中丹双方签署了加强经贸合作的新协议。他说，双方将启动一个中丹食品药品监管合作中心，以促进两国公共部门之间的知识共享。在文化和人文交流方面，拉斯穆森表示，两国将签署双边电影协议，允许中国和丹麦合拍电影。

拉斯穆森还说，丹麦和中国在国际问题上有着密切的合作。"我们都是贸易国和自由贸易、加强全球合作的有力支持者。"拉斯穆森说。从联合国到亚投行，从"一带一路"倡议到气候大会，拉斯穆森说两国在全球舞台上有更多的加深合作的潜力。

拉斯穆森说，他曾在多个场合与习近平主席会面，包括2016年核安全峰会。"我们在所有的会议上都进行了非常亲切和富有成果的讨论。"他补充说，习近平主席在达沃斯世界经济论坛上作了非常精彩的发言，丹麦支持任何为坚持贸易自由化和"更好的全球化"的道路所作出的努力。

拉斯穆森说，目前中国是世界第二大经济体，也必将在未来十年内成为最大的经济体。"中国所做的任何事情不仅在亚洲而且也会在世界其他地区产生影响，"拉斯穆森说，"我们希望在这一行程中加入中国。"

除了政治方面，丹麦公司也希望依托自身长期在环境领域的领先地位，在中国占有成熟技术的稳定市场。丹麦企业正在为中国的"绿色"机遇做好准备，希望尖端的技术帮助他们抢占市场份额，正当亚洲巨人加速向低碳发展的转型时期。一些公司甚至已经推出了自己的2020年战略，以寻求与中国的第十三个国家经济和社会发展五年规划（2016—2020）的契合点。

有的公司正在研究零排放技术，有望在2020年以后应用于中国的车辆。有的公司已经在着眼联合开拓丹麦和中国以外的第三方市场。全球领先的供暖和制冷品牌丹佛斯（Danfoss）深耕于中国，是丹麦首先专门针对中国大型政策趋势制定发展战略的公司之一。一个主要的趋势是经济新常态，反映出中国在保持均衡和可持续的发展的同时，经济增速从高速的两位数增长放缓到每年接近7%的增速。丹佛斯制冷事业部总裁费允德表示："我们必须接受中国经济从高速增长到放缓的转变，而我认为7%的增速仍然很可观。"

费允德说，随着时间的推移，丹佛斯公司已经建立了稳固的业务，包括一个长线的业务链。他说："在中国发生变化的情况下，如果我们的战略是正确的，所有这些优势将帮助我们在中国顺利地拓展业务。"他的公司最近推出了2020年中国市场战略，表明对这家已有数十年历史的清洁技术公司来说，中国仍然是"超级有意思"的市场。费允德说，与印度相比，中国在支持低碳发展方面做得更好，积极性更高。他说："我相信这将给中国和欧洲的公司带来更多的机会。"

在长期展望的鼓励下，丹佛斯供热事业部总裁拉斯·特维恩（Lars Tveen）说，在中国东北的一个回收过剩热能的试点项目应该在更多的中国城市应用。在丹佛斯和丹麦能源咨询集团 COWI 的帮助下，辽宁省鞍山市利用当地炼钢厂过剩的热能为380万居民供暖。多年来，他们在冬季燃煤供暖，成为了空气污染的主要来源。

特维恩说："鞍山项目就像一块投入水中的石头，现在我们已经看到了涟漪。"他补充说，中国更多的城市正在要求企业引进这样的设施，根据特维恩的说法，这有很多好处。首先，可以卖出过剩热能。其次，煤炭的燃烧减少，减少的碳排放量可以在中国承诺于2017年成立的国家碳排放交易市场上出售。

再次，特维恩说，鞍山市城市空气更加清洁，试点项目覆盖了一半的城市人口，二氧化碳排放量减少28.9万公吨。特维恩说："所以在中国，我们不是在说空话，我们正在提供一个方案。"

随着中国制定了更加严格的减少车辆污染物排放的措施，丹麦公司已经为新的机遇做好了准备，尽管这个拥有约 560 万人口的国家没有一条汽车生产线。位于索堡尔格的 Amminex 排放技术公司就是其中之一。这个迅速发展的丹麦清洁技术公司，在柴油机减排业务领域提供了一个氨储存和交付系统，减少了柴油尾气中一些毒素的排放。

首席执行官安妮卡·伊萨克森（Annika Isaksson）表示，该公司的产品非常适合中国市场，雾霾已经成为许多城市的公众关注的焦点。她说："我们正在与我们的中国合作伙伴接洽，我们的目标是在 2016 年年底将我们的产品推向中国市场。"

Dinex 是丹麦一家为排放提供先进测试的公司，公司首席执行官陶本·迪纳森（Torben Dinesen），曾用四年时间与中国领先的汽车制造商东风汽车公司的卡车生产部门建立了商业合作关系。使用 Dinex 设备的东风卡车发动机已经进行了测试。迪纳森说："我们期待着能尽快与东风签署合作协议。"

Dinex 一直密切关注中国排放法规的发展。中国有望在 2017 年实施基于欧 5 标准的国家排放标准，迪纳森表示，到 2023 年欧 6 标准可能会在全国范围内实施。迪纳森说："中国排放法规的更新将推动我们为客户带来新的排放控制解决方案，我们需要对这个巨大的绿色市场充满信心和耐心。"

Dinex 希望东风可以成为其主要客户（东风生产的卡车占中国卡车产量的近 20%）。迪纳森说，他的公司预计在未来 10 年与两到三个客户签约。"这一路上，我们需要为未来在中国的扩展提高我们的研发能力。"他说。

丹麦环境与食品部部长伊娃·赫尔·汉森（Eva Kjer Hansen）说她刚从联合国大会上回来。联合国大会在 2015 年 9 月 25 日采纳了丹麦 2015 年后的可持续发展目标。这些目标是未来 15 年内各成员国同意的与国际发展相关的一系列目标。

"这些目标是宏大的，但对提出解决方案、实现这些目标是非常重要的。"汉森说。她认为这些目标比 2015 年到期的千年发展目标更加宏大。"但最大的麻烦是找到融资，我们的目标是找到更多的企业和资金一起完成联合国的目标。"目标之一是确保到 2030 年可以在世界范围内获得清洁水资源，她说丹麦可以在这方面起到作用。汉森说，她非常骄傲丹麦的一家小公司与 NASA 签订了有关太空水循环系统的合同。

汉森说，一些国家通过辩论碳减排的必要性来躲避在环境保护方面的责任，这是很危险的做法。"我们丹麦人认真对待环境保护，我们希望仍然可以在前面领路。"她说。随着中国通过改善环境质量和提高能源效率来加快经济结构的调整，中国将能够很好地与丹麦企业加强合作，汉森说。她指出，丹麦于 1978 年停止使用含铅汽油，而欧盟直到 2000 年才逐步淘汰了含铅汽油。对环境和可持续发展的重视"激发了丹麦环境科技的发展，避免了空气污染，提高了节能技术的效率，"她说，"中国知道我们在食品安全领域非常突出，这也是我即将进行的中国之行的议事日程优先项。"

非凡的丹麦女王和欧洲王室传统

在书写中丹关系时，王室不可不提。丹麦王国的网站上的语言有丹麦语、英语、法语，令人吃惊的是还有中文。除此之外，女王玛格丽特二世（Queen Margrethe II）和她的丈夫曾于1979年9月访问中国，是中国改革开放后首位访华的西方国家元首。她对中国的文化和历史、古代建筑以及出土文物都表现出浓厚的兴趣。

在她2014年4月24日至28日第二次访华期间，她和丈夫走访了中国的五座城市，北京、南京、苏州、嘉兴和上海。她透露说，她和丈夫都喜欢中国的文化和历史，都喜欢吃中国菜。

他们的两个儿子，王储弗雷德里克（Frederik）和王子约阿希姆（Joachim），也经常访问中国。据新华社报道，他们告诉自己的父母很多有趣的故事。报道还说，相比之下，玛格丽特的丈夫亨里克亲王（Prince Henrik）更熟悉中国，被称为"中国先生"。他几乎每隔一年就会访问一次中国。

事实上，欧洲王室有着与中国建立联系的传统。荷兰国王威廉－亚历山大（Willem-Alexander）的女儿阿玛利亚公主（Amalia），13岁成为王位第一顺位继承人，自2016年9月起开始学习中文。有些人甚至把它称为王室"最聪明的投资"，鉴于中国与荷兰之间不断深化的关系。

荷兰王室并不是唯一接纳中文的人。荷兰邻国比利时的伊丽莎白公主（Princess Elisabeth）、国王菲利浦（King Philippe）的长女，出生于2001年，她正在布鲁塞尔荷语中学学习，她也在研习中文。当菲利普国王在2013年即位时，公主成为布拉班特公爵夫人，这是为她的王位继承权保留的头衔，这意味着她有可能成为欧洲国家中一位会讲中文的女王。

事实上，欧洲的老一代王室一直对中国文化抱有兴趣。虽然91岁高龄的英国女王伊丽莎白二世（Queen Elizabeth II）不讲中文，但她对中国哲学，特别是道家学说有极大的兴趣。2016年威尔士三一圣大卫大学（University of Wales Trinity Saint David），在英国王室部分资助下，成立了汉学院，旨在鼓励博士研究生研究中国古代宗教、文字、语言和历史。自习近平主席成为中国国家领导人后，除了丹麦女王玛格丽特二世，荷兰国王威廉-亚历山大和比利时国王菲利普都已经访问了中国。相应地，习近平主席也访问了荷兰、比利时和英国。

学习汉语在欧洲越来越受欢迎。当我在希腊国家主权债务危机期间采访希腊国会议员期间，其中一位国会议员甚至安排了他正在学习中文的16岁女儿也加入了我们的谈话。

当然，欧洲机构向年轻的官员提供越来越多的中文课。2016年7月21日，当我在参观比利时国庆阅兵仪式时，一位退休的比利时人拦住我，对我说，他年轻的时候曾留学中国台湾数年，在中国大陆生活了十多年。我对他流利的中文感到惊讶。所有这些都是中国人在世界各地越来越受欢迎的证明，这部分归功于中国文明的吸引力和中国不断强大的经济影响力。近年来，中国启动了多个项目，以期更好地与世界其他地区建立联系。其中一个重要的项目是旨在通过基础设施建设提高亚欧大陆互联互通，增加贸易量，增进人民交流的"一带一路"倡议。另一个很重要的项目是建立亚投行，向各国提供资金，以改善亚欧非之间互联互通。

因此，中国需要根据这一趋势来进行创新，传播语言和文化，以满足在欧洲和其他大陆日益增长的需求。虽然中国已经帮助世界上许多国家的大学建立了孔子学院，中文和中国文化课程已成为许多国家的小学和中学课程的一部分，但是我们需要为传播中国文化的真正价值作出更多的努力。

08

第八章

丝路思想者和领跑者的警钟

最后一章专门献给一批意见领袖、思想家，以及来自中国和欧洲的年轻的先锋，他们用自己的思想和行动投身到"一带一路"倡议中来。我在观察了各国在"一带一路"倡议上与中国进行的合作之后，以此为切入点，以更广阔的视角来进行这一章的写作。

欧盟应该进一步探索与中国合作的路径

著名经济学家，比利时前首相马克·埃斯肯思（Mark Eyskens）就是这批领袖和思想家之一。虽然经过我与他的团队一段时间的沟通以后他早已同意接受我的采访，但我们发人深省的对话实际上在原定访谈时间的 6 个月以后，即 2017 年 5 月方才进行。整个访谈轻松流畅，埃斯肯思让我的三位实习生以提问的方式来挑战他。他呼吁年轻人要充满好奇，并保持这种精神，如果他们看到美丽的事物，他们应该凝视这些美丽的事物。随着习近平主席的"一带一路"倡议得到全球认可，他坚信，欧盟应该进一步探究"方式和方法"来寻求与中国一同投资世界各国的大型基础设施项目的协同效应。

"铁路、港口、港口公路、机场等基础设施的建设有着巨大的需求缺口。这些很费钱，解决所需的贷款并不容易。"埃斯肯思在他位于布鲁塞尔的办公室说。他的办公室距离欧盟总部不远。作为学者和欧洲的政治领袖，埃斯肯思已经出版了 58 本书。

他说，地球人口预计将在 21 世纪末达到 100 亿，当今主要的经济问题，也是关于这个世界未来的问题，就是投资。

埃斯肯思说，"一带一路"倡议是帮助解决这些全球性需求的宝贵策略。

在投资方面，他说，欧洲今天的问题是缺少投资，因为欧盟有很多其他优先项要处理，并且它已经在养老和医疗保健上支出了很多资金。虽然欧盟已经作出了一些努力，通过欧洲投资计划（2015—2017）专项资金来增加投资，但是，这个目标不够有力，资金也没有很好地被利用。事实上，欧洲审计院出具的报告批评了欧盟委员会的做法。（欧盟）似乎并没有一个真正创造创新和就业的大战略——这是欧洲投资计划收效甚微的原因。"真正能够推动创新和增长的大型基础设施项目不在欧洲地区，很多都是在亚洲。"埃斯肯思说。他相信"一带一路"倡议对欧盟是非常重要的，欧盟需要找到合适的方式方法把欧洲投资重新引导到世界大型项目上。

参与机场、海港、航道、运河等项目建设是非常重要的。埃斯肯思说，欧洲人对中国在做什么非常感兴趣，也对中国的投资融资方式非常感兴趣。在这方面，埃斯肯思说，中国为建立亚投行所做的工作"非常重要"。"随着一些欧洲国家成为亚投行的股东，亚投行可能成为所有国家的融资工具，"埃斯肯思说，"投资必须是双行道，兼顾所有投资人的长远利益，将公平贸易、法律保障、国内价值和企业的社会责任都纳入进来。"如果能够持续，他说，欧洲投资银行可能有兴趣成为合作伙伴。2017 年5 月 14 日和 15 日在北京举行的"一带一路"国际合作高峰论坛期间，欧洲投资银行与中国政府签署了合作协议。"我们努力说服欧洲投资银行到欧洲以外去，到亚洲这个实现了世界大部分经济增长，创造了创新和就业的地方。2013 年欧洲理事会决定考虑扶持欧洲的产业——像中国和日本政府那样——通过有竞争性的长期贷款获得主要基础设施建设的合同。这可能会发生在不久的将来，使亚投行和欧洲真正地形成互补。"埃斯肯思说。除了基础设施项目之外，他还建议双方在大数据、数字设备与现代通信、信息通信技术和科学研究等领域进行合作。"此外，非常重要的就是在脑力上投资，这当然需要学者、教授和学生在教育和研究方面的交流。"埃斯肯思说。

曾于 1971 年至 1976 年担任鲁汶大学校长的埃斯肯思说，鲁汶大学共培养了约 2000 名中国学生，许多比利时学生正在中国的高等学府读书。他说："对于共同建设未来，大家相互学习是非常好的。"埃斯肯思曾多次到访中国，他曾于 20 世纪 70 年代末担任比利时财政部部长期间访问中国，并对随后几十年中国发生的变化有深刻的印象。

他说，中国通过改革开放的努力改变了拥有庞大人口的中国的面貌给他留下了非常深刻的印象。他补充说，邓小平是一个"非常非常伟大的政治家"。他敦促欧盟与其他经济体一同建立"自由贸易协定网络"。他说："面对今天网与墙的两难境地，很多被我们称为所谓全球化受害者的人们认为他们需要在国家周围用墙代替网。这在心理学上可以解释，但实际上没有任何意义可言。"他还补充说，他是一个欧洲联邦主义者。"这是适得其反的，是与未来逆向而行的，所以我们必须拯救我们的网络并摧毁这些围墙。"

现在中国和欧盟正在就双边投资协定进行谈判，埃斯肯思坚信，新的法国总统马克龙，可能支持欧盟和中国之间的自由贸易协定。作为一名欧洲联邦主义者，他认为欧盟仍然需要付出很大努力才能将其建设成为一个强大的集团。1991年时任比利时外交部部长的埃斯肯思表示，欧洲是一个经济巨人、政治矮子和军事蠕虫。在26年后被问及他的观点是否改变时，他回答说："我的回答是没有、没有、没有。我当时真的是对的，我现在还会这样说。"他继续说："我们在安理会的桌子上没有座位，尽管德国是欧洲最大的经济体，但德国也不在桌子上，这是相当不平衡的。用军事术语来说，欧洲根本就不重要。"

比利时全球化专家学者德里斯·莱萨奇（Dries Lesage）表示，世界大国有两套治理方式来处理与其他国家的事物。一套方式是西方使用的，近500年来已经有了"统治世界"的心态，有时会通过军事干涉的方式。另一套方式是中国的，实行双赢战略，赢得许多国家的"内心认同"。"但西方统治世界的心态应该在500年后走到了尽头。"比利时根特大学根特国际问题研究所主任莱萨奇说。

"这是因为实质上西方的经济和军事实力无法再维持这种方式了。"莱萨奇说，现在世界上的许多麻烦仍然源于西方的旧思维。莱萨奇是比利时在全球治理和建设、国际税收政策以及多极化方面的一个权威的专家。从历史和当前的经验教训来看，莱萨奇也敦促欧盟与美国的外交政策保持距离，塑造自己的愿景。他认为，中国在这个多极世界中为与各方建立良好关系方面树立了良好的榜样。"欧盟不应再参与美国统治世界的构想。"莱萨奇说。

西方近五个世纪以来一直使用这种统治理念，甚至多次用军事手段实现了自己的目标。美国和北约仍然使用这种起源于殖民主义时代的方式。在莱萨奇看来，中国遭受了 19 世纪和 20 世纪西方列强的各种军事袭击，经历了这种西方统治的模式。而且，现在非洲和亚欧大陆的许多问题都是由这种一直存在的西方思维造成的。

另外，他将中国崛起的全球领导力视为当今国际舞台上的一大发展。在详细描述这一观察时，莱萨奇说，中国在扩大国际影响力方面已经变得更加自信了，他认为中国这样的发展不仅符合中国的利益，也符合中国的伙伴国的利益。当特朗普政府宣布打算退出巴黎协定和《跨太平洋伙伴关系协定》的时候，这一发展进程将更加快速。莱萨奇说："现在中国在某种程度上就像是二战后第一个十年后的美国。"

美国 1944 年开始建立布雷顿森林体系，这是让美国受益的多边体系的基本结构。就重量和影响力而言，中国现在正在世界上承担着更多的责任，比如保护巴黎协定、保护开放经济和自由贸易。

所以他相信未来将会发生令人着迷的事情。因此，他坚持认为，欧盟应该通过应对不断变化的全球形势来重新表达对对外政策的愿景，尽管迄今为止欧洲还没有就此达成共识。但是，莱萨奇说，他的"个人和主观的欧盟愿景"是世界必须是多极的，而包括大西洋两岸在内的西方国家的身份仍然存在，但这只是多极世界的一部分。而且，他说，在他看来，欧盟愿景必须展示包容性，这意味着每个国家都接受彼此。他们都必须承认多样性和多元化，必须表现出参与的意愿。他进一步阐述说，相互尊重与平等是国际体系的本质，有助于扩大合作和讨论；与此同时，每个参与者的利益和价值观必须以良好的方式进行调和，他们都尊重这种多极化关系。莱萨奇说："欧洲现在必须知道新的参与者是谁，以及未来的参与者是谁。"

在处理与大国的关系时，他强调说，在乌克兰危机后，欧盟对俄罗斯实施制裁数月以后，欧盟与俄罗斯的关系不能"再差"了。莱萨奇说："欧洲不应该继续与俄罗斯对抗。"他继续描绘他的欧盟愿景的精髓，那就是突出各方双赢、平衡和平等的地位。这样，欧洲必须明白，保护你自己利益并不一定意味着它是一个零和博弈。当被问及欧盟是否开始考量这个新愿景时，他回答说："我看到了这个新愿景中的元素。但我不认为它是一个完全成形的东西。现在做主宰的还是旧心态。"

他警告说，在欧洲层面，这样的愿景变化将会非常缓慢。但他表示，现在中国是支持开放经济和自由贸易，倡导合作和共同发展的领导者。所以在对待中国时，欧洲机构应该实施他所制定的欧盟愿景。"这些应该是欧盟处理与中国关系的愿景。"莱萨奇说。

他表示，中欧在寻求可持续发展和维护巴黎协定方面有同样的立场。令他印象深刻的是二十国集团议程与联合国 2030 年可持续发展目标（SDG）之间的联系。在他看来，2030 年可持续发展目标解决了很多迫在眉睫的世界性的环境、社会、经济和政治问题，为日渐显现的全球危机提供了部分解决方案。他说，

2030 年可持续发展目标是在 2015 年 9 月叙利亚战争和乌克兰危机的笼罩下，在非常艰难的氛围中通过的。但他将 2030 年可持续发展目标视为外交上的一大成就。二十国集团领导人在 2016 年杭州二十国集团峰会上再次认可了该文件，一些二十国集团政策也被放在联合国的 2030 年可持续发展议程上，因此政府将会把这些目标作为政策制定的核心。"2030 年可持续发展目标没有被边缘化，这要归功于中国的二十国集团主席国的地位。持续性是二十国集团的特点之一，这应该从一个主席国传递给另一个主席国。"他说。

根据他的观察，中国在解决地区冲突方面非常积极主动，中国具有成为中间人的"合法性"，可以利用其中立立场的优势提供外交手段。这已经在叙利亚、也门、波斯湾地区、伊拉克、阿富汗和其他地方得到证明。莱萨奇说："中国与西方那些把局势弄得一团糟的大国不同，中国不干涉。在合法性方面中国可以做独立的一方。这样的领导力适合进行调解。"莱萨奇还表示，中国不仅正在成为地区冲突的中间人，而且也提供接地气的解决方案。他举的例子是中国把重点放在商业、合作、发展、建设基础设施上，通过在阿富汗实施"一带一路"倡议营造双赢局面。"这是一个有趣的方法，它赢得了阿富汗人的民心。这也是通过商业发展和合作隔离极端主义分子的一种方式。"莱萨奇说。不过，他表示，北约 2001 年进驻阿富汗，由于军事介入，16 年后该国仍然不稳定。关于欧盟与中国的关系，他说，欧洲对中国来说是"混乱而分据"的，有些人批评它，有些人则把它看作为一个机会。现在，欧盟委员会对提案加强投资审查，特别是对来自中国的投资审查，欧盟坚决对中国施加压力，敦促其减少钢铁产能，从而造成了一些冲突，尽管双方都在所谓的战略合作伙伴关系中。

在这样的情况下，中国会很容易被惹恼。"当朋友批评你时，你更愿意倾听。当敌人批评你时，你会忽略它，"莱萨奇说，"在与中国的关系方面，欧洲正是这种情况。"关于正在进行的针对欧洲战略产业投资保护的讨论，他说："这是一个奇怪的讨论。"他认为，在国家层面上，欧盟成员国已经能够保护这些产业。他说，欧盟也在人权、民主，甚至是市场经济地位方面与中国对抗，这引起了很多矛盾。令他失望的是，欧盟方面并没有考虑布鲁塞尔—北京战略伙伴关系的长期愿景，从根本的情绪和感受上正在朝着另一个方向发展。莱萨奇说，欧盟应该对"一带一路"倡议持开放态度，因为中国的愿景不仅是在商业和投资方面，还包括合作和沟通桥梁的建设方面。莱萨奇表示："欧盟需要通过考虑新的发展来形成与中国持续性合作的愿景，但是现在，除了可持续发展，一切都没有朝着正确的方向发展。"

澳大利亚前总理陆克文（Kevin Rudd）说，中国广受关注的经济"新常态"正在帮助重塑中国的增长方式，"一带一路"倡议将加速这一进程。说着一口流利普通话的陆克文，2011 年以来每年都会在达沃斯的世界经济论坛上与我会面。

他的乐观基于两件事，一是中国领导层决策的本质是推进经济改革，其中包括让市场发挥"决定性作用"；二是那些推动这些政策的人都是非常聪明的人，他们知道自己在做什么。他说，重大决策已经制定，特别是有关金融市场和外国投资自由化的决策。2013 年中共中央十八届三中全会作出决定，第一次明确表明市场的决定性作用。"这是全新的理念。说市场起'决定性'作用，和说它起'重要'作用是不—样的，不是吗？这是一个根本性的哲学意义上的转变。这是通过计划或公共投资进行的传统干预在'新常态'这个概念下并不容易适应的原因。"

陆克文说，他密切关注中国在习近平主席的领导下的发展，他已经阅读了《习近平谈治国理政》的英文和中文版本。在被广泛讨论的所谓的"新常态"问题上，陆克文说："在中国，旧模式最终要退休，'新模式'将取而代之。这个新模式的一部分就是新模式本身，新常态显然是私人消费作为增长的新动力。"

中国的丝绸之路倡议即将扩大连通性。陆克文说："这个想法是东盟思想的延伸，我认为这是一个通过铁路、港口和数字进行连接的好主意。"他说，中国提出丝绸之路倡议所面临的巨大挑战就是传播这一想法。

在这点上我同意陆克文的观点。为促进中国与其他地区的联系，我们需要一个更简单、直接的名字。中国被世界所了解的程度部分取决于复杂的汉语翻译成外国语言的质量，但这样的工作总是具有挑战性的，特别是要将简化的流行语和习近平主席的话语的全部含义翻译成英文的时候，例如，习近平主席通过借鉴历史悠久的丝绸之路的概念连接亚欧的倡议。

随着这些提案由中国和其他国家传播、理解甚至部分实现，他的团队将这两个提案凝结成一个表达，那就是"一带一路"倡议。习近平主席在2013年俄罗斯二十国集团峰会之后不久宣布了"丝绸之路经济带"倡议，我也对此作了报道。中国与新兴经济体共同致力于深化全球金融体系改革，在峰会上成立金砖国家银行已经给我留下了深刻的印象。但我对习近平主席的丝绸之路理念印象深刻，因为这表明中国越来越意识到需要承担更多的国际责任。

习近平主席宣布他的"21世纪海上丝绸之路"倡议时，中国新一届领导层在地区和全球层面的积极主动和有战略性的思想令我赞叹不已。多年来，世界需要这样的全球性解决方案来帮助经济可持续发展，但是很快，我意识到用外国语言向外国人传达这样美丽的想法是一件困难的事情。

陆克文坦率地告诉我，他也认为中国将面临向世界其他国家解释战略方案的"沟通挑战"。中文流利的陆克文说，这个概念非常清楚，中国正在努力做的就是扩大连通性。

他说他支持通过建立丝路基金支持基础设施建设和金融注资的努力，他认为中国的挑战不在于提案的内容，而在于沟通。他说，如果你把"一带一路"直译成英文，那么挑战就变得清晰了。在中文框架中，这是一个可以理解的概念，但是当你用英语"腰带"这个词的时候，人们就会想知道它与互联互通有什么关系。陆克文有他自己的解决方案。他说中国应该把它称为"泛亚洲互联互通议程"，然而，我怀疑陆克文的解决方案对接受这些提案相对较慢的欧洲人的有效性。长期以来，欧洲人特别是西欧人有这样的优越感，即使他们急需摆脱经济停滞，但他们也很难接受泛亚洲理念。

我还和世界银行前首席经济学家、北京大学教授林毅夫（Justin Lin）讨论了沟通的挑战，他说，在他看来非洲一定会被列入"一带一路"倡议，这证实了陆克文指出的困难。我问他关于习近平主席倡议的英文表达的想法。现在是中国领导人高级顾问的林先生想了一会儿说，可以采用"一带一路"倡议这个表达。他相信人们会渐渐明白和接受它，但我并不认同。

这样的表达只不过是一个浓缩的中文表达的一字一句的翻译，其中包含两个提议。在使用这种翻译的过程中，许多层意思已经失去了，即使被普遍接受，美丽与和平的理念已经没有了。因此，根据我的理解，用英文命名这样的多重提案时，我们应该放弃尝试逐字翻译，如果我们不绑定在这个规则上，那么选择就很多了。例如，我们可以称它为现代丝绸之路。或者，如果我们把重点放在连接三大洲的连通性和基础设施建设上，它可以被称为"亚非欧基础设施计划"。但是，当然，这些思想是习近平主席首先提出来的，他在改革、法治、反腐、外交等方面体现的能力和战略管理已经积累了极大的信任和尊重。

如果三大洲通过铁路、公路、海运和数字手段更紧密地联系起来，那么丝绸之路提案对三大洲有着非常重要的经济含义与和平含义。所以我建议"一带一路"倡议的英文表达可以简化为习近平新政。为什么不呢？所有这些想法都是在最近被正式确定为"一带一路"倡议之后出现的。

"一带一路"国际合作高峰论坛与欧洲

要 有效融入这样一个庞大的工程，欧盟应该考虑举办一个紧急会议，来跟进"一带一路"国际合作高峰论坛，一位资深的中国问题专家在论坛召开前这样建议道。

"这对欧盟来说是一个很好的主意，我相信'一带一路'倡议包含了一个非常重要的组成部分，那就是欧洲。"总部位于布鲁塞尔的欧盟—中国贸易协会主席约胡姆·哈克玛（Jochum Haakma）在峰会召开前如是说。哈克玛，荷兰人，曾在香港和上海作了九年外交官，他把自己在协会的使命定位为帮助连接中国和欧洲。

但他已经意识到，在对"一带一路"倡议的重要性的理解上，欧洲和亚洲之间有着反差，"一带一路"倡议旨在通过改善产品、人力资源、资本和其他生产力要素的流动，将亚洲、欧洲和非洲连接起来。在反对保护主义和孤立主义的背景下，一些美洲国家已同意加入"一带一路"框架，据报道近期华盛顿方面也显示出了兴趣。

多达30名国家领导人，其中11名来自欧洲，确认将出席北京论坛。然而，哈克玛说，很明显，与欧洲相比，亚洲国家将更加统一，更加战略性地和切实地进行思考，并且学习如何跟进"一带一路"倡议。欧洲是较少参与，并且没有切实地做任何事情，所以我认为，下一个大型"一带一路"论坛应该在布鲁塞尔举办，哈克玛这样说道。

他甚至说，这应该是一个紧急的后续步骤，应在之后六个月内在布鲁塞尔举办，这将是非常直接的一步。他说，欧盟应证明其认知，表明跟进"一带一路"倡议的政治意愿。但是他说，欧盟仍然缺乏对"一带一路"倡议的重要性的认识，主要是因为欧盟内部总会有反对的声音，因为一些成员国担心在欧洲大陆上有不断增长的中国投资活动。许多欧洲企业家和银行家反而看到了与中国一起合作的重要性。"我觉得这种对中国在欧洲投资的重要性的认识已经逐渐增多，因为英国脱欧和特朗普在白宫就职。"哈克玛说。

因此，现在正是欧盟醒来并且加强与中国紧密合作的正确时机，他补充道。对于创业者来说，参与到如此大型的项目中就像"天堂"一样，因为它在改善全球基础设施条件方面至少有三四十年的生命周期，他说。针对欧洲民粹主义和右翼政治力量的崛起，哈克玛表示，非常重要的是欧洲要团结在一起。

哈克玛表示，中国与欧盟之间的热门话题是全面投资协定，有时双方也就开展自由贸易谈判的可能性进行讨论。不过，布鲁塞尔并没有经常提到"一带一路"倡议，哈克玛说，这是一个非常重要和巨大的基础设施建设项目，是世界上有史以来最大的。

"'一带一路'倡议的另一端是欧洲。而且我认为，如果欧洲加入进来，那么欧洲对中国来说就是一个更好的帮手。就可以一起做更多的事情。"他说。哈克玛呼吁欧洲人提出与中国政府合作的计划，许多欧洲国家已成为亚投行成员。

皮埃尔·德福安（Pierre Defraigne）是布鲁塞尔另一位公正、坦率而又经验丰富的亚洲问题专家。他说，欧盟必须在与北京、华盛顿的三方关系中发展自己的远景和能力，而不是跟随美国的脚步，亦步亦趋。他向布鲁塞尔发出了"最后的机会"的信息，称欧盟是否能听得进去将至关重要，如果欧盟能够采纳他的意见，那么欧盟可以最大限度地发挥其在不断变化的全球系统中的潜力，与北京的关系将更加和睦。

"我们需要的是欧盟协调其与中、美的整体战略的能力。"总部位于布鲁塞尔的智库——马达里亚加欧洲学院基金会执行主任德福安说。德福安是我的一位老朋友，我与他曾在 2016 年年末在他布鲁塞尔的家中进行了很长的对话，他是研讨会和辩论会上受邀最频繁的发言嘉宾之一。他希望激发对欧洲一体化和北京—布鲁塞尔的关系的高质量的讨论，这个想法源于他作为欧盟高级公务员数十年的工作经历。德福安自 2008 年开始了他在智库的工作，他相信布鲁塞尔在应对北京方面已经迷失了方向，因为欧洲把注意力放在了应对大规模移民、恐怖主义、失业率上升和英国脱欧的挑战上。

德福安坐在他书房的沙发上，周围满是书籍，安静的书房用中国艺术品装饰。他说，在贸易、投资、旅游、教育和文化交流方面，中国和大多数欧盟成员之间的关系是充满活力的。在加强战略合作关系的过程中，许多欧洲国家领导人与中国国家领导人习近平主席、李克强总理都建立了很密切的私人关系。"但是当他们（作为欧盟）在一起的时候，他们希望欧盟对中国持强硬立场，"德福安说，"我认为他们玩的是双重博弈，但是由于缺乏团结，这使得欧盟处于一个非常不利的境地。"

德福安表示，这一立场冻结了布鲁塞尔—北京的关系，使得困难不能得到解决。作为资深官员，德福安表示，欧盟与中国的不良的互动不是其想要故意冒犯的结果，而是欧盟在团结成员国方面"无能为力"的反映。在没有统一战线的情况下，欧盟过度倚重华盛顿来决定欧盟对北京的立场。他说这意味着欧盟不再是一个独立的实体。

"这是欧盟——美国领导(的结果)。"他认为。有很多欧盟没有能力来决定如何推动布鲁塞尔——北京关系向前发展的例子。多年来,布鲁塞尔未能解除对北京的武器禁运,也未能承认中国这一世界第二大经济体的市场经济地位。

德福安认为,布鲁塞尔需要华盛顿引领的这一事实意味着它无法作出"看似战略性的决定"。目前,欧盟表示与华盛顿建立更加紧密关系是其议程的优先项。欧盟委员会网站将欧盟和美国的伙伴关系列入十大优先事项之中。

但德福安说,布鲁塞尔必须重新安排优先项。"我对布鲁塞尔将会调整其心态持相当乐观的态度,"他说,"现在,布鲁塞尔需要采取行动,在全球治理改革的框架下推动中国、欧盟和美国的三方关系。"他建议建立一个新的对话平台。德福安说:"理想的情况下,这应该是二十国集团领导人会议的一个子机制。"他认为这样的机制将有助于布鲁塞尔在不断变化的全球系统中获得更有利于自己的位置,他还敦促欧盟和美国要注意中国国内外发生的事情。他说,自2008—2009年始于华尔街的金融危机起,中国很好地实施了结构性改革,这也是导致他呼吁改革资本主义模型的原因。但他说,对美国来说,由于政治原因、市场力量,游说团体和全球性公司已经压倒了政治制度,因此实施这样的改革是非常有难度的。

"我不认为欧盟像纽约和华盛顿一样有着同样的压力,但我们的企业是和美国企业一样强大的,"德福安说,"但关键是:政治手段必须接管市场。当你破坏了系统,你必须改变这个系统。这就是中国正在做的事情。"他说，美国和欧洲也应该效仿中国的国内改革并积累公共财富，这对那些在社会阶层下层的人们来说很关键。

在国际上，德福安说，令人鼓舞的是，北京在诸多问题上，特别是在《巴黎气候变化协定》方面已经起到了引领的作用。中国正在逐步实现向以绿色竞争力为经济增长模式的转变，这将对全球参与可持续发展产生积极影响，他说。

但是，他认为，美国的一些势力对执行奥巴马所做的安排犹豫不决。德福安认为，中国在推动《巴黎气候变化协定》方面扮演的积极角色就像 15 年前中国加入世贸组织一样重要，当时的世贸组织还是由西方国家为自己的利益建立的存在已久的旧结构。他说："现在，中国是这个新分支的创始者之一，中国的影响会变得越来越重要。对我来说，中国加入《巴黎气候变化协定》对于世界和未来来说都是乐见其成的好事。"

中国正在通过多种方式积极参与其中。中国已经公平地完成了作为世贸组织成员的义务，而且经证实是一名忠实可靠的成员。现在人民币已经加入了国际货币基金组织特别提款权货币篮子。他说："除了《巴黎气候变化协定》以外，我个人认为中国正处在正确的轨道上。我们必须认同中国的这一发展，并面对挑战。"至于美国，德福安说，未来应该是要改变态度，变得更加积极主动，而欧洲则应该实现团结一致。"欧洲的团结是今天维护世界经济稳定的一个大问题，是对这个联盟和世界的繁荣来说最严峻的挑战，"他说，"我们对自己的构想一直是发展成为多边主义和友好合作的主要角色，但如果我们不能实现统一，欧盟将在经济上成为对世界的威胁。"

多年来，德福安一直是中国的密切观察者，他也阅读了许多关于中国的书籍。他试图了解中国的历史，他认为了解中国政治的全面发展是非常重要的，因为这是一个独特的体系。在中国，由于儒家传统，很多家庭都有一种归属感，这比市场和技术更重要。他说："我看到中国人的行动，他们正在积极地捍卫自己的利益。他们不是被动的公民，而是积极的公民。如果政府能够抓住中国公民的需求和中国悠久的文明的需求，中国将会有更好的未来。"

中国（海南）改革发展研究院院长迟福林赞同德福安的观点，并对他的提议表示欢迎。在过去的五年时间里，迟院长至少十次前往布鲁塞尔参加与智库和欧盟机构的对话。"我们认为可以和欧方一起讨论关于中国的一般性议题，但是当与我们的欧洲同行，尤其是欧方官员，深入探讨一些问题时真的很难进行，"迟院长说，"德福安的提议是富有远见的，布鲁塞尔应该立即将它纳入考量。"中方和欧方应该考虑发展更多的项目来扩大学术界和智库间的交流。他说："双方都需要把这个问题放在首位，弥合双方在理解上的差距。"

最近，他一直在推动欧盟重新考虑对华政策，通过紧急启动双边自由贸易谈判重置政策优先项的想法，以期双方对全球化作出强有力的承诺。继李克强总理最近号召开展双边自由贸易谈判可行性研究后，专家们表示，这样的行动对缓解一系列全球性挑战带来的不断增多的负面影响至关重要。迟福林说："面对瞬息万变的全球环境，欧盟必须加快步伐，重新考虑应对中国的优先项。我认为，迫在眉睫的重点之一应该是中欧自由贸易谈判。欧盟与数个亚洲伙伴已经开始或者完成了自由贸易谈判。"

迟院长说，以更好地连接亚欧非为目的的"一带一路"倡议得到了全球广泛认可，"一带一路"倡议应该成为欧盟重新设置其对华经济和贸易政策的"新的触发器"。中国提出的广泛的"自由贸易网络"将连接参与"一带一路"倡议的各个国家，这也应该是作为自由贸易和全球化的全球性领跑者和战士的欧盟的利益所在。"所以，从逻辑上讲，许多热衷参与'一带一路'倡议的欧盟成员国，应该与中国合作尽快启动自由贸易可行性研究。"迟院长说。过去几年里，我和迟院长进行过多次交流。他表示，现在中国国内的变化可能会对欧盟政策产生影响，欧洲方面必须认真对待，以促进双向交流。

除了迟院长，我和两位中国知名教授——林毅夫和薛澜的对话也是很有意义的。世界银行前首席经济学家林毅夫先生于2016年4月底有了新的职务，他被任命为北京大学南南合作与发展研究院的首任院长。

林毅夫在世界银行的4年任职期间，热衷于利用中国的经验刺激非洲经济。他说学院的落成是一个里程碑，因为它将开启中国的发展和制度经验的系统共享。事实上，距北京大学数个街区之远的清华大学已经开始这样做了。在公共管理学院院长薛澜的带领下，清华大学已于几年前推出了国际化发展的硕士课程，主要为发展中国家的优秀学生提供探索中国发展秘籍的机会。

这些举措也是为了支持欠发达国家实现自己的奇迹。另外值得一提的是，中国的许多知名高级官员和学术领袖都是20世纪

80 年代、90 年代初从美国、英国、德国等西方国家的大学毕业的。他们很清楚地知道如何将他们在西方获得的知识融入中国的发展现实。

因此，向发展中国家的学生传授这些技能可能是北京大学和清华大学设置的课程的核心内容。多年来，美国、英国、法国、瑞士等许多国家的知名商学院都在中国开展项目，而中国学生和成千上万的管理人员则流向海外，进修商业教育。现在中国大学的商学院也变得更具竞争力了。他们中的一些已经慢慢开始招收海外学生。正如中国在政策上形成了一个很大的发展遗产，中国商人们也从零开始建立了不同规模的商业帝国，并从中获得了宝贵经验。考虑到发展中国家对这种知识的大量需求，下一步可以考虑建立一个南南合作和国际发展的独立大学。总部设在北京，这所大学可以在非洲和其他发展中国家设立分支机构。中国领先的商学院在设计战略时也可以考虑非洲和其他发展中地区的机遇。

林毅夫还认为，中国的成功经验和发展模式可以被待发展的经济体所复制，特别是非洲的经济体。他鼓励埃塞俄比亚领导人走这条道路，中国皮革和制鞋工厂已经开始转向以经济起飞为主要目标的埃塞俄比亚。他的发展经济学的思想显示出了独立性，这也反映在他的 25 本著作中，比如《从西潮到东风：我在世行四年对世界重大经济问题的思考和见解》。中国政府顾问，北京大学教授林毅夫先生，是得到西方广泛认可的中国经济学家。他是北京大学中国经济研究中心的创始人和主任。

林先生详细地谈了他为什么认为中国能够实现长期经济增长，中国与发达经济体之间的差距，中国的成本与潜力以及中国成功的全球意义。与我交谈时，林先生说，如果中国国内深化改革取得成功并且条件允许的话，他对中国有潜力在未来 20 年保持每年 8% 的速度增长非常有信心。"我指的是潜力，我必须强调这一点。" 林先生说。他说："所以中国可以在弥合差距之前继续享有落后的优势。" 当中国经济发展由依靠投资和贸易转向由消费拉动的时候，中国将面临经济低迷。在经济发展模式的换挡过程中，林先生说，中国必须知道如何面对三大挑战：收入差距、腐败和环境污染。前两个挑战已经让中国一般老百姓"不幸福"，如果环境恶化，他说，不论贫富都会感到不幸福。"所以我们必须学会如何面对这样的挑战。"

林先生说，世界上的贫困人口，尤其是非洲的贫困人口，在西方殖民统治期间错失了许多发展机遇，在这之后，他们应该过上更好的生活。在担任世行首席经济学家期间，从 2008 年到 2012 年，他花了很多时间访问非洲。虽然他是第一个坐上这个位置的亚洲人，但他曾经说："更重要的是，我可能是第一个理解发展中国家需求的世界银行首席经济学家。" 他说，非洲国家可以向中国学习诸多发展经验和教训，他建议使用双轨改革的方法，对无法存活的企业提供暂时性保护以维持稳定，同时开放国家具有比较优势的部门。他指的是 2011 年和 2012 年埃塞俄比亚领导人作出决定让中国制鞋厂等工厂转移到埃塞俄比亚。现在，在埃塞俄比亚生产的鞋子已经出口到其他非洲国家和欧洲。林先生说："埃塞俄比亚的案例表明，中非欧可以形成三方合作关系。"

他说，在某些制造业向拥有大量劳动力和资源的非洲地区转移的同时，中国和欧洲将从提供科技、专有技术、资本和出口市场中受益。

林毅夫对欧洲表示担忧，自 2007—2008 全球经济动荡以来欧洲仍处于下滑到第三次经济衰退的风险之中，这将减少中国在欧洲的出口和投资。

"欧盟还没有提出所需的结构性改革来提高竞争力，因此，目前风险还无法消除。"

为了帮助全球经济更好地发展，林先生说，重要的是各大经济体要考虑一个"宏大的基础设施建设计划"，以摆脱经济停滞和危机。林先生说，欧洲在改善基础设施方面还有空间，这些措施将会促进技术和产品的出口。中国计划与其他国家"更好地建立联系"，并通过资金和技术投入鼓励多个非洲国家建设公路、铁路和机场。"这样的措施不仅有助于消除欧元和美元竞争性贬值带来的担忧，而且可以帮助世界避免经济停滞。" 林先生说。

现任英国菲利普亲王（Prince Philip） 环境顾问，彭马田（Martin Palmer） 指出，已经度过 90 岁寿辰的伊丽莎白女王（Queen Elizabeth） 在位的时间比他的年龄都长。

是王室的长寿使得彭马田这位汉学家帮助英国王室解读中国文化的丰富性长达三十年之久。

彭马田每年会与菲利普亲王见面三到四次，他每隔两到三年会与女王会谈一次。他们谈话的主题包括道家、儒学以及介绍中国在应对环境保护和全球变暖的挑战方面的价值观念。

"我认为关于王室，特别是女王的有趣的事情主要是长寿，这是一种重要的中国价值观念。" 彭马田说。彭马田是世界宗教与环境保护联盟的秘书长。这一联盟是由菲利普亲王创立的环保组织，总部位于英国。

彭马田说道家用了几百年的时间研究出的草药和其他元素的神奇配方可以实现长寿。他还补充说："我们的女王似乎已经自主地去这么做了。"

谈到 2017 年两度庆祝的女王的 90 岁生日（按照惯例），他将长寿与中国的价值观念联系在一起。他称赞道："（她身上有）一种极大的责任感，对她而言，很大程度上是基于孝道——一种伟大的儒家美德。"在中国传统中，每个人都要孝敬父母。"她绝对地崇拜她的父亲，视她的父亲为她的英雄"。

彭马田与中国的道家大师共事多年。彭马田说，自从他把道家大师请到白金汉宫和温莎城堡，菲利普亲王和伊丽莎白女王开始对道家显示出极大的兴趣。

彭马田说："英国王室一直想了解更多。"

王室夫妇问宗教如何塑造了中国，冥想的传统是什么，天地人的核心哲学观念是什么。

彭马田回忆说，女王还问道为什么宗教之间没有战争，她对道、佛、儒家不同的传统如何在中国百家争鸣也十分好奇。

彭马田曾经邀请道教大师，张道陵第 65 代嫡孙——一位受人敬仰的道教大师，与女王和菲利普亲王会面。女王和菲利普亲王对认识一个家史可以追溯到比女王的家史还要久远的人非常感兴趣。女王的家族史可以追溯到公元 700 年，而张家则是公元 2 世纪。

1985 年，当彭马田应邀与时任世界野生动物基金会国际主席的菲利普亲王谈话时，他第一次与王室成员见面。彭马田为世界野生动物基金会撰写了一本书，书中就不同的宗教对自然起源的不同看法以及如何看待自然界进行了解读。

彭马田所走的文化之路与习近平主席在 2014 年 3 月访问法国在联合国教科文组织的讲话中提到的文化之路如出一辙。他称习近平主席的讲话是近年来中国主席最有趣的演讲之一。

彭马田表示，习近平主席有力地阐明了中国的文化、传统和文明，彭马田还认为这些应该是中国摆脱其所面临的困境的一些方法。

"中国就在那个临界点上。我的意思是现在有一些存在环境污染问题的城市，现在你知道这个问题，而且你也在说，'好吧，这不仅是我们的一个问题，也是地球的一个问题'，"彭马田说，"我认为你正在加紧努力，这是承担责任，因为我们必须承担责任。"

彭马田说，"生态文明"，是中国政策经常用的一个词，这是一个迷人的表达。2006 年他第一次知道了这个说法。当时他正在中国与道家为保护道教仙山以及道教对中国的道德与精神的影响而工作，这也是他从 1995 年以来一直在做的事情。

他说，这是一种观念，它反映了经历了过去四十年迅速发展的中国人开始不只关心自己，也关心那些不如他们幸运的人，也关心森林、河流和鱼儿。

"这些概念在中国古典文学中已存在了数千年，这是对中华文明的重新发现，因为它可以塑造我们的生活方式，"彭马田说，"所以，据我观察，这一重新发现，是近10年来，对最好的文化传统的重新评估。"

他说，"仁"这个古老的儒家词汇，植根于人性本善。所以当"生态文明"出现的时候，我可以追溯它的历史。

彭马田说，实现分阶段生态文明建设的想法——这已经成为2012年以来中国共产党的优先发展的方向之一，这一想法应得到全球的认可。

问题之一是，西方国家如此贬低自己的文明理念，以至于当一个国家说想要实现文明的时候，西方国家并不完全明白它的意义。

彭马田说："我们能够建立起一个生态文明，这是中国的伟大礼物。所以，我认为生态文明的意义在于它对西方物质世界来说是一个深远的挑战。"

多年来，他把佛教、道教和儒家著作翻译成英文。

他说："我现在正在翻译《三国演义》。《三国演义》的文字和故事中蕴含的智慧是我通过文明领悟出来的。"

彭马田说，他正在制作一部有关丝绸之路的六集电视剧。这部电视剧将审视思想、故事、信仰、宗教和哲学沿着丝绸之路往复传播发展，并塑造出了世界上不同的伟大宗教。

"中国方面对这个想法非常积极，我想他们不会遇到许多像我一样知道这么多中国历史故事的西方人。"他说。

多年来，作为一名基督教徒，彭马田过着简单的生活；他得益于中国智慧的启发，懂得知足常乐，这也是中国古代经典文学里所推崇的。

彭马田说："对我而言，要享受今生美好的事物，但要确保这不是以任何人为代价。"

丝绸之路上"互联互通"的创新方式

2014 年，在习近平主席提出"一带一路"倡议后的一年，两个荷兰年轻人沿着丝绸之路一路驾车。长期以来，中国的中产阶级和年轻人以身着欧式服饰、欧洲皮鞋，戴着欧洲品牌的手表，开着欧系的汽车作为时髦的生活方式。反其道而行之，这两位荷兰年轻人为了挑战"中国品牌不是顶级品牌"的认知，在行驶两万公里，长达三个月的旅程中，他们只使用中国产品。

他们的丝绸之路 11 国朝圣之旅从上海出发，终点是家乡鹿特丹。29 岁的城市规划师马伦斯瑞克（Maren Striker）和 27 岁的营销人员罗杰拜克（Rogier Bikker）驾驶一辆中国汽车，带着中国手机，从里到外穿着中国服装，甚至内衣都是中国制造的，当然也戴着中国的太阳镜。他们将他们的旅程命名为"全新中国"。当他们历时 98 天在 10 月 31 日结束了旅程时，他们受到了中国汽车企业比亚迪、鹿特丹政府及他们家人的欢迎。"我们非常高兴能在中国品牌的支持下完成这次冒险，"斯瑞克说，"我们已经证明，中国不仅仅是一个全球工厂。"他们说，他们驾驶的比亚迪汽车的结实程度在伊朗颠簸的道路上与另一辆车相撞之后充分体现了出来。

"我们最终开着它平平安安地回到了家。" 当他们抵达鹿特丹的时候斯瑞克如是说。这辆汽车贴满了给这两个年轻人提供赞助的所有赞助商的品牌和旅程的路线地图。当驶达鹿特丹市政厅时，这辆后座上堆满的一包包衣物和日用品的比亚迪吸引了不少路人的注意。

除了比亚迪赞助了汽车之外，华为还为他们提供了手机，联想则为他们提供了笔记本电脑。他们用中国品牌的相机拍摄了照片。"我们在中国买了很多内衣，供旅途中使用，尽管这个内衣品牌并不在我们的赞助商之列。" 斯瑞克说。他们将此次旅程划分为三个部分：一个月在中国，一个月在亚洲其他国家，一个月在欧洲。他们说，11 个国家中，他们在每个国家都遇到了出众的中国人。他们沿着古丝绸之路领略了美丽的风景，感受了充满活力的文化和繁华的城镇。

在此次旅行之前，斯瑞克在中国生活了七年，他曾在一家城市规划公司工作，并走访过三十一个中国省份。拜克曾在一家上海公司从事市场营销工作。此前，他因 2010 年 10 天游览 10 个中国省份而备受关注。这两个荷兰年轻人说，他们亲眼看到了中国从世界工厂成为人们在新型公司里设计创新产品的地方。2010年，拜克与一位朋友花了两周的时间在中国来了一次自驾游，一路经过工厂，翻山越岭，困了就在车上睡。

"穿越中国边境是一次史诗级的旅行。开车回荷兰的想法就这样在陕西农村尘土飞扬的道路上驾车时产生了，"拜克说，"但是我们回来之后，朋友和家人们都觉得这个想法太疯狂了，不可能实现。所以梦想仍然是梦想。"斯瑞克也曾考虑去冒险。他想过走长城，骑自行车回荷兰或沿长江从源头到入海口。两年后，两个荷兰年轻人在上海酒吧相遇，并分享了他们的梦想。之后两个人辞去了工作，暂别自己的女友三个月时间，把两个人不多的积蓄都用在了实现这个想法上面。

到2013年秋天，计划逐渐成型。他们签约了赞助商，联系了媒体，安排了车辆通行文书，获得了签证，并且确定了要去拜访的在国外生活的中国人。"花在项目上的时间越长，我们就越意识到这个项目的巨大潜力。因此，我们聘请了特别棒的中国团队来帮忙。"斯瑞克说。他记得，他们的团队给几乎所有有权限在欧洲公路上行驶的中国汽车品牌打了电话或者发了邮件。但汽车厂商们直到2013年圣诞节都犹豫不决，这时其中一封电子邮件转发到了比亚迪市场总监那里，而比亚迪这个品牌的英文名称正代表了"营造你的梦想"。"我们在寒冬里圣诞假期的一天在鹿特丹城郊的工业园见到了他们。"斯瑞克说。比亚迪欧洲总经理何一鹏，在斯瑞克和拜克到达鹿特丹时与他们一同进行了庆祝。何一鹏说："我很高兴在这里看到你们两个一切安好。你们的成功证明了比亚迪产品的质量和耐用性。"当听说他们一度在伊朗遭遇车祸，何先生说，他当时非常焦虑，甚至想过暂停这次旅行，但斯瑞克和拜克决定继续，"我感谢他们对中国品牌的热爱和推崇的热情。"

另外一个事件是，在我报道了中国内地演员靳东主演的《恋爱先生》于2017年8月初在比利时的安特卫普港拍摄后的几个小时内，《中国日报》的微博账户收到了大量的评论、转发和点赞，这让我感到非常兴奋。当然，许多好的评论是给予靳东的，靳东因其近年来扮演的优质男人的角色而赢得了数百万中国女性的芳心。事实上，我对靳东的采访也诠释了他为何如此受欢迎。进一步阅读这些帖子会发现安特卫普的啤酒、巧克力、钻石、时尚、历史港口以及购物街都深深地吸引了中国读者。突然之间，我意识到，通过数字平台，影视剧能够在拉近不同国家的人们的距离上起到神奇的作用。

影视剧的作用可以被扩大并迅速地传播。近年来，中国电视节目制作人为比利时电视频道制作了中国美食系列节目，通过类似的传播策略引起了（公众）极大的兴趣。钱秀玲（1912—2008），一位在二战期间挽救了100多名比利时人的性命、使他们免于纳粹毒手的女英雄，也被演绎为电视连续剧《盖世太保枪口下的中国女人》。

无独有偶。伦敦、巴黎、罗马等城市也时不时在中国影视剧中出现。在中欧，布拉格已经成为中国电影界的理想之地。由著名演员徐静蕾导演的广受欢迎的浪漫爱情电影《有一个地方只有我们知道》就拍摄于布拉格。据中国驻捷克共和国大使马克卿介绍，近年来，随着两国关系不断紧密，捷克的宏伟建筑和壮丽的自然风貌已经出现在多部中国电影中。

在中国与欧洲国家交织的关系的背后，隐藏着需要双方共同探讨的极具意义的话题，以满足数字时代影视剧观众日益增长的需求。从历史到战争、爱情、英雄主义、家庭和美食，难以穷尽其题材。如果更多的故事被搬上屏幕，那么这样的努力将会产生连锁效应。

这不仅是因为中国的影视剧的需求正在迅速增加。中国的一个主要现实是，中产阶级在迅速增长，未来几年内中国中产阶级的规模将达到欧洲人口的总和。他们对娱乐和旅行有着极大的兴趣。一部让人印象深刻的电影会吸引他们去旅行。

预计 2017 年到捷克共和国旅游的中国游客数量将猛增 10 倍，达到约 50 万人。这也是为什么安特卫普的店员，甚至是市长，对正在进行的电影和电视剧拍摄感到十分兴奋。他们期待更多的中国人会在电视剧播出后来安特卫普旅游。事实上，这种效应现在已经开始显现。许多游客都在询问电视剧的拍摄是在哪家酒吧，哪家巧克力店，哪家钻石商店里进行的。

令人鼓舞的是，中国制片人和影视明星们已经采取行动来应对这一需求。一些欧洲人也开始认识到这种潜力。例如，位于雅典的 Silky Finance 的执行合伙人克里斯托斯弗拉乔斯（Christos Vlachos）最近转投中国电影市场。希腊和中国作为两个文明的发祥地，一定适合进行电影制作方面的合作。很多人说双向交流会更有效率。当欧洲制片人和电影明星想到北京、西安、现代的上海或深圳，甚至是中国历史悠久的小镇拍摄时，中国和欧洲的联系就更紧密了。

布鲁塞尔小小的舒曼广场，可能不像北京的天安门广场、纽约时代广场或莫斯科的红场那样著名，但却是欧盟机构和各国大使馆的聚集之地。舒曼广场也已经开始吸引中国游客，其中许多人选择新的方式来参观。

2017 年 8 月中旬，我在广场上碰巧遇到一些幼儿园学生和小学生以及他们的母亲。其中一个喊道："看，一辆中国来的汽车！"

让他如此兴奋的是一辆缓缓驶过的"休闲车"。车上是三名来自中国的画家，他们在与比利时的业界同仁见面后，正驶向他们文化交流之旅的下一站——巴黎。

他们一路从北京驶来，是丝绸之路（休闲车）文化交流代表团的成员，该代表团由从商人转型为博物馆馆长的张国中先生资助，这已经是张先生的第三次欧洲文化交流之行。巧合的是，这些孩子也正在进行一次比利时—荷兰—法国的绘画之旅。

近年来，我在布鲁塞尔遇到过同样鼓舞人心的行者们。2015年2月，我遇到了来自北京的大学生赖立坤和他的同伴张惠，他们从2009年开始骑自行车去环球旅行，他们现在正在为他们的非洲冒险之旅做准备。

那一年，我也遇到了一群驱车横跨亚欧大陆的中国人和欧洲人，他们到访了大熊猫所在的地方。他们以大熊猫为媒介，旨在巩固中欧之间的友谊和加深相互了解。

但是如果你认为只有年轻人才有足够的勇气去进行这样的冒险之旅，那你就错了。2016年，一对来自北京的退休的中国夫妇在大约两个月的时间里驾车行驶约一万公里，到欧盟总部与女儿见面。他们花了六个月的时间准备旅行和申请签证。

亚欧大陆有大约80个国家，地势崎岖。从北京到布鲁塞尔，坐飞机需要10个小时左右。但是我遇到的很多人，比如艺术家、自行车爱好者和退休的夫妇，他们都满怀热情地通过汽车、自行车、海路，甚至是徒步的方式横穿亚欧大陆。

他们渴望沉浸在亚欧大陆的自然风光中，亲身体验语言和文化的多样性。这对退休的夫妇不会说任何外语，但他们仍然成功地从北京来到了欧盟总部旁的女儿的家。这些艺术家除了中文也不会其他语言，但是他们说，"笑脸"是世界各个角落最好的表达善意的标志。

十年前，我在伦敦遇到英国广播公司 BBC 的一名记者，当时我惊讶地了解到他选择从伦敦乘火车到北京来履新。那时候，很多人说中欧之间的差异反映在地铁线路的数量上，一边是北京和上海，一边是伦敦、巴黎和罗马。现在看来，差异不再存在。

由于中国经济的崛起，越来越多的中国人到欧洲旅游，探索欧洲的社会、文化和生活方式。尽管大多数人更喜欢乘坐飞机，但也有一些人选择使用陆路交通工具的方式。欧洲必须为接受这些做好准备。除了采取措施让欧洲更安全之外，欧盟领导人还应该与亚洲领导人合作，通过简化签证申请程序等方式来便利人们交流。

也许丝绸之路沿线的十几个国家应该开始考虑签发类似于欧盟申根签证的"丝绸之路签证"，这将成为增加亚欧之间旅游的开创性举措。

以下是本书作者采访过的人物的头像，其职务是受访时职务。

布拉尼斯拉夫·乔尔杰维奇
塞尔维亚贝尔格莱德国际政治
与经济学研究所所长

迪米特里斯·布兰托尼斯
雅典经济与商业大学副校长

多丽丝·洛伊特哈德
瑞士联邦主席

段杰龙
中国驻匈牙利大使

艾兰妮·龚朵拉
希腊旅游部部长

傅承求
中远集团比雷埃夫斯集装箱码
头公司总经理

胜雅律
瑞士汉学家

胡坤
中兴通讯西欧业务主管

让–皮埃尔·拉法兰
法国前总理

伊凡娜·拉德洁瓦克
塞尔维亚贝尔格莱德国际政治
经济研究所国际合作协调员

扬·科胡特
捷克外交部前部长

雅罗斯拉夫·特夫迪克
捷克国防部前部长

让–皮埃尔·莱曼
瑞士洛桑国际管理发展学院国
际政治经济教授

伊维察·达契奇
塞尔维亚第一副总理兼外交部
部长

靳东
中国演员

伊日·帕劳贝克
捷克前总理

伊日·鲁斯诺克
捷克前总理

约胡姆·哈克玛
欧盟—中国贸易协会主席

约翰·施奈德–阿曼
瑞士联邦前主席

乔·莱恩
欧洲议会对华关系代表团团长

尤哈·西比莱
芬兰总理

基里亚科斯·米佐塔基斯
希腊新民主党主席

李满长
中国驻塞尔维亚大使

马克卿
中国驻捷克大使

马克·埃斯肯思
经济学家、比利时前首相

门镜
比利时欧洲学院教授

施明贤
德国前驻华大使

米洛什·泽曼
捷克总统

彼得·塔姆
汉堡国际海事博物馆主任

曲星
中国驻比利时大使

拉多萨夫·普西奇
贝尔格莱德孔子学院院长

罗马诺·普罗迪
意大利前总理

绍利·尼尼斯托
芬兰总统

史明德
中国驻德国大使

雪莉·卡尔维宁
2016年芬兰小姐

宋嗣海
河钢塞尔维亚执行董事

斯特吉奥斯·比齐奥拉斯
希腊政府经济发展部副部长

李素
捷克翻译家，汉学家

迪莫·力塔卡里奥
芬兰奥林匹克委员会主席

瓦茨拉夫·克劳斯
捷克前总统

弗拉丹·武科萨夫列维奇
塞尔维亚文化部部长

沃伊捷赫·菲利普
捷克议会副议长

薛澜
清华大学公共管理学院院长

杨燕怡
中国驻欧盟大使

张海晏
法国鲁昂诺欧商学院商务孔子
学院院长

邹肖力
中国驻希腊大使

A New Code for Common Peace and Prosperity

FU JING

▼

The Belt and Road Initiative offers game-changing catalysts for China and the EU to reposition development strategies and seek closer connectivity in Eurasia

SPM

Southern Publishing & Media Co., Ltd.
Guangdong People's Publishing House Ltd.
· Guangzhou ·

A New Code for Common Peace and Prosperity
The Belt and Road Initiative offers game-changing catalysts for China and the EU to reposition development strategies and seek closer connectivity in Eurasia

Copyright© 2019 by Fu Jing
Published by Guangdong People's Publishing House Ltd.
Senior Editorial Consultant: Alex Kirby
English Editors: Huang Jiehua, Li Lishan
Chinese Editors: Lu Xuehua, Li Qin
Proofreader: Richard Wong

ISBN 978-7-218-13077-4
First edition July, 2019
Printed in the People's Republic of China

Guangdong People's Publishing House Ltd.
Building 2, No. 204 Xingangxi Road, Guangzhou, China, 510300
Tel: 86-20-85716808
Fax: 86-20-85716872
Website: www.gdpph.com

Centuries ago, when our Chinese ancestors braved their way, either by sea or on land, exploring Silk Road connecting Asia, Europe or Africa, they could be called the very first generation of pioneers of budding globalisation.

Later on Europeans, with Marco Polo (1254-1324), Christopher Columbus (1451-1506) and Ferdinand Magellan (1480-1521) taking a historic lead, started to reshape the destinies of many countries across the world with increased interventions, positively or negatively.

This process gathered momentum at different stages of human history. Coupled with the Americans, Europeans accelerated it after the Second World War, mainly through the expanded activities of multinationals, trade and outward investment. The process has helped China, which has embarked on market-oriented opening and reform drive, increase its economic clout during the last four decades.

Since the beginning of this century, especially since the 2008-2009 financial crisis, the world has also benefited from the consistent high-speed economic growth of China, which has on average contributed more than 30 percent of annual global growth.

How to sustain such a global contribution, how to substantially tap the market potential of almost 1.4 billion people is the exact starting point of the Belt and Road Initiative, which was introduced by President Xi Jinping in the latter half of 2013. The answer lies in increasing connectivity and lifting barriers between the Chinese people and the others who share the Eurasian continent.

Geographically, the Eurasian countries are advantageously placed to grow closer on all fronts. I have been exploring the topic for a long time since President Xi proposed the idea. Seizing the opportunity offered by China hosting the Belt and Road Initiative Forum for International Cooperation in May 2017, I travelled to ten European countries during March-May period, talking as much as I could with politicians, businesspersons and academic people, to seek their views.

1

For the past ten years, I have had both sad and exciting moments in my journalistic career, such as reporting the Sichuan earthquake, evacuating Chinese citizens from Libya, covering terrorist attacks in Brussels and constantly reporting on climate change and the financial crisis. The deep exploration of the Belt and Road Initiative in Europe has enriched my life as a journalist.

The idea of writing a book came into my mind and, through an introduction from the publishing house's European partner Mr. Liu Jinrui, Mr. Xiao Fenghua, president of Guangdong People's Publishing House Ltd., soon accepted my pitch.

Thanks to tremendous help from editors Huang Jiehua and Li Lishan, this book has taken excellent shape in weeks after submitting my manuscript. Particularly, they arranged a pre-launch event for it at the Frankfurt Book Fair in early October in 2017. It was a great privilege that Du Chuangui, general manager of Guangdong-based Southern Publishing and Media Co., Ltd., Helga Zepp-LaRouche, president of the Schiller Institute in Germany, Bernard Dewit, chairman of the Belgian-Chinese Chamber of Commerce and Xiao Fenghua all spoke at the launch and the dialogue on the Belt and Road Initiative and Sino-EU relations which I chaired. So my deep and sincere gratitude goes to them.

I need to extend my heartfelt thanks to my mentor and close friend Alex Kirby, a veteran former BBC journalist from the UK who I have known for years. He has intelligently and skillfully polished my language, corrected my silly mistakes and improved the quality during the summer of this year and has tremendously contributed to turning this book into a readable work. Thank you, again, Alex, and I owe you a beer.

I should also thank Mr. Zhou Shuchun, editor-in-chief of China Daily, other members of the editorial board, and my colleagues for their lasting support and help, which have made possible my intensive travels in first half of this year.

And, surely, thanks also go to my intern colleagues Zheng Jinqiang, Zhang Zhaoqing, Wang Kequ and Chen Junyu, for their help in arranging and participating in the interviews and in the process of my writing this book.

Surely, too, writing means a lot of sacrifice for family and of leisure time. I must thank my wife and my son for their understanding and assistance for years.

Of course, this book is imperfect, and I take responsibility for any fault within it.

CONTENTS

01

CHAPTER ONE

Belt and Road Initiative fits into the recovery goals of the EU, though this bloc sends mixed signals

In September 2013, when Xi Jinping made his debut as Chinese president at the G20 summit in St. Petersburg in Russia, his team was so proactive in presenting the country's ideas that the G20 delegation of China was the first one to hold a press conference hours before the opening of the leaders' gathering. Such vigorous diplomacy was followed by Xi's making public the Silk Road Economic Belt initiative in Astana, Kazakhstan in a speech during the second leg of his tour that year.

I was at the G20 summit in Russia and realised the significance of the Economic Belt proposal, which, I figured, would be dominating the new Chinese leadership's diplomatic chessboard in the coming years. Xi was elected as the highest leader of the CPC in late 2012, and in early 2013 he started his term as Chinese president. His raising the Silk Road Economic Belt initiative, in a speech at a university in Astana, was extended by his idea of constructing the 21st century Maritime Silk Road, which was proposed during his trip to Indonesia in October 2013. As a continued and integrated approach to implementing China's endeavour to open up and introduce reform, the proposals responded to the West's consistent call in recent years for Beijing to shoulder more global responsibility. Since the 2008-2009 financial crisis, these demands have become ever more insistent. It is helpful to have a closer look at how Europe responded to China's initiative in the subsequent years.

In the first half of 2017, starting in Greece and finishing in Switzerland, my intensive odyssey to nail down how European countries are responding to the Belt and Road Initiative, which President Xi Jinping raised more than three years ago, has discovered loads of new thoughts. Patiently talking with about 100 politicians, officials, thinkers, lawyers and business people, and digging out stories in ports, airports, factories and construction sites during the previous weeks, has been an enlightening journey. The interviews have enriched my understanding, even though I have been closely observing this initiative since its announcement. Talks with former Italian Prime Minister Romano Prodi summarised my major findings well : calling it a century-long project that will benefit half of humanity, he says Europeans are competing with each other to find synergy with China's Belt and Road Initiative. He has urged that Italy should not be left behind in this competition. Basically, this proposal is about China's clear-cut message of reinventing universal peace and prosperity, especially given the worsening geopolitical situation in some regions of the world and the continuous negative impact of the financial and debt crisis which originated in the United States and Europe nearly 10 years ago.

For the previous four years, the biggest role the Belt and Road Initiative has played is to have been a catalyst, helping other countries to re-position their advantages and uniqueness in a geopolitical way, while placing Asia, Europe and Africa in a long production supply chain or economic corridor. Many countries have rekindled their passion and found the courage to roll out their long-term national development strategies. For example, Greece is determined to become a regional shipping, energy and transportation hub. Hungary and the Czech Republic have indicated they want to be regional centres for aviation, logistics and finance. The Republic of Serbia aims to be a gateway to the Balkan region. This is inspiring as the ambitions and their implementation will not only develop these countries' economies, create more jobs and improve local livelihoods but also bridge the regional differences in Europe.

It is fair to say that Western Europe so far has shown less passion than the rest of the continent, and its countries have not clearly spelled out their national strategy for finding common ground in implementing the Belt and Road Initiative. This is not worth worrying about. As time goes on, these countries will find more opportunities to catch up. Italy has recently cooperated with ZTE, a Chinese telecommunications giant, in a $1 billion project to boost its telecommunication infrastructure and prepare the country for the 5G era. This means improving connectivity, creating opportunities in the developed economies if both sides are determined to find them. Switzerland has set another example by working as an observer in the cooperation framework of China and the 16 central and eastern European countries. This has created very good conditions for third-party cooperation by involving Switzerland and China in central and eastern Europe.

Nearly all the rich countries in Europe are members of the Asian Infrastructure Investment Bank, and through this vehicle, they will find more opportunities for cooperation. In a nutshell, this initiative is not only about China's outbound flow of capital, technology, human resources and ideas, but naturally includes the inward flow from abroad into China. And it is even more about the meeting in the middle of contributions from both China and Western Europe. Pragmatism dictates that delivering the Belt and Road

Initiative needs patience. Some European countries still need structural reform and their legal systems are complicated, which requires businesses to have second thoughts when finalising their investment plans. Nearly everything takes time to change. In interviewing China's telecommunications giant ZTE's branch in Rome, its slogan of Tomorrow Never Waits also rings a bell with me. To deliver the Belt and Road Initiative's inclusiveness, tolerance and even flexibility will count in achieving mutual understanding and joint action.

GRADUAL PROCESS OF ACCEPTANCE

Back in the early days when the Initiative was shaped, I was probably among the first batch of people to explore the linkage of China's Belt and Road Initiative and the European Union's investment scheme. I proposed in my column, penned in late 2014, about feeling delighted that now it has become a leading foreign policy of the two economies, though its realization is far from complete. The following is the piece which has appeared in *China Daily* in late 2014:

"At first, when Beijing offers its solutions to the world, other powers are inclined to simply turn the other way. One example of this happened when the European Commission's new president, Jean-Claude Juncker, held his first meeting with Chinese President Xi at the G20 summit in Brisbane, Australia in 2014. If the published reports were to be believed, then Juncker, whose main priority should be to drive growth by expanding investment, failed to even mention the Belt and Road Initiative when he met Xi. But China and the European Union had decided, when Xi was in Brussels earlier that year, to work together on the matter. At that time, Juncker was not in power in the EU. Indeed, the Brisbane tete-a-tete was not even mentioned on the EC president's website.

But since Xi presented the proposal, China has gone all out to make it a reality. At home, every provincial region of the Chinese mainland has been asked to submit proposals on becoming part of this Eurasian ambition. In October 2014, Premier Li Keqiang explained the initiative at the Asia-Europe leaders' summit in Milan. Shortly before the Asia-Pacific Economic

Cooperation meeting in Beijing in November that year, Xi even chaired a special meeting to discuss the Belt and Road Initiative, which is an effort to give impetus to China to invest and export overseas after decades of attracting an inward flow of capital and technology. During the APEC Economic Leaders' Week in 2014, Beijing announced a contribution of $40 billion to the Silk Road Fund, after the establishment of the Asian Infrastructure Investment Bank on 24 October that year. Though the Belt and Road Initiative was still in its formative stages in 2014, there was no doubt that it was one of the most decisive measures taken under the leadership of Xi Jinping. The initiatives would directly affect 3 billion people in Asia and Europe and would draw worldwide attention.

Unlike the United States when it developed the Marshall Plan for Europe decades ago, Xi said in September 2013 that the initiatives were aimed at increasing the flow of trade, investment, capital, people and culture while focusing on infrastructure projects. Juncker outlined similar aims in a priority plan he announced before he took office on 1st November 2014, a plan aimed at strengthening the EU market. His team had been working on his priorities for 2015, including details of his proposal to mobilize 315 billion euros ($393 billion) of investment over the coming three years. In 2014, the EU was still on the verge of slipping into its third economic recession in six years, and it was high time it started thinking laterally. China's Belt and Road Initiative could give it a fresh burst of enthusiasm even as it pressed on with long-awaited structural reforms. At the turn of this century, China decided to expand its opening and reform drive to the hinterland by implementing its "go-west" strategy. Nowadays when you consider the EU and its 28 member states, you could be forgiven for having an eerie sense of déjà vu, for Europe's eastern, central and southern regions lag behind those of the west and the north.

Just as the disparity in wealth between Chinese regions gave the central government the impetus to act to fix this, Europe now has similar reasons—and opportunities—in dealing with its economic disparities. For example, some have talked of turning the geopolitically important Greek capital, Athens, into a Mediterranean shipping and financial centre akin to Hong Kong or Shanghai. Consider, too, the EU's rather modest ambitions to upgrade its infrastructure. It has less than 7,000 kilometers of high-speed rail and plans to extend this to 15,000 km by 2030. I say modest because it has had high-speed rail since the 1980s. China, on the other hand, said hello to the age of high-speed rail a little more than ten years ago. Now its high-speed lines stretch for about 22,000 km, and by 2020 they will cover 30,000 km. In imitating China's plan, the EU needs to think ambitiously—for example, building a high-speed railway or highway to link Beijing, Brussels, Paris and even London.

These plans are not pies in the sky but utterly feasible. Beijing and Moscow have been working on plans to link each other by high-speed rail, and Moscow is not far from central and eastern Europe. But the EU, compared with its member states, is still conservative when it comes to expanding its relationship with China. It wants to conclude investment talks between China and the EU first. It is not even willing to start free trade agreement talks with China, which sharply contrasts with the EU's desire to quickly strike such a deal with the US. However, the EU will have not just one but two great chances to put its cards on the table with China in 2015, when they meet at two summits. It may well be then that China's westward stare will meet Europe's eastward glance, and the EU will then have some positive things for Beijing's Silk Road projects."

GREEN AND DIGITAL BRI

The writing above helped me to become the first prize winner of the China Journalism Award in 2015. I am also pleased that during my stay in Europe, I worked with some scholars who helped enrich the concept of the Belt and Road Initiative.

On 17 March 2016 in Paris, *China Daily* and Neoma Business School in France jointly organised a seminar at which the concept of the "Green Belt and Road Initiative" was shaped. Five months later, President Xi started to use the concept of Green BRI while chairing a conference on the initiative. This resulted from a discussion with Professor Zhang Haiyan, Director of the Neoma Business School-Confucius Institute for Business. We decided to use this theme as the topic of China's New Silk Road Initiative Conference in Paris, at which European business representatives and academics expressed confidence that China would offer green industrial technologies to engage countries along Belt and Road Initiative routes to create better connectivity in Asia, Europe and Africa.

The green approach was discussed by more than 150 participants attending the event, including representatives from Confucius Institutes and Chinese and European business representatives from the Bank of China, the Chinese car-maker BYD, the Chinese telecommunications giant Huawei and the French power company EDF. Zhang said there had been rising interest in economic and industrial development between Asia and Europe since the announcement of the Belt and Road Initiative in 2013. But concerns had also been expressed about environmental feasibility and consequences, which had been perceived more as key issues in the implementation of the Silk Road initiative, especially in the context of rising worries about climate change. "This is the background to why we are cooperating with *China Daily* to organise this event. But from the discussions we held, we find that China is keen on promoting green cooperation and realising green development with other countries along the Silk Road," Zhang said.

I am also thinking about the Belt and Road Initiative in the context that we are in the digital era. Mobile phone users in China will not have to pay roaming charges while travelling on the Chinese mainland from October 2017, and people in European Union member countries started enjoying the same concession within the EU from mid-June of 2017. Many in China say the move made by China Mobile, China Unicom and China Telecom was influenced by cell phone users' shift to social media to communicate with friends and relatives. For example, there are more than 800 million WeChat users in China who can all use the app to send messages, buy tickets, order meals, book hotel rooms, and even hail taxis. Many other users prefer WhatsApp or Skype, which means the competitiveness of mobile phone service providers has been eroded.

To some extent, the same reason forced the EU telecom companies to scrap the roaming charges, although the Europeans generally spend less time on social media than their Chinese counterparts. The EU has also been thinking of setting up a single digital market, which is high on the agenda of the European Commission. Cancelling the roaming charges is a decisive move by mobile phone service providers to unite the fragmented telecom market in the 28-member bloc, which is now facing tremendous existential challenges. Operators in the EU and China should now consider other, bigger moves, since they have a combined market of 1.9 billion consumers. China and the EU are now in tough negotiations to achieve a high-level investment agreement. Hopefully, the officials are also discussing the prospects of deeper market penetration by telecom companies in China and the EU. And now that Chinese and EU telecom companies have decided to cancel the roaming charges within their own economies, they should also consider cancelling international roaming charges for people travelling to and from the two economies. Such a move has the potential to expand their digital markets. Although it may be difficult to persuade the telecom giants on both sides to do so, it will be worth the effort as it will make the use of mobile phones less taxing. The telecom operators, in the long run, will have no reason to keep international roaming charges so high. Again, the benefits will be immense if a single EU-China digital market can be formed, as it will remove many communication barriers and help boost the flow of investments.

As the China-led Belt and Road Initiative is aimed at bringing Asia, Europe and Africa closer, the formation of an EU-China digital market with free roaming will be an apt example of how to create an even bigger market. In 2018, the main theme of China-EU ties is tourism. And the two sides would do better to discuss the possibility of cancelling roaming charges for mobile phone users travelling between the two economies, because it will help boost the tourism industries in both economies.

ACCUMULATED RECOGNITION

China has called the Belt and Road Initiative a proposal for achieving common peace and prosperity as the overarching umbrella of its diplomacy, and it will be further expanded by cooperation with the EU. Most of the European Union's member states expressed their enthusiastic willingness to become part of the Belt and Road Initiative at the Beijing forum. Greek Prime Minister Alexis Tsipras has says this initiative highlights a vision of connectivity, cooperation and dialogue across Europe and Asia, but also in other parts of the world. Hungarian Prime Minister Viktor Orban was also one of European leaders at the Beijing forum, saying the old globalisation model was obsolete and "the East has caught up with the West." On the Belt and Road Initiative, he saw it as "another direction of movement, which is specifically built on mutual acceptance. Orban called the modernisation of the 350-km Budapest-Belgrade railway line the "most spectacular" agreement signed between China, the Republic of Serbia and his country.

In participating in the initiative, the countries involved have benefitted not only from infrastructure improvement but also from being connected with a global supply chain. The UK, still a full EU member although Brexit talks have been launched, also supports the initiative with determination. British Chancellor Philip Hammond says the UK, lying at the western end of the Belt and Road, is a "natural partner" in this endeavour, and Britain has for centuries been one of the strongest advocates of an open global trading system. He says Britain can also be a natural partner in delivering infrastructure in Belt and Road countries by supporting the finance and planning needed. The UK has been a pioneer in this regard. When China took the initiative of launching the Asian Infrastructure Investment Bank in early 2015, the UK was the first Western country to respond in spite of America's protests. Now, with the latest member Greece, roughly half of all European countries have joined the newly-born multilateral financial institution. And even the European Investment Bank has recently signed a memorandum of understanding with the AIIB, which has about 80 members now after launching in early 2016.

In spite of the active response from member states and businesses, the EU has not reflected their collective enthusiasm. When Jyrki Katainen, Vice President of the European Commission, addressed the Beijing forum, he said China was at one end of the Belt and Road, Europe at the other. But he still hesitated. He continued: "Done the right way, more investment in cross-border links could unleash huge growth potential with benefits for us all." Katainen was repeating the principles of openness, transparency and sustainability which China had already emphasised in the initiative vision paper published in early 2015. However, experts and China observers had been urging the European Union to speak from the same page as its member states. "The views of EU member states and businesses will be central to implementing the Belt and Road, and the success of the project will be based on building common commercial interests more than anything else," says Duncan Freeman, a research fellow of the EU-China Research Centre of the College of Europe.

He adds that the Beijing forum, held in May 2017, had already demonstrated that the idea of the Belt and Road had attained a significant level of global influence, to which the European Union should pay ample attention. He also says the documents issued at the forum provided a greater degree of detail about how the Belt and Road would be implemented and how they would affect relations between China and other partners to the initiative. "A common understanding between Europe and China of the Belt and Road will be the key to successfully implementing the strategy as a partnership," Freeman says. Romano Prodi, former European Commission president and former Italian Prime Minister, noted "competition among European countries" in exploring synergies with the Belt and Road Initiative, which was encouraging. But he regrets the lack of coordination existing at the European level. "We aroused the interest of many universities and businessmen, and you must know this is an economic and political project," says Prodi, a political guru in the EU. Calling it a century-long project which could offer a better livelihood to half of global humanity, Prodi says: "We have to use all the patience that we need for political cooperation."

Despite that then, Chinese ambassador to the EU Yang Yanyi showed her satisfaction towards the development synergies between the two partners. "It is fair to say that China and Europe share much in common in pursuing shared growth, development and connectivity, including through the Belt and Road initiative, and have come up with a proud record so far," she said.

When President Xi visited the European Union headquarters in early 2014, both sides started to talk about the issue. When Premier Li held a summit with his European counterparts in Brussels in 2015, both sides agreed to support synergies between the Belt and Road initiative and the 315 billion euro European Investment Plan. At the member country level, China and some European countries signed an inter-governmental cooperation document and launched a Belt and Road working group mechanism to jointly advance the Initiative. Bilaterally, China launched a rail freight service with some European countries, including the first direct rail link between China and Great Britain, which went into operation early in 2017. "Bilateral or trilateral cooperation in such areas as railways, ports, airports, power, transportation and logistics between China and European countries have also gathered momentum," Yang says. Looking ahead, Yang says China and the EU should stay committed to free trade and economic openness, to a rules-based, transparent and fair international trading regime and order. She also says time would prove wrong and unwarranted the notion that this project was designed to access new markets for China and presented a challenge and even a threat to the future of Europe.

In fact, more than three years after President Xi proposed his Belt and Road Initiative, many Chinese and European scholars have dedicated their research to it, and they are my frequent contacts. Men Jing, the Belgium-based College of Europe's professor of EU-China relations, is among them. After completing interviews that examined how the mega-proposal could impact relations between China and the European Union in 2016, she found that leading Europeans had come to realise the win-win benefits of the plan, designed to bring the Eurasian continent closer. "Their responses are in general positive and they have recognised the significance of President Xi's proposal," says Men in her campus office in the picturesque medieval town of Bruges during a talk with me in October 2016. She says the survey results came after her team, consisting of three colleagues, intensively interviewed about 40 business people, think tank experts and European officials, starting in June 2016.

As well as holding face-to-face talks, they also sent questionnaires, eliciting replies from the top-ranking 20 think tanks in Europe, which had already published papers on China's proposal to construct a Silk Road Economic Belt and a 21st century Maritime Silk Road. Xi put forward the two ideas when he was visiting central and southeast Asia in September and October of 2013. Essentially, the "belt" includes countries situated on the original Silk Road through central and western Asia, the Middle East and Europe. But Beijing says it hasn't defined boundaries, and all the countries that have shown an interest can consult with each other. Men says many Europeans already know about the proposal, on which China and the United Nations have signed a joint memorandum. "When I talk with them, nobody believes this is a project of strategic threat, but they all trust this will be a mutually beneficial big idea," Men says in response to claims that the China-led proposal may be a threat to the rest of the world. After three years of work, and China's tremendous efforts to make part of the proposal a reality, Men concludes: "Such a misunderstanding has gone."

On 1 April 2014, nearly six months after Xi proposed the Belt and Road Initiative, he visited the College of Europe on the final leg of his first Western European tour as Chinese president. That day, Xi endorsed the setting-up of the college's EU-China Research Centre, which mainly trains personnel for EU institutions. He says the two sides needed to forge a partnership of peace, growth, reform and civilisation. Professor Men joined the college and took responsibility as the EU-China professor in 2008.

As director of the research centre, Men says for the next stage the focus should be on the benefits the opportunities the Belt and Road Initiative has brought. In the past three years, China has signed agreements with up to 30 countries linking their national programmes of economic and social development, and some of them, such as Poland, the Czech Republic and Greece, are in Europe. In June 2015, China and the European Union signed an agreement on synergy between the Belt and Road Initiative and Europe's $350 billion investment plan, which will be expanded in time and scale after three years of operation.

Both sides have reached consensus on exploring the synergies of mega-projects to boost trade and investment flow, and China is the first country outside the EU to join the investment plan. But they have not reached common ground at a technical level. "Reportedly, the European Union side welcomes Chinese investment in the scheme, but is not willing to grant it a voice on the board, which Beijing will not agree with," says Men. "So uncertainties still exist when going into detailed talks."

Men also says southern, eastern and central Europeans are more interested in the project than their peers in the west, who maintain the Belt and Road routes do not cover the western part of Europe. In fact, Xi took the concept from the ancient Silk Road, which extended to Italy centuries ago. "Brussels is truly different from Athens," Men says. She felt "joyful" when talking about her interview experience in the Greek port of Piraeus, where China COSCO Shipping Corporation has established a major presence. It rented its container terminals several years ago and acquired a 67 percent stake in the Piraeus Port Authority this year. "Nobody in the port authority left when COSCO stepped in and I found hardly any Chinese in the building when I was interviewing there," Men says.

"The Greek people I approached were happy about the job-saving deal and they are convinced by the credentials of COSCO in Piraeus." Up to 1,000 Greeks are working in the container terminals, having kept their jobs even during the depths of the sovereign debt crisis, says Men. "And the Greeks are expecting, with help from COSCO, to revive their ship-repairing industry, which has shifted to other parts of the world." But what is even more ambitious is a plan to link maritime transport with railways, which will help make Piraeus one of the largest container transfer ports in the Mediterranean, as well as a gateway to central and eastern Europe. "This is more challenging, and will require deep coordination among different European countries," says Men. She says her field trip to Greece had helped her better understand the tangible benefits China's proposal had brought.

"First of all, it is about jobs, which Europeans badly need." As a professor of EU-China relations, Men says she herself has experienced a learning curve after Xi's proposal. From 2014, she has been invited to speak at various seminars on the topic in China and Europe.

She started organising seminars to explore the views of both sides and how the concept should be further deepened. Focusing most of her research energy on the topic in recent years, she says the academic activities have helped Europeans better understand the proposal. Mao Xinya, Director of the Belt and Road Initiative Research Centre at the China Executive Leadership Academy in Shanghai, went to the College of Europe to work as a visiting scholar in early 2016, and they initiated the research project on the impact Xi's proposal has had on China-EU relations. As well as interviews and surveys, their team has also done research on the role Turkey can play in implementing the synergy of China and the EU's mega-projects. In late 2016, they held a seminar on the outcome of their research in the European Parliament and it was hosted by Jo Leinen, President of the European Parliament's delegation for relations with China. As the Belt and Road Initiative has become a platform for China to deepen relations with the rest of the world, Men says her research centre will focus hard on those areas. "The proposal and its impact on Sino-EU relations will be our research priority for the years to come," says Men. "We hope we can do research in a more innovative way in the future and bring in more outcomes and perspectives."

02

CHAPTER TWO

Reviving the cradle of Western
civilisation by linking with the Silk
Road

E uropean countries have all inherited natural advantages and highly-developed strengths. For example, no other continent has such a stable physical structure (scarcely does an earthquake ever damage it except for Italy and Greece) and temperate weather. On top of that, Greece has its own individual appeal. For Chinese students, the first page of European history has always been dedicated to this country, which has only half of Beijing's population, 11 million.

But that historic pride has been overshadowed in recent years. Since my first trip to Athens in October 2010, when the European debt upheaval had begun to engulf Greece and the rest of Europe, I have had numerous opportunities to talk with officials of various ranks, academics, business leaders and even taxi drivers and jobless people on the streets, in a country which most likely ranks among the world's top ten regarding the assets it holds. Basically, Greece is already in the upper tier of global development geography: its per capita GDP is much higher than that of China and its human development index ranking is also better than China's. But its sky-high debt had disrupted its economic cycle and the government could not sustain its pensions, health care and even civil servant payment, not to mention investment in infrastructural expansion.

In keeping with the Chinese saying that the intelligent people hide among the grassroots, two interviewees gave me their ardent, visionary and clear-cut messages of how to save Greece from crisis amid the wide-ranging depression and even anger voiced by ordinary Greeks in recent years. These two enlightening encounters still stuck in my heart, as their shared arguments are so self-explanatory and inspiring: Greece, the cradle of Western civilisation, deserves the same economic miracle that China has achieved after decades of opening up and reform.

Obviously my two Greek interviewees expressed their insights not directly within the context of the Belt and Road Initiative, which was proposed by President Xi Jinping in late 2013. But the essence of what they argue is roughly identical to China's proposal: Greece must think out of the box and achieve prosperity and peace through bold and innovative strategies of linking its people and businesses with the vast terrain of the Eurasian continent and of Africa.

In late 2011, I met my first interviewee Christos Vlachos, a tall middle-aged Greek, similar to many members of the Greek elite class, who completed his excellent education in the UK. As managing partner at Athens-based Silky Finance, an independent financial adviser who works at assisting companies in restructuring or raising finance, Vlachos has been one of my key contact persons in Greece, and every time I have visited he has met me, showing tremendous hospitality. And I even visited his lovely mother in a traditional community in Athens where we had dinner at a local restaurant which they frequent. I can still remember how the restaurant owner was so delighted to take a photo with me. Vlachos says that when he has visited China he has been treated in the same way, though I have not yet had the chance to be his host in my country.

Back in the winter of 2011, when Greeks were suffering from the wounds of austerity cuts, Vlachos called for inspiration for his people, who he believed still possessed many historic, economic, cultural, social and geographical assets with which to earn a much better future. He believed that political leaders had the means to deliver this if they wanted, adding that the country urgently needed political unity at a time when snap elections came in quick succession.

Vlachos says the leaders needed to show decisiveness, courage and determination to lead the people out of financial chaos. Over dinner he told me in a tone which thrilled me: "Greeks need to be inspired with the leaders' short-term measures and long-term vision." For example, he said, could Greece think about asking for China's investment to build a high-speed railway to link Athens and Thessalonica in the north of Greece, the country's second largest city? He said it was beyond imagination what this 500-kilometre project could give to Greece.

Five or six years ago, high-speed railways had already become popular in China, shortening the distance between cities. Having spent a lot of time witnessing China's speedy changes in recent years, Vlachos strongly wishes to import China's miracles into his country. "We have been waiting a long time for inspiring decisions from our leaders and they should think beyond austerity. We should not be let down again and again," Vlachos demanded in 2011.

My other unforgettable conversation took place in June 2014, when I was interviewing an experienced ship-owner in Greece. His vision, that Athens would become like Hong Kong, a global shipping and financial hub, was so stimulating that it has stayed fresh in my mind ever since. As a veteran industry leader, born in 1942, George Gratsos, President of the Hellenic Chamber of Shipping, had travelled to many thriving ports worldwide, and he strongly believes that China is an example for Greece.

During our interview in his Athens office, just a block away from the Hellenic Parliament, he said in a low voice: "Greece's proximity to south, east and central Europe, and its strong rail links, make the port an ideal distribution centre for goods, and the Greek authorities should cooperate further with a major port operator, preferably from the Far East. COSCO's [the Chinese shipping giant] operation has been a wonderful success, and we support its expanded presence in Piraeus."

He adds, that "Athens has the ability to become the next Hong Kong if both sides share their vision to boost it as a global shipping and commercial centre", and this has become a frequent quote on the many occasions I have written about Greece, a country whose population numbers more or less the same as Switzerland, Belgium or Sweden.

Nearly four decades ago, when China started its first steps in opening up and reform, Hong Kong was an example for the fishing village of Shenzhen to follow. Over the years, Shenzhen has become a success story, growing into a giant city that now houses a population the size of Greece's. And now Shenzhen is an example that will be used as China develops its Xiong'an New Area, another economic zone near Beijing. Certainly, as a gateway between Europe, Asia and Africa, Athens enjoys a good geopolitical position. But the key to whether this is exploited lies in how the Greek leadership turns such an opportunity into action, and how the European Union supports that. If things go well, Greeks will one day enjoy the same levels of development as the people of Hong Kong and Shenzhen, and eventually surpass the living standards of the Swiss and the Dutch.

GREEK TAKEOFF AND THE BRI

Greece is one of the countries which has already developed infrastructure blueprints when talking about implementing the Belt and Road Initiative.

Traditionally, when Chinese or other Asian companies export to western, central or even eastern Europe by sea, the container ship normally travels through the Indian Ocean and the Mediterranean Sea, arrives at Western Europe's ports and then offloads its cargo.

The freight could still take many more days in trucks or trains before it reaches its destination. In recent years, time and cost-saving alternatives have taken shape. By making good use of the improved infrastructure conditions of the Greek port of Piraeus, which is managed by China's shipping giant COSCO, the containers can be uploaded there and directly transported to Budapest in Hungary via Skopje in Macedonia and the the Republic of Serbian capital, Belgrade, by railway. The land-sea express passage, agreed by all the countries along the line, is workable, though it moves relatively slowly right now because the rail tracks need modernising. And sometimes the railway has been disrupted by refugees arriving in Macedonia.

The passage from Piraeus to the cargo's destination is just a tiny part of the Belt and Road Initiative, proposed by President Xi in 2013 to better connect Asia, Europe and Africa by improving infrastructure conditions and boosting trade and investment flows. The Greek government has clearly recognised how this initiative will help realise its national strategy of becoming a regional transport, energy and economic hub in the Balkans, the Mediterranean Sea region and North Africa. Importantly, this can help inject more Chinese investment into the infrastructure to speed up the flow. A high-speed railway linking Budapest and Belgrade is in the pipeline already, and the Greeks are fond of similar projects.

Such developments have helped Prime Minister Alexis Tsipras to conclude that "Greece has a strategic role in this initiative" during the speech he made in Beijing at the Belt and Road Initiative Forum in May 2017. As a leader who took his starting point from the cradle of Western civilisation, Tsipras referred to history. Hundreds of years ago, he says, in 550 AD, the Byzantine Emperor Justinian sent Christian monks to the East in order to discover the secrets of the development of silk: "Apparently, after many adventures, they returned to modern-day Thrace with silkworm cocoons hidden in their staffs, introducing silk to Europe for the first time."

But Tsipras pointed out that if the story of the Silk Road is retold today, the world would recall not only an economic history of cooperation and competition between great powers, religions, nations and commercial interests, but a history of people, their contact and communication. "We would not only see how the Silk Road developed from the top down, but also from the bottom up. The commercial and cultural contacts of the Greek and Chinese people stretch back thousands of years," Tsipras was reported to have said.

Though the Chinese and the Greeks have traded, worked with each other, travelled to each others' lands and inspired each other with their struggles, according to Tsipras, the real acceleration of economic, cultural, educational, research exchanges and tourism has taken place only in the last few years, with the development of the bilateral strategic partnership and then the development of the Belt and Road Initiative.

Tsipras, a leader who never wears a tie, says his understanding was that this Initiative is based on the development of infrastructure and connectivity projects bringing Europe and Asia, as well as other parts of the world, closer together. "But if it remains only a series of projects, it will not fulfill the vision on which it is based. It will not be a vibrant Silk Road of the 21st century. The Belt and Road Initiative gives us a remarkable platform with which to connect initiatives enhancing people-to-people contact and I believe we should make full use of it," Tsipras has stressed. "In general, I believe strongly that the Belt and Road Initiative needs a strong dimension of people-to-people projects to fulfill its vision. A vision that—as we engineers say—needs deep foundations so it can be supported from the bottom up."

Tsipras' supportive policy of privatisation has not come easily. In recent years, successes that political parties of the far left and far right have chalked up in Europe impede the continent's push towards integration even as its economic woes continue.

In European parliamentary elections in May 2014, parties of the far right, which oppose European integration, won more seats than many had expected. In Greece on 26 January 2015, it was a party of the far left, Syriza, that won the elections, and its leader Tsipras, then 40, was sworn in as Prime Minister of the debt-ridden country the next day.

The rise of far-right parties stirred a lot of debates in those days, especially on the issues of how integration should be implemented across Europe in the process of the United Kingdom's leaving the European Union [agreed in the 2016 referendum]. The Syriza Party is not against EU membership and the eurozone. Rather, it advocates the removal of austerity measures and renegotiating with its international debtors about how to pay its sky-high debt of 240 billion, as it was then. Before his election victory, Tsipras said his top priority would be to restore the country's lost dignity, which had been reduced by pension and salary cuts, jobs lost and an exodus of foreign investment over the past few years.

When he was elected, whispers on the streets in Athens indicated that many Greeks were sceptical about whether Tsipras could deliver on his promises. There had been talk that Tsipras' success might cause a political quake and market shockwaves. Is what Tsipras advocating wrong? For a country deep in economic recession, austerity measures are normally not sound policy options. On the other hand, Keynesian economics, featuring infrastructure construction, are the ideal. Greece's situation is far from normal because it also has high fiscal debt, unacceptable on the basis of European accounting rules. This means it cannot sustain its development by issuing more bonds. This is the dilemma that Tsipras must face. While writing off the country's debt is not an option, he could start engaging with lenders to extend their payments.

Returning dignity to the country is about paying off its IOUs. Tsipras and his team have invested a lot of energy and time to negotiate with Brussels and the International Monetary Fund to reach compromises. The other important thing is returning the country to its social and economic dynamics. The country's dignity is also about productivity. But these are all easier said than done. To realise these goals, what is most important for Greece is to attract capital to set up factories and improve the efficiency of its state assets. The previous government had announced extensive privatisation plans, including selling the country's biggest port, Piraeus, in which COSCO had expressed an interest. When Tsipras was elected, the new government put a halt to the sale. That is because Tsipras' party opposed privatisation and foreign investment. Is this feasible in the current global situation?

Back then, in my column, I asked Tsipras to rethink, especially about his need to compromise, which could ensure Greeks to chose between relaxing austerity and a return to economic dynamism. I insisted that Greece had many ways in which it could regain its competitiveness. But Greece needs a middle path that can trigger development without political uncertainties, which are an anathema for both Greeks and investors.

In looking back, Prime Minister Tsipras has made compromises towards his party lines, especially in retaining China's investment. President Xi says that, during the Prime Minister's visit to Beijing in May 2017, that the two countries should expand cooperation in infrastructure, energy and telecommunications, and Greece is an important part of China's new Silk Road initiative. Xi says that at present, China and Greece's traditional friendship and cooperation continued to glow with new dynamism.

Greece's active participation in the Belt and Road Initiative is also shown in its becoming a member of the Beijing-led Asian Infrastructure Investment Bank and participating in the share capital of the new multilateral financial platform. Shortly before the opening of the Belt and Road Forum which the Greek Prime Minister and 27 other global leaders attended, Greece won the membership of AIIB following in the footsteps of many European countries.

In fact, Greece moved comparatively late. Its application process started in mid-2016, about six months after the AIIB's official operation. And in March 2015, the Western European powers, led by the UK, had applied for the bank's founding status in spite of the opposition of the United States. The Greek government believed that the decision was part of the government's "general strategy to develop collaboration with international collective investment institutions, with the aim of security financing for high added value investment plans."

"With Professor Panagiotis Roumeliotis acting as the negotiator and representative of the Greek side, Greece obtained its membership only ten months after its official request was submitted. The AIIB will be able to finance projects by Greek companies in the Middle East, China and the rest of Asia, as well as projects in Greece carried out by companies based in Asian countries," according to the press statement. Greece planned to participate in the share capital with about 10 million euros ($11 million).

Greek President Prokopis Pavlopoulos is also a strong supporter of President Xi's initiative. He was quoted in early 2017 as saying that Greece, as a European Union member state, is encouraging greater cooperation between the EU and China, and it's in this direction that it (Greece) is promoting every initiative that brings Europe closer to Asia.

The Greek president has highlighted the maritime Silk Road by saying it is of particular importance, given that the port of Piraeus is the first European point of entry via the new Suez Canal. He says: "COSCO's investment at the port of Piraeus is an example of the amicable and mutually beneficial cooperation between Greece and China, and showcases Piraeus as one of the most significant hubs in the geo-strategic connection between China, and all of Asia, with Europe."

The president says that Greece "wholeheartedly supports this initiative," within the framework of the strategic cooperation with China; and Greece was ready to work together, resourcefully, in this direction. "As countries that are inheritors of two of the most ancient civilisations, Greece and China have always appreciated and supported each other, developing cooperation on multiple levels," says President Pavlopoulos.

In fact, at the political level, Chinese and Greek leaders have been in close exchanges in recent years to lay the foundations to deepen cooperation on all fronts. President Xi made a technical stopover on the Greek island of Rhodes on his way to Brazil in July 2014 and met ex-Prime Minister Antonis Samaras. Xi met Prime Minister Tsipras in New York in September 2015 before their meeting in Beijing last year during the Greek leader's visit. Samaras met Premier Li Keqiang when he visited Greece in 2014 and Li met Tsipras in Beijing in 2016. During the encounters, deeper and strategic cooperation to match each other's development blueprints were put high on the agenda and all Greece's leaders showed great commitment in attracting Chinese investment, while appreciating China's courage in expanding investment in debt-trapped Greece while some other investors fled away.

During an interview with me in March 2017, Chinese ambassador to Greece Zou Xiaoli famously said in his embassy residence that for the Belt and Road Initiative, the political parties in Greece have formed a consensus despite the fact that they disagree with each other on many issues. Former Greek prime minister Antonis Samaras visited China at the end of July 2017, and he won appreciation from the Chinese Premier, Li Keqiang, who thanked Samaras for his support of the Belt and Road Initiative while he headed the Greek government. They became friends when Li visited Greece in 2015, and then Samaras told Li they were true friends, the sort that can exchange ideas with each other while looking at each other in the eye.

BEING WITH GREECE IN DIFFICULT TIMES

When Samaras was elected prime minister in 2012, Greece was on the verge of collapse, with uncontrolled default, a forced exit from the euro, and social upheaval. In the middle of 2014, in a written response to my interview, he boasted that now all these calamities seemed so "distant" in Greece, while China, among a number of countries, stood on the Greek side during this difficult period. "I cannot express how much we appreciate that and how grateful we feel", Samaras wrote to me. In the present world, Samaras says, Greece was best positioned to be the "gateway" of Europe for international trade with the Far East and the Middle East, all the way through the Suez Canal and the Mediterranean, to and from the markets of central and eastern Europe.

But this required investment on a number of infrastructure fronts, like major ports, highways and railways, and Greece had already made a good start with Piraeus. And now there are plans to expand in many directions, he says.

Shipbuilding is another area of mutual interest, together with the maritime industry in general. After all 15 percent of the world sea trade is conducted by vessels under Greek ownership. And tourism, of course, is an area of cooperation already expanding, with a very high potential. "Greece is the natural first step for Chinese people to visit Europe," says Samaras.

And Greek civilisation offers outstanding attractions for people who can really appreciate time transcending culture. Perhaps Chinese people can appreciate what Greece has to offer in this field better than others, since they themselves are very proud of their own civilisation. "After all, 'Sila' in your language literally means 'the other civilisation', " he says.

"You see, culture is not 'something of the past'. It is a dynamic phenomenon which defines people today and generates strong spiritual relations between countries."

But Samaras says there was a strong commercial element in the economic relationship being built step by step. As a country on the "Mediterranean diet", a host of unique Greek agricultural products—raw, processed and manufactured—can be introduced to the Chinese market, from extra virgin olive oil, to feta cheese, excellent wines and various herbs.

For him, a number of areas of mutual interest included specific investment plans, trade agreements and expanding the cooperation, and both sides were making tangible progress and building a solid relationship with enormous prospects for both countries. During Samaras's period, he says privatisation projects had a slow start due to structural rigidities but they were gaining momentum. There had already been a "breakthrough" in Piraeus, where a pioneering investment by COSCO, back in 2009, had already proved a big success.

"Thus we are now building on this and we are trying to expand it further. I believe that the COSCO investment is only the beginning of strategic Chinese involvement in Greek infrastructure projects, in the process of opening up a major 'European corridor'. "

A number of privatisation schemes that had matured in Greece were candidates for the next concrete steps, including railway projects and even airport hubs.

Samaras strongly believes that the commercial ties between China and Europe—this is actually the "big picture"—should be reshaped in terms of opening up rather than closing down, lowering barriers rather than raising new ones, and of course, on mutually beneficial terms.

"Notice the words I have chosen to describe the strategic aspects of our common prospects: a 'gateway' between China and Europe, in terms of international trade; a 'European corridor', in terms of investment and long-term economic ties; a 'cultural window' between the two oldest and most influential civilisations, in terms of coming together and understanding each other."

"The more we find out about each other, the more we understand ourselves. The more we read and discuss about our past, the more we are inspired for our future." Plato, Aristotle and Thucydides are not only the founding fathers of Greek cultural heritage, but they are an integral part of

Western civilisation. Samaras says: "I believe that Confucius, Lao-tse and Sun Tsu are also an integral part of universal cultural heritage. The more we find out about each other, the more we discover striking similarities, and the more we realise that these unique historical experiences of China and Greece are complementary in nature and universal in their potential. " In this case, he suggested that two sides should no longer keep apart two pieces of "treasure" that together could start up a cultural "chain reaction" of immense dynamism.

"Let's bring them together, creating a critical mass...," says Samaras. For example, Greek and Chinese are the oldest still-spoken languages in the world. They have evolved and grown on an unprecedented scale. Just come and think about all this cultural wealth embedded in both of them through the millennia. So, to get started, he says he would expect and encourage more Greeks to learn Chinese in the years to come and many more Chinese people to learn Greek. Both Chinese and Greeks are fast learners. "I was amazed by some Chinese speaking Greek language fluently. I hear that we already have some Greeks that are fluent in Chinese as well. There are probably a million things we can do to understand each other better. So let's get started by doing something truly bold: by eliminating the language barriers between us...," says Samaras.

Samaras has supported advocating cultural exchanges between China and Greece. As one who is used to preserving the records of an ancient civilisation, veteran Greek librarian Filippos Tsimpoglou is well aware of the significance of a visit by a top representative of another long-standing civilisation—China.

Tsimpoglou, 60, is General Director of the National Library of Greece in Athens, housed in a magnificent building dating from 1832 and holding a wealth of documents on Greek civilisation in a range of languages.

In his office, its walls covered in shelves of Greek classics, Tsimpoglou says that in the spirit of cultural exchange he came up with some reading recommendations for Chinese readers, but they may seem a tad unconventional, coming from a guardian of Greece's venerable culture.

"I thought they have read Greek classics, and so I recommended that they read more about modern masterpieces in Greece," he says. Tsimpoglou has listed the collected works of the renowned modern Greek poet Constantine P. Cavafy (1863-1933), who drew his themes from personal experience and a deep and wide knowledge of history, especially of the Hellenistic era.

"The poet was always using his own life experiences to express internal struggles, fate and dilemmas, and that is what I want to recommend," says Tsimpoglou. He also recommends the works of the writer, poet and philosopher Nikos Kazantzakis (1883–1957).

Tsimpoglou says he thinks that one of Greek civilisation's big contributions is that it has enriched global expression by lending words to other cultures, including such widely used words as "logic, dilemma, economy, ecology and crisis."

While he has had no chance to visit China yet, Tsimpoglou hopes to do so. He respects China's civilisation, stretching back for millennia, which for him, represents the accomplishments made possible by the "effort and energy" of humans. "In this way, our civilisation is just an infant before China's long history," he says.

Like Samaras, he would propose an exchange of classics in each other's language. He says he would like to use his Chinese classics in Greek to exchange for Greek literary treasures in Chinese found in China. "We have some Greek classics in Chinese but we need to add more to our library," he says.

Tsimpoglou has had a long career in library science. Before taking up his new position nearly two months ago in 2014, Tsimpoglou worked at the Greek National Documentation Centre, which preserves research papers and other documents, for 16 years before he served as library director at Cyprus University for 14 years.

He says he likes to broaden his perspectives. His hobbies are travelling and photography. "In this way, you can experience again what you have seen when you carefully look at your photos." Tsimpoglou says he is a little concerned about the economic crisis that Greece is passing through, but he strongly believes in the future of Greece, as "both the geographical and cultural" door to Europe, and as a place that produced philosophers and thinkers who gave rise to Western civilisation.

"So if somebody wants to approach European civilisation, culture, mentality or people as a whole, he or she has to turn to the ancient Greek philosophers," he says. Tsimpoglou uses his building as a metaphor for his country. The library, which he calls a mirror of Greek thought, was partly destroyed by a powerful earthquake in September 1999.

Pointing at the corner and ceiling of his office, he says the authorities had just stabilised it by filling the cracks with concrete. "This is very much like the situation in Greece," says Tsimpoglou.

He explains that Greece flourished for years with borrowed money, spent in part on what he calls excessive public welfare schemes, and that ended when the nation's debt crisis arrived several years ago like an earthquake.

"Then we put our efforts toward stabilising things, not repairing or rebuilding the system and structure," he says. "We still live in a dangerous system that needs fundamental changes. Greece is like our library, we must confess."

He adds that while a growing number of people are keen to turn to reading and knowledge to empower them to find jobs, governments from the United States to Greece to the rest of Europe have cut spending on public libraries. But Greeks, he says, need to turn to his country's civilisation to find a recipe to overcome the crisis and to help them show courage for change and reform.

"This is our hope and this is also our projection for the future," he says.

He says Greece faces not only difficulty but also a dilemma, which is a Greek word Tsimpoglou often uses. "How we maintain our civilisation while changing is one of our current dilemmas," he says.

Greeks have suffered not only from the economic crisis but also from a crisis of values, and the country needs to understand the job it faces and its obligations as well as contributing to the planet.

And Greeks, he says, should take action to determine their fate in order to improve their own lives, just as shown in ancient Greek thought. "I am quite optimistic about the future of Greece. As human beings, we have to be," he says. "Otherwise, we would have stayed in caves. We will pass the crisis, though I don't know if it will be in two or three years or in five years."

He suggests that Greeks need to be more self-disciplined and observe the law. As for Europe, one of its missions is to help keep the peace, given that the continent suffered grievously from two world wars during the past century. "This is the challenge that Europe must face," he says. "China is a different country with a long history of civilisation, a big population and the resources to make something different in history." He adds: "If China cannot achieve peaceful development, no other country can do so."

The Greek president and prime minister's deep understanding of the Initiative has already been disseminated to the officials. Before his departure to Beijing to attend the Belt and Road Initiative Forum for International Cooperation in May 2017, Stergios Pitsiorlas, Deputy Minister of Economy and Development in the Greek government, said both sides were working together to sign a three-year action plan in May to continue attracting inward investment to Greece to achieve the synergy of the Initiative and the Greek development strategy. After his return from the forum, Pitsiorlas says Greece would claim an important share of China's investment programme as part of the development of the Belt and Road Initiative. Transport, telecommunications and energy were the three main sectors where the two countries were going to cooperate.

In their three-year action plan document which both sides signed during the prime minister's visit to Beijing, China and Greece demonstrated how China's proposed Belt and Road Initiative perfectly matches the Greek government's strategy for Greece's multi-dimensional role in the region. "I think the synergy of the Initiative and Greece's development strategy will be opening a new page of bilateral cooperation," Pitsiorlas says. Though China's investment stock in Greece is still on a small scale compared with that of Germany, France and the UK, Pitsiorlas says he believed in the prospects, especially after COSCO had achieved impressive credentials in previous years. "The two civilisations (China and Greece) have deepened their friendship in our hard time (by expanding investment and offering bailout liquidity)," says Pitsiorlas.

In return, Greece helped China evacuate workers in their thousands from Libya in 2011 by transporting them to Crete and then bringing them back to China by plane. Pitsiorlas also praised COSCO's deep involvement in the Piraeus port, which offers a courageous example for other potential Chinese investors.

The minister says intensive engagement with China's real estate multinational Wanda, the e-commerce giant Alibaba and energy heavyweight the Shenhua Group had been made recently, and Greece was ready to offer incentives for Chinese investors to settle their investment plans. "The port of Piraeus is becoming the central heart of transportation in the Mediterranean area. It shows Greece can be a bridge between Asia and Europe," says

Pitsiorlas. As a welcome gesture to encourage Chinese investors, the deputy minister says that very soon many signs in Greek airports and seaports, restaurants and attractions would be in the Chinese language.

Zou Xiaoli, Chinese ambassador to Greece, has disclosed China's strong appreciation of the support and active participation of Greece in the Belt and Road Initiative, feeling confident that Greece will not only walk out of the debt crisis, but will also play a more important role in regional peace and stability by implementing its regional strategy. "This is in line with the interests of not only Greece, but also China and the European Union," said Zou during an hour-long talk with me in the Chinese Embassy in Athens in March 2017. "China-Greece cooperation also bears on China-Europe cooperation and cooperation between different regions of the world, which has important and far-reaching significance." Zou also says he himself has realised that many Chinese investors have flocked to Greece to explore opportunities, especially since last year. And he has received not only businesses but also leaders at the municipal and provincial levels, who have shown great interest in exploring opportunities in Greece by making use of its advantage as a gateway.

Zou contributed to the trend towards the "dragon-head" effect of the COSCO Piraeus project which has attracted more incoming investors from China, which he says is by far the most successful infrastructure cooperation project in Greece and even in Europe. "This has greatly boosted the interest and confidence of Chinese businesses to invest in Greece," he says. Zou adds that projects under discussion between the two sides cover a wide area, including ship-building and repair, ports, airports, power, telecommunications, finance and insurance, tourism, real estate and even energy. And he has recently received two companies, both from Shanghai, to compete for the same bids in Greece. "It is encouraging, and we hope more Chinese investors could come," says Zou.

But Zou says both sides should deepen educational cooperation to further facilitate and support the investment, trade, tourism and cultural exchanges. Compared with other European countries, not many Chinese students travel to Greece to seek further education. Statistics have shown that in Athens' universities, the number of Chinese students will not surpass 20. In Brussels the number is already over 3,000, not to mention the numbers in London, Paris and Berlin. "I think we should offer more incentives to encourage [students]," says Zou.

Tourism is another area for both sides to explore opportunities under the framework of the Belt and Road Initiative. Elena Kountoura, the Greek Minister of Tourism, has been deeply involved in the efforts. Before moving to a political career Kountoura had visited China twice, in 1989 and 1998, when she was an internationally-famed model and working in the fashion sector in Paris and Athens. Promoting the fashion concept in China then, she recalled that the roads were broad in Beijing but, at first glance, what she saw were lines of bicycles. When she looked a second time in 1998, she saw cars moving everywhere.

Now, Greece's graceful model-turned-tourism minister says during a talk in March 2017 that she has been busy preparing her promotional trips to China in May and June, which, she says, are warm-ups and follow-up activities for the visit of Prime Minister Alexis Tsipras. Sitting in her office a stone's-throw from the historic Greek Parliament building in downtown Athens, Kountoura says her trips to China offered profound perspectives for observing this country's rapid changes over several decades. "Now I am excited about my third trip to China," Kountoura says.

She says her mission was to attract more Chinese tourists to visit Greece, with the two promotions in Beijing and Shanghai in May and June respectively. Showing an Athens map in Chinese, she says confidently, "I am ready to welcome China's growing middle class to visit my country with its long civilisation." She expected direct flights between Beijing and Athens would be useful for attracting more Chinese tourists. It is reported that Air China will be relaunching its Beijing-Athens direct flight in 2017 and that it will also stop over in the German city of Munich. Kountoura promised that her ministry would be working to help Chinese tourists to obtain visas from the Greek embassy easily. She says that last year more than 100,000 people in China had applied for tourist visas from the Greek embassy in China, with more tourists coming to Greece via other European countries.

With tourism being the only growth sector of the country's sluggish economy during the depths of the sovereign debt crisis, the Greek government aimed to increase its inbound tourists from about 28 million last year to 30 million this year. Kountoura says China was a growing market for Greece, which has relied on tourism to contribute roughly one fifth of its economic output and job creation. Statistics have indicated that the tourists from China stood at 200,000 last year, but Greece has been determined to boost the annual number to one million by 2021. "If we have more direct flights, it will be easier and more convenient for Chinese visitors. I would like to welcome more Chinese," she says. "I hope the number will be 500,000 next year." She says Greece was promoting the concept of 365-day destinations in the country, expanding its island tourism to include culture, adventure sports, nature and other areas. As to the trends of Chinese tourists, she says when Chinese people come only for Greece, they definitely stay longer than six days, but if they're coming through another country, it depends.

"As we understand it, when Chinese people make such a long trip, they want to see more in Europe. They want to see Greece and another country. And usually they stay more than a week," she says. She also says that Chinese tourists are "good spenders", who spend more than the average. "Because Chinese, American or Australian tourists are coming overseas, they have a bigger average of spending than the Europeans. That's for sure," she says. She adds that many young Chinese couples come to get married or to have a honeymoon in the Greek islands, which have become very popular during the last two years.

"We still want to develop this product to make sure the tourists enjoy their stay in Greece, and they will have a wonderful time," she says. But she pointed out that Greece is not only about islands, and her country had hosted the 1st International Western Silk Road Workshop in Alexandroupolis on 26-27 April, 2017. "Greece is supportive of the Belt and Road Initiative and tourism can contribute to the China-led proposal, especially by promoting cultural tourism," she says.

Apart from officials, the discussion of the Belt and Road Initiative in Greece has gathered momentum among academics as well. Going beyond its bilateral significance, some scholars have already pondered how a new mechanism or institution on regional cooperation should be set up following the May forum in Beijing.

Among them is Dimitris Bourantonis, Deputy Director of the Athens University of Economics and Business, who says the Belt and Road Initiative is in essence advocating regional cooperation and it is vital to set up a platform to discuss how to achieve it in a sustainable way. Bourantonis says Beijing's Belt and Road Initiative Forum in May is just a beginning, and it should be institutionalised. "If the G20 avoids discussing regional issues of great significance, and if this newborn forum could debate regional issues quite relevant to the lives of people and of the region, I think it would be valuable for this forum to continue and to ensure its continuity in the future," says Bourantonis. He says the forum could rotate to different countries from this year. "And of course, why not consider setting up a permanent Belt and Road Forum in Beijing?" says the professor. "As a new invention in global governance, it is acceptable."

The opinion leaders I met even urged the political parties in Greece to adopt a concerted stance on the country's national strategy, to ensure the process of implementation will not be disrupted because of political rivalries. It is encouraging that both the leading parties and their opponents are speaking on the same page when talking about cooperation with China under the Belt and Road Initiative framework. In March 2017, I had an off-the-record talk with Kyriakos Mitsotakis, the son of the former prime minister of Greece and honorary president of the New Democracy political party, Konstantinos Mitsotakis. The young Mitsotakis has been president of New Democracy and the leader of the opposition since January 2016. During the meeting, in the ND headquarters in Athens, although the Greek opposition leader declined to state his opinion on the Belt and Road Initiative, his aides have spoken highly of the proposal, which will help revive the Greek economy. Surely these are very encouraging messages: the Greeks are ready to say goodbye to a decade-long crisis management phase and to debate how to shift to explore sustainable growth.

Greece is a country with a population of around 11 million. In Europe, there is a long list of countries with similar-sized populations that have achieved higher levels of development. And Greece shares similarities with Belgium, the Netherlands and Germany, with its ports developing logistics and with an economic corridor that leads to the interior of Europe. To draw an extreme comparison, Greece enjoys more geographical advantages than land-locked Switzerland but the latter has become an innovation giant and one of the most affluent countries in the world. So, seen either way, Greece has a tremendous opportunity to become a European power. To release such power, an additional shaping of the long-term and visionary development consensus among the Greek people is key. At the same time, the European Union should support Greece as it explores this potential and becomes a new economic engine in Europe, instead of only monitoring its bailout and privatisation programmes and being afraid of its impact on other maritime countries.

CASE: COSCO's GREEK MIRACLE

About 30 years ago, Fu Chengqiu had already became a veteran captain of China's shipping giant COSCO and later on he was sent to set up the multinational's branch in Italy. Since 2010, Captain Fu had been managing the two container terminals in the port of Piraeus after his company took over 35 years of leasing rights, which allowed the terminals to be loaned to the Chinese company.

It is a huge success: Piraeus has shot up to become the 38th busiest port worldwide in 2016, up from 93rd in 2010, in terms of container handling capacity. Up to 1,200 port workers have avoided becoming jobless during the struggles of the Greek debt crisis.

With such convincing credentials, Captain Fu, already in his 60s, has taken the helm of the 35-square-kilometer Piraeus Port Authority after COSCO purchased 51 percent of the leading privatization project in August 2016, paying 280.5 million. And in five years, COSCO will own a 67 percent stake in the Authority (PPA), with its total payment reaching 368.5 million.

"The responsibility is obviously as heavy as the mountains," says the white-haired Fu firmly. He is now the CEO of the PPA, which is almost 90 years old.

Sitting in the sofa area of his classroom-sized office in the cruise ship-shaped PPA building and looking at the ferries and other vessels coming and going outside the windows, Fu says his team has spent nearly half a year trying hard to know "every detail of the new family", including its financial balance, customer relations and the real situation of the staff. Fu admitted that his headache now is how to improve the efficiency of the "ageing Greek state-owned enterprises." Out of the 1,100 staff in the PPA, the average age is 51.5.

What's more, he continued, the PPA needs only about 700 staff to keep it running, and how to handle the redundant workers has challenged him as well. "But the bottom line is that we will not fire one staff member in the name of improving efficiency," says Fu, recalling the days when China was implementing its own state-owned-enterprises (SOE) reforms in the 1980s and 90s. At that time some of his relatives and friends still had hard memories of finding new "iron rice bowls" after losing their jobs.

"However, China offered many chances for job seekers then, but now the situation in Greece and Europe is different," he says. The average unemployment rate in many European countries is still at double digits , and one in every two young Greeks is jobless.

Captain Fu says the PPA's businesses range from container handling to freight, cruise operations, car terminals, ship repairing and the port economic zone. He has already reduced the number of the PPA's branches from 94 to 23. "I finished this task weeks ago, and we must improve management efficiency," says Fu, whose name has been inscribed in the time-line list of the port authority's management chiefs on the wall of the boardroom next to his office.

Initial figures show that Captain Fu's team is capable. Its financial report reveals that its revenues in 2016 amounted to 103.5 million, compared with 99.9 million in 2015. And the profit before taxes in 2016 reached 11 million, an increase of 13 percent from 2015. In addition, staff costs fell by 2.2 million (4.3 percent), to 49.9 million in 2016 compared with 51.5 million the previous year. Administrative expenses were cut significantly too, by 5.5 million (20.2 percent). "I am very happy to see that our revenues are rising, but the cost is reducing right now," says Fu.

Fu says his company is going to invest 190 million in the coming years to expand businesses in the port, with an additional 130 million from the European Union, which mainly focuses on deep-sea cruise terminal investment.

Fu says his company would also expand investment and businesses this year in ship building and repair, international cruise ships and car terminals, and improve the infrastructure of the Pier 1 container terminal. He is confident that with a closer economic relationship between China and Europe, the port will have a bright future in different business operations.

A study has shown that COSCO's investment in Piraeus will boost Greek gross domestic product by 0.8 percent and create 31,000 new jobs between 2016 and 2025. But Fu is very humble. He says: "I don't want to make such an estimate. What I trust is taking action and letting the future speak for itself." He is unwilling to predict how many jobs he is going to bring to the Greeks.

In recent years I have talked with Captain Fu three times in debt-ridden Greece, where mere survival is a daunting challenge for most businesses. But Fu offers a rare example of a success story.

About half an hour's drive from downtown Athens, the container terminals of Piraeus are busier than ever, with giant cranes and tractors constantly on the move and dockers working around the clock. When I met him in 2012 at his office in the port, Fu Chengqiu, then Managing Director of Piraeus Container Terminal SA, a unit of COSCO Pacific Ltd., said his company had made a "record-breaking" success of its operations, despite the European economic crisis. "We have not only survived but have also broken records in handling containers," Fu says. "But these are really hard won."

In June 2010, after winning the contract against stiff global competition, COSCO began operating Piraeus' No. 2 pier and rebuilding No. 3 pier. It signed a 35-year lease, and pays 100 million annually to the Greek government.At that time the global economy had been in recession because of financial crises emanating from the United States, and the European sovereign debt crisis was just beginning in Greece. But after two years of operation, figures from COSCO's running of Piraeus seemed to show a major turnaround in performance.

Fu, who captained a cargo ship before he took the helm of COSCO's subsidiary in Italy, is proud of his company's first years in Piraeus. But although it took just four months to record a profit at a port with a history of losing money, Fu says the challenges were tremendous.

Shortly after his company took over operations, Greek port workers went on strike. A 5-kilometre-long line of container trucks waiting to enter the port built up, along with angry complaints from their drivers sweltering under the summer sun. Ship owners also complained when their vessels were delayed at the port after data for many containers went missing. "The most important thing was to start to work," Fu recalls. He braved negotiations with truck drivers and port workers, promising to settle problems soon.

Fu's management team, with seven Chinese members, closely cooperated with the management from the Greek side, and with a pay rise agreed upon the port workers returned to work. Fu also asked for container data to be properly computerised. "At the very beginning, we spent several sleepless nights tackling the challenges," Fu says.

At first, Greek workers feared COSCO would replace some of them with experienced Chinese workers, but only seven Chinese have been employed at the port, and COSCO's presence has created about 1,000 jobs for Greeks. "Instead of bringing Chinese workers, we have brought China's high efficiency to this port," Fu says.

Despite Greece's crisis being so deep, Fu says he still considers Piraeus a vital gateway for shipping heading to Europe. "The port's geographic advantages and the quality services offered by us have helped deliver rapid progress at a time of crisis," he says.

And then COSCO's success at the port has won the respect of the Greek government and the local workforce. Many Greek officials say Chinese investors are warmly welcomed, and hope others will follow COSCO. With an established and growing reputation, Fu says, COSCO is in a key position to participate in any planned privatisation of Greece's top 22 state-owned enterprises. He says the company is in the middle of carrying out an in-depth feasibility study on becoming involved in various privatisation plans proposed by the Greek government. The outcome of the election in 2012, with a new coalition government in place, may help COSCO in their decisions, he adds.

The Greek authorities have expressed interest in further investment by COSCO and other Chinese companies in plans to privatise a variety of state-owned assets, believed to be worth around 50 billion. Because of his successes overseas, Fu is often invited to speak to company executives in China to pass on advice and share lessons learned.

He says there are four elements ensuring his continued success. First, safety is "an absolute priority" for port managers. Second, workers must work swiftly to meet the vessel's schedule. Fu says his port will be among the most efficient in Europe after he trained Greek workers on the basis of "Chinese speed and experience". Third, the cost of loading and unloading containers needs to be kept at a reasonable level. And finally, services and communication with shipowners must be timely and friendly. "If you can do well in these four areas, the customers will come to you," Fu says.

China has been encouraging its companies to invest overseas, but Fu warns: "This should be done in a cautious manner." He suggests that Chinese investors should invest in their own sector where they have had previous experience. "Only this way is there a chance of earning money." And when I interviewed Captain Fu in 2014, I found that if you ask any local taxi driver to take you there, he'll know right away to go to the container port at Piraeus, just over 10 km from the centre of the Greek capital.

In less than five years, the name of the Chinese shipping, logistics, shipbuilding and repair giant has become synonymous here with success. In that relatively short time, its subsidiary the Piraeus Container Terminal has built its monthly handling ability to around 200 cargo vessels, up from 40-50 vessels when it first started operations there in 2009.

On top of that a four-fold increase in handling capacity, it has created around 1,200 jobs, apart from the countless indirect job opportunities as part of the shipping chain.

All this has been achieved against a backdrop of arguably the worst economic conditions ever to hit Greece in modern times.

It is little wonder then that COSCO's success has been applauded by politicians and business leaders alike, culminating in the visit to the terminals by Premier Li Keqiang on 20 June 2014. Yet despite the impressive growth figures, Captain Fu, managing director of the COSCO subsidiary then, remains sober in his assessment of the past five years' work.

Sitting at his desk in the main COSCO office at the port—with the flags of China, Greece and the EU behind him—Fu is clearly a man who expects high standards. "Our operations in Piraeus have become stable and mature, but I do not think it could be labelled as a success quite yet," he insists, focusing instead on what he describes as the win-win situation for all the sides involved.

Fu says Piraeus has provided a good gateway to transport and sell goods to central, eastern and southern Europe, and North Africa. For the still-struggling Greek government, Piraeus, meanwhile, represents a steady stream of international business, from which could be created economic zones in the future, which could in turn be used to host Chinese assembly plants, the plans of which are already in the pipeline, he adds.

In early 2014, Greece's privatisation agency HRADF shortlisted COSCO alongside four other companies as qualified bidders to take a 67 percent stake in Piraeus Port as a whole. Also in the mix are Ports America Holding Inc., the largest port operator in the United States, and other leading companies from across the world, including from the United Kingdom and the Netherlands.

It is expected that the bidders will soon be invited to submit final details, with a decision due from the Greek government by the end of the year. "We are actively preparing the bid document to increase our strategic presence in Piraeus and if successful, this will ensure more win-win outcomes here," says Fu, without elaborating. The port project is among dozens of privatisation plans by the Greek government, as it seeks to raise money from selling national infrastructure including railways, energy facilities, public utilities and real estate to balance its financial books. If COSCO succeeds in its bid, it would mark a significant milestone for the company after it sealed its first deal five years ago to run and upgrade two of the state-owned Piraeus Port's piers for 35 years.

"We are in the middle of our efforts to turn Piraeus Port into a regional hub, which can generate more jobs and help lead a recovery of the local economy", says Fu. "But clearly our longer-term plans are based on winning the bid."

Piraeus is one of the largest seaports in the Mediterranean and among the top 10 container ports in Europe. It has more than 1,500 employees and provides various services to more than 24,000 ships a year. According to Containerization International magazine, it was the world's fastest-growing container port in both 2011 and 2012, and among the world's top 100 container ports, of which Shanghai ranks at the top, and which Rotterdam leads Europe.

As far as COSCO is concerned, its plans would make Piraeus a key Mediterranean transit hub and the major distribution centre for central, east and southeast Europe, including the Black Sea region. Fu says his team has the ability to attract the likes of giant retail exporters such as HP, Huawei, ZTE and Samsung to use the port as their main regional distribution centre. He already has plans in place to connect its sea terminals with air and railway links, offering more flexible options for customers, while expanding the terminals' capacities.

"Our sea-railway system, especially, has transformed traditional, historic shipping patterns, which marks a really significant shift," says Fu. In late April 2014, the first container train left Piraeus, arriving two days later in Gyor in northwest Hungary. There are now seven container train services running between Greece and countries in central and eastern Europe. Traditionally, goods from the Far East docked in Rotterdam, Hamburg or Antwerp before being transported to central or eastern Europe by road or rail. "But our sea-rail strategy will shorten that traditional transportation cycle by seven to 10 days on average," says Fu, "and that means a huge cost saving for our customers."

Christos Vlachos, the managing partner at Athens-based Silky Finance, an independent financial adviser who works at assisting companies in restructuring or raising finance, says the Greek government—with the help of the European Union, International Monetary Fund and European Central Bank—has managed to restore "some order back into the system", but that despite the business climate changing for the better, "a lot still needs to be done" for a full Greek economic recovery.

"Our politicians are not spending money as they used to, and the sentiment toward Greece overseas has also improved," he says, adding that the planned privatisation schemes will be crucial to the country's recovery. He says COSCO's involvement in Piraeus is a shining light of what benefits further privatisation could bring.

"COSCO's success has been in turning a slow-moving and money-losing port into a suddenly busy terminal with a lot of jobs." This can be copied in other sectors through privatisation schemes. Vlachos says the Greeks and the Chinese understand each other so well because both share similar values, such as in hospitality, business mentality and family. "Our prime minister's understanding of the importance of China is far greater than that of his predecessors," he says, welcoming the involvement of

Chinese state-owned enterprises in Greece's infrastructure and financial sectors particularly.

Theodoros Fessas, President of the Federation of Greek Enterprises, agrees there are strong signs that the country's business climate is improving and that overseas investors are starting to look once again at which opportunities the country offers, tempted by the solidity of its membership in the eurozone and the EU. "Another major factor is that currently nearly all of Greece's assets are attractively priced and once the recession bottoms out, prices will pick up, and investors will get a return." Fessas forecasts that China will soon become the world's largest economy, and that Greece represents a perfect import/export hub, linking it to the rest of the European market. "China's entrance into Europe needs a key multi-functional hub, and Greece can be one of the strongest options," he adds, noting that Chinese investors will certainly be eyeing investment opportunities in Greek ports and airports. Fessas says he expects the leaders to encourage more multinationals from China to invest in Greece and set up their European headquarters in Athens.

George Gratsos, president of the Hellenic Chamber of Shipping, has also been a strong supporter of COSCO's investment in Piraeus.

"We are extremely happy that COSCO's investment is growing and working so well," he says. He adds that Li's visit underlines a strong friendship between two countries that has lasted for "many, many, many years". Greece's proximity, he says, to south, east and central Europe, and its strong rail links, makes the port an ideal goods distribution centre, and he urged the Greek authorities to cooperate further with a major port operator, preferably from the Far East.

"COSCO's operation has been a wonderful success, and we support its expanded presence in Piraeus." Using Greece as its gateway to Europe is also good for China and made-in-China products, given that Chinese exporters could avoid paying EU import duties by using the port, he says. "Athens has the ability to become the next Hong Kong if both sides share their vision to boost it as a global shipping and commercial centre."

Despite that, the Greek workers in the container terminals have clearly shown that the Greek government, facing the double-digit unemployment rate, has done the right thing in leasing the two terminals to COSCO. The 39-year-old Melissis Dimitrios and his colleague John Stamatelopo, 40, have been responsible for offloading containers in the port since COSCO started to manage the terminals in late 2009. They worked five days a week and earned about 1,200-1,300 a month, which is relatively high and stable by Greek income standards. "Conditions are quite good and we are happy. Many Greek people admire us and they want to work here," says Stamatelopo beside a high-rise cargo ship. After loading the containers, the trains, twice every day, trucks and even small cargo ships will transport the goods to other parts of Europe. "I hope more people could come, and it is good for us," says the worker delightedly.

It can become true. In addition to other job opportunities in the expansion of the port, Captain Fu has promised that by 2018, the container terminals in Piraeus will be handling 5 million TEUs (20-foot equivalent container units). "By then it will be entering into the fleet of the world's top 30 container ports," says Fu, seriously but soberly. And in the long run, Fu's company has shown its determination to boost the container handling capacity to 10 million TEUs, which would create more jobs in the long chain of port business. Pointing to a framed photo of his cute grand-daughter on his office desk, Fu says she is the source of tremendous joy after his strenuous work. "Whenever I see the photo, I am happy," says Fu, smiling broadly. "I do treat the port and our Greek people like a big family as well."

Greek shipping executive Andreas Potamianos seems younger than his 79 years when he talks about the Chinese government's support for investing in Greece and its potential to boost the economic recovery of the nation.

The enthusiastic septuagenarian, who has long led Epirotiki Lines, one of the country's renowned family shipping businesses, has taken it upon himself to prepare an investment priority list for China. Potamianos' list includes railway construction, port management and tourism. But topping the list is his suggestion that China invest in construction of mega-cruise vessels that can meet the holiday needs of the growing market of middle-class travellers. "It is the right time for China to start cruise businesses and investments to satisfy market demand," says Potamianos, Honorary President of the Greek Shipowners' Association for Passenger Ships.

He says he sees great potential in working with China to construct a new generation of cruise vessels of advanced design and with energy-saving systems.

Potamianos, whose company operates seven cruise vessels that the family built, says his people are engaged in negotiations with Chinese companies and they hope to announce some breakthroughs during Li's visit in 2014. There is no doubt that as the chairman of the Greece-China Friendship Association, he is convinced of the need to boost bilateral relations by linking Greece's competitive shipping industry with China's developmental abilities. "I just want to say China should accelerate its pace in earning its own piece of the pie in the market," says Potamianos, whose family has interests in both cargo and passenger shipping.

Potamianos was speaking in his office facing the Piraeus passenger terminals, the biggest in Greece. He pointed to a model of his family's first vessel, which plied the waters back in 1850.

He says China has shipyards capable of building cruise ships, and great market potential to explore. "And we have expertise both in vessel building and crew training to share with our Chinese friends," says Potamianos. He says he proposed a shipping alliance to former premier Zhu Rongji when he held the position from 1998 to 2003. But during that period, Potamianos says, China had other development priorities.

Now things are different. China stands to be among the first group of Asian countries to build large cruise ships, he says. Cruise ship construction is still dominated by European and American companies, though China has made rapid progress in mega-cargo ship construction.

In Asia, Japan and South Korea have begun working with other countries to build cruise ships, now that the cruise business in Asia is growing rapidly.

With China's per capita GDP surpassing $8,000, China's government has been encouraging the development of the cruise industry. International experience has shown that when per capita GDP reaches $5,000, the cruise industry is ripe for growth. A GDP of $10,000 is a precursor of a golden age for developing such leisure businesses. The Chinese government has predicted that by 2020, the cruise industry will contribute about $50 billion to the nation's economy. In the United States, the industry currently generates about $40 billion yearly and employs 350,000 workers. "So you can see the huge potential in China in developing the cruise industry," says Potamianos. In addition to jointly developing cruise vessels, Potamianos says Greeks feel comfortable with China expanding its presence in Greece because China concentrates on doing business. "But some other countries don't do it this way and they want to dominate in Greece, which is not acceptable for us," he says.

"China and Greece have a long history of friendship and understanding", he says. With China, "we don't have such a kind of fear of being dominated."

The economic situation in Greece has also made the country eager for partnerships. "Psychologically, Greeks feel the situation is getting better, but the reality is that Greece has done very badly. There are many promises on TV but concrete measures are few to get the economy out of crisis," Potamianos says. Many Greeks have become impoverished, suicides have risen and a lot of companies have closed. Greeks have felt a distance grow toward the European Union—while they didn't quit the EU, the European community did little to protect the Greeks, Potamianos says. "Against this background, a growing number of Greek people have turned their eyes to China," he says.

Greece would like China to become its top trade partner, he says. China currently is Greece's No.17 export destination and No.5 import source.

Potamianos says that Greeks would like to see the giant, state-owned COSCO participate in privatisation plans for Piraeus port management, in addition to the company's expansion in container terminals in Piraeus.

"Everybody has talked about COSCO since it brought jobs and hope to us," he says. Potamianos says he would like to see China invest in infrastructure improvements in Greece. One such opportunity would be investment in a new freight railway linking Athens and Budapest, which would give the seaport in Athens a bigger role and allow Budapest to become a logistics centre in central and eastern Europe.

"Of course, we also look forward to China's investment in improving passenger railways between Athens and Budapest," he says, adding that it would bring more jobs and tourists to Greece. "On top of that, we look forward to more and more Chinese tourists traveling in Greece," he says.

To encourage that, Potamianos says he hopes the Greek government would make visiting easier and also launch direct flights from major cities in China to Athens. "We need also to design tailor-made tourist packages to attract the Chinese," he adds. Though he is about to turn 80,

Potamianos' enthusiasm for business, and for life, has not dimmed. He is still active, taking part in water skiing and going on walks on weekends. He works from nine in the morning to seven at night, and hopes his efforts to expand ties between China and Greece will bear fruit. "I have spent a lot of time on working as a business bridge between China and Greece," says Potamianos.

Many people hope Potamianos' efforts pay off despite the fact that Greece has grabbed a lot of the world's headlines in recent years in comparison with most European countries. But most of the stories have been about one of three subjects: prolonged bailout talks with international creditors, frequent elections, and the nation's privatisation process.

During my stay in Europe that began in 2010, these stories have taken much of my energy. The stories have been about whether Greece could keep afloat in the face of possible bankruptcy caused by the severe sovereign debt crisis and financial austerity programmes. Amid the UK's triggering of negotiations to leave the European Union, Grexit is basically no longer a threat, and though the Greek economy is still fragile, some locals are unsatisfied with belt-tightening reforms, and some others are still afraid of structural reforms. With the figures now showing Greece has left years of recession behind it, it is still a hard job for this country to embark on a new economic cycle, mainly because the miserable business climate in the country has not inspired confidence among global investors.

However, what impressed me most during my interviews in early 2017 was that many Greeks were following the consultant Vlachos and veteran shipping leader Gratsos, discussing the national strategy of positioning itself as a centre for regional shipping, logistics and even energy, by taking advantage of the fact that its southern boundaries are in the Mediterranean Sea and its north leads into eastern and central Europe.

And their major arguments are that Greek strategy is also in line with China's Belt and Road Initiative. Both are about increasing connectivity and the flow of goods and other productive elements.

03

CHAPTER THREE

China and the Czech Republic
energise traditional friendship by
linking together

In recent talks with friends, a sudden thought comes to my mind: Greece and the Czech Republic are on the way to transforming their national fates, in bridging the gap between Western Europe and themselves, with their leadership being so keen on forging closer relations with China, especially through matching the Belt and Road Initiative with their own development strategies. The findings during my trips to the Czech Republic in 2016-2017 supported such an assumption. And I can even assume that, probably, no other leader in this world other than President Milos Zeman has currently shared such a busy and full agenda of engaging China.

Commandeering two spacious halls in his magnificent presidential building, the marvellous Prague Castle which commands a stunning view of this renowned tourist city, Zeman invited up to 1,500 business persons, experts and officials on 18 July 2017, mainly from his country and China, for a dinner gathering after the forum on investment and the Belt and Road Initiative. This must be among the largest events organised overseas after Beijing convened the first Belt and Road Initiative Forum in May 2017. In his address, Zeman himself says he was also impressed by the activeness and responsiveness the European and Chinese participants showed in echoing President Xi Jinping's proposed initiative.

A Chinese saying puts it this way: the fire burns high when everybody adds wood to it. Since President Xi came up with the proposal to better connect Asia, Europe and Africa, China was clearly insisted that this is a shared vision and action. Zeman has shown tremendous political wisdom and commitment and set an extraordinary example in understanding this initiative and its approach. Apart from the July encounter with the business community, Zeman, within three months, also separately met young football players, student pilots and media representatives from China and his country in his castle, offering very generous hospitality. And he flew to Beijing to attend the May forum as well.

Prime Minister Bohuslav Sobotka displaced equal political commitment in cementing cooperation by advocating his country's "driving role" in implementing the Belt and Road Initiative in central and eastern Europe. Sobotka says his land-locked country's ambition is to become a regional financial and aviation hub, similar to London, Paris and Frankfurt in Western Europe, by forging synergies between its development strategy and China's proposal. Obviously, the Czech Republic, now economically growing at the fastest pace in Europe, has already reaped early benefits. When he spoke at the forum in Prague in July, Sobotka admitted his quarter-hour-long speech would not exhaust the list of projects both sides had been implementing or planning.

For example, several Chinese financial institutions have already established branches in the Czech capital. The number of tourists has grown from 50,000 in 2012 to an estimated 500,000 this year. And direct flights between Prague and Beijing, Shanghai and Chengdu have already started, with two more routes, between Prague and Shenzhen and Kunming, joining them soon. Maybe no other country outside Europe would launch five direct flights to link to a country with a population of only about 10 million, half Beijing's size. The Shanghai-based CEFC China Energy, an active Chinese investor in the Czech Republic has already invested in various sectors of finance, aviation, real estate, football, brewing, machinery and e-businesses. In addition, after the first freight train linking Prague and Yiwu, a famous commodity distribution city in China's economically booming Zhejiang Province, started operating on 19 July 2017, the province is also seeking to construct a logistics park, initially covering a square kilometre, in the Czech Republic. This project is expected to create 3,000 new jobs.

All these encouragingly incremental developments in business and people-to-people exchanges show that Zeman's political wisdom has already paid off. Surely this momentum can only increase, because both sides have just opened the first page of delivering their visions and ambitions. President Xi has called the Belt and Road Initiative a century project in terms of the lasting efforts needed. His Czech counterpart Zeman, who has met Xi six times in previous years, echoed him by calling it a "global dream." With such visionary understanding, turning Prague into a regional financial and aviation hub is not only in the interests of the two countries, but is also useful in bridging Europe's regional disparity, which should be at the top of the EU's agenda as well. And, hopefully, the experiences shared by China and the Czech Republic in successfully aligning their development strategies can be copied by other countries.

If so, Zeman's political wisdom will create a spillover effect. Such an effect is evident in the heart of the old town of Prague, where the representatives of the central Bohemian region of the Czech Republic and southwest China's Sichuan province sit together on the ground floor of an ancient building. In Chengdu, capital of Sichuan, they are jointly opening promotion centres as well. The centres in Prague are filled with Czech publicity material; those from Sichuan include panda souvenirs, local tea, Changhong TV and other specialties. On the top floor of this building is the New Silk Road Institute, which was founded by Jan Kohout, adviser to President Zeman, to advocate President Xi Jinping's proposed Belt and Road Initiative. As an architect of bringing the region and Sichuan province closer, Kohout says he has very good reason to put the centres and his institute together. "It is an innovative mixture of the government's promotion centres and a think tank," Kohout says during our meeting in April. "We need to think big on the one hand and promote specific projects on the other."

Just returning from Chengdu, provincial capital of Sichuan, Kohout, the former foreign minister, says he has already travelled to Sichuan more than twenty times. And now he is involved in the efforts to persuade the province to build an industrial park in his country—and even to try to bring in pandas. Previously, the Sichuan-based TV maker Changhong had already expanded its investment in the Czech Republic, and the direct flights between Chengdu and Prague had already been launched. "What I understand is that a political highway has already been built between the two countries, and we need to increase the traffic by expanding cooperation in various areas," says Kohout.

The political highway he referred to is the closeness of the strategic partnership formed in recent years, and the frequent high-level exchanges. In May 2017, Kohout accompanied Zeman to attend the Belt and Road Initiative Forum for International Cooperation, and this was Zeman's third visit to China during his presidency. That day I met Ma Keqing, Chinese ambassador to the Czech Republic. She agreed with Kohout that the frequency of high-level political exchanges between China and the Czech Republic is unprecedentedly high. "Within three years, President Xi and President Zeman have already met six times on various occasions, and Zeman is going to make his third tour of China within his presidency, which shows the closeness of our top leadership," says Ma. "We need to carry on the momentum."

Xi paid a historic state visit to the Czech Republic in March 2016, and Ma says both countries' action to boost their relationship to a strategic partnership level is shown by the Czech Republic's recognition of the importance of China, because it has such relations with only six countries, including the United States and Russia. Following such high-level mutual recognition, in November 2015, China and the Czech Republic signed a memorandum of understanding on jointly building up the Belt and Road Initiative, which was the first such document signed between China and a central European country. And in November 2016, both sides turned their Memorandum of Understanding into a Belt and Road Initiative work programme. Ambassador Ma says that in the Czech Republic the support for boosting pragmatic cooperation by seeking synergies in each other's mega-projects to implement China's Belt and Road Initiative is generally active. Ma says in her official residence: "They responded even more actively after President Xi's visit last year."

"It is evident how firmly the Czech Republic supports the initiative and now the most important thing for us is to enrich it by institutionalising the platforms and designing suitable projects," says Kohout. "Another point I want to address is that the Belt and Road Initiative should be a two-way platform." He says both sides should also help investors in the Czech Republic and the rest of Europe to explore more opportunities in China.

In an effort to fulfill the Czech Republic's proposal of making Prague as China's financial centre for central and eastern Europe, its central bank has recently approved the business licenses for the Industrial and Commercial Bank of China (ICBC). Ma says China's investment in the Czech Republic has soared by attracting $1.1 billion in 2016. "It is not significant compared with our investment in the entire country but it has grown from a low base," says Ma. "But before 2014, China's total investment in the country was less than $300 million." She says the number of Chinese tourists to the Czech Republic stood at 350,000 last year, a 22 percent year-on-year increase, and the first quarter of this year has seen a 50 percent year-on-year increase.

While helping the Czech Republic realize its ambition of becoming a regional hub of finance and aviation, China is also trying to forge deeper cooperation in industrialisation and advanced manufacturing sectors, says

Ma. "In addition to infrastructural and other investments, we should also aim to improve China's competitiveness in industrial competition by enhancing cooperation with the Czech Republic," says Ma. "In this regard, it is an excellent partner, as this country has followed in the steps of Germany very closely."

In fact, during trips to the Czech Republic in 2016, in which President Xi paid a historic visit to the country, exchanges with politicians, businessmen, shop owners, writers, sports coaches and even passers-by on the streets showed me that the Czech Republic is a "New Land" in terms of China's Belt and Road Initiative. My excitement arose mainly because the Czechs are well prepared to match China's proposals, equipped with a long list of ideas to engage the Chinese who are already involved, ready to turn those ideas into reality.

Such a proactive attitude developed roughly three years after President Xi came up with his mega-proposal to closely connect Asia, Europe and Africa with better infrastructure, growing trade and financial vehicles, smoother talent flow and more cultural exchanges. The Czech Republic is on its way to becoming one of the leading lights of matching the Belt and Road Initiative together with the UK, France, Pakistan, Russia, Indonesia, Greece and others. Beijing's stance is crystal clear: this proposal is offered for the world to generate prosperity and eradicate poverty, but the participants should offer concrete ideas to enrich it. To put it succinctly: this is China's proposal, but a world opportunity. The Czech Republic has understood this concept well.

President Xi Jinping's Belt and Road Initiative is essentially a peace project, which is about more than economic benefits alone and is connecting people of different countries. Jan Kohout, an adviser to Czech President Milos Zeman on Chinese matters, told me when I met him in 2016: "President Xi's Belt and Road Initiative is a solution for the world to walk out of wars and conflicts and bring about prosperity. It is not only about business but focuses on bringing people closer, leading to better communication and cooperation. The world is filled with troubles and challenges ranging from those in the Middle East, Syria, Afghanistan, and North Africa. And avoiding misunderstanding and conflicts is essential, and in my understanding this is basically what this initiative is about." Calling Xi the "Father of the Belt and

Road Initiative", Kohout, who has twice been foreign minister of the Czech Republic, says the initiative is political, but China has no geopolitical motives. "China is not pushing each country to join, and China is not applying pressure. This is mutual. It is up to every county to decide."

Based on his long engagement with Chinese leaders, businesses and academia, Kohout set up the New Silk Road Institute Prague in September 2015 in response to the ongoing and accelerating geopolitical and economic changes in the world. Kohout says his institute, above all, is similar to the spirit of Xi's proposal, which aims to assist in building a better world of communication, not a world of purposeless confrontation. Kohout says that within the framework of the Belt and Road Initiative his institute will create a positive environment for cooperation and offer suggestions to the leaders and governments of both sides. He believes that the driving force behind the New Silk Road is definitely the economic benefits available for both continents, which increase connectivity between Asia and Europe, such as high-speed railways, a network of highways, smart air and sea infrastructure and high-speed data networks and sustainable energy infrastructure.

"Nevertheless, this idea should not be reduced to economic benefits only. We should not understate the importance and effects it has on areas such as education, culture, mutual understanding and ideological interactions," says Kohout. "All these are integral components of the new grand project design."

And the institute will focus on more specific areas and give more concrete suggestions especially on feasible infrastructural and logistic projects, financial cooperation and energy technology. "We focus on highways, high-speed trains and infrastructure prospects, and also focus on soft projects. This is what we are aiming for. But right now, we are looking forward to President Xi Jinping's visit, which is historic for us," says Kohout. Calling his institute a pioneer in Europe, he says, during Xi's visit both sides would look at cooperating more deeply on the Belt and Road Initiative.

Kohout says President Zeman is a great supporter and promoter of Czech-China relations and strongly supports the Belt and Road Initiative. "The Czech government and business have also shown strong support for this initiative. So all these are very encouraging," he says. "So we can start to implement more focused projects on infrastructure, trade and finance, for example."

China has prepared mega-programs to build connectivity, which is the core element of the Belt and Road Initiative. The Republic is a land-locked country whose total population is only half that of Beijing. The big idea is to finish a water corridor linking the Danube, Oder and Elbe rivers to enable the Czech Republic, the only country among the 28 EU members without direct access to the sea, to reach the Black Sea, Baltic Sea and North Sea. Czechs are keen to seek help from China to fulfill that dream.

And of course, as many European countries use "gateways" to describe their geographic advantages, the Czech Republic has also offered to work with China to turn Prague into an aviation and financial centre. The Republic has already worked with Sichuan province to construct a high-tech industrial zone. Chinese companies, though still only on a small scale, are starting to invest in media, football clubs, and entertainment in this country, which, according to top Czech politicians, has realized the importance of catching the development train with China. Apart from these business ideas, the Republic has already mobilised a lot of resources to offer ideas and facilitate coordination. The government has set up a special working team to deal with China affairs, in which six vice-ministers are involved. The group reports directly to the Prime Minister and the president. Meanwhile a thinktank specialising in Belt and Road Initiative research has been set up and is offering suggestions and advice for the top decision-makers. All these moves are really fresh and encouraging. It is rare to see other countries taking such concerted actions to echo the Belt and Road Initiative from different directions.

And they are even thinking of "minds connecting with minds". During my final day there, I had a lunch interview with prolific middle-aged Czech translator Zuzana Li, who pointed out that China-Czech cooperation is not only about business and trade. She has translated up to ten books of modern and contemporary Chinese fiction and poetry into Czech. And she has even started to offer online materials for secondary school teachers in the country to introduce Chinese literature, which she says is another window on China. This reminds me of a saying by the famous writer Lu Xun, which goes: "basically there is no road in the world; the road takes shape because more people walk on it." For the Belt and Road Initiative, it badly needs ideas and active contributions from the people of the world, and they are expected to be as proactive as the Czechs in turning China's proposal into their own agenda.

This is the process of developing a road of common prosperity, which we urgently need in a world of conflicts, wars, terrorism and economic turmoil in some regions.

Veteran politicians' keenness

In 2016 and 2017, I had opportunities for deep exchanges with Czech thinkers and politicians. I have not seen their collective and active sharing and engaging journalists in any other country, and it has been among the most joyful moments of my career. I met the former President of the Czech Republic Vaclav Klaus in his office in suburban Prague shortly before President Xi's visit to his country in early 2016. He says Xi's visit was "of historic meaning and a logical development," which showed how both sides were serious about developing a strategic relationship. China, he says, should feel it was in its strategic interests to develop such high-profile relations with a European country like his. He was President of the Czech Republic from 2003 to 2013 and also served as Prime Minister for a long time. He himself set up a research institute on global affairs in Prague after his retirement.

Klaus has visited China several times and now it is logical for his country to start to engage China. In 1993, the Czech Republic and Slovakia split, and Klaus says it was natural that the Republic should develop a sound relationship with its neighbours first. So it had been inward-looking for quite a long time. And trade with European countries had amounted to nearly 80 percent of its total volume at that point. "Xi's visit is the logical development of the situation. I myself have a good relationship with China," says Klaus. "But we used to be more inward looking and concentrate on Europe, on our tasks, on the domestic agenda after the Czech Republic was set up in 1993 during the dramatic years of political and social changes."

He says the Republic should be busy with establishing good relations with neighboring countries first, which are closer to it. "Now it is for us to keep closer ties with China as well," he says, adding that the Republic takes Xi's visit seriously. "When President Xi decided to visit, we found that China was also very serious about recognsing the role of the Republic in the Sino-EU relationship framework," Klaus says. "We are happy that President Xi does not visit the UK, France or Germany, but the Czech Republic; so finally he arrives in the heart of Europe, geographically." Klaus says countries in central and eastern Europe used to have similar political systems, and it is relatively easy for them to better understand China, compared with other European countries.

As a senior economist, Klaus is optimistic about China's economic outlook, saying that the slowing down of the Chinese economy is very often discussed in Europe and the United States. "I am the first opponent of this topic. When looking at China's growth dangling between 6 and 8 percent, you dare to have the courage to take it as a slowdown in a continent where there is roughly a zero rate of growth for a long period of time," says Klaus. Klaus says he knows that China has been faced with challenges, but the debate should not be the growth rate itself. "And the debate should be about whether China will bring us positive growth, and my answer is YES," he says.

A former Czech Prime Minister, Jiri Rusnok, has never visited China, but the names of many Chinese cities and businesses are in his mind. When President Xi Jinping flew to the Czech Republic for his state visit from 28-30 March in 2016, Rusnok says it was time for his country to catch up and deepen cooperation in "all areas", following the steps of its European peers. "In many, many areas, the bilateral relationship was not as good for some years as it could have been in past decades. Many of our peers are a long way ahead of us," says Rusnok, who started to work as Governor of the Republic's Central Bank soon after President Xi's visit. For the visit, he believed it should be the highest level and the most important visit for the Republic, and it did prove the bilateral relationship was at its highest point ever.

"I am sure this will boost our relationship in many areas," says Rusnok, adding that the relationship will be deepened from business to culture, health, education, research, transport and scientific cooperation. Sitting in his office at the Central Bank in Prague, Rusnok says this was great because there was so far unused potential to boost cooperation further. But Hungary, Poland and Western European powers such as Germany, France and UK have already set up strategic cooperation partnerships with China. "So it seems we are catching up on something we missed in the recent decade, and I welcome the progress made by my president and prime minister during the last two or three years," he says.

Rusnok says the reasons behind the changes were a natural development inside Czech politics and the fact that most of the political representatives had realized that their country had missed some opportunities in developing a relationship with China and gaining more of China's market. "We definitely, in my opinion, made some mistakes in the past. So there are some pragmatic approaches from us. I am glad of that and it's nothing special," he says. "And we have followed our partners in the European Union, and they are a few years ahead of us."

Asked if the Czech Republic should consider joining the Asia Infrastructure Investment Bank, he says his country should do so as many of its European Union peers had done. "So I should not say there is no reason that we are not part of the bank. Because I am sure that if we join, facilitating our businesses to become tenders to bid for some projects financed by this bank is possible," says Rusnok. Meanwhile, he says, it was obvious Asia and East Asia were regions with high development potential. "So I think we should not miss this opportunity. I think the Czech government should consider this opportunity to join the bank," says Rusnok. "But I am not sure whether it will be discussed or not during Presdient Xi's visit." As to cooperation, Rusnok says both sides should consider transport as a priority because of the European gateway location of the Republic, which links East Asia and Europe. "And Prague airport still has potential for both passenger and cargo transport," he says.

In addition to other flights, Rusnok says direct flights between Chengdu and Prague were important as he believed Chengdu was an ideal transfer airport for Europeans travelling to southeast Asia or southern Asia. "Chengdu airport is an interesting place for us as it still has capacity compared with Beijing and Shanghai," says Rusnok. For example, every year more than 300,000 Czechs visit Thailand, and if only 20 percent use the route via Chengdu, that will help it to become economically feasible. And freight transport prospects were also encouraging, as many Asian investors had launched their businesses in the Czech Republic's manufacturing and industrial areas, which are very competitive. "They need to transport electronic parts from China and so freight transport by air is also important," he says.

Ten years ago, when Jiri Paroubek was Prime Minister of the Czech Republic, he was visionary enough to fly to Beijing and hold talks with his Chinese counterpart Wen Jiabao to strengthen the Republic's business relationship with China. And at minimum China's TV manufacturing company Changhong set up a new factory then, which was part of the success he helped achieve. After he stepped down in September 2006, Czech politicians were mainly inward-looking and until now, Changhong's trade volume within the European Union still accounts for the lion's share of the total. In the last two or three years, the Republic has once again renewed its efforts to deepen its economic and trade relationship with China.

"I am very happy with this change, following my talks with the Chinese leadership about considering our strategic partnership ten years ago," says Paroubek, born in 1952, during a talk with me in 2016. He says he appreciates the "courage and vision" of the leaders of both sides to consider upgrading the relationship to a strategic level, and President Xi Jinping's visit has brought tremendous positive changes to their bilateral relationship. Paroubek says President Xi is a "visionary, serious and down-to-earth" global politician and he knows very well what Chinese people need most. "President Xi has made great efforts in fighting corruption and keeping the Chinese economy on track, which has already impressed me."

And what has also impressed him is Xi's visionary capacity in guiding China to the global stage by taking proactive steps to engage the world and contribute to its development. "And this is clearly seen by the world regarding China's contribution," he says. While his country is ready to cooperate with China, especially in boosting bilateral trade, now the trade partners for this land-locked country are still in Europe. He boasts that industrial competitiveness in the Republic is very strong and the quality of its products could compare to those made in Germany, which has become far more progressive than the Republic in terms of its trade relationship. "We have the same quality (as that of goods made in Germany) but our prices are lower. So we need to catch up to boost exports to China," says Paroubek.

Meanwhile, he says, the Republic should make even greater efforts to find synergies within China's Belt and Road Initiative. But he admits it is a mistake that the Republic did not become a founding member of the Asian Infrastructure Investment Bank (AIIB). "I hope we can do something in this regard to catch up," he says. Apart from possible engagement with the AIIB, Paroubek also says it would be meaningful if both sides considered cooperation to build a high-speed railway in the Republic and also improving logistics and freight transport. Paroubek says both countries should go beyond normal business and try to explore opportunities in music, painting, art and films and to enrich the minds of the people of each country. Paroubek also says this visit is vital for China to boost its relationship with countries in central and eastern Europe. "This is the first time for him to come to this region after taking office as president and I am sure this visit will be very important to boost China's relationship with countries in central and eastern Europe," says Paroubek.

He also believes that President Xi would deliver a message to the European Union, which he visited in 2014. He says it is of great importance to boost the Beijing-Brussels relationship but, in many areas, Brussels is influenced by Washington. "We can see the European Union lacks independence, as some of its policies, such as on refugees, the Ukraine crisis and relations with Russia, are influenced by the United States," says Paroubek. As to China's market economy status, Paroubek says the European Union should recognise it, recognise China's economic contribution globally, and recognise China's contribution to European development during previous decades. "The West should know these very well and recognise them," says Paroubek. "But for some reason, the United Sates is still exerting its influence on the European Union."

In early 2014, Xi Jinping made his first European tour, after being elected as Chinese president in March 2013, by visiting four western European powers and the EU headquarters. He also attended the World Nuclear Security Summit in the Hague in March 2014 and in early 2016 visited the Czech Republic before flying to the Washington summit on world nuclear security. This was his first tour as president of the central and eastern parts of the European Union.

And between China and the UK, which has vowed to become the former's best partner in the West, began a golden decade of strategic partnership after President Xi's state visit in October 2015. Xi also joined global leaders at the Paris climate change summit at the end of 2015, helping to achieve a global deal on curbing greenhouse gas emissions. Taking stock of all of Xi's "landmark" European tours, other Chinese leaders have paid many visits to European Union countries in the last three years while their European counterparts have increased the frequency of their Chinese visits. All these top-level political and diplomatic moves have been accompanied by encouraging and diversified business and people-to-people exchanges.

In spite of that, I was asked the same question on many occasions by European friends: Beijing and Brussels are determined to set up a strategic partnership, but Beijing is busy deepening ties with member states while scaling up cooperation with countries in central and eastern Europe. Why is that? Basically, this is a false proposition. China is absolutely correct in engaging all the countries with sovereign rights while adhering to its principle of helping to push European integration. On the practical level, President Xi clearly stated that China is determined to forge a partnership of "peace, growth, reform and civilisation" when he closed his tour in 2014. Against the realities of the European Union and its member states, the four fronts serve both the targets and the competitiveness of European countries and the European Union.

So my answer to the question is a slogan: find the ways that work. It means that if China has been working in the direction of delivering such goals, any contact and engagements at different levels should be encouraged. So it is meaningless to ask who Beijing should engage, especially when Europe is struggling with various challenges—economic growth, terrorism, immigration and the integration process. China's proactive and pragmatic Europe policy is what Europe badly needs.

Beijing is not only offering proposals and ideas. The politicians, business leaders and even ordinary people (tourists, or people sending their children to Europe for a better education) have acted. Though bilateral trade activities have been affected by the global slowdown, two-way investment is still active while Chinese investors have targeted Europe as the first destination of their merger and acquisition expansions.

It is obvious that European member states have welcomed China's approaches, which aim to explore more win-win opportunities economically, to achieve better understanding among peoples and to shoulder more global responsibilities jointly. For example, the UK has vowed to become China's best friend in the West, and here in Prague the two countries decided to scale up their relationship to a strategic level.

Encouragingly, many European countries have joined Beijing's Belt and Road Initiative for better connected infrastructure, trade and flow of personnel. Up to 20 European countries have joined the Beijing-led Asian Infrastructure Investment Bank as founding members, and some are on the waiting-list. When looking back ten or twenty years later, all these decisions made by Chinese and European leaders within the last two years should be seen as historic, strategic and meaningful.

All in all, the world now is still short of mega-ideas for making the Earth a peaceful and prosperous place. The Chinese have proposed, and the Europeans have echoed them, though some other Western powers have opposed them or at least hesitated. This should be recognised as the biggest achievement when assessing the China-EU partnership over the last several years. But this is just beginning of a real strategic partnership.

When talking about President Xi Jinping's visit in 2016, Vojtech Filip, Deputy Chairman of the Chamber of Deputies of the Parliament of the Czech Republic says it had shown a recognition of this European country's role in helping to boost the Sino-EU relationship and build a multi-polar world, which is in the interests of the Czech Republic. "We believe President Xi's visit is a milestone event for our bilateral relationship dating back 67 years, and we aim to build a strategic partnership towards the 21st century, the themes of which are about shaping a multi-polar world," Filip told me during an interview before Xi's visit. At the end of March, Xi met Filip and other parliamentary and party leaders. Filip, the chairman of the Communist Party of Bohemia and Moravia, the biggest party in the Czech Parliament with 42,000 members, met Xi before when he visited China,.

Filip said Xi was a man of vision, with tremendous knowledge of Europe and the world situation, and a sophisticated communicator. "He is a man with charisma and I think 90 percent of Czechs like him and are keenly expecting his visit," says Filip, adding that his first talk with Xi happened in 2011 in Beijing, when he was still Vice-President of China. "He is confident, visionary and has a lot of ideas." As to the visit, Filip also saw it as a new starting point after the two countries forged a close relationship in the 1950s and Czechoslovakia (as it then was called) was among the first group of countries in the world to recognise New China. He says that was the foundation for the bilateral relationship, and that Czech President Zeman had started to forge a closer relationship after the 1990s and especially when he was Prime Minister.

And now, after Zeman was elected as president in 2013, the two sides had accelerated their pace in building a closer relationship. "Obviously, both the president and prime minister have taken a closer relationship with China as a priority and during the last three years, the Czech Republic and China have had important meetings and visits among top leaders. It is important for us," says Filip. He says the strategic partnership of both sides would be forged facing the 21st century, in which a multi-polar world was key. China and the European Union are essential parts of this multi-polar world and the Czech Republic has shown strong support for China deepening its relationship with the EU. And now it is obvious that China has played a responsible and active role in the world, and Xi Jinping's Belt and Road initiative is seen as China's solution to offer an "economic foundation" for a peaceful world. He says Xi's visit to the Czech Republic was happening seventy years after the end of World War Two. "And it is meaningful to think about how the global powers contribute to world peace, and China has set an constructive example," says Filip.

Jaroslav Tvrdik, former defence minister of the Czech Republic, also says that from political conviction to family linkage, both Czech President Milos Zeman and Czech Prime Minister Bohuslav Sobotka have treated China as a "strategic partner" for a long time under their leadership, according to their top adviser Tvrdik. "They have their detailed a prioritised agenda to deal with their relationship with China, into which I believe they have put a huge amount of energy," says Tvrdik.

Now he acts as special adviser for the Republic's highest leadership and he was responsible for helping coordinate President Xi's visit arrangements from the Czech side. Zeman visited China in 1999 when he was the Czech prime minister, and twice since he became president. He met President Xi several times. "He is a long-time supporter of the Sino-Czech relationship, and this is a long-term vision," says Tvrdik. "He has invested a lot of personal passion and love in developing relations with China since the early stages of his political career. His policy has remained consistent."

So it is with Prime Minister Sobotka. He and his father both visited China in 2015. The Prime Minister aimed to boost the relationship with China and then invited President Xi to visit his country, ahead of schedule (it was originally scheduled for mid-2017). To celebrate his 70th birthday, his father flew from Prague to Beijing at the end of September to refresh the memories he gathered when working in China as an engineer about two decades ago. "It is special also because the prime minister bought the flight tickets as birthday gifts for his father and his colleague, who was with him in around 2000," says Tvrdik.

The prime minister's father and colleague had worked in China for three years in Tianjin. Most likely, his experiences during his stay in China influenced the prime minister's views on this emerging power. According to Tvrdik, the prime minister's father happily accepted his son's gifts with only two requests. First, he needed a translator to accompany them. And secondly, he needed a T-shirt of China's military parade to celebrate the 70th anniversary of victory against fascism and Japanese aggression, which was held on 3 September 2015. "And finally, the prime minister's father wore the T-shirt during the whole of his trip to China in September 2015," says Tvrdik. "He was aged 70 by then, too."

The prime minister began to carry on the "family linkage" with China, and in 2015, when he visited China at the end of November, he also took his children with him. Before their departure, their grandfather gave the children a tutorial on where to visit in China. When the prime minister had completed his talks with President Xi, they had a light moment. Xi says, according to Tvrdik, he had a deep impression of the Czech Republic, "because when I was young, my father bought me a pair of leather shoes when leaving the Czech Republic for home—my first pair of leather shoes in my life."

Xi's father Xi Zhongxun, then Vice-Premier of China, visited Czechoslovakia, as it then was known in 1959. The prime minister also shared his family's stories about China with President Xi. "I am proud that my father was working in China, and I am carrying on this friendship," Tvrdik quotes the prime minister as saying. Sobotka visited China in 2007 for the first time, and set up a working group on Chineses affairs when he started his premiership. "China is the only country for the Czech to set up such a coordination team shortly after he took power as prime minister," says Tvrdik, who was deputy head of the group.

CONNECTING MINDS

After holding intensive political meetings, engaging in lively exchanges with young football and ice hockey players, and signing cooperation documents during his March 28-30 visit to the Czech Republic in 2016, President Xi and his Czech counterpart Milos Zeman visited the 850-year-old Strahov Library in Prague. After being introduced by the museum curator to the collections on Chinese-Czech exchanges dating back 300-500 years, the two presidents stepped onto the veranda to get a bird's eye view of Prague while sipping their farewell beer.

Shortly after Xi left for Washington to attend the Nuclear Security Summit, I too had the chance to visit the stunningly magnificent library, which consists of the Philosophical Hall, which houses the Czech language collection on Confucius and the early comprehensive introduction to China, and the Theological Hall, with its stuccoes and paintings. The books on China, some of which are original manuscripts, were mostly written by missionaries during their stay in China or after their return hundreds of years ago.

Jan Parez, curator of the library's manuscript section who was responsible for preparing the items for Xi, says the president had a deep understanding of and respect for Czech society and culture. Thanks to Parez, I had the privilege of visiting the two halls, which are now open to tourists, and enjoying the panoramic view of Prague and soaking in the glory of the place where the two presidents drank their farewell beer.

Xi says it was a rare experience to see such a rich artistic and cultural treasure. Some other journalists who reported on his visit called it the most beautiful library in the world. It is a beacon of knowledge and beauty, and delivers a strong message. Both presidents are extremely keen readers with a preference for books on history and civilisation. And by saying that a long history and bountiful cultural heritage are the precious wealth of the

Czech people, and that China is an ancient civilisation with a history of more than 5,000 years, Xi highlighted the great potential for the two countries to learn from each other and expand their cultural exchanges following the establishment of a strategic partnership during his visit. The two presidents know that increasing people-to-people and cultural exchanges is the key to laying a firm foundation for the development of bilateral relations.

During his visit to the Czech Republic, Xi promoted mutual cultural respect. But there was more to his visit than economic and cultural exchanges. Xi visited the Czech Republic shortly after China announced the 13th Five-Year Plan (2016-20). By the time the plan is completed in 2020, China's per capita income is expected to reach $12,000, making it a relatively high-income country. Also, Xi has vowed to end extreme poverty in China by 2020.

Given these facts, one can say Xi's visit to the Strahov Library also signifies his vow to offer enough public goods to those in need. And this is an area where Europe has a lot of experience to offer to China. For example, it has already used the index of the number of books a child has access to at home to measure people's living conditions in a region.

China needs to identify the poor and needy in the country, as well as build more libraries to allow children from poor families to have access to more books because these can help them emerge out of poverty. Going by European standards, building more cultural venues such as libraries, museums, theatres, sports centres and swimming pools should also be given priority in order to help propel China's economic development and lift people's incomes, as well as their living standards.

When President Zeman was giving a speech in Renmin University of China in late 2014, he received a special gift: a Czech version of *The Four Books*, a novel by the remarkable Chinese writer Yan Nianke. The translated work on China's development in the 1950s and 60s, which Yan, also a professor at the university, took twenty years to plan and two years to write, won the international Franz Kafka literature prize that year.

Suzana Li, from the Czech Republic, was the translator of the masterpiece and other titles by Chinese writers such as Su Tong and Liu Zhenyun. Recalling the gift Zeman received, Suzana says fruitful exchanges between China and her country and Europe also heavily rely on building up trust in ordinary people's minds and hearts. "And literature and films are perfect vehicles to achieve that," Li told me in a lively coffee bar in Prague before Zeman left for Beijing to attend the Belt and Road Initiative for International Cooperation. Then Li said she wanted to deliver that message to the participants at the forum, that they should strongly support the translation of literature and bridge the gap in understanding between cultures, even in the era of digital transformation.

"Films have taken the upper hand now, but literature is essential as well in shortening the understanding gulf," says Li, who started to learn Chinese in the 1990s. She was even busy earning her doctorate in Chinese literature in Peking University ten years ago. Li loves the accounts of love, hardships, despair, sorrows and success of Chinese people's daily lives described in literature. An industrious middle-aged Czech translator of Chinese into her mother tongue, she has lived a very simple life; she spends six days a week in her quiet study in Prague translating. Every day, she works for six hours, and if there is a deadline, she works even on Sundays, and her hours of work are even longer. Her leisure time is spent reading and watching Chinese movies to help enrich her understanding of society and culture. Of course, she adds: "I spend roughly the same time on reading after getting tired in translation. And sometimes, I struggle to understand various writers' narrative styles."

But she says being occupied by those plots of how ordinary Chinese live their lives, how they earn their daily bread, how their fates change, is the most delightful thing. Her hard work helps her complete translating at least two books of contemporary Chinese literature into Czech every year. "This is my love and I am lucky because not everyone can live such a quiet life," says Li. "If I don't translate, I cannot imagine what else I could do; and I do think our exchanges will go beyond business and also focus on cultural and literary exchanges."

Such a focused way of life, being immersed in books on China, has helped Li shape her own yardstick to measure this country's progress in recent years, which is also shown in the birth of a group of excellent writers whose terrific works should win a Nobel Prize. "Writer Mo Yan winning a Nobel Prize, for sure, is a huge success for China," says Li. "But I think there are many Chinese writers who deserve the utmost honour." Li's academic and reading experiences ranged from British to American literature before she obtained her doctorate in China. "So I believe that Chinese writers have produced high quality works as writers have done in other countries," says Li.

But her conclusion is drawn from action. In the 1990s, she found it difficult to locate Czech-language novels and stories by Chinese writers and she could not understand why, because she had studied for a year in China and knew it as a country rich in literature. She contacted one publisher in an attempt to fill the gap, but that failed because the publisher knew nothing about China. Later on, she met a publisher from Prague's publishing house Verzone, who came to China and fell in love with it. "And she felt it was a shame that such fewer Chinese books were translated into the Czech language," Li recalls. "I trust more Czech-language readers share the delight of reading these stories and plots."

Li's latest translated work is *The Explosion Chronicles*, also by Yan Nianke, whose theme is how a village in his home province Henan, in Central China, was transformed in the previous three decades while China achieved an economic miracle. Li says her translation of Yan's *The Four Books* and *The Explosion Chronicles* will also help readers in her country understand the tracks of China's development in previous decades. And another book completed was *I Did not Kill My Husband*, by the renowned writer Liu Zhenyun. While translating, Li was impressed by Liu's style of writing, which she considers very humorous, easy to understand and accessible to readers. "It's witty and funny and illustrates the everyday lives of Chinese people. That's why also the Czech publisher was most interested in the book. So I think it's also a good way for Czech readers to see Chinese people's lives," says Li.

Because of Li's stunning skills in translating modern Chinese literature, she has received subsidies from the Confucius Institute headquarters to support her work. In August 2016, she was given an achievement award by the Chinese government for her lasting efforts in literature translation, and Vice-Premier Liu Yandong even received the 19 outstanding sinologists all over the world. On the Belt and Road, she says: "In my view, it is a colossal enterprise, which needs patient and piece-by-piece work for years. I am confident that what I am doing to help the Czechs know ordinary people's daily lives via translated bestsellers is laying a foundation, which is vital, essential and effective."

In addition to exchanges of literary works, China and the Czech Republic have launched a new round of personnel exchanges and cooperative agreements, which is implemented by China's State Administration of Foreign Experts Affairs and the Czech Association for Science and Technology (CAST). In an interview, Jaromir Volf, chairman of CAST, says Xi Jinping's visit to his country in early 2016 took place after the Czech president and prime minister's visits to China, and he was quite sure that President Xi's historic visit had brought the bilateral relationship to a far-reaching level, covering areas from business, trade and investment to personnel exchanges. Describing the visit as "the most important political event between our two states," Volf says CAST, an independent legal entity made up of 67 technical and industrial associations with nearly 100,000 members, was an important channel for the Czech government to communicate with technical staff. "We have such a big database and we are ready to cooperate with the Chinese government to select the proper experts China needs," says Volf.

Volf has visited China three times and now he has become the first Czech expert to be working with China under the new cooperation framework." I am starting to work and commute between China and the Czech Republic frequently and to spot experts for both sides," he says. Volf, an engineer, he will start work in Shandong Province in late 2016 and a five-year contract has already been signed. "I am very excited to work as a bridge-builder to deepen mutual cooperation," he says. Every time he received a Chinese delegation, he says, they had shown great interest in working with Czech experts, and had great passion for agricultural and technical areas. He believed there should be huge potential synergies in these areas between the two countries. In the agricultural sector, Volf says, the Czech Republic is competitive in planting wheat and corn, and producing the ingredients for brewing beer. "China has already shown interest in this area," he says.

As an advanced industrial country, the Czech Republic is also strong in mechanical technology, automation, building, Robot technologies and electronics. "We are ready to cooperate with China in these areas if China requests," says Volf. He adds that China is very competitive in science and technology now and it has advanced universities in Shanghai, Hong Kong, Beijing and other cities. "The level of science and technology is very high and we have a possibility to deliver two-way exchanges," he says.

Sports exchanges between China and the Czech Republic is also a focus. With China and the Republic ready to launch large-scale sports diplomacy, ice hockey coach Slavomir Lener still remembers what he described as a "crazy but great" experience in teaching Chinese players in freezing weather, at minus 30-40 degrees, in northeast China twenty years ago. He had never experienced that temperature at home in a country of ice hockey and football. And he had not visited China after that. He told me in early 2016 how excited he felt when a group of young players accepted his supervision to prepare themselves to compete in the 2022 Winter Olympics, which will be held in Beijing and Zhangjiakou, Hebei Province.

"We have started the first stage to prepare them to become the core of China's national team in the 2022 Winter Olympics", says Lener, who had spent about six months in China in 1995 coaching the national team. He was speaking during an interview at the Czech Ice Hockey Association. Twenty young Chinese players started their eight-day training in Prague on 24 March 2016. Lener was supervisor of this camp, responsible for scheduling and arranging the best coaches to teach and organise three games for the young players. "This is the first contact, and we will see if cooperation will continue after this training." This happens when President Xi is going to pay a 40-hour state visit to the Czech Republic before he flies to Washington to attend the World Nuclear Security Summit. And before he left for that visit, Xi, himself a football fan, chaired a meeting on the preparations for the 2022 Winter Olympics.

When President Zeman visited China in September 2016 and Prime Minister Bohuslav Sobotka visited China in November that year, both of them talked about sports cooperation with Chinese leaders.

In late 2015, when former president of the Chinese Olympic Committee Liu Peng visited Prague, he showed a strong intention to learn from the Czech Republic's winter sports and experiences in organising events in the run-up to delivering the 2022 Olympics. "I found the Czech Republic has a lot we can learn from in winter sports," Liu is quoted as saying. And it is highly possible that both sides will announce plans to deal with this during Xi's visit, the first by a Chinese President to the Republic in 67 years. "During Xi's visit, young football players will also compete while Chinese ice hockey players accept training," says Jiri Kejval, President of the Czech National Olympics

Committee. "And sport is about friendship. This is preparation and we know that China will not only organise a Winter Olympics but also be part of it by participating in the game."

Kejval says his country is ready to help China to catch up in the next six years. Now, China ranks 38th in global ice hockey competition and the Chinese ice hockey team can only take part in the 2022 Olympics if it is ranked among the world's first 18 national teams. Kejval is quite confident that his coaches are qualified to achieve that goal. In the 1950s Czech coaches taught the Russians and now their teams are ranked among the highest in the world. Kejval was a roller and during his time, he says, there had been no roller in China. But now China was also very good at ice rolling sports, within the space of just a few years. "So I am 100 percent sure China could produce highly competitive ice hockey players despite the fact that team sports are more difficult than individual sports," says Kejval.

Quoting his experiences in China, Lener says China was ready to win. He says Chinese players were very focused, eager to learn and compete. "And we are going to train their sense of hockey as this is a game of ten persons, not an individual game," he adds. Both he and Kejval praised the fact that China had made tremendous progress in sports and event organisation, calling the 2008 Beijing Olympics Games "spectacular." "And now you start to shift to winter sports, which has brought a lot of opportunities for us to begin cooperation," says Kejval. He thought China could also cooperate with the Czech Republic in football as this had begun to become a widely-promoted sport. He says it was not only China which learned from the Czechs; this was a two-way street. "We can learn from China in volleyball, table tennis and other sports," he says.

With Chinese investors enjoying a spree of investment in prestigious football clubs and world-renowned players in Europe, CEFC—China Energy Company Limited, one of the country's top private businesses, based in Shanghai—has a different apple in its eye. About two years ago, when this quickly-growing company targeted SK Slavia Praha, a football club set up in the Czech Republic in 1892, it found that its players were not being paid properly, the management was in chaos, and its ranking had fallen to a historic low, which shocked and disappointed its fans. A Prague court had decided to declare it bankrupt. But three days ahead of the court's deadline,

CEFC China, which focused on energy and financial investment overseas, injected a moderate sum of money (which it was unwilling to disclose), paying off the debt for the club, buying it and its players, and becoming the new owner.

"CEFC China moved in at a critical time," says Tomas Buzek, board member of Slavia Praha. "The historic football club of the Czech Republic was saved."

From ordinary people on the streets to Prime Minister Bohuslav Sobotka, and his son, the club once boasted a million fans. The country has a population of around 12 million. Almost immediately after CEFC China's purchase of the club in September 2015, there was a sharp improvement, and the club moved up the ranks by six places (compared to the previous season). After eight long years, it also returned to European Cup competition. Its worst situation was between 2013-2014, when it faced downgrading to a lower league.

Buzek says the stabilisation of the club's financial situation, strengthening its management, setting up standard control mechanisms and investments in a players' squad, brought success right in the first season when Slavia returned to the European Cup competitions again. "At the same time, these steps laid the foundation for success, and the club, a few rounds before the end, enjoyed a leading position in the league table and chased for victory in the national cup," says Buzek, speaking in the Eden Arena football stadium, about ten minutes' drive from downtown Prague. With a capacity of 21,000 seats, the stadium is also owned by CEFC China now and has become the home venue of SK Slavia Praha and occasionally the Czech Republic national football team.

Last September the club decided to appoint 56-year-old Jaroslav Silhavy, a household name in the Czech Republic, as head coach, and the management was radically strengthened. Soon the Chinese company's investment proved to be a huge success: its team never lost a game in 23 matches, and during the ongoing Czech First League season it has secured first place. Its fans have returned to the stadium. "Now, for most matches, our stadium is full when our team is playing," says Buzek happily. But at the worst time, only one out five seats were filled.

What made Buzek happy is that the value of the club has increased and some players have become commercially competitive. Citing numbers,

Buzek says the club was assessed at a value of six million euro when CEFC China decided to invest in September 2015. But now it has soared to twenty million euros, though it is still worth far less than the top clubs in Europe. "What's more, a few players are outstanding worldwide," says Buzek. Of 25 club members, the market value of the most competitive one ranges from six million to ten million euros.

But Buzek says CEFC China has no intention of "making a profit" from this project. "We have aimed to restore happiness and joy to its fans and we want to share this responsibility," says Buzek, also vice-president in charge of CEFC China's European operations. This club boasted a stunning record, winning 17 championships in the Czech First League, but it could not sustain itself financially before the Chinese company moved in. "CEFC China is still investing in us and I think very soon we will become financially sustainable", he says.

The club also relies on revenue from ticket sales, advertising and TV broadcasting." Though our players are competitive and valuable, we don't have a plan to transfer them to other clubs when offers come. This would destroy our team," says Buzek. His club has also invested in boosting exchanges among young players between China and Europe. In March 2016, when President Xi visited Prague, the Slavia International Cup made its debut and several teams of young players from both countries took part. Xi and the Czech President Milos Zeman met the players.

When Chinese and European players came to this year's matches on 21-23 April, Zeman met those from both sides before leaving for his third presidential visit to China in May. "Though I am not a keen football player, I do know this game is full of fun and joy. And I hope you can grow into stars that will not be forgotten by your fans," he says in Prague Castle, where the president's office is located. He recalls he only played football once in his life. "But I will cheer for the young boys from China and the Czech Republic," he says.

Film is also a medium shared by the two countries. The filming of a popular romantic drama, *Somewhere Only We Know*, which was directed by and starred the award-winning actress Xu Jinglei, took place in Prague several years ago. According to the Chinese ambassador to the Czech Republic, Ma Keqing, the magnificent architecture and stunning natural beauty of this country have already been captured in several Chinese movies in recent years, as both countries have tightened their relationship. Behind China's interwoven relations with European countries hide tremendously meaningful topics for both sides to explore, with the aim of satisfying the growing demands of moviegoers and TV audiences in the digital era. Ranging from historic themes to topical exchanges, war, love, heroes, family and food, they are inexhaustible.

If they put more stories on screen, efforts like these will cause a chain effect. This is not only because the demand for movie and TV series in China is expanding rapidly. One dominating reality in China is that this country's middle class is expanding rapidly. Its size will equal the total population of Europe within a few years. This middle class has a huge appetite for entertainment and travel. When its members are impressed by a movie, they think about traveling. The number of Chinese tourists to the Czech Republic soaring tenfold to an estimated 500,000 this year is a typical example.

In addition, film lovers among Chinese tourists are especially welcome to visit a film poster gallery in downtown Prague, which has exhibited 1,200 original movie posters from 1936 to 1961. Named Gallery Spectrum, it is situated in the centre of Prague and is designed for families, pupils, students, foreign and Czech tourists. "Now we are trying to attract more and more Chinese visitors, as many Chinese tourists are flocking into Prague," says Petra Paroubek, senior consultant of the gallery. She says the visit of President Xi Jinping will make Prague more attractive to Chinese tourists, and she believes more and more of them will be coming to Prague and the Czech Republic. "We believe many Chinese tourists are moviegoers who would like to have a look at these original posters," she says.

Paroubek also says her team is contacting tourism agencies to introduce the gallery. At the same time, the team is developing Chinese-language products such as posters and Chinese-version websites. According to Paroubek, the gallery is a unique collection from the golden era of Hollywood and European movies. Visitors can see big stars such as Marlon Brando, John Wayne, Sophia Loren, Marlene Dietrich, Alain Delon, Jean Gabin and others. "Visitors can get a poster copy or have it printed on a T-shirt," she says. The gallery's waxworks of World War II leaders are mainly for students and school pupils and were handmade in the1950s and 1960s in the original way, not cast like most wax figures. "All the items exhibited here come from a private collection," says Paroubek.

BUSINESS OPPORTUNITIES

More than 10 years ago, when Lian Yongping, at the age of 25, moved from southwest China to the Czech Republic to start helping his company to build a factory from scratch, he felt he was a total stranger in the country. He even puzzled about how to express himself at first when meeting with local staff.

Now, with the factory producing up to a million TV sets last year, Lian, general manager in charge of European operations for Changhong, a famous household appliance brand, has had a threefold dream of expansion after ten years of learning and operations in the Czech Republic. "My ambition has resulted from our experiences, and we found it is urgent, feasible and doable," says Lian in the factory, about 50 km from Prague. "It is time to be ambitious."

He says sales of his factory's TVs has grown rapidly in the last three years at an average 20 percent. Now his company is competing against products from South Korea and Japan for the European market. "Once our TV sales surpass one million, 3 percent of the European market share, it is relatively easy to overtake two million compared with our first ten years of progress," says Lian. "But the key is how to realise this in a smart but integrated way."

First, he says, his company has decided to set up a research and development centre next to the factory. At the same time, it will also shift to manufacturing refrigerators, washing machines and other appliances, with production lines for the European market opening soon.

"This is designed to be our home appliance production base for Europe, and we aim to promote our own brand," Lian says, pointing to the empty land which his company has already purchased beside his factory. Secondly, Lian says he has been motivated to enlarge the production chain to take care of the life cycle of his products. "We aim to set up our own logistics centre, expand our business to sales, after-sales service and maintenance, which are even more profitable than manufacturing," he says.

Lian says his parent company has shown strong support for his ideas for expanding the business chain, or as he puts it, like constructing a highway. "Once we have our own complete business chain, we can also use this platform to offer services for other electronic products as well," says Lian.

His factory has already rented storage space near Prague as a pilot step to implement the ambition. "And thirdly, I want to get involved in attracting more Chinese investors to the Czech Republic and helping construct a high-tech industrial zone in Nymburk, where my factory is based," says Lian. "I want to share my experiences and lessons, and then we could work together to contribute to Czech development."

Right now, Nymburk and Sichuan province, where Changhong is headquartered, have already begun cooperating to construct a high-tech industrial zone beside Lian's factory. The government of Sichuan province has already started to attract more investors to settle in the zone, which covers about four million square metres. "We started from nothing ten years ago and I am quite confident that this industrial park will take shape in another ten years," says Lian.

Lian says the visit of President Xi Jinping paved the way for the business expansion as mutual political trust was hugely boosted. And at the same time, Lian says Xi's visit also helped Czechs and Europeans to recognise again the competitiveness of made-in-China products, with this country aiming to upgrade its manufacturing capacity to a higher level. "We are quite encouraged by the Chinese leadership's global win-win vision in introducing the Belt and Road Initiative to better connect China and Asians, Europeans and Africans," says Lian. "From a businessman's point of view, this is creating opportunities and facilitating goods flow for us."

With capital, technology and a market network at hand, Lian says Chinese investors should also have second thoughts on how to expand overseas while the Chinese government is taking a proactive approach. He says the Czech Republic is an ideal location for Chinese investors to expand in Europe because of its gateway advantages there, despite it being landlocked. But it has highway, railway and aviation access to the rest of the Europe and the world.

Meanwhile, Lian says, Czechs are well-educated and its labourers are hardworking, while wage standards are lower than those of Western Europe. "This is, from my point of view, an ideal choice for Chinese investors," says Lian.

But he says Chinese investors should be modest enough, as most European countries have already experienced technological, industrial and management "revolutions" in terms of factory operations and business expansion in previous decades, which have left them with huge legacies. "We can only learn first and then consider innovation while learning, which should be a viable choice," says Lian. His factory has already achieved automation in the assembly process, and the management depends heavily on digital software applications. With his senior team, he has developed a management software application which uses about 500 key data inputs and criteria to describe his 400 managers' and workers' performance in a single system. "I just need to take care of the performance of the managers in charge of production, sales and procurement and finance, and if I need to check, I just open my mobile to see the progress shown in the application," says Lian. "If the targets could not be met before the deadlines, I will be alerted and then I will warn the managers." But normally, Lian Yongping says, he is very relaxed. "Because everybody knows their duty and the system will alert them automatically."

In addition to the greenfield project, Chinese and Czech researchers successfully developed a railway engine capable of speeds of more than 500 km/hr, says Petro Kouvaliuka, president of Czech Technical University in Prague.

Kouvaliuka announced this achievement before President Xi Jinping visit the Czech Republic from 28-30 March 2016. The breakthrough was made jointly by a team from his university and CRRC Dalian R&D Co., Ltd in northeast Dalian city, which specialises in high-speed engine development. The two sides entered into a partnership four years ago and Kouvaliuka says he was told about the achievement recently.

"The researchers from China and the Czech Republic made the breakthrough and the outcome, a speed over 500 km/hr, is feasible," Kouvaliuka told me in an interview in early 2016. "It is fast and it is commercially feasible." The two teams joined efforts to use the high-speed engines on the 2,000 km railway linking Beijing and Chengdu, capital of Sichuan province, says Kouvaliuka. "After that, they will be trying to sell it in Europe or the United States."

Asked if the engines could be used in the Czech Republic, Kouvaliuka says it was impossible now because of the many curves on the Czech railways caused by rivers, mountains, villages and towns. The maximum speed of Czech trains was 160 km per hour. "But maybe we can build a high-speed railway linking Prague and our second biggest city, Brno, about 200 km away," Kouvaliuka says.

As China has offered the Belt and Road Initiative to better connect the Eurasian continent by improving its infrastructure, some Czech politicians have shown interest in building high-speed railways in the Republic, though it faces huge obstacles such as environmental impact assessments and slow decision-making processes caused by public participation. On whether the country should consider involving China in building a high-speed railway, former Prime Minister Jiri Rusnok says the Republic was underdeveloped in this area and there should be a long-term intention to consider such programmes. He says Czechs know that China is helping to develop similar programmes in other central and east European countries. "We will take this as a kind of reference project—and why not reach further into central Europe, to the Czech Republic, if it is successful?" says Rusnok.

Jan Kohout, former foreign minister of the Czech Republic, also says his president was impressed by China's high-speed train from Tianjin to Beijing, as were other officials. "They believe it is high-end technology, and there is no doubt about Chinese companies' competitiveness in building the railway," says Kohout. "And technology is needed not only here but also in Central Europe." He says China was helping to construct a high-speed railway between Budapest and Belgrade, and possibly, this would be extended to south and north. The Czech Republic and Germany were going to build a high-speed line between the German city of Dresden and Prague, reducing the journey time from 2 hours 15min to just 50 minutes. "This is a small start, but it is difficult to implement big infrastructure projects due to environmental impact assessments and the public joint decision-making," says Kohout. But if Chinese companies wanted to invest in such projects in

Europe, they should come two or three years before the tender opened. "It is important to get involved locally before you jump in the sky for tendering," Kohout says.

Despite the high-speed line being still under discussion, the first freight train between Prague and Yiwu, a famous commodity distribution city in China's economically booming Zhejiang Province, began its maiden trip on 20 July 2017 from the Czech Republic capital. The inauguration of the freight rail link was hailed by both President Milos Zeman and Prime Minister Bohuslav Sobotka as another important milestone of bilateral cooperation under the framework of the Belt and Road Initiative proposed by President Xi Jinping in 2013.

On 19 July, the country's top leaders endorsed the project while addressing more than 1,500 participants attending the annual China Investment Forum, at which Liu Yunshan, member of the Standing Committee of the Political Bureau of the CPC Central Committee, also delivered a keynote speech. The officials from Yiwu highly praised the geographic importance of the Czech Republic, saying this landlocked country had easy access to most European countries within a radius of 1,000 kms. "The Czech Republic has its special geographic advantage...nearly the whole of Europe has been covered," says Lin Yi, Mayor of Yiwu, introducing the cooperation blueprint between his city and the Czech Republic before the Provincial Governor Yuan Jiajun and the Chinese ambassador to the Czech Republic, Ma Keqing.

Lin says his city aimed to boost the frequency of the freight trains running between his city and Prague, where exports from China could be easily distributed through the rest of Europe. "Ideally, we hope every day there will be a train leaving from both Prague and Yiwu for each other," he says. The first train was laden with more than 80 containers of crystal products, auto components and beer from the Czech Republic and it took sixteen days to arrive at its destination.

"The duration is much shorter compared with shipping by sea, though the cost will be higher," says Lin. "Now more and more auto producers have started to use this mode of transport to distribute their components in China." With support from the provincial government, Lin says, his city planned to start construction of a logistics centre covering about one square kilometer in the Czech Republic by the end of 2017, though he didn't reveal its location.

He says the project would generate about 3,000 jobs for the country. Firmly supporting the Belt and Road Initiative, President Zeman says he expected that the freight express between Prague and Yiwu to help boost agricultural exports from his country to China. Since the Belt and Road Initiative was launched in 2013, the freight trains have been running in their thousands between Chinese and European cities, efficiently bringing economic cooperation closer for both sides.

Before Yiwu had explored the geographic importance of the Czech Republic, some cities in Germany and Poland had been playing a bigger role in the increased freight movements on the Eurasian continent since 2013.

To encourage more active economic exchanges between China and the Czech Republic, Chinese think tank experts have been delivering positive messages. During his recent visit to this country, Li Daokui, professor of Tsinghua University and also a member of the Chinese People's Political Consultative Conference (CPPCC), the national political advisory body, said China's economy would slow down in 2017 and would grow at 7.0-7.5 percent during the 2018-2019 period, believing that China's growth rate would be 6.9 percent in 2017 while the economy would level out, with growth regaining upward to the range of above 7 percent.

After his speech delivered at the China Investment Forum in Prague in July, Li made these points during an interview with me. The Czech Republic Prime Minister, Bohuslav Sobotka, and Liu Yunshan, member of the Standing Committee of the Political Bureau of the CPC Central Committee, who was visiting the country, delivered keynote speeches at the forum, calling for increased cooperation under the Belt and Road Initiative framework.

Li said the consistent recovery of the global economy, China's successful economic restructuring and the local governments' growing passion in driving new investment would be "three positive factors" behind his "cautious optimism" over China's upward trends. "I am cautiously optimistic about the prospects if we can continuously manage the risks at home and abroad properly," says Li. "Based on our research outcomes, China has potential to explore to keep its growth above 7 percent for a few years." If Li's estimate goes well, it means that China will say goodbye to the downturn in the economic cycle from 2012 to 2016, which saw growth of 7.9 percent, 7.8 percent, 7.3 percent, 6.9 percent and 6.7 percent respectively.

Fredrik Erixon, Director of the European Centre for International Political Economy, also says China's growth will remain in the current range throughout the year. "China has already acknowledged what needs to be done—to re-balance its economy, to open up more sectors for competition and help to drive growth in services, innovation and technology adoption," says Erixon. He also says, Beijing has already identified the importance of moderating credit growth and getting the capital market allocate money in better ways. "If faster economic growth will be maintained, the challenge ahead is to continue delivering on these objectives," says Erixon.

Home Credit Group, an international consumer finance provider based in the Czech Republic and also the country's biggest investor in China, is one forerunner trying to boost investment in China further. "We will also aim to build partnerships with Chinese companies to invest in other countries, and this is our new strategy after ushering in the Belt and Road Initiative," says David Minol, Chief Executive Officer of Home Credit Philippines, who had worked in China as chief financial officer. Home Credit has formed a partnership with Dongguan-based Chinese smart-phone manufacturer Oppo Electronics Corp, and they have already jointly increased their presence in Vietnam and the Philippines by offering loans to mobile phone buyers.

Minol says his company is also exploring such cooperation with other smart-phone producers such as Huawei in third-party countries. Home Credit Group has recently gained two billion yuan (278 million euro) "immediately" from PAG Asia Capital, a Hong Kong-based private equity firm, says the group's top management. This cooperation aims to help the group's China operation to be listed on the stock market eventually.

Jiri Smejc, Chairman of the Home Credit Group, made the announcement recently, while the two companies signed cooperation agreements in July 2017, which will enable the Home Credit Group to accelerate its pace of localisation by seeking a Chinese shareholder after it has been present in China for up to ten years. It expects that it will take another three to five years to complete the process of approval from the regulatory bodies to make the PAG the group's shareholder in China.

Smejc says his group's partnership with PAG has showcased its confidence in the stability and promising prospects of China's financial market, adding that China's regulatory bodies have made tremendous efforts to beef up the robust market in previous years. The registered capital of Home Credit Group's operations in China amounted to 7 billion yuan and the new input will make PAG a minority shareholder. "The investment will be in place immediately," says Smejc. He says this partnership was finalised after two years of negotiations, and for a long time his group had been trying to identify "qualified" local partners and investors. "This is a very big and strategic decision for us, which has showcased our confidence and commitment to this dynamic market," he says.

"We are very pleased to form a partnership with one of the world's most innovative consumer finance providers," says Shan Weijian, Chairman of PAG Group, which boasts one of Asia's largest private equity firms. Shan says his company will contribute its knowledge in the China market to help Home Credit further grow and better serve its customers, while both sides have set a goal of "eventually listing Home Credit China's operations on an internationally recognised stock market," after going through all necessary regulatory approvals.

According to their agreement, both sides have committed to develop a healthy consumer finance sector in China while recognising the great potential of this sector. Home Credit says partnering with PAG will enable it to open a dialogue with more local partners regarding strategic cooperation and investment. Smejc says China is his group's largest and fastest-growing market with 7.5 billion euro in total assets, over 13.2 million active customers by the end of March and 178,00 sales points across the country. Thanks to its successful operation in China, Smejc says his company is also the biggest consumer finance provider in several countries in Asia, except India. "But very soon, we will be the most competitive one in this country as well," says Smejc, adding that his company mainly offers small loans for those on the lower rungs of society.

A high-level official of the Czech National Bank says his country welcomes foreign investors increasing their stakes in financial sectors. In elaborating the country's openness, the official, who has spoken on condition of anonymity, adds that 70—80 percent of the country's financial sectors are in the hands of foreign investors, and the country's financial sector is competitive.

Apart from businesses, both Chinese and Czech banking watchdogs have demonstrated their willingness to support increased activity by banks and financial companies in each other's markets under the Belt and Road Initiative, which will boost connectivity throughout Eurasia. They also have decided to deepen cooperation on cross-border crisis management to prevent the impacts of any financial crisis.

Shang Fulin, then chairman of the China Banking Regulatory Commission, and Miroslav Singer, governor of the then Czech National Bank, made the commitment during President Xi Jinping's visit in early 2016.

While boosting the bilateral relationship to a strategic level, both countries have been determined to deepen pragmatic actions to realise the Belt and Road Initiative, which was proposed by Xi in 2013. It comprises the Silk Road Economic Belt and the 21st Century Maritime Silk Road.

"While deepening supervision and crisis management cooperation, we strongly encourage our banking and financial sectors to participate in the initiative and diversify financial services to facilitate investment and trade activities between the Czech Republic and China," Shang says.

Singer says: "The initiative creates potential for mutually beneficial economic cooperation between the two countries, and we are keen on expanding cooperation with Chinese partners." Shang's commission and the Czech National Bank signed an enlarged memorandum of understanding to share experiences on crisis management. Shang adds that his commission, in line with President Xi's proposal, is in the process of forming the Asian Financial Cooperation Association, which will be a platform for banking and financial sectors along the Belt and Road routes. The Czech Banking Association is very supportive and will be a member of the association. "Right now, great potential for cooperation on both sides has been released and both sides have shown huge intentions to further deepen cooperation," says Shang. "We are ready to keep closer relations with the Czech National Bank."

Shang says the Czech Republic is an important country along the routes of the Belt and Road Initiative and China supports financial cooperation with the country. In August 2016, Bank of China set up a branch in Prague, which has become a financial platform for enterprises on both sides.

Shang says his commission has actively supported setting up branches or subsidiaries of banking and financial companies in the countries along the Belt and Road routes. He adds that by the end of 2016, nine Chinese banks had set up 56 branches in 24 countries along the Belt and Road routes, and 20 countries along the routes have set up 56 branches of commercial banks in China.

China and the Czech Republic have also tightened cooperation in aviation. In addition to an increased number of flights, a group of students from Sichuan Airlines are working for their pilot certificates at the flight school FAIR, about an hour's drive from Prague.

Michal Markovic, director of the flight school, says the students will stay for 14 months to complete their integrated pilot licence course, which consists of almost 900 hours of theoretical knowledge and 230 hours of flight training.

"In the end, the students should obtain a European licence and this is the first time we have invited a large group from China," says Markovic, who believes that his project plays a useful part in deepening people-to-people exchanges between China and the CEE countries.

CHAPTER FOUR

Switzerland and the Republic of Serbia, both European countries outside the EU, show ample passion to link with China

The two countries, Switzerland and the Republic of Serbia, are both outside the EU but have contrasting stages of development. But they have actively approached China by enriching the Belt and Road Initiative in different ways. Switzerland, the first country in Europe to have set up a free trade partnership with China, believes this initiative will help all economies to come closer, while the Republic of Serbia is counting on the Initiative to enhance its infrastructure, re-industrialise its economy and improve its role in the region. All the aims are rational and compatible.

SHARED VALUES BETWEEN CHINA AND SWITZERLAND

For Switzerland, it played a unique role for the Belt and Road Initiative Forum for International Cooperation on 14-15 May 2017: President Xi Jinping announced China's hosting the crucial gathering when he delivered a speech in January at the annual meeting of World Economic Forum in Davos during his state visit. Xi's Swiss counterpart Doris Leuthard swiftly confirmed her attendance during Xi's visit.

Prior to Xi's visit, Leuthard has pinned high hopes on enhancing cooperation with China, announcing that she shared the "same values" with Xi during an exclusive interview with me in January. After Xi's speech, Leuthard restated the message in the Congress Hall of Davos when I was asking her how she responded to Xi's visit. In my interview experience, it is my first time to interview a state leader twice within one week. The easy-going Leuthard is an excellent example of the Swiss, for whom, it seems that there is no word "no" in their life dictionary. Switzerland, by far, has been one of my most frequented countries during my journalistic career. Not to mention other interview assignments, I have covered all the Davos summits from 2011-17, which are enlightening and enriching journeys for me, though it is always hard to find a bed in the crowded skiing town during the busy seasons.

In May when she was in Beijing, Leuthard formally stated her country's stances on the Initiative, following its decade-long pioneering role, among the Western countries, it has played leading role in deepening partnership with China. "Only openness and an open economy have better results, and nowadays, we can not avoid going global," says Leuthard with me on the 12 January 2017 during an exclusive interview in Bern, the Swiss capital. "We fight against protectionism and President Xi shares the same values and philosophy."

Saying she had "a lot of honor and pleasure" to receive President Xi and his wife Peng Liyuan then, Leuthard revealed that the two countries were going to send strong signals to drum up global cooperation and fight against closed-door policies during Xi's stay in Switzerland from 15-18 January. "I think many countries are on our side and they know cooperation is much better than isolationism and protectionism." In such a spirit, both countries announced to upgrade their free trade agreement, which entered into force in July 2014 and helped waive the majority of tariffs in two-way trade. However, Leuthard says both sides have decided to reduce more tariffs to nothing or low rates to facilitate trade flow. "We have found that there is still room to improve and so we decided to upgrade our free trade partnership," she says, adding that the global financial market is not stable and so is the situation in Switzerland, the seventh biggest financial market in the world. "I am keen to learn how Xi will share his view on the challenges," says the Swiss Federation president.

Leuthard has the intention that both Geneva and Zurich, traditional financial centre, to compete to attract Chinese banks to expand their businesses in the two cities. "Competition is a good thing and we welcome Chinese banks to invest in Switzerland," she adds. Financial cooperation was part of agreements which both sides signed during Xi's visit. She also said that both sides would be deepening cooperation in the energy sectors after they had already entered into agreements in dealing with environmental problems. "I know pollution is quite severe in China and that's also why we want to share our experiences and technologies in expanding cooperation in energy and environment," she said. Citing an example that in some urban regions in China, heating still relies on coal burning, she says affordable replacements and technologies already exist. "It is not about cost but adapting to changes," she says. But Leuthard forecasts that China will be moving faster than expected in dealing with pollution and smog. She recalls Switzerland had such bad experiences in the industrialization process but it took about 40-50 years to root out the problems.

Having visited China in August 2016, Leuthard, took over from Johann N. Schneider-Ammann as president of the Swiss Confederation from the beginning of 2017. Schneider-Ammann paid a state visit to China in April 2016, and during the meeting with President Xi, agreed on an innovative strategic partnership, which he says gave an adds dimension and fresh impulse to Sino-Swiss bilateral relations. During the visit, Switzerland signed up as an observer of the partnership agreement between China and sixteen central and east European countries. The Swiss government is made up of the seven members of the Federal Council, each of whom has the same status, rights and obligations and are elected by the United Federal Assembly for a four-year term of office. Each member of the Federal Council heads one of the seven departments of the Federal Administration and the president of the Swiss Confederation is elected for a one-year term.

Geng Wenbing, Chinese ambassador to Switzerland, says that more countries have shown growing interest in free trade talks with China, mainly because Switzerland has already benefited from the high-level trade partnership established in 2014, making its export to China grow steadily. The official figures from the Swiss government has indicated that its exports have slowed down in October and November last year but the export volume to China has kept a double-digit year-on-year growth in the two months, which is encouraging against the backdrop of bleak global trade. Specifically, its exports to China have increased 11.5 percent year-on-year in November while the pace in October was as high as 24.1 percent. "Such rosy results have led more countries to become interested in free trade talks with China and even some of them asked me for the agreement texts sealed by China and Switzerland," Geng says. "I am sure that every country that enters such trade arrangements with China will become winners."

Geng has based his argument on the fact that China has been restructuring its investment and trade-led economy into a pattern depending on consumption and innovation, which will create tremendous import opportunities. Geng says Xi's visit to Switzerland took place against the rapid and complex evolution of the global geopolitical situation and rising pickup of trade and investment protectionism. In December 2016, the European Union, United States and Japan, the leading global economies refused to fulfill its promises it made 15 years ago when China joined World Trade Organization in recognizing China as an equal trade partner. But Switzerland, joining dozens of WTO members, recognized China's market economy status in 2007. Apart from the efforts in boosting trade partnership, Geng says the leaders will upgrade their political relationship to a new level. Switzerland was the first Western country to established a diplomatic relationship with the People's Republic of China in 1950. And in April 2016, when former president of the Swiss Confederation Johann N. Schneider-Ammann visited China, both sides decided to enter into an innovation partnership.

Schneider-Ammann, now, head of the Federal Department of Economic Affairs, Education and Research, says that Switzerland has been following "with great interest" the Belt and Road Initiative because his country is an export-led and open economy, and closer connectivity among different countries is in its interest. In recalling his state visit to China in 2016 when he was rotating federal president, Schneider-Ammann says he learned a lot about this initiative in detail during the meeting with President Xi. "One year later, we will have a new president (Leuthard) and she will present our Swiss stance soon in Beijing," said Schneider-Ammann during an exclusive interview with me in early 2017 in his office in Bern. Now, though the discussion about the initiative is still not wide among the public in his country, he says the politicians, the government and the parliament already known about the initiative and the new president herself has her team and China experts and contacts exploring this initiative.

Though he could not offer more details on the Swiss position at the moment, Schneider-Ammann says his country has always been the forerunner in strengthening firm partnership with China. These pioneering relationships range from recognizing New China among the first Western countries, exporting advanced technologies, admitting China's market economy status, entering into a free trade agreement and innovation partnership with China, to becoming a founding member of the Asian Infrastructure Investment Bank.And it even has become an observer country in the cooperation framework between China and the sixteen Central and

Eastern European countries. "Now, our frequent political exchanges have demonstrated how we are steadily pushing our partnership," says Schneider-Ammann, recalling that President Xi generously shared his views with him during the state visit in April last year, especially during the State dinner. "I learned a lot and we fixed a lot of practical issues," says Schneider-Ammann. "Though it was my first time to meet President Xi, what impressed me was his statesmanship, sincerity and readiness to talk with a small European country.

Schneider-Ammann also says President Xi frankly talked about present challenges that China faced and during this visit, he found that President Xi has a very, very respected personality while both sides exchanged in very detailed ways regarding an innovation partnership, with China listing it high on its development agenda. "We spent a lot of time on this topic and President Xi had been keen to know the detailed policies and practices of my country," says Schneider-Ammann, adding that now both sides have already held technical meetings on advancing the free trade agreement while the two sides will regularly review the agreement every two years.

Apart from political and economic exchanges, both sides are exploring opportunities in education, tourism and even sports. Schneider-Ammann also says that Xi has shown great interest in the vocational education system in Switzerland. Yves Fluckiger, Rector of the University of Geneva says his university and Tsinghua University have launched the Geneva-Tsinghua Initiative, which has developed into an ambitious joint education program about the United Nations Sustainable Development Goals, supported by a local foundation in Geneva. His university has launched two activities which will be linked through the Geneva-Tsinghua Initiative, and lead to research and development relevant to the One Belt One Road Initiative. "The huge ambition and scale of the Belt and Road Initiative will surely lead to many fascinating research projects and education opportunities, in everything from advanced engineering to issues of international law and intercultural communication," says Fluckiger. "And of course, once this amazing infrastructure is in place, we can expect it to have a major impact on student mobility throughout the Eurasian continent."

Marc Luthi, CEO of SC Bern, an ice hockey team in the Swiss capital, recently met Chinese ambassador to Switzerland Geng Wenbing, discussing how to explore opportunities to develop winter sports in China. "President Xi's visit in January and China's upcoming hosting of the Winter Games have offered chances for us to explore and we are ready to start," says Luthi. During President Xi's visit, the leaders of both sides agreed to deepen cooperation in winter sports. Simon Bosshart, Director of Global Accounts and the Director for Asia Pacific for Switzerland Tourism also says the winter sports have already become a selling point even when attracting more Chinese tourists. Bosshart says the worsening safety situation in Europe and terrorism attacks have affected the amount of those group tourists from China. "But we have noticed that the number of individual tourists from China has been increasing, which is the new trend for us," says Bosshart.

CULTURAL BONDS LINK CHINA AND SWITZERLAND

Is there any country in the West which has earned huge success by putting ancient Chinese wisdom into governance and use? Probably, Switzerland has done so, though in an unconscious way. The German philosopher Leibnitz (1646-1714) said about the relationship between China and Europe that each side had something that it could give to the other side to its advantage. For instance, Switzerland could get precious inspiration by many thoughts transmitted by the ancient Chinese book of wisdom *Tao Te Ching*.

Since the end of the 1990s, Swiss sinologist Harro von Senger had planned to decode the ways behind his country's governance by referring to the ancient classic of the philosopher Lao-tzu, who allegedly lived more than 2,500 years ago.

So he started to do preparations by reading intensively and buried himself into writing in German in recent years. The book, *Das Tao der Schweiz (The Tao of Switzerland)*, consisting of six chapters and about 70 pages of notes and references made its debut in early May in the renowned Publishing House of Neue Zürcher Zeitung. "Switzerland has basically realized Lao-tzu's ideal of governing a small country," said von Senger, from the Swiss Institute of Comparative Law in Lausanne during an interview in early 2017.

Sitting on the first floor of the restaurant Bären in his hometown Einsiedeln, which is about one hour away by train from Zurich, von Senger pointed to the Benedictine abbey through the window, saying he obtained eight years of middle school education there. During the time, von Senger learned Latin for eight years, ancient Greek for six years, French for seven years and English for two years while he was a native speaker of German.

After entering the University of Zürich, von Senger started to show great interest in Chinese language, and he wrote a doctoral thesis in legal history on sale contracts in traditional China. But soon he shifted to the more than 80 sayings of Lao-tzu, who he quoted within each chapter, using more than 1000 references to illustrate the linkage of Swiss success with China's ancient thoughts. "It is a successful country, and behind its success lies the profound thoughts of Lao-tzu," says the 1.95-meter-tall von Senger in fluent Chinese.

Switzerland of course has not consciously acted according to the *Thoughts of Lao-tzu*, but its success can be explained by the profound thoughts of Lao-tzu. "Let there be a little country without many people": This is a line from the 80th chapter of Lao-tzu's work *Tao Te Ching*. With a population of less than 9 million, Switzerland is kind of country that Lao-tzu had dreamed of in size, says von Senger.

And Lao-tzu advocated to be weak, gentle, modest and inactive. He said, when a plant is starting to grow, it is small and weak, which is the sign of blossoming; but when a plant is about to wither, it is big and stiffening, which is the sign of death. "We are small and weak," says von Senger, who was born in 1944 and studied in Peking University in the 1970s.

"These are good things for us as we are not considered dangerous by other countries." In addition, von Senger says that Switzerland has also practiced the thoughts of another famous thinker, Zhuangzi, who lived in the same era as Lao-tzu and they shaped the essence of Taoism. Zhuangzi said in his works: All men know the use of the useful, but nobody knows the use of the useless. Switzerland profits from the use of the useless, von Senger says. Citing the example of the Swiss army, which he says could be considered to be the most successful one in the world because it has not been defeated and has never killed a single foreigner for more than 200 years.

"Thanks to our Taoist-like policy of neutrality which makes Switzerland 'useless' for any foreign power and also thanks to good luck, the Swiss army has finally achieved such a big success," he has explained. But he has further emphasized that his country's "uselessness" is "useful" for hosting, at the international level, international organizations in the dozens and helping to offer platforms in solving conflicts to contribute to global peace and prosperity.

All these link to another important part of Taoism, which is *mouliie*. He says this thought has not been properly expressed in Western languages. For example, one American scholar, who is said to be "one of the US government's leading China experts", translates "mouliie" as "deceptive strategy", which is very superficial, he says.

So he coined the English world supra-planning, which he says is superior to "strategic thinking" considered in the West to be the highest level of planning. "Sometimes, we need to coin a word to catch the attention at unique phenomena of another civilization," says von Senger. He says supra-planning, or *mouliie*, is a broadly based art of planning only developed in China. von Senger explains *mouliie* with the *yin-yang* symbol. The *yang* part refers to laws, regulations, customs and routine. But the *yin* part refers to hidden ways to solve problems, which need wisdom and creativity.

von Senger is an industrious scholar and from his studies in Beijing 1975-77, von Senger read Chinese-language newspapers, such as People's Daily and Guangming Daily. His books on *Chinese Mouliie* are published in 15 languages. In addition to the *yin-yang* peculiarity of supra-planning, von Senger says its other feature lies in long-term thinking.

He says nowadays, China's leadership has proposed two centenary goals, to double the 2010 GDP and per capita income of the Chinese and to complete the building of a moderately prosperous society by 2020 and to build a prosperous, strong, democratic, culturally advanced and harmonious modern socialist country and realize the great renewal of the Chinese nation by the middle of the century.

The public debate on the two goals did not become popular in China until 2011 but he has already written about it in his book *Moulüe* published in German in 2008. It is the only Western book on this topic. He took an article published in *Neue Zürcher Zeitung*, an influential German-language newspaper in Switzerland from his bag. The publishing time of this newspaper article was on 19 April, 1985. "This is an article which I had written on the goal of 2049," says von Senger, adding that China had already discussed such a long-term goal in 1980s and it aimed to be a developed country then.

"Thirty-two years ago, I knew China had a very long, long-term goal," says von Senger. von Senger says that having a long-term goal is one dominating feature of supra-planning but Western strategic thinking could not last so long. Normally, Western strategies, like the Lisbon strategy launched in March 2000 by the European Union, last only ten years. But still, his country is an exception. He adds: "Switzerland has also had long-term thinking, which is about its neutral position."

SOFT POWER OF SWITZERLAND

Just as Professor von Senger points out, Switzerland boasts international organisations in their hundreds, and their attitudes towards the Belt and Road Initiative are helpful to know. Umberto de Pretto, Secretary-General of the International Road Transport Union, based in Geneva, says the Initiative, a vision originating from China, serves as a set of "global ambitions" that will have far-reaching benefits of economic stability and prosperity for communities across the world. "While the initiative is the vision of the Chinese government and primarily concerns China and the countries along the Belt and Road routes, the ambitions are global," he says."It encourages a more globalised, integrated approach to achieve an open, inclusive and balanced regional economy and I believe the initiative will have far-reaching benefits of economic stability and prosperity for communities across the world." Ahead of the Belt and Road Initiative Forum for International Cooperation in May 2017 in Beijing, de Pretto says that countries across the world were being reminded that prosperity and peace were achieved through enhanced trading relationships. That is a strong message that is compelling for both the Chinese and international community. According to him, the initiative has already won wide recognition in Europe since it was first proposed by President Xi Jinping more than three years ago, with many Europeans believing that it will help connect new business zones and landlocked countries with major European and Chinese markets. This conclusion was reached, he says, after his organisation, which had been promoting standards and safety for the global road transport network for seven decades, hosted a conference on transport and the Belt and Road Initiative in Brussels in November 2016.

At the conference, he says the opportunities and challenges for Europe under the Initiative were specifically examined. During the conference, which brought together 300 of Europe's leading transport professionals, de Pretto said, it was widely agreed that the Initiative would have significant potential to increase trade, stimulate economic development and reduce transport times.

De Pretto also says that his organisation, representing the interests of the international road transport industry and with members and activities in more than 100 countries across the world, is keen on promoting the Belt and Road Initiative. De Pretto says China has been encouraging the countries along the Belt and Road to achieve economic policy coordination and to undertake broader regional cooperation. He says China had ratified an international transit system based on a UN convention implemented at the global level by allowing customs-sealed vehicles and freight containers to transit countries without border checks. And it had also ratified the World Trade Organisation's Trade Facilitation Agreement, demonstrating China's integration into global transport and trade norms, says de Pretto. "This has shown that China has set an excellent example to improve global connectivity by lifting barriers," says de Pretto. The Chinese government has already expressed its determination and willingness to actively develop international road transport networks and to build a modern international road transport system by 2020. But de Pretto also says that though China shares its frontiers with 14 countries, the highest number in the world, its road transport currently accounts for only 10 percent of international goods delivery, illustrating vast untapped potential. He says China's international road transport industry does not match the geographical and economic significance of the country. For example, China has approximately 300 companies engaged in international road transport services for goods transit, compared with smaller countries, like Turkey, which has 2,000, and Poland, with 6,000.

Switzerland is competitive in soft power. The typical example is the World Economic Forum's annual gathering where politicians, business gurus, journalists and celebrities from across the world gather at the annual "thought fair" in Davos, Switzerland. Because of the importance of the Forum and the huge number of representatives, some beds in Davos hospitals are even said to be "rented out" to delegates. Given the mad rush, I've not been able to book a hotel room in Davos during any of the past seven Forums, and instead I have had to check into a hotel in a nearby town and commute for an hour by train to and from the venue every day. Nevertheless, the Forum, thanks to the new ideas, trends, debates and conversations it generates, has been a regular feature on my calendar. Despite being a small country with a population of only about 8 million, Switzerland has occupied a prominent place in the world of economics and business. Now Davos has a sister gathering—Summer Davos, held in Tianjin and Dalian in rotation—in addition to other important regional meetings in Africa, the Middle East and other parts of the world. Apart from that, Geneva is the second headquarters of the United Nations and home to dozens of international organisations, including the World Trade Organisation and World Health Organisation. And all these have increased the soft power of Switzerland.

By learning from Switzerland, China can shape its own soft power. Since President Xi became China's highest leader in late 2012, with the world being too big and the challenges too many, he has says China will adopt proactive approaches to embrace and tackle all of these problems. Apart from Chinese politicians' continuous efforts to provide solutions for global problems, China is also trying to improve the capacity-building of its think tanks. And a group of 25 academic organisations were recently encouraged to come up with quality intellectual results. All these developments indicate that China is keen on playing a proactive role to help provide solutions to global problems and make the world a better place. In this context, Switzerland offers at least two sets of references for China. First, China has to invest energy, time, patience and inputs to build platforms to come up with influential thoughts and ideas. And to make debates interesting and fruitful, the government, businesses, the media and the world of academia should play their respective roles. Businesses, for example, should fulfill their social responsibilities of offering financial support to build such platforms.

The World Economic Forum reached its influential position because it has been developing for more than four decades. The China Development Forum, the Bo'ao Forum and Summer Davos are held every March, April and September, but they only focus on China or regional agendas. But since the Chinese leadership aims to offer more global solutions to maintain peace and development across the world, China has to offer more platforms to produce thoughts that will have a global impact. Moreover, China should host more global and regional conferences. Geneva, as well as New York, are excellent examples for Beijing, Shanghai and other Chinese cities to follow. In this regard, the establishment of the Shanghai Cooperation Organisation's Secretariat and the Asian Infrastructure Investment Bank's headquarters in Beijing, and the BRICS New Development Bank's headquarters in Shanghai are welcome developments because they will help strengthen China's soft power. Still, China has to make more efforts to play the global role that matches its economic power.

Right now, the world faces a pressing challenge that global stakeholders are not willing to cooperate, and in a nutshell, globalisation is at risk. China, however, is still a driving force to call for increased efforts in reshaping the multi-polar world and improving global governance. And encouragingly, Klaus Schwab, founder and Executive Chairman of the Geneva-based international organisation, invited President Xi Jinping to deliver the opening address on 17 January 2017 after he had paid a state visit to Switzerland. Xi visited the Lausanne-based International Olympics Committee and the headquarters of the World Health Organisation in Geneva, and spoke at a high-level conference at the United Nations office in Geneva before wrapping up his first overseas tour of 2017. Schwab, whose organisation started cooperating with China in 1979, has attached great importance to President Xi's participation in the annual event, the first time China's leader has attended. He says President Xi's participation was relevant to the theme of the Forum, which was "Responsive and Responsible Leadership". As the

the world is in transition towards a multi-polar geopolitical and economic structure and China now equals the United States in terms of economic power, he expected President Xi to show that China would play a positive role in global affairs.

Ahead of Xi's arrival, Schwab says: "In 2017 we are living in a truly multi-polar world where declining levels of global cooperation around our key shared challenges is a very real possibility. Against this backdrop, our theme reflects the clear need for those in positions of power to act responsively by listening and understanding the expectations of their people, and responsibly by being bold in providing and delivering a vision for a future that is sustainable and socially inclusive." He says the areas where responsive and responsible leadership was needed most included fostering growth, ensuring the global economy was more sustainable and socially inclusive, designing systems for better global cooperation, and preparing the world for the Fourth Industrial Revolution.

He also says: "The last area was of critical importance, as technology and innovation have the propensity both to eliminate so many jobs and positions and also to help humanity by creating millions more roles and building stronger societies. The imperative is to act now so that we have the governance and the values in place so that technology serves humanity rather than challenges it."

According to Schwab, China is an emerging superpower and we expect the country to play an increasingly active role as a responsive and responsible global leader. Areas where we are already seeing this happen are in galvanizing support for protecting the environment through the COP-21 Paris Agreement, acting as a champion for international trade and investment and in supporting development and infrastructure finance, and moving to develop and expand the global digital economy.

He says that as China becomes better known for its innovative strength, the world expects Chinese expertise to play a greater and more visible role in many critical areas of discussion, whether on infrastructure development, clean power, or the Internet, just to name just a few. It would also take encouragement from the innovative approaches China had taken in the fields of infrastructure finance, through the AIIB and NDB and trade and investment through the Regional Comprehensive Economic Partnership (RCEP) and One

Belt, One Road initiatives.

Schwab says he liked President Xi's use of a well-known Chinese proverb at that year's G20 summit when he said: "People with petty shrewdness attend to trivial matters while those with great wisdom attend to the governance of institutions." This to me perfectly sums up the importance that global governance holds for the collective health of our international community and reflects China's willingness to contribute to a fairer, more prosperous and sustainable planet.

When I asked: "Clearly, the West entered a financial and economic crisis in 2008-2009 before the world came together to find solutions. How do you comment on the *status quo* now? And, currently, black swan events have happened within G7 one after another. How do you comment on the 'political crisis' confronting the West now?" Schwab responded: "Political events in 2016 have made it very clear that levels of trust between political leaders and those that elected them have come under great strain. The burdens placed on leaders in today's complex and interconnected world have never been greater and the imperative now is for leaders to work together to strengthen our global systems, and to re-imagine new ways for international cooperation. One of the greatest challenges facing many of the G7 countries is the fact that income inequality has been allowed to increase, and leaders have lost their ability to listen to the needs of people."

I was quite curious how Switzerland, which is a tiny country but with huge competitiveness and soft power, had made it. Schwab says Switzerland had a great number of competitive strengths: it was home to a number of world-class innovative companies and possessed excellent academic research establishments that worked well with the private sector to commercialise new technology. It also had a highly efficient, flexible labour market and stable macro-economic environment. Switzerland's small size in terms of population had acted as a strong incentive to develop deep trading relationships with the EU and other partners around the world and to invest in developing its richest natural asset, its people, to help them develop entrepreneurial talents. "Openness to trade and to developing innovation and entrepreneurial talent are all areas that China and Switzerland can work together on," says Schwab.

Born in almost the same era as Schwab, Jean-Pierre Lehmann, world-renowned for his work on globalisation, has shaped his own way of observing China's evolution of openness. He has stored, in his laptop, the photos of Chinese politicians from Mao Zedong to Xi Jinping, which have captured their historic moments on the global stage. In particular, Lehmann, a professor at Switzerland's International Institute for Management Development (IMD) has kept nearly all of the photos of President Xi Jinping shaking hands with leaders from the rest of the world. Now, still teaching global affairs at IMD and at Hong Kong University, he has used the photos to illustrate China's gesture of embracing the rest of the world and to observe what he calls "Asia in the new global disorder". "I must say all of the photos of President Xi shaking hands are impressive, and the messages showcase a new era that we're talking about," said Lehmann during an interview in late April in the office of the tranquil IMD campus beside Lake Geneva in Lausanne. Patiently introducing the photos, he continued: "It is evident no other leader has shaken so many hands in such a short time. This is China's coming out, and it's a gesture. But it's also a symbol."

President Xi became China's leader in late 2012. He has travelled to about 50 countries in the past four and a half years and hosted the APEC, G20 and Belt and Road Initiative summits in Beijing. Lehmann, recalling China's history, calls Xi's proactive meeting with politicians worldwide "fantastic news," which has shown the emerging country's determination to engage with the rest of the world. These are in sharp contrast with some leaders' tendency to construct walls and favour isolationism.

Though Lehmann says he prefers Barack Obama to Donald Trump, he was very critical of Obama's China policy regarding the Trans-Pacific Partnership, which excluded China from this Asia-Pacific trade deal. But Trump announced the American withdrawal from it after entering the White House. "Obama said we needed to write trade rules without China. Why say that? Why not say let's write the rules together?" Lehmann, a globalist, has asked. "It is a new era, so there has to be an adjustment." Lehmann has shown his concerns over global protectionism: the WTO's Doha Round talks are dead because of the refusal of the Western powers and Japan to adjust to the new realities; Trump also threatened to withdraw from the Paris climate change agreement; he thinks Western Europe is very complacent and inward-looking, though central and eastern Europe are more open-mind. Against global dismay, he sees China's intervention over globalisation as a big revolution.

While warmly shaking hands and talking with global leaders, Lehmann says President Xi and his country have been thinking in terms of a grand vision and a grand plan, which would bring together different parts of the world. According to him, the Belt and Road Initiative is an essential part of China's portfolio of solutions. But it is still a vision, which needs to be developed into different strategies with the rest of the world. He suggests that China should not avoid using the expression "strategy," because it is basically neutral. "Trump's wall is a bad strategy, but increasing connectivity is a good strategy," says Lehmann. He says he always tells his audiences that the Belt and Road Initiative is still at a very early stage and it is normal to have some critical opinions. But he continues: "The opinions don't mean anything strategically, though that's correct at this moment. It is still a vision for which strategies will follow." To the criticism that this initiative is in China's interests, he responds: "You have no country in the world that will ever do something just for the other's interests, without mentioning its own." He adds that China has already clearly made clear in the vision paper that it is a win-win initiative. Some people in the West have also criticised the fact that the initiative has involved only talks, without concrete measures. "I don't think this case is true," he says.

Of course, now there should be debate and discussion because this idea is only three or four years old. Lehmann even warns that there will be "difficulties and obstacles" to transform the vision into strategy in the coming five to ten years. "But my position has been that it should be welcomed rather than contained," he says. For example, he says he was "extremely critical" of the Americans and the Japanese for not becoming founding members of the Asian Infrastructure Investment Bank, which now has grown into a multilateral financing vehicle with up to 80 members. Between 14-15 May 2017, the US and Japan sent representatives to attend the Belt and Road Initiative Forum in Beijing.

Taking his trip to a Belt and Road Initiative forum in Xi'an in 2015 as an example, Lehmann says he was tremendously encouraged that there were representatives from all over the Eurasian continent, ranging from Iran, India and Pakistan, to Ukraine, Georgia and other countries in Europe. "But there were no Americans and no Japanese. This is a global initiative and you need to do something," he says. He argues that the business sectors across Eurasia and Africa have started to accept the idea. And the world must recognise China's courage in making the initiative an open, global and inclusive platform. However, as a global expert, he says not only in Europe, but also in Asia, suspicion, apprehension and anxiety over China are also mounting as it moves to the centre of the global stage, and this is not fair. China was at the global centre historically for a long time, he says, and now when China returns there some see it as a "new kid on the block"—a kid as big as China! In this situation, Lehmann says, China still has a lot of work to do to better communicate with the rest of the world. "China has to make efforts in soft power and so the initiative has to be well marketed by the Chinese," he argues. He recalls how, when he was 18 or 19, there was a tremendous amount of apprehension that the US was going to conquer the world, which is an automatic apprehension people have the new kid on the block. "But then you have to make efforts to reassure, to engage the rest of the world in a sophisticated manner," he says.

Lehmann says China has a tremendous amount to offer culturally, economically and technologically to the world. He joined the IMD almost twenty years ago and retired in 2012, though he is still teaching occasionally. He is also teaching at Hong Kong University, saying that the students from Asian business sectors have consistently enriched his perspectives on how to look at the changing world as well. "I've enjoyed the teaching environment here. The birds are singing outside and the spring is here. It's very pleasant," he says at his IMD office. As a French citizen, he moved to Switzerland in 1997 and lived outside France for that long time, with stints in Japan, Sweden, the UK and the US. For the previous five decades, Lehmann worked professionally in Asia and was able to witness the dramatic changes taking place there. Lehmann believes in the world's shared values, despite his support for discussions on Western and Chinese values. "But I think in many cases our values are the same, though the expression is somewhat different," he says. Lehmann says, at Hong Kong University, he has taught many young parents from China, the rest of Asia and other parts of the world. What they want is for their children to be brought-up well, to be happy and to contribute to the rest of the world, he says.

He admits that sometimes he feels embarrassed by the tone of Western politicians when they raise the topic of values. "As if we were pure, and there's an assumption that the American global order is benign and the potential Chinese order is malign," he says.

THRIVING DREAM OF THE REPUBLIC OF SERBIA

The Republic of Serbia is a country with 7 million citizens, roughly the same size as some big prefecture-level Chinese cities. It will enjoy rapid economic growth from last year's 2.8 percent to the projected 3.5 percent in 2019. According to the World Bank's latest updates, the prospect is even rosier than that of EU economies, which average around two percent annually. This promising outlook has partly resulted from the country's plan to become a regional transport hub which has expanded investment in roads, railways, urban expansion and even high-tech park construction, similar to the growth engines in some of China's cities. In April 2017, I made my first trip to this country and there I found how it can follow the example of China in shaping its competitiveness and improving its people's livelihoods.

Also, Chinese investors have contributed to the increased investment intensity in this country by exporting capital and know-how and creating jobs for local people. "China's investment scale for those projects in progress and in the pipeline in the Republic of Serbia totals about $10 billion," Li Manchang, Chinese ambassador to the Republic of Serbia, told me during an exclusive interview in his embassy in Belgrade. In the meeting room, Li, a veteran diplomat, showed me models of the projects which have already been completed in the country. The models, displayed on the tables of the embassy meeting hall, include buses, power stations, bridges and other projects. Li says the outcomes had mainly resulted from the high recognition by the Republic of Serbian leadership of the significance of China's Belt and Road Initiative, on which both sides signed a cooperation memorandum in

2015.

Citing the Serbian leaders, Li says they had repeatedly emphasised that the initiative proposed by President Xi Jinping in 2013 would help the global economy walk out of the stagnation it experienced since the 2008-09 financial and economic crisis. "So the top Serbian leaders urged their country to grasp the chance to find synergies with the initiative," says Li.

Ivica Dacic, the first Deputy Prime Minister and Foreign Minister of the Republic of Serbia confirmed that Serbian President Aleksandar Vucic, who was still Prime Minister in April, would head the delegation of his country at the upcoming "Belt and Road Forum" in Beijing. "This speaks volumes about the importance that the Republic of Serbia attaches to this significant global initiative," Dacic told me in an interview. Before Vucic's visit, President Nikolic paid a state visit to China early in the year, following President Xi's visit to the Republic of Serbia the previous June and Nikolic's attending the commemoration of the 70th anniversary of the victory of the Chinese People's War of Resistance against Japanese Aggression and the World Anti-Fascist War in 2015.

The foreign minister says he also looked forward to the direct air route between the Republic of Serbia and China while his country had attached special importance to the modernisation of the Belgrade-Budapest railway line, a pioneering undertaking of transport networks on the land-sea link between China and Europe. "This is an opportunity for the development of the region and greater sale of goods and flow of goods and people," he says.

He says the Republic of Serbia aspired to having the closest possible connections with the world. "In that context, we wish to see even stronger momentum in cooperation with China in infrastructure investment in order to make the Republic of Serbia the regional transport hub," says Dacic. Following his national strategy, Ambassador Li rolled out "several firsts" in bilateral cooperation in the embassy's guest hall.

He says the first bridge China had built in Europe was located on the Republic of Serbia's Danube River section. China's first high-speed railway in Europe, connecting Belgrade and Budapest, is planned also partly in the Republic of Serbia, and the project is expected to be kick-started within the year after the European Commission completes the loan agreement supervision. And within Europe, the Republic of Serbia is the first country to grant Chinese passport holders visa-free entry for a stay of up to 30 days. Li says that right now Chinese companies were constructing highways and electricity generators in the Republic of Serbia, and investors from China had already signed contracts with Belgrade's municipal government to construct its ring road.

China is also on the way to improving the Republic of Serbian capital's waste water treatment facilities and heating supply network, while another electricity generating project, of which the investment totals up to $900 million dollars, is also be targeted. Out of the 10-billion-dollar projects, China will also help the Republic of Serbia to construct an industrial park which will cover 300 hectares in its first phase, says the ambassador, adding that after signing a memorandum in 2015, both sides will be ready to sign an agreement by the end of this year to pave the way for breaking ground next year. "At least other Balkan countries have shown 'envy' towards the Republic of Serbia, which has seized a good opportunity to enhance cooperation with China," says Li. "I think the Republic of Serbia has taken the lead in this regard, and other European countries may follow suit."

Considering the current political and economic situation in the Balkans, it is easy to understand the importance of participation in the Belt and Road Initiative, not only for the Republic of Serbia but for all countries in the region, says Branislav Djordjevic, Director of the Institute of International Politics and Economics in Belgrade. He says that though his institute had long had an interest in China, it is true that this interest developed particularly after the conclusion of a strategic partnership between the two countries. Now it had focused much attention on the Belt and Road Initiative. "It is an old truth that prosperity brings peace and stability," he says.

He also says that China's Belt and Road Initiative helped the Republic of Serbia become more qualified as a EU member. "Since each of these countries is looking for membership in the EU, it would be easier for them to be absorbed as economically and politically stable countries," says Djordjevic. "With certain necessary adjustments coming along with synergy with the Belt and Road Initiative, the Republic of Serbia itself could be an engine of such a process."

According to Li, on the heels of former prime ministers Romano Prodi of Italy, Jean-Pierre Raffarin of France, Waldemar Pawlak of Poland and other high-ranking European political figures, former Serbian President Nikolic has shown an initial intention to contribute to Belt and Road Initiative cooperation with China after he steps down soon. Prime Minister Aleksandar Vucic replaced the 65-year-old Nikolic on 1 June after the April election. "During his recent visit to China, President Nikolic was considering setting up a Belt and Road Initiative office in Belgrade after his retirement," Li told me. Similar to the example set by American politician Henry Kissinger, now aged 93, Nikolic will focus his post-retirement work on promoting the relationship with China, and the office he proposed will cover every front of China-Serbian relations, says Li.

Li says Nikolic had come up with the idea during his recent visit to China, saying China's Belt and Road Initiative was of great significance to the future and destiny of people from all nations of the world. During his presidency, Nikolic upgraded the strategic relationship with China, and last year President Xi visited his country, jointly agreeing to remodel the two countries' relationship into an example for China and other European countries. Since President Xi came up with the Belt and Road Initiative in 2013, many European think tanks have put their research capacity into the proposal. With a growing number of politicians joining in support for these efforts, Prodi, also a former president of the European Commission, and Raffarin have stood out enriching the content of Belt and Road-themed research, launching academic projects and organising debates and dialogues.

Apart from Nikolic's passion, Serbian scholars have also shown strong interest in setting up China-themed think tanks in the Republic of Serbia, which they say is a gateway country in the Balkan region. The Institute of International Politics and Economics in Belgrade is a renowned academic organisation with a history stretching back 70 years. Ivona Ladjevac, its coordinator for international cooperation, says the Chinese Academy of Social Sciences was the key contact in China, and both sides had implemented joint research programmes smoothly under the 16+1 framework, which includes China and the 16 central and eastern European countries.

"Out of our 30 research staff, five of us have focused on Belt and Road Initiative research," says Ladjevac, who has got involved in it and has started to learn Chinese.

Dusko Dimitrijevic, former Director of the Institute of International

Politics and Economics, says his institute had already organised a high-level Silk Road forum last year during President Xi Jinping's visit, together with the CASS (Chinese Academy of Social Sciences). "We intend to set up a joint centre for research cooperation to promote think tank networking under the 16+1 framework," says Dimitrijevic. "We hope we can become coordinators for our region in the future in terms of academic cooperation with China." He says his institute had a new intention based on years of sound cooperation with China.

Listing China, with the US, Russia and the EU, as one of the country's four strategic priorities, Dimitrijevic says it was essential to set up such a coordination centre in the oldest institute in the region in terms of research in international relations. During the last seven decades, he says his institute had also shaped a sound relationship with 200 or more institutes worldwide. Commenting on Dimitrijevic's proposal, Ambassador Li says both China and the Republic of Serbia were making efforts to improve the exchange mechanisms and platforms to catch up with the momentum of a bilateral relationship. "It is encouraging, and I think think tank cooperation will be promoted as well in the future," says Li. "If President Nikolic takes the lead in setting up a China—Serbia cooperation office after his retirement, I propose that think tank cooperation should be part of his efforts."

Radosav Pusic, Dean of the Confucius Institute in Belgrade, agreed with Djordjevic, saying the Republic of Serbia was a small Balkan country, and at every critical historic moment, his country had been a victim. "When powers play games, a small country suffers. Belgrade has been destroyed more than 40 times in history, and we even suffered from wars in the 1990s," says Pusic. And since the wars ended, this country has stood still economically for some years, with the financial crisis making its situation even harder. Many young people are leaving the Republic of Serbia. But Pusic says it was a "historic moment" for the Republic of Serbia as economic and investment activities with China had become more frequent than ever under the Belt and Road Initiative cooperation framework.

"This has resulted from a firmer political and strategic partnership between the countries, which has laid a solid foundation for other encounters," says Pusic, a renowned China scholar who has already written or translated up to thirty books on China's classical writings, poetry and philosophy. "Against this background, many people in the Republic of Serbia have shown interest in the Belt and Road Initiative," says the scholar. "But if it had been raised ten years ago, this recognition would not have been that easy."

Pusic says more efforts were still needed, especially on the cultural and publicity fronts. "The Silk Road Initiative is a concept with tremendous historic significance, and so this also offers another perspective to learn more about China," says Pusic. "I will do more in helping Serbians understand China's traditional cultures," he says. Pusic is now immersed in writing a book on China's ancient philosophical history.

REVIVING A STEEL FACTORY AND SAVING JOBS

For twenty years, Svetlana Radosavljevic, one of a few Serbian blue-collar ladies working in the front lines of the country's biggest steel mill, Zelezara Smederevo, has been monitoring the steel and iron manufacturing in the glass-walled control room of an old production building.

This mill, located less than an hour's drive from Belgrade, could run only one of its two production lines for years. It was losing about $10 million every month, many of its 5,000-strong workforce were idle and not in the mood for work. Prolonged low competitiveness had forced it gradually towards bankruptcy. But since China's giant Hesteel Group, based in north China's Hebei Province, purchased this company for 46 million euro a year ago, the 105-year-old mill, has been given a new lease on life. Two lines of Hesteel the Republic of Serbia, the new name of the mill, have been running at full speed; its production will reach two million tons this year, the maximum quota agreed by the EU and the Republic of Serbia, and it ended a seven-year loss and started to earn a profit at the end of last year.

More importantly, workers are rejoicing that all of their jobs have been secured and their wages increased by 8 percent on average compared with their pre-takeover level. "Now it is safer, production is better and I am more focused on my job as I don't need to worry about being jobless one day," Radosavljevic says happily as she overlooks the hot-rolling manufacturing line, introduced by the legendary Yugoslavian leader Josip Broz Tito (1892-1980) in the 1970s. Even now, there are only three such lines in Europe. Her control room is about 50 metres from the end of the line, where rolls of steel plate are produced. President Xi met some of the Serbian workers and management team in Radosavljevic's control room during his visit last June.

They recalled that Xi's visit injected a huge spirit of confidence for making huge changes in this Serbian company. In addition to the front-line workers, even Prime Minister Aleksandar Vucic, now also president-elect of the Republic of Serbia, felt excited about the performance sheet achieved within such a short time. "I was talking to the prime minister about our revenue target this year, which would reach about $800 million," says Song Sihai, executive board member of Hesteel the Republic of Serbia, who was responsible for the company's management, during a recent interview. "Vucic urgently asked his assistant to calculate the ratio of the amount (which has doubled the company's historic high) to the country's total economic output."

Sitting in his office, Song, a high-level executive from the parent company in Hebei, cited Vucic's conclusion, saying the contribution of Hesteel the Republic of Serbia's revenues this year will surpass 2 percent of the Republic of Serbia's GDP. "Surely, this will hugely help revive its economic development," says Song, speaking confidently and loudly. Previously, Vucic had said China's takeover of the Serbian state-owned company would help his country to achieve a 3.5-4 percent economic growth rate in 2017, which would bring the Republic of Serbia closer to the EU standard. When analysing the miracles his team has achieved, he says it had mainly resulted from the high competitiveness and advantages of the parent company had developed for decades during China's high-speed process of industrialisation and urbanisation.

"By using our strengths, we have brought the Serbian mill into our global operation cycles," says Song, adding that his company is already a global heavyweight. For raw materials, the Serbian mill mainly depends on imports, while it sells products mainly outside the Republic of Serbia, which accounts for just one fifth of its sales. "This is a typical company, with both ends being outside the production country, and so cost reduction is the key," says Song.

His parent group boasted of millions of tons of annual production capacity, and it has a decisive say in raw material procurement in some countries. "For our Serbian company, we rely on our global purchasing platform to buy raw materials, and the cost is much lower," says Song.

Meanwhile, the parent company took a controlling stake in Swiss-based Duferco International Trading Holding in 2014, and now Duferco is helping explore a cost-saving market for the Serbian mill. In the past, the mill mainly sold its products to Western Europe, and then to the former Yugoslavia and other Balkan regions. "In our industry, we must factor in a shorter sales radius to reduce transport costs," says Song. He cited an example: the cost would be $1-2 per ton if the product was sold in the Republic of Serbia, but if it was transported to Italy the cost would soar to $33 dollars per ton on average. Now, he says, the lion's share of the market was in the former Yugoslavia, amounting to roughly 50-60 percent of total sales. It is also exploring the targeted market along the Danube River, which mainly includes Germany and Bulgaria, as transport by water is also cheaper, though the EU is highly protective of its market.

"We have even managed to find opportunities in the United States," says Song, adding that sales in the US would overtake 20,00 tons in April 2017. He says the UK market was also in the pipeline, while the process of its departure from the EU was launched. In addition to sales and procurement benefits offered by the parent company, Song's team has focused a lot of energy on controlling and improving product quality and improving environmental standards.

Last year, his parent company invested $120 million in cash to ensure that the sluggish mill ran at full strength. "Even when we started formal operations at the very beginning after taking over, we ran two lines in an effort to find what the loopholes for future management were," says Song. And this year his company has poured another $120 million in to upgrade the production equipment. In the operation, Song says, he also found much potential for cost reduction. For example, now the mill is powered by natural gas, but so far the waste heat and energy recovery and recycling technology is still not being used.

Basically, the mill's capacity can be further boosted. If the lines are equipped with upgraded modern facilities, its production capacity will reach

40-50 million tons, doubling the current level. "But we have no plan to boost capacity, but instead to focus on production safety, product quality and environmental standards," says Song. In the long run, his company will be targeting high-end production, such as steel for the auto industry. It will also improve the environmental standards of the mill. "We will try to meet European environmental standards in a few years," says Song, adding that the competitiveness and environmental standards in most of China's steel and iron companies are now even higher than those of European competitors.

He says: "So I am very confident that we can turn the Serbian mill into the most capable steel and iron company in Europe." Linking it to China's Belt and Road Initiative, Song says it was against this big background that his company's competitiveness could help promote connectivity and the flow of production elements worldwide. He recalled that, at the beginning of his country's Opening-Up and Reform, China was eager to introduce capital, technology and human resources. In his steel and iron sector, some Chinese companies had even moved parts of European mills to China to follow up these aims.

"Now it is China's turn," says Song. "We rely on our sharp competitiveness to upgrade a Serbian company, and we aim to contribute to this country's re-industralisation process." He adds: "In the context of the Belt and Road Initiative, we contribute to our partners positively and we aim to set an excellent example."

REVIVING MOVIE MEMORIES

For many Chinese, the plots of former Yugoslavian films such as *Walter Defends Sarajevo* and *Bridge* have stayed in their minds. President Xi himself says he knew how to whistle the melody from *Bridge* when he met the Serbian President Tomislav Nikolic and his delegation recently in Beijing.

Even in June 2016, prior to Xi's arrival in the Republic of Serbia, he says in an article published in a Serbian newspaper that the two movies had rekindled the mounting patriotic passion of the two countries' people. "Both the Chinese president and the premier know well about the two films," Vladan Vukosavljevic, the Serbian culture minister, told me in an exclusive interview shortly after his Beijing trip with his president weeks ago. Resulting from the *Bridge* effect, Vukosavljevic says both sides had basically agreed to strengthen film cooperation in an effort to produce one commercial movie very soon. "We have this idea to refresh people's minds and basically it will be a commercial movie, which could attract movie-goers worldwide," says Vukosavljevic in his office in Belgrade in April 2017.

To achieve this goal, he says, China had already offered excellent TV and film studios in Beijing, with very graphic photography. In recalling his recent visit to Beijing, the minister says President Xi himself says he knows how to whistle the melody from the movie *Bridge*. "He says: 'I like that tune.' Those were his words. Premier Li Keqiang says the same thing. So it's very popular." Vukosavljevic says the film should be shot in both the Republic of Serbia and China, because the Serbian people did not know very much about China. "I was impressed with the huge economic development that I saw last year during my first visit and this year too. People in the Republic of Serbia should see this," says Vukosavljevic.

He suggested that such progress should be wrapped into a modern story of young people, about how they live, how they think, how they love, how they look at the world around themselves. "But inside that story, some deep roots of our cultural cooperation and connections should be shown. There are some tunes for those old movies with scenes from those movies," Vukosavljevic says.

"But the story should be contemporary. And I would like that movie to be seen by many audiences in China, in Europe and worldwide." He even suggested that both sides have a good opportunity to make an excellent movie that will not be only a way to show cultural potential, traditions or tourism, but something more. "But what we must try to make is a really good and nice movie which should visit international film festivals," he says.

He trusts that China's movie directors and artists have great potential to cooperate with their Serbian peers, saying that many artists from China in the field of movies, visual arts and contemporary art were becoming known globally. "Excellent film directors have won many prizes worldwide. So China is not only economically jumping into the future," he says. "It is also jumping with big steps into the modern contemporary world of culture. China has a lot of things to show the entire world." He also says the leaders of both sides were highly supportive of building a Chinese culture centre in Belgrade. In return, the Republic of Serbia would build a similar centre in Beijing. The Belgrade centre, covering an area of 6,000 square metres, would be built on the site of the former Chinese embassy that was destroyed by a NATO bomb in May 1999 in what was then the Federal Republic of Yugoslavia.

Recalling the bombing, which was dropped deliberately, the minister says the centre to be built on the site will be part of a Chinese culture and business promotion building, which will cover 30,000 square metres in total. It will be completed in 2018. "For its part, the Republic of Serbia will open a contemporary culture centre in Beijing, and I can openly say this is a historic step in our cultural cooperation," Vukosavljevic says.

05

CHAPTER FIVE

Hungary and Poland take lead in Silk Road Initiative to reshape their regional importance and relationship with China

Every European country has the habit of boasting of its gateway advantage when attracting foreign investment. But the reality is that in central and eastern Europe (CEE), and even in the south, no ports can compete with Rotterdam, Antwerp and Hamburg; no airport is busier than Frankfurt, Paris, Amsterdam and London, and financial hubs are only story about President Xi whistling the melody from in the West Europe. In lifting themselves out of the negative impacts of the financial and European debt crises of 2008, the CEE countries have aimed to improve their competitiveness by exploring their potential.

They have taken notice of the revival model of the Asian economies, especially the secrets of China's lasting boom. They started to improve their infrastructure by ambitiously expanding highways, ports and airports, building high-tech parks and attracting foreign investment. China has already met such demands.

In 2012, China and sixteen CEE countries started their annual summits in Warsaw, Bucharest, Belgrade, Suzhou and Riga to discuss and implement concrete plans in various areas. By 2016, only up to 50 projects in areas such as infrastructure, energy, education and finance had been completed, and they even designed work programmes towards 2020. At the Riga summit held in 2016, they rolled out a list of dozens of tasks, which will be reviewed at the upcoming summit in Budapest.

In an interview, Duan Jielong, Chinese ambassador to Hungary, says that after President Xi Jinping proposed the Belt and Road Initiative in 2013, a new impetus had been injected into the cooperation between China and the CEE countries. "Within the background of President Xi's Belt and Road Initiative, new opportunities and perspectives have occurred regarding cooperation between China and central and eastern European countries," says Duan. In his eyes, China's investment in the region started to become active.

Duan says the number of Chinese businesses investing in Hungary had reached 40 by the beginning of this year. "Last year, the number was around 30," he says, not specifying the investment amount but revealing that the businesses mainly invested in auto parts, the chemical industry and electronic products. He says the railway project linking Budapest and Belgrade was a landmark one, and the governments of the three countries involved had maintained close communication in an effort to launch the project by the end of this year.

The European Commission is now reviewing the project report before it gives the green light. Apart from the land-sea expressway which means that containers in Piraeus in Greece can be offloaded and directly transported by rail to Budapest via Skopje in Macedonia and Belgrade, Serbia's capital, the countries have reaffirmed their support for the cooperation initiative involving ports on the Adriatic, Baltic and Black seas, and along the inland waterways.

They know that Adriatic-Baltic-Black Sea port cooperation would help widen the scope of China-CEE practical cooperation and contribute to greater synergy between the Belt and Road Initiative and the development strategies of CEE countries and the EU's Trans-European Transport Network.

Meanwhile Poland, Hungary and the Czech Republic have already benefited from the China-Europe rail freight service, which was launched in 2011 and has become an important part of the Belt and Road Initiative. Xinhua reported that by the end of March 2017 a total of 3,557 freight trains have run so far, with services reaching 27 Chinese cities, and 28 cities in 11 European countries.

After the announcement of Xi's initiative and the implementation of the initial projects, with their aim of connecting Asia, Europe and Africa by improving infrastructural connectivity and boosting investment and trade, the countries' "gateway advantage" of regional and even cross-continent importance have become prominent.

The Czech Republic aims to build itself up as a regional aviation and financial centre, says Ma Keqing, Chinese ambassador to the country. The leaders of Poland, with a population of around 40 million, have decided to turn it into a regional and European centre. And even Greece, a country always hitting the headlines and struggling with bailout talks, has designed a national strategy of embedding itself into the Belt and Road Initiative and becoming a regional energy, shipping and logistics centre. "Greece has been implementing its national development strategy while participating in the Belt and Road Initiative," says Zou Xiaoli, China's ambassador in Athens.

To further engage in the Belt and Road Initiative, Czech President Milos Zeman, the Hungarian Prime Minister Viktor Orban and his Polish counterpart Beata Szydlo have joined other leaders from Europe and the rest of the world at the Belt and Road Initiative Forum for International Cooperation in Beijing on 14-15 May 2017. The leaders from the CEE countries offered their opinions between how to expand cooperation in infrastructure, industry investment, economic and trade cooperation, energy and resources, financial cooperation, people-to-people and cultural exchanges, ecological conservation and maritime cooperation.

And to further explore opportunities, the China-CEE Institute, a think tank, was set up in Budapest in April by the Chinese Academy of Social Sciences (CASS) to focus on cooperation between China and the CEE group. The president of CASS, Wang Weiguang, says the setup of the new institute was a milestone for China's think tanks to go global. Huang Ping, General Director of the Institute of European Studies of CASS, also heads the China-CEE Institute. "This should be the first think tank we set up in Europe, and it will play a big role in the context of boosting the Belt and Road Initiative," Wang says. In fact, with a population of 123 million people, the sixteen countries' trade volume with China amounted to $50 billion in 2012, equalling to the value of trade between China and Italy. And China's investment in the sixteen countries equalled its investment in Sweden, while their investment in China was no greater than Austria's.

Meanwhile the CEE countries have a great demand for road and railway construction, port and power plant expansion, and are hungry for China's investments. Now, according to the Chinese Ministry of Commerce, the trade volume between the two sides has grown at a moderate speed amid ableak situation globally, but the investments have increased by a big margin in many countries.

HUNGARY'S SYNERGY WITH THE BELT AND ROAD INITIATIVE

After a recent meeting with the 41-year-old Ye Xiaorong, who comes from Qingtian County in Zhejiang Province and now lives in Budapest, I suddenly have realised that a new type of Chinese town is emerging. And China's Belt and Road Initiative is giving his dream a timely push. In many

Chinese communities of European towns, Chinese restaurants, groceries, traditional Chinese medicine clinics and even tourism sit next to each other in one or two or several streets. These streets and shops were usually built by the local municipalities for the Chinese to rent.

"I like markets where we can bargain. I like bargaining," says Ye with a sober but enthusiastic tone while serving Chinese tea to me in his office on the outskirts of Budapest. While we drank our tea, he told me how exploring business opportunities with partners is an essential part of his daily life.

I know many have equated typical citizens of Ye's hometown with Jewish people, who are sometimes regarded as business-savvy. When he talks, he shows traits such as courage, flexibility and pragmatism. And he is shy of revealing the annual revenues his business group has earned. I think readers need to be very careful in this section. Many readers in the UK and other parts of Western Europe and North America, for example, would consider it racist to define any ethic or racial group—such as Jews—as "business-savvy", even if the description is not meant in a critical or hostile sense.

"I can tell you I dream of turning the place around us into a modern Chinese town, with hundreds of wholesale shops to satisfy the Europeans' living needs," says Ye, now President of the Building Material Market in Budapest, smilingly skipping my questions on his detailed business figures. With a long tradition of citizens leaving their hometown to live globally, Ye's mountainous rural county now has around 500,000 residents. But the number of those who have left and are now outside China has reached 300,000. Nine out of ten are in Europe as restaurant owners and shopkeepers.

Ye, the architect behind a brand-new Chinatown in the Hungarian capital, has made a difference. Being slightly stout, Ye told me he grew up in a humble rural family with five brothers and sisters. Quitting school in the early 1990s, like many Chinese businessmen during those years, he started out with limited opportunities, selling ice-lollies with his brothers in their hometown. Earning one or two cents delighted him.

When he went into the wholesale garment business, he had lost so much money that even his mother ordered him to give up the business altogether. After a seemingly-endless quest, she lent him 1,000 yuan to restart his business and he made a profit of about 300,000 yuan before leaving for Budapest in 1999, with help from his relatives. "I learned a lot from losing money at the very beginning," says Ye.

Like many Chinese in Budapest who used the Hungarian capital as a gateway to other countries, Ye soon began selling garments and other cheap Chinese products wholesale to neighbouring countries in the old China-Europe business centre, which was as crowded as a shantytown. The centre still hosts 2,000 shopowners. But Ye dreamed of a clean, orderly and decent business atmosphere.

In 2001, he started a real estate investment company and began building a new Chinatown on vacant land about a kilometre from the old business centre. The construction was accelerated in 2008 and now the new Chinatown, consisting of three streets, is filled with garment wholesaling, a restaurant, a supermarket and even law firms. The restaurant offered menu items so tasty that Hong Kong's action movie star Jack Chan visited it during his Hungarian tour in April.

That achievement has not stopped Ye. Three years ago, he and his younger brother launched another plan to build three more streets within 5-8 years for wholesale sales of building materials, wall bricks, lamps, heating and cooling equipment, and auto parts. "My goal is clear that we must become the biggest player, at least in the region," Ye told me.

Now the first new street has taken shape, with wholesale shops lining two sides and up to 40 merchants, half of them Chinese and half Hungarian, have already moved in. Finally, he says, the three streets will be host to 500 wholesale enterprises and will generate at least 3,000 jobs for Hungarians. The Chinatown and Ye's planned building materials shop streets are metres away from the main railway link between Budapest and other European capitals. China, the Republic of Serbia and Hungary have already agreed to upgrade the railway between Budapest and Belgrade under the Belt and Road Initiative framework.

Ye is certain that this line will be become much busier as many goods will be transported via the land-sea express linking Greece and Hungary and other parts of Europe. So he asked the Budapest railway authority to build a small freight station beside the market. This is still under discussion, while the station would help him save the transport costs of loading goods from another railway station, which cost about 400 euro for each container. Combining the six streets together, Ye believes that this will be a novel Chinese business community, serving Europeans and creating jobs for Hungarians with a long chain. He also says the market's suppliers are worldwide, ranging from Turkey to Germany, though most of the building materials still come from China because of its lower price.

Standing beside the railway line, Ye told me: "When our blueprint finally turns into reality, our Chinatown will be an attraction in Budapest." He even plans to usher in hop-on and hop-off tuk-tuks for sightseeing tourists.

Ye's six-street market dream is truly a facelift for Chinatown. Hungarians always say they are the only Europeans with eastern roots. This is proved by their lasting passion to absorb China's Zen and Kung Fu cultures.

During my interviews in Hungary, in addition to Ye's ambition, the 32-generation of Shaolin Temple warrior monk Wang Deqing, who moved to Hungary in 1999, also impressed me by his way of spreading Chinese culture. He has been appointed to coach in Hungary's National Police School, to be the chief coach of the Special Police Forces and coach of the president's bodyguards, the Escort Unit.

"Many may think I will equip them with Chinese Kung Fu," says Wang in his International Chan Wu Federation on the outskirts of Budapest, which he set up in 2003. "That's not true, specially when training the president's sniper team."

In his practice, Chan, which means Zen Buddhism, and Wu, which means martial arts, are equally important. And on his arrival in Hungary, his federation aimed to spread Chinese culture with the combined philosophy of uniting Chan and Wu. "I mainly used the Chan to cultivate the minds of the Hungarian snipers, who had always been working in high-tension conditions," says Wang. "I have taught them how to be calm and have a peaceful mind even in super-dangerous and critical situations while working alone and concealed."

His years of effort in Hungary have been recognised. He was working as the executive chairman of the China-Hungary Police Exchange Association, which is linked with Hungary's Ministry of Interior Affairs. The former Hungarian Prime Minister Peter Medgyessy recently invited him to dinner and thanked Wang for his contribution to boosting Chinese culture in Hungary.

Wang says it was with Medgyessy's enormous help (when he was prime minister earlier this century) that Chinese traditional medicine, acupuncture, Kung Fu and even the Chinese language had started to be greatly promoted in Hungary. "Prime Minister Medgyessy is a visionary and respected Hungarian leader in boosting Sino-Hungarian exchanges," says Wang.

Apart from Wang's contribution to the police and bodyguard units, he has trained European Chan Wu coaches, and now there are about 30 branches of the Chan Wu Federation worldwide, many of them in Europe. It is estimated that up to 200,000 practitioners worldwide have embraced this form of Chinese cultures. "I think it is most popular in Hungary, and one Hungarian coach told me he has already taught about 1,000 students," says Wang. "This is an amazing achievement."

Wang says all the students are asked to preserve and promote authentic traditional Shaolin Kung Fu as it was taught to him by his masters in the Shaolin Temple itself. These include the traditional etiquette and disciplines, encouraging students to cultivate martial virtues and establish harmonious and happy attitudes and values. Chan Wu has established nine ranking systems to recognise its students' achievements in martial arts practice through examinations.

Now, Wang says, among practitioners in Europe, some have benefitted from the training, which has changed their attitudes. Wang is still observing a simple way of life despite his achievements and the recognition he has earned. "If I was not practicing kongfu, I would be among those who were abandoned by the mainstream," he says.

Wang was born in Zhejiang in 1974, and was extremely naughty. So at the age of nine his parents sent him to a sports school near the Shaolin Temple in central China's Henan Province. Three years later he joined 15 others to form the Shaolin Temple Martial Arts Team and became a novice monk. "I was fascinated, but soon I found that being hungry was one of the biggest worries in the temple," Wang recalled. At the age of 18, Wang became known and turned to being a warrior monk, receiving his monk's name, Shi Xinghong.

Soon he started to spread Kung Fu culture worldwide. Wang's concept of combining martial arts and mind cultivation even attracted the Spanish government before he settled down in Hungary, and he was invited to work with juvenile offenders in Spain.

Wang recalled that he could not carry on after a year coaching there because he was given a spacious ancient villa by his Spanish hosts. He says: "I am used to a simple life in the temple, and that was unacceptable, though my coaching was useful for young offenders."

THE 350-KM BUDAPEST-BELGRADE RAILWAY: AN ICONIC PROJECT

B oth Chinese and Hungarian officials have confirmed that China's participation in the modernisation of the 350-km Budapest-Belgrade railway line is on a smooth track, while the European Commission is reviewing the related design and financing arrangement report.

"Both sides have already signed construction contracts and the financing scheme memorandum, and we are involved in efforts to start the crucial project as early as possible," says Duan Jielong, Chinese ambassador to Hungary, speaking in an exclusive interview.

Duan says China would help to make the railway a double-track line; the design of the section in Hungary was already completed, and China and Hungary have formed a joint entity to invest in and implement the project.

The construction company from China's side was also ready to break ground in the Serbian section. Reliable sources from the Republic of Serbia say in a recent interview that the European Union might give the green light to this project "very soon." Hungary's Foreign Minister Peter Szijjarto also says the modernisation of the Budapest-Belgrade railway was the "flagship project" of cooperation between China and the CEE countries, which his country had been actively pushing forward.

"This is because it involves the creation of a new model of cooperation in cross-border infrastructure investments enhancing regional connectivity," says Szijjarto in an interview.

He also says it was an integral part of the Belt and Road Initiative as a section of the China-Europe Land-Sea Express Line, and would possibly provide the fastest, highest-capacity transport route connecting the Greek port of Piraeus with Western Europe. He says this line would benefit many countries in industrial transformation. "Similarly to Hungary, the countries along the line can connect to the China-Europe Land-Sea Express Line with industrial parks and logistics centres, and, obviously, their products can be exported to China," says Szijjarto.

His country welcomed the initiative from the very beginning as a unique opportunity for attracting investment and much-needed new financing options necessary for infrastructure projects implemented in the CEE region to improve connectivity, with particular focus on freight transport.

"The Budapest-Belgrade railway line is a significant project in this regard," says Szijjarto.

He says China was the target country of his country's Opening to the East strategy launched in 2010, and the Belt and Road Initiative fit well into the country's development blueprint.

Both Duan and Szijjarto commented on the significance of the Budapest-Belgrade railway project before Prime Minister Viktor Orban left for Beijing to join the Belt and Road Initiative Forum, which was an opportunity for all countries involved in the initiative to jointly conduct talks and to discuss existing best practices and experiences.

Orban paid an official visit to Beijing in May, and in addition to a bilateral meeting with Premier Li Keqiang, Orban was received by President Xi and top legislators. In Beijing, Orban says the old globalization model was obsolete and "the East has caught up with the West".

He sees the Belt and Road Initiative as "another direction of movement, which is specifically built on mutual acceptance." Orban describes the modernisation of the Budapest-Belgrade line as a "most spectacular" agreement.

In participating in the initiative, the three countries have not only benefited from infrastructure improvement, but also from being connected with the global supply chain.

Under the Belt and Road Initiative framework, Szijjarto says that, Hungary had been gaining an increasingly important role as a financial centre of the region, promoting renminbi transactions.

Ambassador Duan also says the economic and trade relations between the two countries had become closer after they implemented the Belt and

Road Initiative. Duan says China was Hungary's biggest trade partner outside Europe, with trade volume exceeding $8.89 billion in 2016 and gaining 10.1 percent year-on-year, against bleak global trade figures. Duan also says that in 2016 Hungary's exports to China had broken all previous records, reaching $3.46 billion with a growth of 20.5 percent. The prospects were particularly good for high-quality agricultural and food products, which are attracting growing demand in China.

Right now, Hungary is China's biggest investment destination in the CEE countries, and accumulated investment stock has surpassed $4.1 billion. Duan says Huawei, ZTE, Bank of China joined up to 40 Chinese companies in investing in Hungary and the investment has already created 7,400 jobs.

Among the Chinese investors, BYD, China's leading electric auto supplier, is the newcomer to Hungary. Isbrand Ho, Managing Director of BYD Europe, says his company would invest some 20 million euro in the three years leading up to 2018 in the new plant, which is about 50 km from Budapest. It would create 300 jobs, the vast majority being taken by locally-recruited Hungarians with a technical background, who would assemble up to 400 electric buses a year in two shifts.

"Those buses will be exported to customers across continental Europe," says Ho. "Initial output will be electric buses and coaches but other products will soon follow." Ho says the Belt and Road Initiative aimed to create the world's largest platform for economic cooperation, and many companies had signed cooperation agreements for projects along the routes. "Not only BYD Europe but also our customers, suppliers and other counterparts benefit from these improved connections," says Ho.

He says the BYD was very conscious of Hungary's strong heritage of bus making in the immediate region, and nearby factories in Hungary had built thousands of buses every year to supply the former eastern bloc. With the Hungarian government trying to re-establish that industry, Ho says BYD was proud to be at the forefront of this endeavour and expected to be a strong partner in helping Hungary to implement public transportation electrification. "We anticipate a significant rise in sales of electric buses in Europe, and the plant improves our ability to meet customers' needs," says Ho.

POLAND AND CHINA: RE-POSITIONED
PARTNERSHIP WITH SRI ESSENCES

As the hometown of the world-renowned composer and pianist Frederic Chopin (1810-49), his Polish hosts organised a concert for Xi and his delegation during his visit, featuring Chopin's compositions. In 2016, when I interviewed Polish President Andrzej Duda, he says his Chinese counterpart Xi's arrival in the CEE region for the second time in less than three months signalled his full recognition of the region's dynamics and importance. "I have no doubt President Xi perfectly understands the dynamic in this part of the world. We are developing fast, so is China," Duda told me in a written interview.

Duda, aged 44, says his country was well prepared to welcome Xi and his wife Peng Liyuan to Poland after his trip in the Republic of Serbia. At the end of March, Xi had paid a state visit to the Czech Republic, beefing up political ties and signing dozens of economic and trade projects.

"This second trip (within less than three months) underlines how important central and eastern Europe is becoming for China," says Duda, who visited China last November. Recalling that he was deeply impressed by China's thousands of years of history and heritage during his first ever trip to China, Duda stressed that President Xi would perceive Poland and the whole region as an extremely attractive market, a land of boundless opportunities for deeper economic cooperation. During his trip to China in November of 2016, China and Poland signed a cooperation document on the Belt and Road Initiative and Poland officially became a member of the Asian Infrastructure Investment Bank.

"We see it as an opportunity to find new ways of funding ambitious infrastructure projects in Poland and other countries in central and eastern Europe," says Duda. The Polish leader says that Poland had to improve the North-South axis, which had been neglected since it joined the European Union in 2004, and it needed to build more motorways and more railways, which would form a link between the Baltics and the Balkans.

"I am convinced this would give an enormous boost to all of us," says Duda. "And China can play an important role in this area."

"On the other hand, we also hope that Polish companies will benefit hugely from the Belt and Road Initiative," says Duda, adding that they had experience and a highly qualified workforce, and he was sure they could establish long-lasting and fruitful partnerships with Chinese firms.

Duda says he realised that Beijing was playing an increasingly crucial role in the international arena; many Chinese companies were well-known and respected abroad, and China had seen millions of people emerging from poverty over the last few decades.

He says one of the biggest challenges these days was social inequality and uneven growth between urban and rural areas, and he knew how much the Chinese authorities had done to tackle this issue.

"On the other hand, many European nations have had to cope with the very same problem recently," says Duda.

Duda says dozens of bilateral agreements would be signed during the visit, which would be the foundation for further cooperation between China and Poland. "But our relations should not be solely of an economic nature," says Duda.

"I am sure both President Xi and his wife Peng Liyuan will fall in love with Polish culture, Polish music and, last but not least, Polish cuisine as well."

China and Poland laid solid foundations to forge a synergy between the Belt and Road Initiative and the 2030 development strategy, as this central European country was actively pushing economic diplomacy, says Li Wei, Minister of the Development Research Center of the State Council, a top think tank for China's central government.

"China's Belt and Road Initiative has created vital opportunities for both sides to deepen their trade and economic relationship, and Poland's long-term development strategy has echoes the initiative well," says Li. The Polish long-term strategy 2030 was aimed at achieving high-level modernity, and President Xi came up with the Belt and Road Initiative in 2013 to boost connectivity in Asia, Europe and Africa. In terms of Chinese-Polish economic relations, Li says China was an important investment destination and the biggest trade partner of Poland in Asia, while Poland is China's biggest trade partner and the most important investment destination in central and eastern Europe.

"Right now, Poland has been greatly increasing its investment in infrastructure construction, which has brought tremendous opportunities for Chinese companies," says Li. Historically labelled as the eastern gateway of Europe, Poland has already become an active participant of China's Belt and Road Initiative, he says. And among all the rail freight expresses linking China and European countries, six of them will be entering their destinations via Poland.

President Xi attended a ceremony during his visit, at which various freight lines between Chinese and European cities were united under one brand, "China Express", which is up to 10 days faster than transport by sea.

Li says the Initiative was being given top priority by China, with the central government and all of the provinces, municipalities and autonomous regions having already mapped out their own blueprints on how to make the Belt and Road Initiative a reality. Externally, Li says, China had already signed agreements with more than 30 countries such as Mongolia and Kazakhstan to seek synergies for each other's major projects. In 2015, China and Russia announced that they would find ways of linking the Belt and Road Initiative and the Russian-led Eurasian Economic Union, which so far consists of five countries. China and the European Union have also signed an agreement to deepen cooperation between the Belt and Road Initiative and the EU's 315-billion-euro Investment Plan, known as the Juncker Plan.

"In implementing the Belt and Road Initiative, we have also made a lot of progress in infrastructure construction and trade and industrial park projects," says Li.

For example, the 770-km high-speed railway linking Moscow and Kazan, the Jakarta-Bandung high-speed railway and the China-Laos railway are under construction, and China has gained a big stake in the projects by offering technological solutions, financial sources and engineering experience.

Li says China had already entered into currency swap agreements with sixteen countries along the routes of the Belt and Road Initiative. Apart from the Asian Infrastructure Investment Bank and Silk Road Fund, China had been working to set up joint financial vehicles with nations in Africa, the EU, Russia and other countries and organisations. "We are trying to sort out the problem of financial constraints," he says.

Li also says China and 46 countries had already signed agreements to waive visas for each other's territories, and another 19 countries had agreed to issue visas on arrival for Chinese citizens. "The measures have greatly facilitated people-to-people exchanges, travelling, economic cooperation and trade flows," says Li.

China and Poland upgraded their strategic partnership to a "comprehensive level" during President Xi Jinping's visit in 2016 to this fast-developing country. And the scaling-up of the bilateral relationship, five years after establishing the Sino-Polish strategic partnership in 2011, would be happening after Poland's adjustment of its foreign policy in recent years by engaging all global players, instead of mainly the West. "Our bilateral relationship had made tremendously solid progress on all fronts in previous years, and both sides recognised such benefits during President Xi's visit," says Xu Jian, Chinese ambassador to Poland.

Xu, having also served as ambassador to Romania, says the burgeoning development of partnership between China and the CEE countries was also the reason behind the "re-positioning" of the China-Poland relationship during Xi's visit. Xi visited Poland in 2016 after his three-day state visit to the Republic of Serbia, which lies at the crossroads between central and southeast Europe. "I think our relationship is already at the level of a comprehensive strategic partnership," says Xu.

During Xi's visit to the Czech Republic in March 2016, the two countries established a strategic partnership. And for an overall relationship between China and the EU, which Xi visited in early 2014, a comprehensive strategic partnership has already been forged.

In recent years, especially after the 2008 financial crisis, the CEE countries have started to readjust their foreign policies after years of closely engaging the Western countries. And China's economic dynamics and market have also become magnets to draw them closer. Among the sixteen countries in the region, Poland, Hungary and the others have become active pacesetters in developing a partnership with China; while other countries, such as the Czech Republic, have vowed to catch up. And in early 2016, this effective cooperation framework even attracted Switzerland as the first country with observer status of the China and central and eastern Europe partnership, known as the 16+1 group.

"I believe President Xi's second visit to the region within three months has clearly demonstrated how my country values the relationship between China and the sixteen countries, and the partnership between China and the EU as well," says Xu. The pragmatic cooperation between China and Poland has been smoothly implemented in recent years. Now both sides are showing great interest in exploring cooperation in infrastructure projects in Poland.

Xu says Poland had asked China to get involved in its airport construction, highway building and high-speed railway project. Poland joined the China-led Asian Infrastructure Investment Bank and actively supported the Belt and Road Initiative. And recently the president of the AIIB, Jin Liqun, visited Poland, which is seeking alternative financial sources outside the EU to fund its infrastructure projects.

China and Poland signed a new document on the Belt and Road Initiative during Xi's visit, to further narrow down meeting points in infrastructure cooperation.

Both state and private investors from China pledged to inject fresh capital and technology into Poland and other regions of Europe under the framework of the Belt and Road Initiative, with its aim of boosting Eurasian connectivity. They announced their commitments at the two-day annual Silk Road Forum organized by the Development Research Centre of the State Council and its global partners while President Xi was paying his three-country tour to the Republic of Serbia, Poland and Uzbekistan in 2016.

"China and Poland, similar to other European countries, have faced the same challenges of restructuring economies and developing sustainability, and we are keen on investing in infrastructure, energy saving, high-tech and innovative sectors in Europe," says Jin Qi, Chairman of the Beijing-based Silk Road Fund. The medium-and-long-term fund was established at the end of 2014, with a first-phase financial injection of $10 billion, while Xi pledged that the total investment will be $40 billion.

China and the European Union were negotiating putting a joint fund in place to connect Belt and Road initiatives and the EU's 315-billion-euro investment scheme. Jin's fund is expected to become one of the Chinese founders of the joint fund, likely to be unveiled at the Sino-EU leaders meeting in June 2017, "We are determined to forge synergies of mega-projects between China, the EU and its member states," Jin told the annual forum, the third one after those held in Istanbul and Madrid in 2014 and 2015 respectively.

The forum in Poland has touched on the standardisation of the Eurasian transportation system on land and by sea, innovative ways of financing, global governance and sustainable development, and cooperation between China and Europe at regional levels.

Ding Xuedong, then chairman and CEO of China Investment Corporation, says his organisation was also ready to fill the financial gap when Poland and other countries in Central and Eastern Europe needed funds. Ding says the sixteen countries in the region are expected to need at least one trillion dollars in the coming ten years to improve their infrastructure by building roads, highways, airports and other facilities. "Facing such a huge amount of capital demand in infrastructure construction alone, investment from the government could not satisfy the needs and the countries need to channel more resources," says Ding.

Even the Western European powers face the challenges of filling the capital gap when upgrading their infrastructure, says Ding. "So the effective mechanism is to pool the resources from the governments, policy loan vehicles, investment funds and private sectors," he says, adding that Poland and the rest of Europe were investment targets of this state fund.

Apart from the Chinese investment giants, private investors have also attached growing importance to Poland and other European countries. Among them is Wu Daohong, Chairman of Beijing Shenwu Environment & Energy Technology Co., Ltd., who says that China's private companies had the advantages of cooperating with European partners in high-tech sectors. Wu says he had even brought with him three patent technologies on biomass and clean energy, especially on using coal in a cleaner way; the talks with Polish partners were continuing. "We are quite sure that our technologies in the coal sector are advancing, and Poland and China, both rich in coal reserves, could boast huge opportunities if pollution can be avoided in coal use," says Wu.

Stephen Perry from the London-based 48 Group Club says the Belt and Road Initiative, a continuation of China's opening-up drive, will last for 20-50 years, and one of the key determinants will be the response of the West. He says China wanted Western involvement, as it has many of the key advanced technologies and has funding and various capabilities in finance, technology and management that this project will require. "If the West gets invested in this project, we will get large rewards and growth of our own," says Perry.

CHAPTER SIX

Western European countries vary in their acceptance of the Belt and Road Initiative while ties with China have grown tighter

Germany, France, Italy, the UK, Belgium and Luxembourg could be treated as the six founding countries of the European peace project, and now the European Union includes 28 members until the UK's impending departure from the bloc actually happens. During the previous four years, after President Xi announced the Belt and Road Initiative, these countries have shown various degrees of acceptance, with the UK taking the lead but Belgium losing the chance of becoming a founding member of the Asian Infrastructure Investment Bank. Some in Italy have proposed competing with Greece, which has already become a pioneer in promoting the initiative. Germany believes it is a project which could align with its international development strategy while in France the opinion leaders hope the new president could become proactive in engaging China. And tiny land-locked Luxembourg has even linked with central China's Zhengzhou with Silk Road in the air, a freight airline.

In fact, during the first seven months of 2017, there have been four global occasions for the leaders to debate the international agenda, including the G7 and G20 summits, the World Economic Forum's Davos gathering in January and the Belt and Road Initiative Forum in Beijing. After the Beijing gathering, between 14-15 May, of all the hundreds of foreign participants, Italian Prime Minister Paolo Gentiloni and Germany's Minister for Economics and Energy Brigitte Zypries could have been the key messengers in spreading the forum's consensus that tearing the walls down could achieve peace and prosperity. This is simply because Gentiloni, who joined state leaders from across the world in Beijing, would have hosted the G7 summit in the Sicilian town of Taormina between 26-27 May, and Germany was to chair the G20 Leaders' Meeting in Hamburg between 7-8 July. Zypries attended the forum on behalf of German Chancellor Angela Merkel, who could not attend due to a scheduling conflict.

The two countries were responsible for agenda-setting for the upcoming summits, and Gentiloni and Zypries should have noted the proposals, solutions and suggestions that were emerging from the two-day gathering in Beijing. What China was basically proposing with the Belt and Road Initiative is that the world should engage in joint consultation and cooperation in pursuit of peace and prosperity, rather than engage in confrontation which would lead only to conflict. This revival of the Silk Road spirit was something the G7 and G20 summits urgently needed to embrace. When the meetings wrapped up in early 2017, the G7 finance ministers and central bank governors failed to adopt a firm stance against protectionism, mainly because of the opposition of the United States representative.

The G20 finance ministers were also not on the same page at their meeting in March as they dropped their commitment to take "no single protection measure", a practice adopted in the depths of the global economic recession. However, it was not just the United States that was taking a protectionist stance. The European Union announced anti-dumping measures against China's exports of iron and steel pipes and tubes in May. But the leaders who gathered in Beijing issued a communique highlighting their consensus in support of deepening cooperation and building more opportunities by connecting different countries, regions and cultures through better infrastructure, innovative financial tools and measures to encourage the flow of other productivity elements, such as capital, technology and human resources.

The task of spreading this message would fall on Italy and Germany's shoulders when they hosted the forthcoming summits. It is true that they were being held at a difficult time, as French President Emmanuel Macron had only just begun his five-year term, Donald Trump had taken office in January, and Gentiloni had started to lead the Italian government last December. British Prime Minister Theresa May was also a new face. But the leaders should not only spend their time laying the "foundations for trust", which always appears to be a core task of their gatherings. They now need to be decisive in delivering concrete outcomes. They must fight against protectionism, collectively learning from the Silk Road spirit that was evident in Beijing during the Belt and Road Forum. And they must secure the harvest of global efforts to fight against climate change. If so, that would pave the way for the G20 summit in Hamburg, for which the theme was connectivity.

In many ways, this theme already reflected some of the outcomes of the Belt and Road Initiative, and the participants should have been encouraged to debate and find ways to achieve not only greater infrastructure connectivity via roads, highways, railways and ports, but also through financial openness and digital transformation. In Beijing, World Economic Forum founder Klaus Schwab called the Belt and Road Initiative proposed by China a model for fostering economic development and international cooperation. He plans to deepen the scope of the WEF's debates and discussions by linking the Initiative with its research and agenda-setting process on various occasions. In acting as timely messengers and transforming the world into a better place, Italy and Germany were enabled to follow the example set by Schwab and use the Silk Road spirit of peaceful exchanges to guide the G7 and G20 summits.

GERMANY AND THE BELT AND ROAD INITIATIVE

B asically, the Italian presidency of the G7 failed to discuss the Belt and Road Initiative at the meeting in late May, while on China's diplomatic chessboard the significance of Germany and other European Union member states can be gauged from the frequent visits President Xi Jinping has paid to those countries. In fact, he arrived in Berlin paying another state visit to Germany before attending this year's G20 summit in Hamburg.

China has always attached great importance to Germany. This is Xi's second state visit to Germany after his previous one in March 2014. What's more, the Chinese president's visit this year follows just one month after Premier Li Keqiang's tour of Germany. And Li also paid a visit to Germany in 2014.

Germany attaches equal importance to China, and German Chancellor Angela Merkel has visited China many times during her term in office. An official in the chancellor's office says Merkel probably doesn't attach such importance to any other country. Germany is a competitive exporter and manufacturer, and thus an ideal model for China. Its social welfare and market system have been widely debated in China, which is undergoing market-oriented reform. And for decades, Germany has had a big share in China's market. For example, German car brands, such as Volkswagen, Audi, BMW and Mercedes, are omnipresent in China.

And since Chinese investors have just started to explore the opportunities in the high-end product market, Xi is likely to discuss with German leaders how to further boost bilateral ties and become bigger players in each other's markets by removing trade and investment barriers.

Globalisation faces increasing challenges, especially with the United Kingdom's departure from the EU and US President Donald Trump's inward-looking policy to "make America Great Again", which is nothing but trade protectionism. Trump has also pulled the United States out of the global climate change agreement, which almost every UN member state welcomed and signed in Paris in 2015.

Germany has been championing free trade and closer global connectivity and remains committed to fighting climate change. And at the World Economic Forum in Davos, Switzerland, in January, Xi affirmed China's commitment to globalisation and free trade, a commitment EU commentators and politicians alike have repeatedly cited and welcomed. For China, Germany is not only a market but also a platform to explore the entire EU economy. In recent years, Beijing has been viewing Sino-German ties beyond the two countries' markets, whose consumers add up to 1.9 billion people.

That's one of the reasons Xi proposed the Belt and Road Initiative. Germany's positive response to the Initiative prompted other EU countries to join it. For example, China initiated the Asian Infrastructure Investment Bank, which many EU countries joined as founding members to explore more opportunities in third-party markets.

After the G20 summit in Hamburg, I did a comparative reading of the outcome documents reaped there and those produced at the Washington gathering, the first such meeting between rich and emerging economies' leaders held just two months after the fall of financial giant Lehman Brothers in 2008. A comparison like that can lead to both encouraging and worrying observations.

Obviously, after intensive diplomatic efforts by German Chancellor Angela Merkel's team, (she is possibly the only leader who has participated in all 12 previous G20 summits), the topics put on the agenda went far beyond risk management, financial market regulation, financial liquidity guarantees and the urgency of reviving economic growth, which were heavily debated at the very beginning. Then the major task of the international community was to avoid global market dysfunction by engaging emerging economies such as China to contribute to the world's growth, while at the same time the international community has accumulated urgent capital resources to the global financial institutions to ensure it was workable.

In the depths of the global economic recession, the most damaging since the 1929-1933 Great Depression, China contributed half of the global economic growth, and even now the share of its contribution, according to the International Monetary Fund, stands at around 30 percent. In return, China gained some of its due say in established international economic governance: the renminbi was put in the global currency basket, it was increasingly exchanged at bilateral level and recently it was even bought by the European Central Bank as a reserve currency.

China has taken the lead in setting up new multilateral financing platforms such as the Asia Infrastructure Investment Bank and the BRICS bank (the New Development Bank), respectively based in Beijing and Shanghai. And it proposed the Belt and Road Initiative to make the global economy grow even stronger and more inclusive. With China's contribution (as shown in the Hamburg documents), the outcomes of this two-day meeting held in tight security in the German port city expanded widely and built on the results achieved at previous summits, which typically focused on the fact that rich countries were eager to talk with developing economies.

The G20 leaders seemed to reach a consensus on open economy, free trade, energy and sustainable development, the digital economy, a partnership with Africa, health, and women's empowerment, which were condensed into a 15-page declaration and several annexes. This gives the impression that they agreed on everything except climate change, where the United States showed that it opposed the G19 by immediately stopping contributing to the global deal on fighting climate change.

The agreements are encouraging as the leaders knew well the significance of making global economic growth stable, sustainable and inclusive, aiming to benefit everybody in the world. Compared with the vision they showed at the G20 summit in Washington, it was a great leap forward. However, just as in the economic crisis of 2008-2012, during which the leaders coped successfully to some extent, the world is facing another crisis, a lack of collective global leadership and international political trust.

With economic growth being on the right track generally, India is provoking China at their border, the United States is aggressively demonstrating its military presence in the Asia-Pacific region, the differences between Europe and the United States are expanding, and relations between Russia and the

West are unfriendly. All the players were at the G20 summit in Hamburg, and their mutual trust had a huge influence on their economic consensus. In the documents from the G20 Washington summit, and even those in London and Pittsburgh of the US, words like "refrain" were frequently used, and then most of the players turned their words into action by extinguishing the fires and offering incentives to growth.

Now it is obvious that this political will from some economies, at a better economic time, is becoming weaker. Some are turning to domestic market protection, geopolitical calculations and military showcasing, instead of finding ways to offer more global public goods to really turn the Hamburg consensus into reality. Comparatively, it is growing hard to make compromises among the powers now. The United States, as with its trick over the Kyoto Protocol, once again confirmed its stance by withdrawing from the Paris Climate Change Agreement. That is damaging to international cooperation, as every other player believes the biggest economy should be a trustworthy partner and should implement an agreement it has agreed and ratified.

The situation is worrying. If such political trust cannot be deepened, the spirit of compromise cannot be sustained, and the G20 consensus will remain only a paper consensus, and what it could deliver will be curtailed.

While Western Europe differs from the rest of the continent, Michael Schaefer, former German ambassador to China, says Europeans were forming a "joint attitude" towards China's proposed Belt and Road Initiative, which is expected to stabilise the vast region between China and Europe. He adds that Xi had used bilateral meetings and even the G20 platform to further explain the significance of this century project, which will benefit not only China but also the rest of the world. "From their reluctance at the very beginning, the Europeans have started to shape their joint attitudes towards the Belt and Road Initiative," says Schaefer, who served as German ambassador to China from 2007 to 2013, during an exclusive interview with me in Berlin. "I am very vocal in supporting the Initiative, and Europe needs a more active response."

As chairman of the BMW Foundation in Berlin, Schaefer says he was not sure whether the Initiative would be discussed at the G20, but at least, he says, President Xi could discuss the topic when he met national leaders for bilateral talks. He thought China could do more to gain trust and interest in explaining the vision of this grand initiative, which would bring stability for those potentially fragile regions. Schaefer says that now the European Union has shown its great interest in the initiative, and many people in Germany have also improved their understanding of the project since it was proposed by President Xi in 2013.

"I believe this is an intelligent approach to create dynamics in potentially fragile areas," says Schaefer, pointing out that this initiative would go far beyond the symbolic and historic linkage of China to the Eurasian continent and a matter of infrastructure. Instead, Schaefer says, this project made a lot of sense when talking about the linkage of not only markets but also people. "I think it is in the common interest for the EU, Central Asia and China to participate in this initiative and contribute to stabilising the countries still in a relatively fragile situation," says Schaefer. "In this sense, this is a project which will be stabilising a huge area between China and Europe."

He says such stability, to be brought about by increases in human well-being through development and cooperation would be crucial for Eastern Europe and China's immediate neighbours, and even for those in poor regions of northwest China. "That is why Europe should act much more positively," he says. Schaefer also says that the maritime section of the Belt and Road Initiative was very important, as the world needed a safe maritime passage linking Africa, China and Europe, which could help Africa to develop their visions of development.

He adds that fragility was not only bad for foreign businesses, but also not good for the development of the people within the regions concerned. He has even urged that all countries to participate in this initiative should have long-term vision because it might last for thirty to fifty years. Schaefer says: "We need to understand this is not a project that will be done within one year, five years, but we need to contribute in the coming thirty or fifty years."

Schaefer had accompanied Xi to visit Germany in 2009, and found Xi to be a "very serious and impressive man with huge interest in history". "We had discussed a lot of things then," says Schaefer. He also says that during his seven-year stint as ambassador in Beijing, German Chancellor Angela Merkel had visited China six times, but not during election years. Schaefer says China was a unique country and its Reform and Opening-Up was extremely successful in bringing so many people out of poverty in such a short time. A massive group of 400 million people now formed a middle class. He says Xi Jinping was now bringing China into the centre of the international community which it deserved in terms of history, population and economic clout and was earning the respect it was due.

Schaefer says Xi had understood very well that in the 21st century that development can be achieved only through cooperation, instead of using the hegemonic approach some countries had used in the last century. "I think Xi has done two impressive things since becoming China's leader," says Schaefer. "One is fighting corruption, and the other is coming up with the Belt and Road Initiative to forge global cooperation and connectivity."

Shi Mingde, Chinese ambassador to Germany, also says that for the Chinese president and premier to visit Germany (in the same year) once again was a rarely-seen diplomatic move in Sino-German relations, and even in China's history of foreign relations it was extremely rare. "So this has gained mounting attention from the world," he says, adding that Xi paid his first state visit to Germany in early 2014, and during that year Premier Li also visited Germany, holding an annual high-level consultation meeting with the German government.

Shi regards Germany as a "core power" in Europe, with the most powerful and comprehensive strength, and on the global stage it exerted great influence. "China and Germany have shared growing common grounds in developing bilateral relations, solving regional and global difficulties and exploring development opportunities," says Shi. Such overlapping consensus on various fronts have helped Germany become China's biggest trade partner in Europe for 42 consecutive years, according to Shi. And last year, replacing the United States, China became Germany's largest trade partner. The trade flow between China and Germany already accounts for one third of the total between China and the 28 countries within the EU, Shi says, citing figures from German sources. "Germany has shown great confidence in China's market potential and economic prospects; China has recognised the importance of Germany's high-tech industry and management experiences," says Shi.

Shi added that, for years, Germany had also been the most generous country in Europe in regard to technology transfer to China. Xi's visit would see the 45th anniversary of Sino-German diplomatic relations, which Shi highly praised. "Our relationship has seen the best time ever in history, and this bilateral relationship has become the driving force of the Sino-EU partnership," says Shi.

Shi says that during his visit, President Xi would be outlining the future development blueprint of his bilateral relationship with the German leaders. "I believe new impetus will be injected into the sound relations during Xi's visit," says Shi. Shi revealed that President Xi would be inaugurating the Panda Garden in Berlin and would be present at the Sino-German youth football match. Shi says that Xi would be discussing with German leaders how to deepen cooperation under the Belt and Road Initiative framework, which would be one of the most important topics on the leaders' agenda.

Shi says Germany had already realised that the initiative was an important global public good, and its attitudes towards the initiative had undergone a "huge change" in the previous three years. When China was hosting the Belt and Road Initiative forum in May, Angela Merkel said her busy domestic agenda would not allow her to attend the gathering, so she sent her representative to indicate Germany's commitment to supporting the initiative. Shi says Germany was one of the Western countries that had shown timely support for China's proposal and was the fourth largest shareholder, after China, India and Russia, as well as the biggest non-regional shareholder, in the Beijing-based Asian Infrastructure Investment Bank. "Many cases occurring in previous years have shown that China and Germany can cooperate with each other to explore even more market potential in Asia, Africa and other parts of the world by participating in the Belt and Road Initiative," says Shi.

VIBRANT GERMAN-CHINESE RELATIONS

President Xi is a soccer fan and so is German Chancellor Angela Merkel, and during the past three years they have made consistent efforts to expand their two countries' soccer partnership. During his first trip to Germany as Chinese President in early 2014, Xi met young Chinese soccer players who had been trained in Germany. And when Merkel visited China in June and September of 2016, she even discussed with Xi how they might explore more soccer cooperation.

The efforts have paid off. When Vice-Premier Liu Yandong visited Germany in late 2016, the Chinese and German governments, their soccer associations and leagues formally entered into an agreement to deepen cooperation. Merkel met the Chinese delegation and had up to one hour of talks with Liu, during which much interest was directed toward soccer. Against the backdrop of a tough international situation, Germany and the European Union's recent hardening stance against China's investment and trade, it is laudable that the two countries explored a fresh frontier for bilateral relations.

China aims to participate in the World Cup and would like to host the competition one day and even win it. The fact that its soccer development still has some way to go to achieve these goals has motivated China to seek help.

It's starting with its kids. For example, one of China's goals is to prepare a reserve of 50,000 soccer coaches in schools and set up 15,000 soccer schools nationwide by 2020. Germany has helped China achieve its economic takeoff by investing, trading and exporting its high-tech know-how for years. Having won the World Cup four times, Germany is also a natural partner to help China achieve its soccer ambitions. Germany is likely to get the opportunity to train Chinese school coaches or even send their own coaches to some of China's schools.

Of course, China's leaders believe the promotion of soccer goes far beyond the aims related to the World Cup. And soccer cooperation between China and Germany can produce other opportunities for them to tap into China boasts 500 million soccer fans, and many support German teams. A long chain of business opportunities offering fun and enjoyment for the fans are waiting for China and Germany to explore.

On the hardware side, China plans to construct 70,000 soccer pitches by 2020. In addition, it is also ready to allow private and foreign investors to get involved in soccer development funds. Germans could also explore business opportunities by helping China realise these aims. Nowadays, the majority of Chinese people are seeking to improve their quality of life and are willing to invest time and energy in leisure and sports. And parents are encouraging their kids to follow sports, or to play them. So China and Germany could even exchange ideas about how to improve the quality of life through the promotion of sports.

While entering into the agreement, Merkel jokingly expressed her worry that Germany was helping to cultivate a competitor in the soccer world. But Germany should not worry. There are many advantages for the country. Basically, there are no global or EU regulations that restrict Germany from exporting soccer coaches, experience, and management professionals to China. However, it will have to compete with other countries. Within Europe, Italy, France, the UK, Spain, Portugal, and even Poland and the Czech Republic can compete with Germany for soccer opportunities with China. And other rivals exist in Africa, South America, and Asia. Such competition is valuable as nations work with China while it strives to attain its soccer goals.

For years, the middle-aged photographer Zhao Hui has been snapping the smiling faces of those ordinary Chinese in the mountains, on the streets and even in the temples. Then, in the theme of China Story, he exhibited them in the United States, the European Union headquarters and elsewhere to help them see glimpses of China through his photos. In the last two or three years, Zhao and his wife Li Chen have been doing something in the reverse direction. They aim to put bright foreign faces in front of the lens, and then showcase them in China.

Zhao, who was born in Jiangsu Province, studied photography in the United States in the 1980s and settled in Beijing, has targeted Italy and Germany. Germans often wear serious expressions, some are camera-shy, and many of them are not glad to be photographed by strangers. These are challenges for Zhao, who has long used his lens to show happy and smiling moments of ordinary people. "You must have a long and state-of-the-art lens, and you can only do that from faraway, without being noticed," he says during an interview in Brussels.

Zhao and his wife Li Chen are now driving across Germany to spot those inspiring moments on the streets, roads and forests, in the villages and even on the islands. This is the fifth time they have toured Germany in recent years, and Zhao's work has won high recognition, with the office of President Frank-Walter Steinmeier inviting him to take photos in the presidential building during President Xi Jinping's visit in early July. The couple has every reason to be proud of this recognition, which has been gained through their diligent efforts. Every time when they travel to Germany to take photos, they spend three or four weeks there and drive about 5,000 kilometres, leaving their lovely daughters at home.

Zhao joked that their total German mileage of 25,000 kilometres had already doubled the length of the historic trek of the Red Army's historic Long March in the 1930s. "We have reaped nearly 60,000 stunning photos, which are rare treasures for us," says Zhao. In addition, Zhao says they were journeys to explore the German character, to dig down into the country's culture and look into its history.

The smiling and happy moments of ordinary Germans, such as postmen, shopowners and waiters often become Zhao's targets. When asked what was the difference when Chinese and Germans smiled, he responded with wit: "All the happy people are the same." Out of the photos in their thousands, Zhao says he liked the shot of a dedicated German postman, with a ring of keys from his neighbourhood being attached to the belt round his waist. Zhao says he was told those were not the keys to the mailboxes, but to the homes in the village. "That is the trust, simple and deep trust in a small community, which shows the unsophisticated side among some Germans," says Zhao.

During his trip in March 2017, he was invited to take photos when the football teams Bayern Munich and Borussia Dortmund were competing. "This was my first experience of photographing a football match," says Zhao. "Of course, the bravery and the moments of furious running should be part of a typical German story." In addition to the photos of people, Zhao also says buildings and natural landscapes were part of his selection. He loved his photo of Hamburg's Elbphilharmonie Concert Hall, which opened at the beginning of 2017 and hosted the G20 leaders with a concert. "This is a landmark German building, with a red-brick base and glass structure on top, curved windows and a roof that resembles the crest of a wave," says Zhao. "In my opinion, this is a mixture of modern and traditional elements of Germany, which is why I love it so much."

This year marks the 45th anniversary of Sino-German diplomatic relations. The German Embassy in Beijing already agreed to organise a

German story photo exhibition for the couple, and a collection of photos could be published soon. His wife Li Chen accompanied him all along the way, driving him to every spot where he believed stunning photos would be captured by his cameras. "He is devoted, crazily critical of quality, and always desperate for the best shot," says Li.

While the leaders of both industrialised and emerging countries gathered in Germany's port city to discuss the world's pressing challenges between 7-8 July, they were offered a relaxing moment to enjoy music in Hamburg's newly-built landmark concert hall. But Peter Tamm, Director of the International Maritime Museum in Hamburg, had also made a historic offer: up to 120 treasured items chronicling the history of China's Maritime Silk Road from the 13th to the 17th century were on exhibition in his museum.

"The leaders should come to know how different cultures and civilisations were exchanged and understood in an amazingly peaceful way during this period," Tamm says in the museum in the heart of the tranquil port. "The exhibits reveal the unbelievable achievements China made in those years."

The exhibition, from June to September, was jointly arranged by Tamm's museum and Guangdong Museum, from Guangdong Province. The items will be moved to Rome for another exhibition later this year. The themed exhibition of the Maritime Silk Road was on the second and third floors of the museum, which were professionally and delicately decorated. The exhibition included shipwreck relics, porcelain, plants, religions and cultures. Tamm's maritime museum, an eleven-floor building, was opened in 2008 by his father, whose life-long hobby was to collect maritime models and relics. Before he died last December, his father often said that oceans were essential for mankind to exchange and trade with other peoples and nations, and he was always excited by China's maritime and trade history.

"As my father's motto goes, we are thrilled to have this exhibition and we are happy that more and more museum-goers are interested in Chinese culture and Silk Road history," says Tamm. Deeply involved in ship brokering, media and culture businesses, Tamm says this had shown how German people and other Europeans were impressed by Chinese culture. He says all the items were treasures and he was extremely impressed by the unique items from the Nanhai 1 and Nan'ao 1 shipwrecks, which were recovered off the coast of

South China. The colossal vessels had been used to bring China and the rest of world closer through trading and cultural exchanges.

"They are symbolic of a period in China's history that is little known here in Germany," says Tamm. "The routes were used during the Middle Ages to bring luxury goods from China to the Middle East and from there on to Europe." He says the exhibition had helped explain China's Belt and Road Initiative, which aims to bring common prosperity, mutual understanding and closer connectivity through cooperation, trade and investment. Tamm says an average of about 125,000 visitors came to his museum every year, but the exhibition, themed as East Meets West, the Maritime Silk Road during 13th-17th centuries, had already helped increase the visitor flow.

Without giving specific figures, Tamm says the number of visitors to his museum had increased by 35 percent year-on-year in June. His museum and Guangzhou Museum have also produced a book in German and English to introduce the history and items of the exhibition. In the preface to this collection, Luo Shugang, China's culture minister, says that through the multidimensional content reflecting cultural and commodity exchanges, historic relics and underwater archaeology, the exhibition had shown the common progress across the oceans between different civilisations during that period. "I am certain that this exhibition will contribute to further understanding between China and Germany," says Luo.

CHINA'S PROPOSAL INCREASES BELGIUM'S COMPETITIVENESS

In 2015, when all the Western European countries except Belgium applied to become founding members of AIIB, Belgium's former Prime Minister Elio Di Rupo expressed both excitement and regret during an exclusive interview with me China about two crucial decisions involving Beijing. Di Rupo says he was delighted to see how quickly China had moved two of its pandas to Belgium. In a matter of 24 hours after he met with Premier Li Keqiang in September 2013, the 15-year loan was agreed upon and in less than a year, the two pandas had arrived in Belgium.

The animals came to Belgium's Pairi Daiza Zoo in February of 2014, with King Philippe of Belgium and President Xi Jinping unveiling the panda garden a month later. Di Rupo says he could not believe that the pandas had already been living in Belgium for a year, noting "how time flies". The deal, he added, was an exact reflection of the nations' close bilateral ties.

Now the Mayor of Mons, Di Rupo was aiming to promote the city through the European Capital of Culture programme in 2015. According to the European Union, the title of European Capital of Culture is "awarded to two cities from two EU member states with the aim of supporting European cultural cooperation". But regret kicks in when Di Rupo talked about the Belgian government's reluctance to join the AIIB, which attracted applications from more than 50 countries. Admitting that he is not tracking the new bank issue, Di Rupo is shocked his country didn't apply. He says he will ask the national government and Prime Minister Charles Michel why Belgium did not follow in the footsteps of other Western European countries who applied.

That same day, I also met Zhang Haiyan, Director of Neoma Business School's Confucius Institute in Rouen, France, and he concluded that Beijing's leading role in setting up the AIIB had resulted in split opinions within some Western countries, though he didn't believe Belgium was being cautious because of its close ties with China.

A level of caution, however, can be seen in the United States, which did not apply to be an AIIB founding member, though Jacob Lew, as Secretary Treasury, paid a last-minute visit to Beijing before 31 March, the deadline for submitting an application to the bank. Former US Secretary of State Madeleine Albright recently said Washington's decision not to seek membership was "miscalculated". Some Belgians say it's financially unfeasible for their country to apply to the new bank. Some say the Belgian government is in a difficult position in trying to coordinate all three of its regional governments. While it's believable that Greece is too financially strapped to apply to become a founding member, Belgium is not in the same position. When Belgian banks, among other European banks, were required to increase their saving ratios during the European sovereign debt crisis of 2011, Belgians responded swiftly.

I gather that Belgium's reluctance has resulted from a miscommunication among the parties. Of course, Belgium is different from the US, which is engaging China while attempting to contain it on many fronts.

There is likely an inefficiency in the decision-making process among Western countries, which has already sparked widespread criticism among experts. Take their activities in fighting the financial crisis, for example. Many analysts have said that the long-standing debates among EU parties involved forced member countries to miss windows of opportunity in finding solutions and policy readjustments, thus prolonging the crisis. Europe is still in economic stagnation.

I have been asking Europeans how the political system in Europe should be reformed to improve the decision-making process and avoid political instabilities, such as what's happening in Greece. Many shrug their shoulders and shake their heads. They have no answers but they do have a simple reply: this is Europe.

Fortunately, Belgium has changed its attitude. It became an AIIB member, rather than a founding member, in March 2017, and many in Belgium took this as a sign of the country's increased competitiveness. In presenting her country's advantages, Iascale Delcomminette, CEO of Belgium's Walloon Export and Foreign Investment Agency, even mentioned its joining the AIIB as one of Belgium's advantages in attracting foreign investment.

Being one of three regions in Belgium, Wallonia, with a population of less than four million population, will be playing a "useful role" in exploring synergies with the Belt and Road Initiative, says the regions' senior official. "We are a member of the AIIB," she says while pointing to her country's gateway position, mature market, openness and other merits. When all the countries in Western Europe followed the UK in early 2015 in applying for founding membership of the China-proposed Asian Infrastructure Investment Bank, Belgium failed to move in a timely fashion and only became a member of this new multilateral financial vehicle in late 2016. She pledges that Belgium will be joining China in defending free trade and globalization, while other regions of the world—hopefully for a short time—don't believe anymore in free trade and international cooperation. "China and Europe share those common objectives," Delcomminette says.

She says her region's "strategic location" in the centre of the most developed part of Europe will be helpful in partly turning the Belt and Road Initiative into reality. Delcomminette says that during the past two years many Chinese people have been coming to visit Europe through Liege Airport in her region by taking chartered flights, and there are frequent cargo flights between Liege airport and Shanghai, Guangzhou and Hong Kong. She also says Wallonia's ideal location has allowed it to offer its convenient connections as the main gateway to European markets, and its various transport solutions have made it a European logistics hub. "Goods arriving from China by air, by train or by sea and waterways can rapidly be dispatched and delivered to all major European cities," Delcomminette says. "Wallonia has offered plenty of opportunities for Chinese economic operators to lock into this well-developed European transport network."

With some countries fearful of attracting China's investment, she cites the American investment strategist Keith Fitzgerald, saying in an interview in 2012: "A powerful China is coming, and we have two choices. Either we're at the table, or we're on the menu." Delcomminette also says Belgium was one of the six founding members of the EU back in 1958, and it had been part of the eurozone from the beginning. "Most importantly, we have no anti-Chinese fear," she says. "We are confident that the EU will play a major role to promote win-win cooperation with China and defend the interests of all its countries and partners."

But she says Belgium is not afraid of Chinese investments. "On the contrary, we welcome them," Delcomminette says, adding that her country has a long tradition of welcoming foreigners, boasting of Belgium being one of the most foreign investment-friendly countries in the world. She says her country's way to consider a win-win foreign investment relationship is to ensure that the investor can develop its business successfully and benefit from all the local expertise and incentives they will need. She says the major Chinese investment in Wallonia is the ongoing CBTC (China Belgium Technology Centre) project in Louvain-la-Neuve, and now 22 people are working within the Chinese investor United Investment Europe for this project. The project, involving high tech, biotech, digital, electronic and green sectors was officially launched on 20 June 2016 and the first stone was expected to be laid in June 2017. She says this project, which will be completed by 2025, will create 1,300 jobs in total, of which 40 percent will be Chinese expats and 60 percent (780) local staff, as the contract has shown.

Delcomminette says that for the Chinese, the creation of 780 local jobs is not such a big deal. "You have to keep in mind that Wallonia is much less populated than China," she says. "The 780 jobs in Wallonia are equal to 300,000 jobs in China (because the sharp difference of scale of population). You then realise how important this investment is."

The word "but" is probably the one most frequently on the lips of Qu Xing, China's ambassador to Belgium, when describing the achievements of this small country in Western Europe. Qu, who took up his diplomatic role in late 2014, has been impressed with the strengths of Belgium, a country with only half the population of Beijing. "It is a small country, but it has tremendous global influence," Qu says. Sitting in the guest room of the newly-refurnished Chinese embassy, on an avenue lined with dense trees on the outskirts of Brussels, Qu notes that the country is home to the European Union headquarters, NATO, many think tanks and major media, along with lobbying and commercial organisations in their thousands. Behind him hang the flags of China and Belgium, typical of an embassy setting.

"After Washington, Brussels should be the second symbol when we talk about the West," Qu says, referring to the wealth of soft power that makes Belgium different from other European countries. After setting the scene, Qu, a professor-turned-ambassador, goes into detail about Belgium's advantages in the fields of research and development, foreign trade, education and logistics. The list would be impressive, even for a large nation.

Because China has been in the process of restructuring its economy and boosting outward investment, Qu has been busy exploring cooperative opportunities for Chinese and Belgian businesses, putting as many on-site visits as possible on his daily agenda. Neatly dressed in a grey suit, he just returned from a visit to the headquarters of Agfa, a leader in colour printing and healthcare solutions, located half an hour from Brussels. "I was impressed by its cutting-edge research capacity," he says.

Agfa is among the global top three in colour printing, along with Kodak in the United States and Fuji in Japan. Qu has also visited companies in fields such as pharmaceutical, civilian nuclear technology and the microelectronics sector. He's been impressed at every turn. Belgium is not a big market—"but", he emphasises, "it has a strong hold on research and development".

By using the country's geographic location in the heart of the European Union as a gateway, Belgians are inclined to develop international trade and explore markets that value the country's competitiveness in research. In addition, Belgium boasts convenient transportation hubs that can easily connect with Paris, Luxembourg, Amsterdam, Frankfurt and other European cities by water, land or air.

Qu notes that Belgium has several universities in the world's top 200. All of these factors contribute to its vitality in trade and investment. Qu has spent a lot of time in Europe. He lived in Paris from 1986 to 1992 while earning a master's degree and a doctorate in political science at the Paris Institute of Political Studies. Between 2006 and 2009, he worked as Minister, Deputy Chief of Mission, at the Chinese embassy in France.

Qu says Belgium, which is nestled between the powers of France, Germany, the UK and the Netherlands and is a convergence point for the Latin and Germanic cultures, "is genetically inclusive, tolerant and open". It was also among the earliest countries to become industrialised.

Qu says he now has the great responsibility of helping to deepen the bilateral relationship between Belgium and China in several areas. A renowned professor who was the assistant president and vice-president at the China Foreign Affairs University from 1995 to 2006 and the president of the China Institute of International Studies from 2009 to 2014, he is adept at listing data and forming new narratives in describing the bilateral relationship.

He says businesspeople in China and Belgium today handle trade flows which every seven hours are equal to an entire year of trade 45 years ago, when the two nations first forged diplomatic ties. The fact is, among the many factors cited by Qu that illustrate the closeness of the partnership the two nations have forged over the past few years, their bilateral trade may be the most impressive feature of their relationship. In 2015 it reached $23.2 billion. "That's 1,150 times the trading volume at the beginning of our diplomatic relations," he says proudly, adding that the annual growth rate over the past five years has been 16 percent.

He says companies from both nations are more interactive than ever and are investing in each other's enterprises. For example, Volvo's Ghent plant has been booming since China's Geely took over, Qu says. Every minute, the 5,300 local employees produce one automobile, a production rate that yielded a record high 250,000 automobiles annually. With such high performance, the company has fared well in a relatively sluggish global automobile market.

Since October 1971, when the two nations established diplomatic ties, the partnership has made big strides, he adds. "One of the indicators of our close relationship is the high frequency of high-level exchanges," Qu says.

In March 2016, Brussels was attacked by terrorists who set off explosions at the airport and in subway stations after the earlier attacks in Paris. Qu says the incidents had a "negative" impact on tourism in Belgium, with some agencies and individuals cancelling their plans. The number of tourists has been decreasing overall because of safety concerns. "But," Qu says, "Belgium is still attracting a lot of Chinese investors because of its lasting advantages. We can see the trend is still on the rise because the investors, generally, have a longer-term view when making strategic decisions." He notes that, in fast-changing surroundings, it is hard to predict the danger of a terrorist attack, and every country must bear the brunt of such a risk. "But," he says, "continuing with normal life in society is another way to fight terrorism." "It is not Belgium alone," he says. "In this sense, terrorist attacks will not discourage investors."

LINKING ITALY AND CHINA: THE SILK ROAD

Italy was the European destination of the old Silk Road, which once brought Chinese and European civilisations to meet. In seeking synergy with the China-proposed Belt and Road Initiative, which many Europeans now call the new Silk Road, the Italians have shown profound passion in taking this opportunity to revive their economy. Among them are Italian President Sergio Mattarella, who has pledged that Italy will be responsive in becoming part of this initiative proposed by President Xi Jinping more than three years ago. During a six-day visit to China in February, he said the two countries could "write a new chapter in history" in implementing the connectivity-themed proposal, given his country's geopolitical advantage in connecting Asia, Africa and Europe.

Paolo Gentiloni, the new prime minister who replaced Matteo Renzi in December 2016, joined up to 30 state leaders worldwide at the Belt and Road Initiative Forum for International Cooperation in Beijing on 14-15 May. Gentiloni is quite familiar with China after close meetings with his Chinese counterparts when he was serving as Foreign Minister in Renzi's cabinet from 2014. He was also Minister of Communications when Romano Prodi, an economist and close China observer, served his second term as Italian prime minister from 2006 to 2008.

In May 2016, Gentiloni, as Foreign Minister, agreed with his Chinese counterpart Wang Yi that both sides should promote three major strategic alignments, namely the linking of China's Belt and Road Initiative and the development strategies of Italy, the linking of "Made in China 2025" and Italy's "Industry 4.0", as well as the linking of China's "Internet plus" strategy and the technological innovation plan of Italy. "The Italian side earnestly expects to be considered as a key cooperative partner by China in jointly building the Belt and Road, and hopes that more Italian businesses would have opportunities to participate in the relevant cooperation in the Belt and Road initiative," Gentiloni was cited as saying in an official statement.

In November 2016, when President Xi made a technical stop on the Italian island of Sardinia on his way to South America, former Prime Minister Renzi also promised during their meeting that Italy would actively participate in the Belt and Road Initiative construction. "Italian leaders have shown a strong will for cooperation. President Mattarella has indicated full confidence in the Initiative and on many occasions Prime Minister Gentiloni has also shown his strong support of the Belt and Road Initiative," says Li Ruiyu, Chinese ambassador to Italy.

In addition to the Italian leadership's high level of recognition for the Initiative, the business sectors also showed strong interest in exploring the win-win opportunities available by embracing it. "The Italian side has organised a lot of themed promotional activities to boost economic and trade cooperation to a new high, and I have attended many of them," says Li. One of the latest was organized by Luigi Gambardella, President of ChinaEU, a

Brussels-based business-led international association. Li spoke at this seminar on digital cooperation, which was held in Rome on 3 May, and says China and Italy shared tremendous opportunities in both countries' industrial and digital transformation process.

Gambardella, who is Italian, also says both countries can explore third-party cooperation in the 5G era by improving the digital and telecommunications traffic infrastructure along the Belt and Road routes. He says he was going to propose the idea of a digital Belt and Road initiative while at the Beijing forum. Ambassador Li says the trade flow between China and Italy had surpassed $43 billion in the last year while the investment stock of China flowing to Italy had already surpassed $12 billion by the end of 2016.

"And our Chinese companies have participated in some heavyweight projects in Italy," says Li, adding that China and Italy will renew their cooperation action plan soon. The two countries' three-year 2014-2016 cooperation agreement has now expired.

Among the Chinese investors in Italy is ZTE, China's telecommunications giant, which won the one-billion-dollar bid to upgrade Italy's telecommunication infrastructure at the end of 2016. Hu Kun, ZTE's chief in charge of the company's operations in Western Europe, says his branch in Italy was busy recruiting local professionals to join the company.

"In addition to this project, we are also about, probably, to win the bidding for several other projects in Italy. So we are short of manpower and also need to rent more offices," says Hu, in his ZTE Italy office in the industrial zone of Rome. For the billion-dollar project, ZTE is going to upgrade Italy's telecommunications infrastructure to make it ready for the 5G era, he says. "When the project is finished, Italy will be the forerunner in Europe in terms of telecommunications infrastructure," Hu says.

And in implementing this project, he says, the contractors would also create up to 2,500 new jobs for Italy over the next two and a half years. Hu says his company was also expanding its business in smart city and research facilities in Italy.

John Hooper, the correspondent of the London-based *Economist* magazine for years, has been closely watching how Italy could benefit from the dynamics of Asia, especially the development of China.

He says Italy was traditionally an exporting country and its economy could be easily influenced by external factors. And now the country needed structural economic reform to further release its potential. "This country needs outside demands to develop its economy, especially that of China," says Hooper.

He says that design, luxury goods, tourism and fashion were attracting China's rising middle class. "But Italy is still a country dominated by families and SMEs (small and medium enterprises), which has made it difficult to engage China's demands and penetrate the Chinese market," says Hooper. "What I suggest is to let the Italian SMEs form alliances region by region to engage the Chinese market to boost their presence in this big market."

European political guru Romano Prodi twice accepted my request for exclusive interviews. In April 2017, in Rome, he told me that China's Belt and Road Initiative would change the lives of half of humanity in the coming decades, and global leaders should unify their determination at the upcoming forum for international cooperation to be held in Beijing to grasp the chance. "This is a very important meeting, which will signal a green light from Beijing that the countries which agreed to participate in the initiative can get down to business," says Prodi, calling the Initiative "a century project" that would last for decades, mainly improving the connectivity of Asia, Europe and Africa.

Prodi, who had served as Italian Prime Minister twice and also as European Commission President, says what had impressed him most was that this Initiative would be changing the lives and fates of people in less developed countries, especially in Asia. Prodi says the first and more visible consequence of implementing the Belt and Road Initiative would be that many countries in Central Asia would cooperate with China to develop and improve their infrastructure. "This will not be constructing roads and railways but changing the daily lives of the people in these countries. I do expect this, as it will be a new page for these countries," he says.

Now, after three years of publicity and promotion, European countries had been "competing to seek synergies" with the Belt and Road Initiative, which he was delighted to see. "But this will also be a difficult project, which will last for decades, and the most important thing is to gain increased political will, endorsement and support from the countries along the routes," says Prodi.

But he says he was quite confident of progress because the Initiative had already been widely accepted during the previous years of publicity by the Chinese government, businesses and think tanks. "After three years of preparation, the Beijing forum will be seen as an occasion of giving a green light, of coming up with larger-scale cooperation," says the 77-year-old Prodi, who himself has been busy promoting the Initiative.

Still teaching in Tianjin and Beijing, Prodi has been shuttling between China and Italy. Just returning from a one-week lecture visit to Beijing, Prodi says he had met a more recent Italian Prime Minister, Paolo Gentiloni, before his departure to China to attend the forum. Prodi didn't reveal their talking points, apart from saying that Gentiloni, who was Communications Minister in Prodi's cabinet during the 2006-2008 period, was a firm supporter of the Belt and Road Initiative. When President Xi Jinping visited Central Asia and Southeast Asia in September and October 2013, he had raised the idea of jointly building the Silk Road Economic Belt and the 21st-century Maritime Silk Road.

Prodi says the Belt and Road Initiative was a combination of being envisaged and implemented through the routes by land and by sea. "As a European and Italian, I should say the bulk of the goods flow is still by sea and the role of the Mediterranean region is vital in implementing the Initiative," says Prodi.

The leaders from Spain, Greece and Italy, from the same region as Italy, were to attend the Beijing forum. Prodi also says the initiative originated from the concept of the historic Silk Road, of which Italy was the destination while the worldwide household figure Marco Polo, who brought China to Europe more than 700 years ago, was from Venice. "So I propose the next summit should be organised in Venice, which has the symbolic meaning that President Xi's initiative links the past with the future after the Beijing forum," says Prodi with a smile.

In preparing my recent interview trip to Italy on the Belt and Road Initiative, I longed to meet Siro Polo Padolecchia. He is the only living descendant of Marco Polo (1245-1324), who wrote *The Travels of Marco Polo*, a book that described to Europeans the wealth and prosperity of China centuries ago. Because he now lives in Monaco, our schedules could not fit; but the elderly Padolecchia sent me a timely five pages of answers to my questions, answers which were thoughtful, emotional and vivid and compensated for our inability to meet.

Padolecchia and his father's generation have not lost close contacts with China that his ancestor had established. He went to China at the age of 8 because his father was doing business there, and he spent three years of his childhood in China. So he wrote to me: "This interview could not have been more appropriate without incorporating the knowledge my Chinese friends so generously shared with me during my long stay in China."

He says my questions had helped him to absorb and improve his vague notions of China during his childhood. Padolecchia recalled that before his arrival in China, he had been very curious to discover this other part of our planet, so far from the place where he was born, and fearing he would be unable to understand China, its language, its culture, its jokes and its moods. But now, his memories were as poignant as Marco Polo's.

For him, China's charms are its people's kindness, the seasons full of lovely white magnolias and other flowers, the lakes with floating lotus flowers and small boats navigating slowly, undisturbed and happy. Padolecchia even told me how, for him, China had become such an unquestionably significant place that any of the 126 other countries of the world he had travelled to in his life could not compare.

For years, he has tried to promote communication between Europe and China, by creating the EURO-CHINA International Business Advisory Council, and by expanding the activity of the Marco Polo Society. He is particularly proud that it has become a very long-established organisation and the continuation of the principles of his ancestor, Marco Polo, and is regarded as a bridge between different communities under the auspices of the United Nations and of the European Union. Asked what he thinks has changed in China since his first arrival there, he says it was the attitude of people who have developed a sense of satisfaction that you can read in their eyes, and not only in the large cities but also in the smaller ones and even in rural villages.

He suggested the best way to learn about China is to pay a visit; as a Chinese proverb says, "it is better to see it with your own eyes than to read it one hundred times." Now he has focused a lot of attention on President Xi's Belt and Road Initiative, and says its mission of improving connectivity between China and Europe, promoting development and trade between Asia and Europe, will enhance stability and security for the states in this historically turbulent region.

He believes a number of huge Chinese projects in Africa and in Central Asia have contributed to increasing confidence in the ability of China to operate and create similar infrastructure projects domestically and abroad. Citing the opinion of Italians and Europeans, he says the Belt and Road Initiative concept attempts to realise a mega-foreign policy project of building peace and common prosperity.

Calling President Xi the architect of this peace project connecting Asia and Europe, Padolecchia says it covers almost the same lines as those traced by Marco Polo in the 13th century. Putting the project under the lens of a long view of history, he says that if the 20th century was dominated by the concept of the American Dream, in the 21st century the concept of the Chinese Dream will prevail, referring particularly to the freedom, opportunities and positive image of a new China.

FRANCE ALSO AIMS TO COOPERATE

In France, veteran politician Jean-Pierre Raffarin says the Belt and Road Initiative was "an invitation for Europe" to look more to the East. He was speaking after being named as the special representative of French President-elect Emmanuel Macron to attend the Belt and Road Forum in Beijing scheduled for 14-15 May 2017. Raffarin says Macron had made the decision shortly after winning the French presidential election by defeating the National Front's Marie Le Pen. "Indeed, I am leading the French delegation for the Belt and Road Initiative Forum, invited by President Xi Jinping," said Raffarin during a written interview with me before attending the May forum.

Raffarin said the decision was announced after President Francois Hollande and President-elect Macron came to an agreement to choose him as the special representative at the forum, in which up to 30 state leaders attended.

On behalf of the president, Raffarin said, he would be delivering the message that the Belt and Road Initiative would assert the strategic and geopolitical place of the Eurasian continent by improving connectivity. "This is an invitation for Europe to look more to the East," he says.

"I don't underestimate the other messages of boosting economic growth and advocating peace, in particular." As to the two countries' bilateral relationship after the election, he says President Macron would be maintaining a strong friendship and strategic partnership with China.

"In my country, since General de Gaulle we have always had a major interest in the Sino-French relationship, putting aside our internal political differences of various parties," says Raffarin. He says priority would be given to global equilibrium for peace and development because both sides had shared trust, which relied on a common vision of a multi-polar global system and multilateralism.

Meanwhile, he says, both sides would seek to strengthen vibrant economic exchanges and to promote cultural partnerships. "I am convinced that President Xi and President Macron will agree to put innovation and research at the heart of our cooperation," Raffarin says.

He added that the two countries' relationship with Africa could also be added to the priority list. He confirmed that President Xi and President Macron had had a very "positive and constructive" phone discussion. According to the Xinhua News Agency, President Xi congratulated Macron on his election as French president, calling on both sides to carry forward friendly ties, strengthen strategic mutual trust, accommodate their respective core interests and major concerns, and expand practical cooperation in various areas. Macron says he would continue to pursue France's positive and friendly policy toward China, stick to the one-China policy and deepen practical cooperation in such areas as diplomacy, trade and industry as well as in the framework of the Belt and Road construction. "As far as I know, they have touched on numerous topics on the phone," says Raffarin.

He is not alone. Back in 2015, ahead of Premier Li Keqiang's visit to France, and President Xi Jinping's participation in the United Nations climate summit in Paris at the end of that year, France intended to become the first country in Western Europe to back China's proposals to establish a modern Silk Road. This all stands in stark contrast to Washington's recent upgrade to its containment measures against Beijing, of course, giving the cold shoulder to any new ideas. France's signal of support came from Laurent Fabius, who served as prime minister between 1984 and 1986 and is now Foreign Minister.

On 12 June, he made an eloquent speech at a forum about China's Belt and Road Initiative organised by the French Regional Council of Haute-Normandy.

As Foreign Minister then, he says he had just wrapped up his 10th visit to China, adding that the frequency of his visits was higher than to the US, indicating the importance his country had attached to China. Zhai Jun, the Chinese ambassador to France, responded by saying he was jealous that the 69-year-old Frenchman got to visit Beijing more often than he did.

In a historical and global context, France has no reason to ignore the rise of China, which has been "writing the new chapters of world history", Fabius says in his speech. He says the Belt and Road Initiative, the proposed Silk Road Economic Belt and the 21st Century Maritime Silk Road, indicates that China is actively taking global responsibility.

Therefore, from a strategic point of view, France must endorse and participate in the new Silk Road proposals to make sure it is a "Sino-French Road", he says. Xi has turned a new page in China's Opening-Up and Reform, and France cannot afford to lose the opportunity to back the country's initiative. He also admitted that France had not responded well enough to embrace the development opportunities offered by China.

The minister's understanding of the importance of the Belt and Road Initiative won applause. Chi Fulin, a scholar and adviser to China's leadership, hailed Fabius as the first top foreign diplomat to elaborate "clearly, solidly and comprehensively" on Xi's proposals.

Proving he was serious about engaging with Chinese businesses, Fabius also stayed to listen to other speakers at the forum throughout the morning and during lunchtime. The foreign minister is a native of Normandy, an area rich in tourist and commercial resources, and he says the area would benefit from the Belt and Road Initiative and by seizing the opportunity for exponential growth in Chinese investment and tourism. The number of Chinese tourists to France is expected to increase from two million to five million in the next three years, and Fabius says the benefits of the Initiative could go beyond tourism.

The routes proposed as part of the Initiative are much longer than the ancient Silk Road used by merchants 2,000 years ago, and Fabius says they could have an effect on far more than just trade. France had played a constructive role in the 50 years since Charles de Gaulle had taken courageous steps with the Chinese leaders to establish a diplomatic relationship.

CHAPTER SEVEN

Finland and Denmark represent Nordic countries shaping New Silk Road ties with China to enter into the global production chain

Though I have been on dozens of trips in their dozens in Europe during my previous seven years of posting, I did not have a chance to do an interview in Finland until President Xi Jinping's visit in early April 2017, a state visit before his tour of the United States. I was part of a ten-day media tour in this advanced country in 2008, but sadly a devastating earthquake happened in my home province just a few hours after I landed in Beijing upon my return. While I was penning this part of my book, a less powerful but still damaging quake occurred in my home province. What a saddening coincidence.

In 2017, what excited me most was that I did short but face-to-face interviews with both the Finnish president and the prime minster. It was a great recognition of my paper and my career, and during my long stay in Europe, this has been exceptional.

Before meeting President Xi, Finnish President Sauli Niinisto told me in Helsinki in the Presidential Palace that he was well prepared to host the Chinese president and discuss free trade and the Paris Climate Change Agreement, going beyond bilateral relations. Shortly after American President Donald Trump took office, the Finnish president praised his Chinese counterpart for his "stable and deep" thinking. "It is a short visit but we are doing our best to make our great visitor President Xi and his wife feel at home," Niinisto told me in fluent English, with reassurance and confidence.

Niinisto says he was prepared to listen to President Xi's opinions on what was going on in the world while discussing how to develop their countries' bilateral relationship to a new stage. Recalling four years ago, during his visit to China, Niinisto says he agreed with President Xi that there would be a new kind of strategic partnership between the countries. "What have we seen in concrete terms? We have seen a lot of development in business but also in our political contacts," says Niinisto when mentioning his first meeting with Xi after he became China's leader in 2012.

Niinisto says he had established a sound personal relationship with President Xi after several meetings in previous years on various occasions. And President Xi and his wife even prepared a birthday party for Niinisto's wife four years ago when the couple paid a visit to China, attending the Bo'ao Forum in Hainan Province.

Niinisto says both sides had been discussing their partnership agreement and had a shared view that it could go further. As Finland marked the centenary of its independence in 2017, he said his country was very honoured to have President Xi visiting in a way that respected Finland's independence since 1907, which was important for Finland. "So we do appreciate it a lot," says the president.

He says now the world was seeing many problems worldwide and it was more and more important to have key contacts between leaders. "Now President Xi is continuing from here to the United States. And I think the whole world is looking at how that visit will go," says Niinisto.

Niinisto says he had just met the Russian president at the Arctic Forum held in Russia before agreeing to my interview, adding that he appreciated the points President Xi had raised at the World Economic Forum in Davos earlier in the year, and especially his point on free trade: "His opinions are very similar with the stances in the European Union and Finland, which certainly support free trade very strongly."And Niinisto says that he had also heard him speaking about the importance of maintaining the Paris Climate Agreement, and this was the other issue in which the EU and China shared similar positions. "Apart from other questions—these are very big ones—and how we enhance that kind of thinking is important. That is also one element why we are so eager to see what is going to happen," says Niinisto.

In the EU-China relationship, he says, both parties shared common views on big issues,which is a sound basis for a way to go further on other issues too. Niinisto says his Nordic friends were very curious about the summit in Helsinki between Xi and himself. "Certainly we are going to discuss with them the idea of how all the Nordics may build better cooperation with China," says Niinisto.

The president also says that both sides should assure the business sectors that there would be plenty of room for cooperation, and that innovation was one of its elements, pointing out that innovation in clean tech is important because this is essential when urbanisation is still booming in China. And on the other hand, he says, Chinese companies were interested to invest in Finland and right now, some intended to invest in renewable energy.

Niinisto used to be President of the Finnish Football Association, and says football was a "common language" between him and President Xi, though Finland was not a strong footballing nation. "However, we are very competitive in winter sports and I think both sides could deepen cooperation in this area," says Niinisto.

"All in all, I am going to invite Xi to discuss how to develop the relations between our countries. And I am very interested to hear his opinions on the Belt and Road Initiative," says Niinisto.

During my early morning interview with the Finnish Prime Minister Juha Sipila before Xi's arrival, he insisted that during the conversation, it was an interview just between us, with none of his staff sitting beside us. For the photo session, however, his staff moved in.

Like his president, Sipila has pledged that his country will join China in advocating free trade and globalisation, even as the concepts come under attack in some parts of the world. "First of all, free trade is very important," Sipila says on the eve of President Xi's visit, talking in his office in downtown Helsinki. He says he had been preparing and waiting for the visit "very eagerly", and both sides had "a lot of issues" to discuss.

Amid rising threats of isolationism and protectionism, he recalled that at the recent European Council meeting, European leaders had especially discussed Xi's speech at the World Economic Forum's annual meeting in Davos, Switzerland, in January. President Xi was going to visit Finland between 4-6 April before meeting American President Donald Trump. This would be Xi's first visit to the Nordic region since he became China's president in 2012.

Sipila says President Niinisto would focus on political and foreign affairs with Xi while Sipila himself concentrated on economic issues. Returning to Xi's speech in Davos, Sipila says it had been encouraging because it supported free trade when there was discussion in the US about imposing trade barriers to protect American industries.

"My understanding is that the president is flying to the US after his visit to Finland. For Europe and for Finland, it's also very important that China and the US have a very good relationship, and that free trade continues, because that affects us as well." Sipila says the prospect of a US-China trade war concerned him. "But I think in the end common sense will prevail." He says: "Maybe there will be some renegotiation of agreements. I don't know. But I think it's in our common interests to continue free trade."

China's investment in Finland is increasing. Right now, according to the prime minister, Chinese companies have invested around one million euros in each of two projects in the north of the country, and there are plans for investment in two bio factories. Sipila says that China and Finland would sign investment agreements during Xi's trip, but the details had not been finalised.

Tourism has also been increasing. The number of tourists from China has doubled in recent years as many Chinese have dreamed of visiting the homeland of Santa Claus. Sipila says that Finland had a strong record of innovation in its universities and business start-ups which could complement China's manufacturing capabilities, although he noted that China too had made major improvements in innovation. Other areas of cooperation could include bio-fuel, clean technology, green energy, ICT, metallurgy and forestry, he added. Some people in Europe viewed Chinese investment with suspicion, but Finland and the EU put no barriers on Chinese investment. "I am a friend of free trade and without limitations. So Finland is a supporter of free trade and investment flows," says Sipila.

Within three months in 2017, President Xi Jinping flew to Europe twice. Following his attendance at the annual meeting of the World Economic Forum and his state visit to Switzerland in January, Xi arrived in Finland on 4 April 2017 before holding talks with United States President Donald Trump.

Certainly, the two European tours contained tremendous messages on how China expected this world, now filled with protectionism, populism and even threats to peace by some countries, should evolve, and what role China would play. Using Switzerland and Finland as platforms to communicate such stances and commitments, they embody China's belief that all of the global players, including Europe and the US, should fulfill their due responsibility in building a prosperous and peaceful world, instead of merely observing what actions China would take.

Beyond such global and geopolitical significance, President Xi also knows well how his visits could help to promote his domestic priorities especially when his hosts' strengths perfectly match China's national strategy of improving innovation and competitiveness. In 2016, China announced a three-step roadmap to achieve this. Firstly, by 2020, China is aiming to become an innovative country, which means its input to research and development would surpass 2.5 percent of total economic output and the knowledge-intensive service industry should contribute to at least 20 percent of the economy.

By 2030, the 2.5 percent ratio should climb to 2.8 percent, while China's businesses should move up to the medium and high-end global supply chain. China will be among the leaders of global innovation. By 2050, China aims to become a global power in science, with its economy mainly driven by innovation, science and technology breakthroughs. Then China will be building some of its universities and research institutions into world-class entities, and the talents in science and research will become the backbone of its national strategic resources.

Such innovation goals are going hand-in-hand with China's economic restructuring efforts, poverty reduction, dealing with ageing challenges and improving people's livelihoods. Though China has made rapid progress in its innovation capacity in recent years, it knows the gap is still wide. Based on the World Intellectual Property Organisation's annual report, China ranked 25th in 2016, moving up nine places from 34 in 2012, when Xi became China's leader.

With Switzerland, always taking first place in global innovation rankings, and Finland being among the world's top five, China has chosen perfect partners to run with. This is because the Swiss and the Finns are modest, inclusive and willing to share, contribute, compete and grow together to transfer knowledge and technology. Such openness has resulted in tremendous benefits after the two countries, with less than ten million people each, integrate into a big market of up to 1.4 billion people.

In addition, such cooperation is complementary, as the countries' positions along the global value chain vary. Even in the process of China's upgrading its position and competitiveness, openness and globalisation will help the research institutions and businesses of both sides work together and benefit each other more. Encouraging innovation policy in China has penetrated into every part of its national programme. For example, Guizhou Province, the poorest place in China, has targeted Switzerland as a pace-setter in achieving poverty-reduction goals, as the province and Switzerland share similar land-locked and mountainous terrain, though their development levels are in sharp contrast. This province has combined innovation and poverty reduction in one shot. Such comparison and cooperation would help this province know its potential. For example, now they are injecting resources into environmental protection, infrastructure construction, tourism and education to remodel Guizhou into China's Switzerland.

They have undertaken actions they aim to achieve, while China and Switzerland have built their innovation partnership at a national level. Similarly, in Finland, China also has a lot to learn along the way to fulfilling its dreams.

The 24-year-old Shirly Karvinen, Miss Finland in 2016, is doing something special. Her father is a typical Finn: modest and shy and soft-spoken, while her Chinese mother is open-minded and more easy-going. But they share one characteristic: both are hard-working.

Karvinen says she was lucky that she could embody her parents' combined personalities; she herself started to earn money at the age of 14 by selling Finnish magazines by telephone. "I could earn 400 euro a month when I was 14," says Karvinen, who was crowned Miss Finland in May 2016. "And I think nobody else in my class could do it this way."

So she says independence is another advantage she shares with her parents.

"I think what I inherited from my parents' genetic advantages made me a little bit darker than ordinary Finnish people, which let me stand out in the Miss Finland competition last year," says Karvinen, with a height of 170 cm. The typical Finn is white and in previous decades, three ladies of mixed colour had won the annual crown, she says. Being half-Chinese and half-Finnish, Karvinen says she felt "proud and honoured" that President Xi was visiting Finland before his American tour.

"I am very happy that I am half-Chinese and half-Finnish and I am proud of being having two motherlands," says Karvinen. "I am very much looking forward to President Xi's visit and I believe this visit will promote two-way understanding." Karvinen says she was keen on promoting China-Finland exchanges, which would hugely benefit both sides. "I feel like I have two motherlands, especially now that I'm older. I really think that it's a special thing that my mom is from China. I am very proud of my Chinese roots."

Already graduating from university in Helsinki, Karvinen says her mother, who is from Hubei Province, met her father in Africa, and she spent seven years there before her family moved back to Finland for her to attend primary school. Recalling her childhood experiences in Africa, where her parents were working in different countries, she says she could manage to accept everything, and she was too young to actually realise where she was going.

"You're just going around. But I think that it's a very good thing, because it gave me a very international background. I'm very good at coping in new situations, in new environments. So I think that actually taught me a lot when I was very young," she says happily. When she was a little girl, her Finnish grandfather discovered her potential, and was always saying that some day, when Shirly was old enough, she would go on to be a Miss Finland competition winner.

"It all started just like a childhood dream, but then when I got older, and especially when I moved to Helsinki, like three, four, five years ago, then I realised that that was something I really wanted to do some day," says Karvinen. "I wanted to be different, I wanted to show an example that there are all kinds of Finnish people and different-looking people and it was always my dream. I decided that I wanted to go after it."

Along with chasing that dream and completing her education, Karvinen continued her part-time job from the age of 14. "I don't know how many part-time jobs I have done, and those taught me to stand on my own two feet," she says. "So I think there was a very big advantage for me. I've lived abroad, and I worked since I was 14 years old, so I was very mature. I knew that Miss Finland was not just a title, it was a responsibility and honour, and more importantly it was a job to do."

Since last May, Karvinen has been working as Miss Finland to promote her country on various occasions. This job finished in September in 2017, as that year's competition had been postponed until then. Among all her activities, Karvinen says she felt most interested in hosting TV and radio shows. "After my Miss Finland year I really would have loved to have my own TV show or work on the radio or maybe even abroad somewhere. It would be really nice to have had the opportunity to work internationally," she says.

She says she had touched on many broad topics on TV and radio. And one topic was very close to her heart: school bullying. "Apart from fun stuff, I've also been speaking against bullying very strongly," says Karvinen, recalling that when she was young, she lived in a smaller town in central Finland and looked very different from everyone else. So sometimes she was bullied.

Lowering her voice, Karvinen says: "So now as Miss Iceland I have been talking very strongly against bullying, speaking about my own experiences and trying to help people who are in the same situation."

Timo Ritakallio, who became President of the Finnish Olympic

Committee in November 2016, says Finland should explore more potential for cooperation in winter sports with China, which was determined to develop these areas when preparing to host the 2022 Winter Olympics.

"The 2022 Winter Olympic Games to be hosted by China will bring new development not only for Chinese sports but also for the international sports family," says Ritakallio, adding that Xi's visit would bring the two countries closer and deepen cooperation in winter sports.

Recalling that Finland President Sauli Niinisto used to be President of the Finnish Football Federation and knows both the national and international level of sports, Ritakallio says he believed that President Niinisto and President Xi would touch on sports cooperation because Xi himself is also a football fan. One example is that with support from President Xi and German Chancellor Angela Merkel, both of whom are passionate football fans, China and Germany established a football cooperation partnership last year. "I understood that China has been putting more and more focus on developing winter sports. China and Finland have had good relations for a long time, so it's an opportunity that the Finnish government should take," says Ritakallio.

He says Finland was a very strong winter sports country, competitive in cross-county skiing, snowboarding and ice hockey. "In this area we have the world's top level coaches and I think China is developing these sports and teams. It would be good to have connections with the world skiing sport organiations, and sport institutes that would offer help to China," he says.

Apart from exporting coaches and experience, Ritakallio says Finland was also strong in knowing how to produce artificial snow and ice in an environmentally friendly way. "Due to climate change and global warming, even in Finland we must rely on artificial interventions on some occasions to have enough snow and ice to meet the minimum standards of such sports," says Ritakallio.

He says the Finnish clean-tech companies were well prepared to transfer their know-how to China, adding that the Finnish company Snow Secure had already entered into a cooperation agreement with the 2022 Olympics Organising Committee in China. Ritakallio says ice hockey is very popular in Finland, and even in small cities the ice hockey halls are built by using artificial ice. The country has also built small snow houses providing artificial snow for cross-country skiing.

"Apart from the Olympics, we can also cooperate to promote these sports (among non-professionals) as China has already planned to do," says Ritakallio, adding that Finnish business and sports sectors were keen to develop cooperation with China. As it is a voluntary position, Ritakallio's term of office as President of the Finnish Olympic Committee will be ending after the 2020 Tokyo Olympic Games.

"This is a voluntary job, and I work for the investment sector," says Ritakallio, President and CEO of Ilmarinen Mutual Pension Insurance Company in Helsinki. He says his company had invested about a billion euros in equities and other financial products in China so far. He says: "I visit China regularly because it's a universal response to feel that China is like the future. It has the best opportunities."

Denmark: a country that holds lasting ties with China

The Danish prime minister, Lars Loekke Rasmussen, loves pandas. Before his meeting with Chinese leaders in early May 2017, he paid a special visit to see the two pandas in Chengdu, in Sichuan Province. The pair will be sent to Denmark through a loan contract, as with other European countries.

In addition to love of pandas, this Nordic country has been well prepared to endorse President Xi Jinping's proposed Belt and Road Initiative, calling it "a future dynamo" for the growth and prosperity of Asia and Europe. Pledging that his country will actively participate in it and he would use the visit to further boost his country's relationship with China, Rasmussen made the comments in a written interview with me ahead of his tour in China from 2-5 May 2017. "The Belt and Road Initiative is indeed a very interesting foreign policy strategy," says Rasmussen. "Further connecting Europe and Asia firmly through trade and bilateral cooperation can hopefully be a future dynamo for growth and prosperity for both continents."

President Xi, Premier Li Keqiang and Chairman of the Standing Committee of National People's Congress Zhang Dejiang met or held talks with Rasmussen during his visit, exchanging views on bilateral ties and issues of common concern. Rasmussen's visit was among the recent high-level exchanges between China and the Nordic countries. Shortly after Xi's visit to Finland in early April, Norwegian Prime Minister Erna Solberg paid a visit to China to enhance bilateral relations.

Rasmussen served as Danish prime minister from 2009 to 2011 and visited China in 2010. His current term started in June 2015. Rasmussen says the Belt and Road Initiative could hopefully provide economic stability and development for Central and South Asia—gateways between East Asia and Europe. "This will be crucial for trade between the two biggest concentrations of economic power," he says, adding that his country, as one of the world's foremost shipping nations, has been engaged in linking the two continents for centuries.

This visit happened several days ahead the highly-anticipated Belt and Road Initiative Forum for International Cooperation on 14-15 May 2017 in Beijing. Rasmussen says his country's representatives would be attending and would "be happy to contribute" positively on both the political and the business level during the conference.

He says China was Denmark's largest trading partner in Asia and his country was the first Nordic country to sign a comprehensive strategic partnership with China. "We will now take our bilateral relationship to a new high," he says. "I am particularly pleased that we will launch our first 'Joint Work Programme' during my visit."

Rasmussen revealed that the programme contained 58 concrete joint cooperation areas, covering the approach towards 2020, between 80 Chinese and Danish state institutions, and he says this would take the cooperation between the institutions of both sides one important step further. During his visit, both sides signed new agreements to strengthen economic and trade cooperation. For instance, he says both would launch a Chinese-Danish Food and Drug Regulatory Cooperation Centre that would help facilitate knowledge-sharing between public authorities in the two countries. In terms of cultural and people-to-people exchanges, the prime minister says the two countries would sign a bilateral film agreement allowing China and Denmark to work on co-productions.

Rasmussen also says that Denmark and China had close cooperation on international issues. "We are both trading nations and strong supporters of free trade and increased global cooperation," says Rasmussen. Ranging from the United Nations to the AIIB, the Belt and Road Initiative and climate change, Rasmussen says both countries had much more potential to deepen cooperation on the global stage. Rasmussen says he had met President Xi on several occasions, including at the Nuclear Security Summit in 2016. "We've had very cordial and fruitful discussions during all our meetings and it has led to many of the results that we are now finalising in China during this visit," he says, adding that President Xi gave a very fine speech at the World Economic Forum in Davos in January, and that Denmark supported any efforts to stick to the road of trade liberalisation and "better globalisation". Rasmussen says China was currently the second-largest economy in the world and was set to become the largest during the next decade. "Anything that China does will have an effect not only in Asia but on the rest of the world," says Rasmussen. "We wish to join China on this trip."

In addition to politicians, Danish firms hope for a ready market in China for technologies developed thanks to their long-term environmental leadership. Businesses in Denmark are preparing for "green" opportunities in China, hoping their cutting-edge technology will help them grab market share as the Asian giant speeds up its transition to low-carbon development. Some companies have even rolled out their own versions of a 2020 strategy to seek synergy with China's 13th Five-Year Plan (2016-2020) for National Economic and Social Development, which will focus on a cleaner policy portfolio for growth.

Some are doing research on zero-emission technologies, which may be applied to vehicles after 2020 in China. And some are already thinking of jointly exploring third-party markets outside Denmark and China. Danfoss, a global leader in heating and cooling, has been in China a long time and is one of the pioneering Danish companies that has tailored its development strategy to China's mega-policy trends. One leading trend is the so-called economic new normal, which reflects China's economic growth slowing from a sizzling double-digit rate to closer to 7 percent annually while maintaining balanced and sustainable development. "We have to come to terms with the transition from booming to slowdown in China, while I think 7 percent growth is still a lot," says Jurgen Fischer, President of Danfoss Cooling.

Fischer says the company had established a solid presence over time, including a long business chain. "Amid changes in China, all these advantages will help us expand our business smoothly in this country if our strategy is correct," he says. His company recently rolled out a 2020 strategy for the China market, indicating that China is still a "super interesting" market for the clean-tech company, which has been expanding there for decades. Fischer says that compared with India, China is better prepared and more active in supporting low-carbon development. "I believe that this will bring more opportunities for both Chinese and European companies," he says.

Encouraged by his long-term outlook, the president of Danfoss Heating, Lars Tveen, says a pilot project in northeast China that recycles surplus heat should be used in more Chinese cities. With help from Danfoss and the Danish energy-consulting group COWI, Anshan city in Liaoning Province has tapped into the surplus heat from a local steelmaking facility to provide heating to 3.8 million residents. For years, they primarily burned coal, a major source of air pollution, to provide heat during the winter.

"The Anshan project is like a stone dropped into water, and now we have seen the ripples," says Tveen, adding that more cities in China were inviting companies to introduce such facilities. There were a number of benefits, according to Tveen. First, surplus heat could be sold. Second, the burning of coal was reduced and the reduction in the carbon quota could be sold in the national cap-and-trade market that China promised to set up in 2017.

Third, Tveen says, air in the city was cleaner, with the pilot project covering half of the urban population, living with carbon dioxide emissions reduced by 289,000 metric tons. "So in China we are not only talking and talking. We are offering a recipe," says Tveen.

With China toughening its measures to cut pollutants from vehicles, Danish companies have been preparing for new opportunities, even though this country of about 5.6 million people doesn't have a single auto assembly line. Amminex Emissions Technology, based in Soborg, is among them. This rapidly growing Danish clean-tech company, in the diesel engine emissions reduction business, offers a system for ammonia storage and delivery, which reduces emissions of some toxins from diesel exhausts.

Annika Isaksson, the chief executive, says the company's product is ideal for the Chinese market, where smog has become a public concern in many cities. "We are approaching our China partners and we aim to bring our products to China's market by the end of 2016," she says.

Torben Dinesen, CEO of Dinex, a Danish company that offers advanced test centres for emissions, spent four years building a commercial relationship with the trucks unit of Dongfeng Motor, a leading vehicle manufacturer in China. Dongfeng's truck engines have been tested using Dinex's equipment. "We are expecting to sign cooperation contracts with Dongfeng soon," says Dinesen.

Dinex has kept its eye on the development of China's emissions regulations. China is expected to implement Euro 5-based national emissions standards in 2017, but Dinesen says it was likely Euro 6-based standards would be put into effect by 2023 nationwide. "The updates of China's emissions regulations will push us to bring new emissions control solutions to our customers, and we need to have confidence and patience for this huge green market," Dinesen says.

Dinex is eager to keep Dongfeng as a key customer—the company produces nearly 20% of China's trucks—but Dinesen says his company expected to sign up two or three customers in the next 10 years. "Along the way, we need to improve our research and development capacity in China for future expansion," he says.

Eva Kjer Hansen, who was appointed Danish Minister of Environment and Food in June, says she just came back from the United Nations General Assembly, which adopted its post-2015 Sustainable Development Goals on 25 September 2015. The goals are a set of targets for the next 15 years relating to international development agreed upon by member states.

"They are ambitious, but it is important to deliver solutions and fulfil such goals," says Hansen. She says they are more ambitious than the millennial goals, which expired in 2015. "But the biggest trouble is to find financing, and we aim to find more businesses and funds to work together to help achieve the UN goals." One of the goals is to ensure access to clean water around the world by 2030, and she says Denmark can help with that. Hansen says she is proud that one small company in Denmark has signed a contract with NASA for a water recycling system in space.

Hansen says some countries have used the debate over the need for carbon reduction to dodge their responsibilities in environmental protection, which is dangerous. "We Danes are very specific in every front of environmental protection, and we hope we can still lead the way," she says. With China speeding up the restructuring of its economy by improving environmental quality and boosting energy efficiency, the country would be well served by strengthening its cooperation with Danish companies, Hansen says. She notes that Denmark stopped using leaded petrol in 1978, while the European Union phased it out in 2000. The emphasis on the environment and sustainable development "has triggered development of environmental technologies in Denmark that prevent air pollution and improve energy efficiency," she says. "And China knows that we are very strong in food safety, which is also high on the agenda during my upcoming visit."

Marvellous Danish Queen and European Royal Tradition

In writing of relations between China and Denmark, the royal family must be mentioned. The website of the Danish monarchy is presented in the Danish, English, French and, astonishingly, Chinese languages. Apart from that, the royal couple, Queen Margrethe II and her husband, visited China in September 1979, the first Western head of state to pay such a visit after the start of China's opening up and reform policy. She has shown great interest in China's culture and history, ancient architecture and unearthed cultural relics.

On her second visit from 24 to 28 April 2014, she and her husband travelled to five Chinese cities, Beijing, Nanjing, Suzhou, Jiaxing and Shanghai. She revealed that both of them love Chinese culture and history, and both of them like eating Chinese food. Their two sons, Crown Prince Frederik and Prince Joachim, often visit China, too, according to Xinhua, and they told their parents a lot of interesting stories. Xinhua also says that, by comparison, Margrethe's husband Prince Henrik is more familiar with China and is known as "Mr. China". He often visits China, almost once every other year.

In fact, royal families in Europe have a tradition of forging their links with China. King Willem-Alexander's daughter Amalia, the 13-year-old heir to the throne, started to learn Chinese in September 2016. Some have even called it the royal family's "smartest investment" given the deepening relationship between China and the Netherlands.

Dutch royalty is not alone in embracing the Chinese language. In nearby Belgium, Princess Elisabeth, the first child of King Philippe, born in 2001, studied Chinese in a Dutch-medium school in Brussels. When King Philippe acceded to the throne in 2013, the princess became Duchess of Brabant, a title reserved for the heir apparent, which meant she could become the first Chinese-speaking queen of a European country.

In fact, the older generations of royal families in Europe, similar to that of Denmark, have had an interest in Chinese culture for a long time. Although Britain's Queen Elizabeth II, 91, doesn't speak Chinese, she has enormous interest in Chinese philosophy, especially Taoism. In 2016, the University of Wales Trinity Saint David, partly supported by Britain's royal family, established the Academy of Sinology with the aim of encouraging doctorate students to study ancient Chinese religions, texts, language and history. In addition to Queen Margrethe II of Denmark, King Willem-Alexander of the Netherlands and King Philippe of Belgium have already visited China since Xi Jinping became China's leader. And in return, Xi has visited the Netherlands, Belgium and Britain.

Studying Chinese is becoming popular across Europe. When I was interviewing parliamentarians in Greece during the country's sovereign debt crisis, one of them even arranged for his 16-year-old daughter, who was learning Chinese at the time, to be present during our conversation.

For sure, European institutions are increasingly offering Chinese-language classes to young officials. On 21 July 2016, while I was walking with participants in the Belgian National Day parade, a retired Belgian stopped me to say that in his youth he had studied Chinese in Taiwan for a few years and had spent more than 10 years on the Chinese mainland. I was amazed at his fluent Chinese. All these are proof of the trend that Chinese people are becoming popular across the world, partly because of the attraction of Chinese civilisation and China's growing economic clout. In recent years, China has initiated several projects to better connect with the rest of the world. One is the Belt and Road Initiative, which is aimed at improving connectivity in Eurasia through infrastructure construction, growing trade flow, and increased people-to-people exchanges. Another project is the establishment of the AIIB, which offers funds to countries to improve connectivity between Asia, Europe and Africa.

China therefore needs to innovate in order to respond to this trend to spread its language and culture, in order to meet the rising demands in Europe and other continents. Although China has already helped set up Confucius Institutes in many universities in countries across the world, and Chinese language and culture classes have become part of primary and secondary schools in many countries, more needs to be done to spread the real values of Chinese culture.

It's time China intensified its cooperation with other countries to turn some of the schools into bilingual or trilingual institutions, where Chinese language and culture can be taught at least one day a week. Britain, the US, Canada, Japan, France and other countries have set up many schools in China with their own curriculums.

CHAPTER EIGHT

Wake-up calls from Silk Road thinkers and pioneers, who play vital roles in constructively enriching and communicating the initiative

This final chapter is devoted to selected opinion leaders and thinkers, and young pioneers from China and Europe, who have devoted much of their thoughts and actions to the Belt and Road Initiative. I approach this chapter from a wider perspective after examining how each country has cooperated with China in this regard.

THE EU SHOULD FURTHER EXPLORE MEANS TO WORK WITH CHINA

The 84-year-old renowned economist, and former Belgian Prime Minister, Mark Eyskens is among this group of selected leaders and thinkers. Although I contacted his team over a long period and he had agreed to talk with me, our thought-provoking discussion was able to actually take place only in May 2017, nearly six months after the date we had originally agreed. The talk was light and flowing and he allowed my three interns to challenge him by asking questions. He urges young people to be curious and to keep that spirit, so that if they see beauty they will keep their gaze on it. With President Xi's Belt and Road Initiative now globally recognised, he insists that the European Union should further explore "ways and means" to seek synergies to invest with China in massive infrastructure projects worldwide. "There is a huge need to build, to construct infrastructure such as railways, ports, roads to ports, airports. This will be very costly and it will not be easy to arrange all the lending required," says Eyskens in his office in Brussels, not far away from the EU headquarters. The scholar and European political guru, who has already published 58 books, says the essential economic issue today, and also for the future of this world, is about investment, with the Earth's population expected to reach 10 billion by the end of this century.

Eyskens says the Belt and Road Initiative is a valuable strategy for helping to cover these global needs.

On investment, he says the problem for Europe today is a lack of investment, because the bloc has other priorities and has spent a lot of money on pensions and health care, though the EU has made some efforts to increase investment by earmarking money in the European Investment Plan (2015-17). But, he says, it is not targeted enough, and the money was not well used. In fact, a European Court of Auditors report criticised the European Commission's approach. There does not seem to be a grand strategy to truly create innovation and employment—which is why the results are meagre. "The big infrastructure projects that can really spur innovation and growth are outside Europe, and many are in Asia and China," says Eyskens, believing the Belt and Road Initiative is very important for the EU, which needs to find the ways and the means to re-orient European investments to the big projects in the world.

For instance, how Europeans should get involved in the projects of building airports, seaports, channels and canals and so on is very important. Eyskens says Europeans are extremely interested in what China is doing, including the way that it finances investment. In that connection, Eyskens says what China did to create the AIIB is "very important". "With some European countries becoming stakeholders of this bank, this may become a great instrument for all," Eyskens says. "Investment must be a two-way street, with long-term benefits for all, embedded in multilateral agreements regarding fair trade, legal security, in-country value and corporate social responsibility." If that can be sustained, he says that the European Investment Bank could possibly be interested to work as a partner. During the Belt and Road Initiative Forum held in Beijing on 14 and 15 May 2017, the European Investment Bank signed a cooperation agreement with the Chinese government. "We've tried to persuade the European Investment Bank also to go outside Europe, to Asia, where most of the world's economic growth is realised, and thus where innovation and employment are created. In 2013 the European Council decided to consider ways to assist European industries— as the Chinese and Japanese governments do—to acquire major infrastructure contracts through competitive long-term loans. This may happen in the near future and make the AIIB and Europe truly complementary," says Eyskens. Apart from infrastructure projects, he also suggests that both sides can cooperate on big data, digital devices and everything that has to do with modern communication, ICT and scientific research. "In addition, it is also very important to invest in brains, and that requires of course education and research exchanges of scholars, professors and students," says Eyskens.

He says the University of Leuven, where he was chairman between 1971 and 1976, hosted about 2,000 Chinese students altogether, and many Belgian students are studying in China at the big universities. "That's wonderful for building the future together and learning from each other," he says. Eyskens has been to China several times, and when he was finance minister he visited China at the end of the 1970s and was impressed by the changes during the following decades.

He says he has been extremely impressed by China's reform endeavours, which have transformed China, with its huge population, and adds that Deng Xiaoping was a "very,very great statesman." He has urged the EU to construct "a web of free trade agreements" with other economies. "Confronted by a dilemma between a web and a wall, many people today, who we call the victims of globalisation, think that they have to replace the web by walls surrounding countries, which is psychologically explicable but makes no sense at all," he says, adding that he is a European federalist. "It is counterproductive and it's against the future, so we have to save our webs and destroy the walls."

With China and the EU now considering a bilateral investment pact, Eyskens strongly believes that the new French President, Emmanuel Macron, may support a free trade agreement between the EU and China. As a European federalist, he believes the European Union still needs a lot of effort to build itself into a strong bloc. In 1991 Eyskens, then Belgium's Foreign Minister, says Europe was an economic giant, a political dwarf and a military worm. Asked after 26 years whether his views have changed, he responds: "My answer is no, no, and no. I was indeed right then and I am still right now with that sentence." He continues: "We have no seat around the table of the Security Council. Germany is not around the table, although it is the biggest economy in Europe. This is quite unbalanced. In military terms Europe is simply insignificant."

Dries Lesage, a Belgian scholar of globalisation, says there are two sets of dominating approaches used by world powers to deal with the rest. One is used by the West, which for nearly 500 years has had a mentality of "ruling the world", sometimes through military intervention. The other approach is by China, which implements a win-win strategy to win "hearts and minds" in many countries. "But the mentality of the West for ruling the world should come to an end after predominating for 500 years," says Lesage, Director of

184

the Ghent Institute for International Studies at Belgium's Ghent University.

"This is because materially the West's economic and military weight cannot sustain that way any more." Nowadays many of the world's troubles are still rooted in the West's old mentality, says Lesage, an authoritative voice in Belgium on global governance and its architecture, international tax policy and multipolarity. Arguing from both historic and present lessons, Lesage also urges the European Union to keep its distance from American foreign policy and shape its own vision. He believes China has set an excellent example in forming a sound relationship with every partner in this multi-polar world. "The EU should not join the United States in its own vision of ruling the the world any more," says during a lunch interview with *China Daily* beside the EU headquarters before heading for an important consultation meeting organised by the Belgian government.

For the last five centuries, the West has been using this vision of ruling and many times it realised its goal by using military means. For example, Lesage says, the United States and NATO still use that approach, which originated from the age of colonialism and has lasted through the end of the Cold War era. China suffered from this vision of Western dominance in the 1800s and 1900s in various military attacks by the Western powers, according to Lesage. What's more, many problems nowadays in Africa and the Eurasian continent have resulted from this lasting Western mentality of the West, he says.

On the other hand, he regards China's rising global leadership as a big development on the international stage right now. Elaborating on this observation, Lesage says that China has become more assertive internationally in terms of expansion of influence, but he sees the development as not only in China's interests but also those of its partner countries in the world. This development has evolved faster, while Donald Trump's administration announced its intention of withdrawing from the Paris Agreement and the Trans-Pacific Partnership. "China now is similar, to some extent, to the United States in the first decade after World War II," says Lesage.

The United States started in 1944 to establish the Bretton Woods system and the United Nations, which are still the basic structures of the multilateral system from which the United States has benefited. In terms of weight and clout, China is now taking more responsibility in the world, as shown by its protection of the Paris Agreement, an open economy and free trade.

So he believes that what will happen in the next months and years is fascinating. Therefore, he insists, the European Union should reshape its vision of foreign policy by responding to the evolving global situation, though so far there is no European consensus about this. But his "personal and subjective EU vision", says Lesage, is that the world must be multi-polar while the Western identity, which includes those across the Atlantic, still exists but is just one part of this multi-polar world. Furthermore, he says, his EU vision must showcase inclusiveness, which means each player accepts the others. They must all recognise diversity and pluralism and must show willingness to engage. In further elaboration, he says mutual respect and equality are the essence of the international system and they can help expand cooperation and discussion; meanwhile, the interests and values of every player have to be reconciled with good ways and show respect for such multi-polar relationships. "Europe must know who are the new players now, and for the years ahead," says Lesage.

In dealing with relationships with the great powers, he stresses that a relationship with Russia cannot be "this bad" after EU sanctions against Russia lasted for months after the Ukraine crisis. "Europe should not continue confrontation with Russia," says Lesage. And he continues to map the essence of his EU vision, which also features a win-win, balanced and equal footing for everybody. In this way, Europe must understand that protecting your interests does not necessarily mean it being a zero sum game. Asked if the EU has begun to think about this new vision, he responds: "I see the elements of it. But I don't see it as something fully formed. Now what dominates is still the old mentality."

And he warns that such a change of vision will move very slowly at the European level. However, he says, now China is a leader in supporting an open economy and free trade, and advocating cooperation and mutual development. So in dealing with China, the EU vision he has formulated should be implemented by European institutions. "These should be the EU's visions in dealing with its relationship with China as well," says Lesage.

He says China and the EU have shared the same language in pursuing sustainable development and in maintaining their commitment to the Paris Climate Change Agreement. What has impressed him is the linkage of the G20 agenda and the UN's 2030 Sustainable Development Goals (SDGs).

In his opinion, the SDGs, addressing a lot of pressing planetary issues environmentally, socially, economically, and politically, have offered part of the solution to the global crises emerging right now. He says the SDGs were agreed in a very difficult atmosphere in September 2015, amid the unfolding Syrian war and the Ukraine crisis. But he sees them as a big achievement diplomatically. The G20 leaders endorsed the document again at the G20 summit in Hangzhou in 2016, several G20 policies have been attached to the UN's 2030 sustainability agenda, and so governments will be putting the goals into the centre of policy-making. "The SDGs are not being marginalised, thanks to China's G20 presidency. Continuation is one characteristic of the G20, and this should be kept from one presidency to another," he says.

Based on his observations, China has become proactive in solving regional conflicts, for which China owns "legitimacy" to become a broker to offer diplomatic solutions by taking advantage of its neutral stance. This has been shown in Syria, Yemen, the Persian Gulf regions, Iraq, Afghanistan and elsewhere. "China is different from the West and other powers, which have really made a mess of it," says Lesage. "China is not involved. China can be a respected party in terms of legitimacy. Such leadership is found in mediating."Lesage also says China is not only becoming a broker in conflict zones but also offers solutions on the ground. The example he gives is that China focuses on business, cooperation, development, building infrastructure, and creating win-win situations by implementing the Belt and Road Initiative in Afghanistan. "This can be an interesting approach, which has won the hearts and minds of Afghans. And it is also a way to isolate extremists through business development and cooperation," says Lesage. However, he says NATO moved into Afghanistan in 2001, but after 16 years the country is still not stable, because of military involvement. Regarding EU-China relations, however, he says Europe is "confused and divided" towards China, with some criticising it and some taking it as an opportunity. Now the European Commission's proposal to beef up screening on investment, especially from China, and its unbending attitudes, pushing China to reduce its steel and iron production capacity, have caused confrontations, though the two sides are in a so-called strategic partnership.

In such a situation, China will be easily annoyed. "When a friend criticises you, you are more willing to listen. When an enemy criticises you,

you will just ignore it," says Lesage. "Europe is struggling with this kind of situation in terms of its relationship with China." Regarding the ongoing investment protection discussion against Europe's strategic sectors, he says: "This is a strange discussion." He believes that, at national level, EU members can already protect these sectors. He says the EU has also been confronting China on human rights, democracy and even over the market economy status, which has caused much ambivalence. To his disappointment, from the EU side, the visions of the Brussels-Beijing strategic partnership are not there, and fundamental sentiments and feelings are going in the other direction. Lesage says the EU should become open to the Belt and Road Initiative because the Chinese vision is not only about business and investment: it also includes cooperation and bridge-building. "The EU needs to form visions to engage China consistently, by factoring into new development," says Lesage, who is hugely concerned. "But now, everything except sustainable development is not going in the right direction."

Former Australian Prime Minister Kevin Rudd says China's widely talked-of economic "new normal" is helping reshape the way the country will grow and the Belt and Road Initiative will speed up that process. Rudd, a fluent Mandarin speaker, has met me at the World Economic Forum in Davos every year since 2011.

His optimism is based on two things. One is the nature of the Chinese leadership's decision to press on with economic reform, including giving the market a "decisive role". The second is that those who are driving these policies are highly intelligent and know what they are doing. Significant decisions have already been made, in particular those relating to financial markets and foreign investment liberalisation, he says. Decisions made in the Third Plenary Session of the Central Committee of the Communist Party of China in 2013 were the first clear statement that the market would be regarded as decisive in determining other economic policy. "That's new. Apart from this, saying the market plays a 'decisive' role is not the same as saying it plays a 'significant' role, is it? That's a fundamental philosophical shift. That's why traditional intervention by way of planning or public investment does not easily fit under the term 'new normals'."

Rudd says he has closely watched China's development under Xi Jinping's leadership and has read English and Chinese versions of Xi's new collection on *Governing China*. Of the so-called new normal, which has been widely debated, Rudd says: "In China, the thing about old models is that they eventually need to be retired, and the feeling is that 'new models' need to replace them. So part of this new normal is the new model itself, and the new normal is obviously that the new driver for growth is private consumption."

China's Silk Road Initiative is about expanding connectivity, Rudd says. "The idea is an extension of the ASEAN idea, and I think it's a good idea to link through rail, port, digital." The big challenge that China faces with the Silk Road initiative is communicating the idea, he says.

I agreed with Rudd on that point. To boost China's connections with other regions, a simpler, more direct name is needed. The extent to which China is understood by the world depends partly on the quality of translation of the complicated Chinese language into foreign language. But such work is always challenging, especially when translating the full meaning of simplified buzzwords and phrases into English. An example is President Xi's initiative to connect Asia and Europe by borrowing the concept of the historic Silk Road.

With these proposals being disseminated, understood and even partly made into reality by China and other countries, his team has condensed the two proposals into one expression, which is the One Belt and One Road Initiatives (in Chinese, literally *yi dai yi lu*). Xi made public his Silk Road Economic Belt initiative shortly after the G20 summit in Russia in 2013, which I covered. China's efforts and joint contribution with emerging economies to deepen reform of the global financial system and establish the BRICS bank at the summit had already impressed me. But I also came away impressed by Xi's Silk Road idea because it shows China's growing awareness of its need to shoulder more international responsibility.

When Xi publicised his Maritime Silk Road proposal, the new Chinese leadership's proactive and strategic thinking at the regional and global level awed me. For years, the world has needed such global solutions to help sustain the economy. But very soon, I realized it would be a difficult job to deliver such beautiful ideas to foreigners in their own language.

Rudd frankly told me that he too thinks China will have a "communication challenge" explaining the strategic proposal to the rest of the world. Rudd, who speaks Chinese fluently, says the concept is very clear, and what China is trying to do is to expand connectivity.

Saying he supports the efforts in infrastructure construction and financial injections by setting up a Silk Road fund, Rudd says the challenge for China is not so much the content of the proposal, but the communication of it. If you translate *yi dai yi lu*, or One Belt and One Road, directly into English, the challenge becomes clear, he says. It is an understandable concept in the Chinese framework, but when you use "belt" in English, people have to wonder what that's got to do with connectivity, apart from keeping your trousers on, he explains. Rudd has his own solution. He says China should call it a "pan-Asian connectivity agenda". However, I doubt the effectiveness of Rudd's solution among Europeans, who have been relatively slow in accepting these proposals. For a long time Europeans, especially those in Western Europe, have had such a sense of superiority that it is hard for them to accept a pan-Asian idea, even though they badly need a way out of their economic stagnation.

I also discussed the communication challenge with Justin Lin, former World Bank chief economist and professor at Peking University, who says he thinks Africa will certainly be included in the Belt and Road Initiative. This shows the difficulties Kevin Rudd identifies. I asked about his thoughts on the English expression of Xi's proposals. Thinking for a while, Lin, now also a top adviser for China's leadership, says the expression "One Belt and One Road Initiative" can be used. He believes that people will gradually come to understand and accept it. But I am not convinced.

Such an expression is simply a word-for-word translation of a condensed Chinese expression, which includes two proposals. In using this translation many shades of meaning have been lost and even the commonly accepted, beautiful and peaceful idea of the Silk Road has dropped away. So, in my understanding, when naming such combined proposals in English, we should abandon attempts to do so by translating them word for word. If we are not tied to this rule, the options are many. For example, we could name it the Modern Silk Road. Or, if we're focusing on connectivity and infrastructure construction to connect the three continents, it could be called the Asia-Africa-Europe Infrastructure Plan. But, of course, these ideas were first proposed by Xi, who has accumulated a huge amount of trust and respect as a result of his capable and strategic governance in reform, rule of law, fighting against corruption and diplomacy.

The Silk Road proposals contain immensely significant economic and peaceful connotations for the three continents if they are more closely connected by rail, road, sea and digital means. So I suggest that the English expression for the One Belt and One Road Initiative should be simply Xi's Deal. Why not? All these thoughts emerged after it was officially nailed down recently as the Belt and Road Initiative.

BELT AND ROAD INITIATIVE FORUM IN EUROPE

To become effectively integrated into such a huge project, the European Union should consider hosting an urgent conference to follow up on the Belt and Road Forum for International Cooperation, a senior China expert advised ahead of the event, which was held in Beijing between 14-15 May 2017.

"It is an excellent idea for the European Union to catch up, as I believe the Belt and Road Initiative contains a very important part, which is Europe," Jochum Haakma, chairman of the Brussels-based EU-China Business Association, says before the meeting. Haakma, a Dutchman, worked in Hong Kong and Shanghai for nine years as a diplomat, and he still considers helping to connect China and Europe his mission at the association.

But he has realised that there is a contrast between Europe and Asia over understanding the significance of the Belt and Road Initiative, which aims to connect Asia, Europe and Africa by improving the flow of goods, human resources, capital and other elements of productivity. Even against a backdrop of protectionism and isolationism, some countries in the Americas have agreed to join the Belt and Road framework, and Washington has reportedly shown interest in it recently.

Up to 30 state leaders, including 11 from Europe, confirmed that they would attend the Beijing forum. However, Haakma says it became very clear that Asian countries were much more aligned than European, thinking much more strategically and also practically, and learning how to follow up with the Belt and Road Initiative. Europe is less involved and not really practically doing anything, and so I agree that the next big Belt and Road Initiative forum should be organised in Brussels, says Haakma.

He went so far as to say that this should be an urgent follow-up step, which should be organised in Brussels within six months, which would be a very straightforward step. He says the European Union should demonstrate its awareness and also show the political willingness to work together with China to set up working groups to follow up on the Initiative. But he says that the EU still lacked awareness of the significance of the Initiative, mainly because within it there would always be opposition because some members feared China's growing investment activities on the continent. Many entrepreneurs and bankers in Europe had seen how important it was to work together, he added. "I think this awareness, realising the importance of China's investment in Europe, has been gathering because of Brexit and (US President) Donald Trump's taking office in the White House," says Haakma.

So the time was right for the European Union to wake up and work closely with China, he added. For entrepreneurs, it was like "heaven" to be integrated in such a big project, because it had a lifecycle of at least three to four decades in improving the world's infrastructure conditions, he says. Against the rise of populism and right-wing political forces in Europe, Haakma says it was very important for Europe to stay together. Even in its relationship with China, Europe as a strong entity working together economically and politically would be a much better counterpart for China to deal with, he says.

Between China and the European Union, Haakma says the hot topics are comprehensive investment agreements, and sometimes both sides have discussed the possibility of launching free trade negotiations. But Brussels has not mentioned the Belt and Road Initiative very often, says Haakma, adding that it was a really important and huge infrastructure project, and describing it as the world's biggest ever.

"The other side of the Belt and Road Initiative is Europe. And I think if you add Europe in this fashion, you are a much better counterpart to China. You can do much more together," he says. Haakma has urged Europeans to come forward with plans to work together with the Chinese government to design projects via the AIIB, of which many European countries had become members. He says he would be delighted if one of the outcomes of the forum in Beijing was to set up a Belt and Road Initiative technology fund. To achieve this, the first important thing was that the right players would be there at the forum. Then they could sit together and form a few working groups to kick off, he says.

Pierre Defraigne is another candid and veteran China hand in Brussels. He says the EU must develop its own vision and capabilities within the triangular relationship involving itself, Beijing and Washington, instead of merely following in the footsteps of the United States. He sent this "last chance" message to Brussels, saying it was vital that the EU listened if it was to maximise its potential in the evolving global system and to be on better terms with Beijing.

"What we need is the capacity of the EU to coordinate its general strategy with China and the US," says Defraigne, the executive director of the Brussels-based think tank Madariaga—College of Europe Foundation. Defraigne, an old friend of mine, with whom I had a long talk in late 2016 from his home in Brussels, is among the city's most frequent speakers at seminars and debates. He hopes to trigger quality debates about European integration and Beijing-Brussels relations—ideas that grew out of his work over many decades as one of the EU's senior civil servants. Defraigne, who has been in his think tank role since 2008, believes Brussels has lost its way in its dealings with Beijing, as Europe has focused on dealing with the challenges of mass migration, terrorism, rising unemployment and Brexit.

Sitting on a sofa, surrounded by books in his quiet study decorated with Chinese art, he says relations between China and most EU members are vibrant in terms of trade, investment, tourism, education and cultural exchanges. And many European state leaders have forged closer personal relationships with their Chinese counterparts, Xi Jinping and Li Keqiang, as they have deepened strategic cooperation. "But when they are together (as the European Union), they want the EU to be tough with China," Defraigne says. "I think they are playing a double game, and it puts the EU in an extremely uncomfortable position because of this lack of unity."

He says the stance freezes the Brussels-Beijing relationship and means difficulties cannot be solved. As a veteran official who has worked as a cabinet head for two European commissioners, Defraigne says the EU's poor interaction with China is not the result of its wanting to cause offence, but a reflection of its being "helpless" to unite its members. And in the absence of a united front, the EU has relied heavily upon Washington in formulating its stance toward Beijing. He says this means the EU is no longer a separate entity.

"It is EU-American leadership," he contends. There are many examples of the EU's inability to make the decisions needed to move the Brussels-Beijing relationship forward. For years, Brussels has failed to lift an arms embargo against Beijing. It has also failed to grant market economy status to China, which is now the world's second-biggest economy. He says it seems as if Brussels is not ready to fulfil the commitments it agreed to when Beijing was admitted to the WTO, something Defraigne was closely involved in while working as cabinet head for Trade Commissioner Pascal Lamy.

Defraigne believes the fact that Brussels takes its lead from Washington means it is not able to make "seemingly strategic decisions". Currently, the EU says a stronger relationship with Washington is high on its agenda. The European Commission's website puts the EU-US partnership among its top 10 priorities.

But Defraigne says Brussels must reprioritise. "I am quite optimistic that Brussels will adjust its mindset," he says. "Now, Brussels needs to take action in pushing forward the triangular relationship of China, the EU and US, under the framework of global governance reform." He suggests the construction of a new platform for dialogue. "Ideally, this should be a submechanism under the G20 where leaders can meet," Defraigne says. He believes such a mechanism would help Brussels better position itself in the changing global system and urges both the EU and US to note what is happening with China, at home and abroad. He says China has done well in implementing structural reforms since the 2008-2009 financial crisis that originated on Wall Street, something that led him to call for the reform of the models of capitalism. But he says the United States has found it extremely difficult to implement such changes because of political reasons, market forces, lobbyists and global companies that have overwhelmed the political system.

"I don't think the EU is under pressure to the same extent as New York and Washington, but our firms are as big and powerful as the American ones," Defraigne says. "But the key point is there: politics must take over from the markets. When you have broken the system, you have to change the system. This is what China is doing." He says the United States and Europe should also follow China's lead in domestic reforms and accumulating public-sector wealth, which is crucial for those on the lower rungs of the social ladder.

Internationally, Defraigne says, it is encouraging that Beijing is taking the lead on issues, especially in pushing the Paris Climate Change Agreement into effect, which happened on 4 November 2016. China is on the way to achieving changes in its economic growth pattern toward green competitiveness, which will positively influence global engagement on sustainable development, he says.

But he believes some forces in the US are hesitant to implement the obligations taken on by President Barack Obama. Defraigne believes China's active role in pushing the Paris Agreement forward is as important as its joining the WTO 15 years ago, when it was an existing structure built up by the West for its own benefit. "Now, China is among the founding actors of this new branch, whose impact has become more and more important," he says. "For me, China's joining the Paris Agreement is a good move for the future and the world."

And China is actively engaging in many other ways. It has fairly completed its mandate as a member of the WTO and proven to be a faithful member. Its RMB currency has now joined the basket of currencies in the Special Drawing Rights category of the International Monetary Fund. "And, in addition to the Paris Agreement engagement, I personally think China is on the right track," he says. "We have to enjoy that development and now be up to the challenges." As for the US, Defraigne says the future should be about changing its attitude and becoming more proactive, while for Europe it should be about achieving unity. "The unity of Europe is a huge problem for the stability of the world economy today. It is the most serious challenge for this union and the prosperity of the world," he says. "Our vision of ourselves is always developing to be a main actor in multilateralism and cooperation but if we are not able to achieve unity, the EU will become a threat to the world economically."

For years, Defraigne has been a close China watcher and has read many books on the country. He has tried to understand its history and believes it is important to know the full development of politics in China because it is a unique system. In China, because of the Confucian tradition, many families have a sense of belonging, which is more important than markets and technology, he says. "When I observe the actions of the Chinese people, they are actively defending their interests. They are not passive citizens but active citizens. If the government can capture the demands of Chinese citizens and China's long civilisation, it will have a better future."

Chi Fulin, President of the China Institute of Reform and Development, shares Defraigne's opinion and welcomes his proposals. In the last five years, Chi has travelled to Brussels at least ten times to participate in dialogues with thinktanks and EU institutions. "We felt it was workable, discussing general topics about China, but it was really hard to deeply explore issues with our European counterparts, and especially with officials," says Chi. "Defraigne's proposal is visionary and Brussels should give it immediate consideration." Chi says both China and the EU should consider developing additional projects to expand exchanges within academia and thinktanks. "Both sides need to make this a priority, to bridge the understanding gap between the two powers," says Chi.

Recently, he has been pushing the idea that the European Union should reconsider its China policy and reset its priority portfolio by starting bilateral free-trade talks urgently, allowing both sides to make a strong commitment to globalisation. Following Premier Li Keqiang's recent call for a feasibility study on bilateral free-trade talks, experts says such actions were essential in cushioning the rising negative impacts of a string of global challenges. "Against the fast-changing global environment, the European Union must accelerate its steps to reconsider its priorities in dealing with China," says Chi. "I believe one pressing priority should be EU-China free-trade negotiations, which the EU has already started or concluded with several Asian partners."

Chi says the wide global recognition of the Belt and Road Initiative, which is mainly aimed at better connecting Asia, Europe, and Africa, should work as a "new trigger" for the EU to reset its economic and trade policy portfolio as it relates to China, with China proposing a wide "free-trade network" that would connect all countries participating in the Belt and Road Initiative, which should also be in the interest of the EU, which is a global forerunner and champion of free trade and globalisation. "So, logically, the EU, of which many member states have been passionate about participating in the Belt and Road Initiative, should engage with China in launching freetrade feasibility studies as soon as possible," says Chi. I had numerous talks with Chi over the past years. Now, he says, China's domestic changes can have impacts on

EU policy, which the European side must take seriously to stimulate two-way exchanges.

In addition to Chi, my talks with two of China's leading professors, Justin Yifu Lin and Xue Lan, were also meaningful. Lin, former Chief Economist of the World Bank, acquired a new position at the end of April 2016 when he became the inaugural Dean of the South-South Cooperation and Development Institute of Peking University. In September that year, enrolled students from developing countries were able to study the experiences and lessons of China's development in previous decades.

Lin, who became passionate about using China's experiences to spark African economies during his four-year stint at the World Bank, says the inauguration of the institute was a milestone event, as it would begin the systematic sharing of China's development and institutional experience. In fact, Tsinghua University, just a few blocks away from Peking University, has already begun this. Led by Xue Lan, Dean of the School of Public Policy and Management, the university launched a master's programme in international development several years ago, mainly focusing on offering outstanding students from the developing world chances to explore China's recipes for development.

Such initiatives are also designed to offer support for less-developed countries to bring about their own miracles. It is also worth mentioning that many renowned high-level officials and academic leaders in China graduated from universities in the United States, the United Kingdom, Germany and other Western countries in the 1980s and early 1990s. They well know how to blend the knowledge they acquired in the West into China's development realities.

So teaching such skills to students from developing countries would probably be the core of the curricula in the programmes offered by Peking and Tsinghua universities. Over the years, nearly all the renowned business schools in the US, the UK, France, Switzerland and many other countries have launched programmes in China, while Chinese students and executives in their hundreds of thousands have flown overseas to further their business education. But now the business management schools of China's universities have also become more competitive. And some of them have started to take small steps towards enrolling students overseas. Just as China has shaped a great development legacy on the policy front, so its business persons have also gained tremendous experience in building up various-scale business empires starting from scratch. Considering the massive demand for such knowledge from developing countries, the next step might be to develop an independent university for South-South cooperation and international development. With its headquarters in Beijing, it could set up branches in Africa and other developing countries. China's leading business schools could also consider the opportunities in Africa and other developing regions when designing their strategies.

One night in May 1979, as China was launching its reform and opening-up drive, a young soldier from Taiwan is said to have braved the Taiwan Straits by swimming from the outlying island of Quemoy to the mainland using basketballs as a floatation device. Justin Yifu Lin went on to gain a master's degree in political economics at Peking University, and then a doctorate in economics at the University of Chicago. He gained global prominence, once serving as the World Bank's chief economist.

While he sharpened his free market thinking, he tailored it to the Chinese vision of the balanced roles of the government and the market's invisible hand. Partly because of the contributions of scholars such as Lin, China has achieved more than three decades of rapid growth. And he believes that with some adjustments, the country still has the potential to sustain the miracle for another 20 years.

Lin also believes that China's successful experience and development patterns can be copied by economies that are still catching up, especially those in Africa. He has encouraged Ethiopian leaders to take that path, and Chinese leather and shoemaking plants have started to shift to Ethiopia, which is primed for an economic takeoff. His thoughts on the economics of development show an independent streak, reflected in his 25 books, with titles such as *Against the Consensus: Reflections on the Great Recession*. Lin, an adviser to the Chinese government and professor at Peking University, is the Chinese economist most widely recognised in the West. He is the founding director of the China Center for Economic Research at Peking University.

Lin spoke at length on why he thinks China can achieve long-term economic growth, the gap between China and developed economies, China's costs and potential, and the global significance of China's success. In talking with me, Lin says he was quite confident China has the potential to maintain an annual growth rate of 8 percent for the next 20 years if its deepening of domestic reforms are successful and if global conditions allow. "What I mean is the potential, and I must emphasise that," Lin says. In 2008, China's per capita income was 21% that of the United States as measured in purchasing power parity, which indicates that there is still a large technological gap between China and advanced economies, he says. "So China can continue to enjoy the advantages of backwardness before closing the gap." China is faced with an economic downturn while it has begun to shift its economic engines from relying on investment and trade to being driven by consumption. During the process of shifting economic development patterns, Lin says, China has to come to terms with three major challenges: income disparity, corruption, and environmental pollution. The first two challenges have made ordinary Chinese "unhappy", and if the environment worsens, neither rich nor poor will feel happy, he says. "So we must come to terms with such challenges."

Lin says the world's poor, especially in Africa, missed many development opportunities during colonial rule by the West. They deserve a better life, he says. During his term as the World Bank's chief economist, from 2008 to 2012, he devoted a lot of time to visiting Africa. While he was the first Asian to occupy his position, he once said, "More importantly, I may be the first World Bank chief economist who understands the needs of developing countries." Among the development lessons he says African countries can learn from China, he cites the dual-track approach to reform, offering transitory protection to non-viable firms to maintain stability while liberalising the sectors in which the country has comparative advantages. He refers to the Ethiopian leadership's decisions in 2011 and 2012, which led to a shift of China's shoemaking and other plants to Ethiopia. Now shoes made in Ethiopia have been exported to other African countries and to Europe. "The Ethiopian case has shown how China, Africa and Europe can form a relationship of trilateral cooperation," Lin says.

In shifting some manufacturing to Africa, which has plenty of labour and resources, China and Europe also benefit by offering technology, know-how, capital and export markets, he says.

Lin is concerned about Europe, which is still at risk of slipping into a third recession since the 2007-2008 global economic turmoil, which would cut

China's exports and investment in the continent.

"The risk cannot be removed right now as the European Union, (especially in the eurozone), has not come up with the necessary structural reforms to improve its competitiveness."

To help the global economy grow faster, Lin says it is important for the major economies to consider a "grand plan of infrastructure construction" to shake off economic stagnation and crisis. Europe still has room to improve its infrastructure, and such measures would boost its exports of technology and products, Lin says. China plans to become "better connected" with other countries and is encouraging several African countries to build roads, railways and airports with capital and technical inputs. "Such measures can help dispel fears that the euro and dollar will competitively depreciate and also help the world stave off economic stagnation," Lin says.

As an environmental adviser to Britain's Prince Philip, 62-year-old Martin Palmer notes that Queen Elizabeth, who has already celebrated her 90th birthday, has reigned longer than he has been alive.

It's that longevity that has allowed Palmer, who is also a sinologist, to help interpret the richness of Chinese cultures for the British royal family for three decades.

Palmer meets Philip, who is 96, three or four times a year and talks with the queen once every two or three years. Taoism, Confucianism, and the introduction of Chinese values in dealing with challenges of environmental protection and global warming are among their talking points.

"I think the interesting thing about the royal family and in particular about the queen is primarily longevity, a prime Chinese value," says Palmer, Secretary-General of the Alliance of Religions and Conservation, a UK-based environmental organisation founded by Prince Philip.

Palmer says Taoists spent hundreds of years trying to work out magic formulas with herbs and other elements to achieve longevity, and adds: "Our queen seems to have done it by her own free will."

For the queen's 90th birthday, celebrated (as always, according to tradition) twice this year, he links longevity to Chinese values. He credits, first, "a tremendous sense of duty, which in her case is very much founded upon filial duty—a great Confucian virtue". In Chinese tradition, everybody must honour their parents, and she "absolutely adored her father and he was her hero".

Palmer has been working with the Taoists of China for years, and Prince Philip and Queen Elizabeth have both shown enormous interest in Taoism, Palmer says, ever since he took Taoist masters to Buckingham Palace and Windsor Castle.

"They have always wanted to know more," he says.

The royal couple asked how religion shaped China, and what were the traditions of meditation and the core philosophical concepts of heaven, earth and humanity.

Palmer recalls that the queen also asked why there were no wars between Chinese religions, intrigued how the different traditions of Taoism, Buddhism and Confucianism worked side by side in China.

Palmer once took a senior Taoist master, the 65th direct descendant of Zhang Daoling—a venerated Taoist—to meet the Queen and Prince Philip, who were fascinated to know someone who could trace their family back even further than the queen could. Her roots date back to around AD 700, while Zhang's go back to the second century.

In 1985, Palmer met the royal family for the first time when he was invited to talk to Prince Philip, who at that time was the international president of the World Wildlife Fund. Palmer had written a book for the WWF, looking at how different religions viewed the natural world, depending on what they believed about its origins.

Palmer was following the same cultural path as President Xi Jinping did in his speech to UNESCO in March 2014, when he visited France. He called Xi's speech one of the most interesting speeches by a Chinese President in recent years.

According to Palmer, Xi spoke powerfully about China's cultures, traditions and civilisations, and thought they should be part of a recipe to bring China out of the dilemmas it faces.

"China is at that tipping point. I mean you have got some of the polluted cities, but now you know it and you are also saying, 'Well, it is not just a problem for us, it is a problem for the planet'," Palmer says. "And I think you are stepping up to the mark, it is taking responsibility as we had to take responsibility."

Palmer says "the ecological civilisation", a phrase often used in Chinese policy, is a fascinating expression that he first came across in 2006 when he was working with the Taoists in China on protecting their sacred mountains and on their moral and spiritual influence on China, which he has been doing since 1995.

This is a concept, he says, which reflects the notion that the Chinese have begun to care not just for themselves, but also for people who are less fortunate than they are, and for the forests, the rivers and the fish, after the rapid development of the past three decades.

"These had been shown in the Chinese classics for thousands of years, and this is a rediscovery of Chinese civilisation, because it could shape how we live," Palmer says. "And so I've watched over what is now 10 years, this rediscovery, re-evaluation of the best of cultural tradition."

The old Confucian phrase of benevolence, or *renli*, is rooted in what it is to be a good human being, he says. "So when ecological civilisation came along, for me, I could trace its history."

Palmer says the idea of having phases of ecological civilisation—which has become one of the overriding developmental components of the Communist Party of China since 2012—should be given global recognition.

Now one of the problems is that the West has so devalued its own notion of civilisation that it doesn't quite get it when a country says it wants civilisation, he thinks.

"This is China's great gift, that we can have an ecological civilisation, which will come into being. So I think that the significance of ecological civilisation is that it is a profound challenge to a Western, materialistic world," says Palmer.

For years, he has translated Buddhist, Taoist and Confucian texts into English.

"I'm translating at the moment the *Sanguo, The Romance of the Three Kingdoms*, and the wisdom that is embedded in those texts and stories, that's what I understand by civilisation," he says.

Palmer says he is in talks with different organisations in China, including the Party's cultural and communication units, about making a six-part TV series tied to the Silk Road. It would look at the way ideas, stories, beliefs, religions and philosophies travelled back and forth along the Road and shaped the great religions of the world.

"The China side is very excited by this. I suppose they don't meet many Westerners who know as many stories from Chinese history as I do," he says.

For years, as a Christian, Palmer has led a simple life, and also has benefitted from Chinese wisdom, which is about enjoying what one can legitimately enjoy, as written in the ancient Chinese classics.

"For me, it is about enjoying the good things in this life," Palmer says, "but making sure that that is not at the cost of anyone else or at the cost of creation."

INNOVATIVE WAYS OF CONNECTIVITY ON THE SILK ROAD

Nearly one year after President Xi's Belt and Road Initiative, in 2014, two young Dutchmen drove along the Silk Road. For a long time, the Chinese middle class and young professionals have dressed in European clothes, wearing European leather shoes, strapping on European watches and driving European cars as essentials of a trendy lifestyle. Turning that logic on its head, the two young Dutchmen challenged the perception that Chinese brands are not worthy of top-tier consideration by taking a 20,000 km, three-month journey, during which they used only Chinese products.

On their 11-country Silk Road pilgrimage from Shanghai to their home town of Rotterdam, urban planner Maren Striker, 29, and marketer Rogier Bikker, 27, drove a Chinese car, used Chinese mobile phones, dressed in Chinese clothes down to their underwear and, of course, wore Chinese sunglasses. They dubbed their journey "Brand New China." On the day they wrapped up their 98-day journey on 31 October, they were welcomed by the Chinese auto company BYD, the Rotterdam government and their families. "We are extremely happy finishing this adventure with the support of Chinese brands," Striker says. "We have proven that China is not just a global factory." They say that after their BYD car was hit by another vehicle on Iran's bumpy roads, it proved the car's toughness.

"We finally drove it home safely," Striker says when they arrived. The car was adorned with the names of all the sponsors whose products the two young men had used, and a map of their journey's route. It attracted quite a bit of attention from passers-by when it arrived in front of Rotterdam city hall, with bags of clothes and daily necessities heaped in the back seat.

In addition to BYD providing a car, Huawei provided mobile phones and Lenovo equipped them with laptops. They shot pictures with a Chinese camera. "We even bought packs of underwear in China to use along the way, though the brand is not on our sponsorship list," says Striker. They divided their journey into three parts: a month in China, another elsewhere in Asia, and a month in Europe. They say they met remarkable Chinese people in each of the 11 countries they travelled in. Their journey along the old Silk Road took them through beautiful landscapes, vibrant cultures, bustling towns and a whole lot of nothingness.

Before the trip, Striker had spent seven years in China working for an urban planning company and had visited 31 Chinese provinces. Bikker had worked in marketing strategy at a Shanghai company. He previously attracted notice in 2010 by travelling in 10 Chinese provinces in 10 days. The pair say they witnessed China changing from being the factory of the world to a place where people designed innovative products in new types of companies. In 2010, Bikker did a road trip through China with a friend, passing factories, crossing mountains and sleeping in the car for two weeks.

"This epic trip could only be surpassed by leaving the borders of China. And so the idea for a drive back to Holland originated while driving on the dusty roads of rural Shaanxi province," says Bikker. "But upon our return, friends and family regarded the idea as too crazy to happen, so the dream remained just that: a dream." Striker was also contemplating adventure. He had thought of walking the Great Wall, cycling back to the Netherlands or following the Yangtze River from its source to the sea. Two years later, they met in a Shanghai bar and shared their dreams. They then quit their jobs, leaving their girlfriends for three months, and spending the small savings they had on their idea.

By the autumn of 2013, the plan was taking shape. They signed up sponsors, contacted the media, arranged car documentation, obtained visas and found Chinese people living abroad to visit. "The more time we spent on the project, the more we realised the huge potential of it. So we hired great

Chinese team members to help out," Striker says. He remembers that they
called or e-mailed nearly all Chinese auto brands authorised to operate on
European roads. But the car companies hesitated until just before Christmas
2013, when one of their e-mails was forwarded to the marketing director of
BYD, which, appropriately, stands for Build Your Dreams. "We met them
at the BYD European headquarters at an industrial park on the outskirts of
Rotterdam on a cold day between Christmas and New Year's Day," Striker
says. Isbrand Ho, BYD Auto Europe's managing director, celebrated with
them on the day they reached Rotterdam. "I am delighted to see you both
here, safe and well," Ho says. "Your success has demonstrated the quality
and durability of BYD's products." When he heard they had been in a traffic
accident in Iran, Ho says, he was very anxious and even thought of halting
the trip, but they decided it would continue: "I thank them for so passionately
loving and promoting Chinese brands."

In another development, I am thrilled by an avalanche of comments, re-
postings and likes, within hours, on my newspaper's Weibo account (similar
to Facebook) after reporting that China's middle-aged actor Jin Dong had
been starring in a romantic TV series *Mr. Right* in Antwerp, a Belgian port,
in early August, 2017. Certainly, many nice words are due to Jin Dong, who
always plays a role as a model man and has won the hearts of millions of
Chinese ladies and girls of various ages. Indeed, my interview with Jin proved
that he deserves his popularity. Further reading of those postings will find
that Antwerp's beer, chocolate, diamonds, touch of fashion, historic port and
shopping streets have all attracted Chinese readers. All of a sudden, I realised
how magical a role a TV series and movie, through digital platforms, could
play to bring people in different countries closer nowadays.

And their role can be multiplied and speedily spread. In recent years,
Chinese TV producers have managed to produce a Chinese food series
for Belgian TV channels, which has stirred up much interest by similar
communication strategies. And Qian Xiuling (1912-2008), a Chinese-Belgian
heroine who saved up to 100 Belgians from death at the hands of the Nazis
during the Second World War, had also been brought into a TV series,
Chinese Woman Facing The Gestapo's Gun.

Belgium is not alone. From time to time London, Paris, Rome and other
cities are included in Chinese films and TV series. In central Europe, Prague

has also become an ideal place for the Chinese movie sector. The filming of the popular romantic drama, *Somewhere Only We Know*, which starred and was directed by award-winning actress Xu Jinglei, took place in Prague several years ago. According to the Chinese ambassador to the Czech Republic, Ma Keqing, the magnificent architecture and stunning natural features of this country have already been captured in the scenes of several Chinese movies in recent years, as both countries have tightened their relationship.

Behind China's interweaving relations with European countries, there are hidden tremendously meaningful topics to explore for both sides, with the aim of satisfying the growing demands of moviegoers and TV audiences in the digital era. Ranging from historic themes to present-day exchanges, war, love, heroes, family and and food, they are inexhaustible. If more stories reach the screen, such efforts will lead to a chain effect.

This is not only because the demand for movies and TV series in China is expanding rapidly. One dominating reality in China is that this country's middle class is also expanding rapidly, and its size will equal that of Europe's entire population within a few years. They have a huge appetite for entertainment and travel. When they are impressed by a movie, that prompts them to think about travel.

As an example, Chinese tourist numbers visiting the Czech Republic will soar tenfold to an estimated 500,000 this year. That is also why shopkeepers in Antwerp, not to mention the city's mayor, feel excited about the ongoing film and TV shooting, expecting that more Chinese will visit their city after the series goes out. In fact, this effect is starting to become obvious right now. Many visitors are asking which bars, chocolate shops, or diamond stores the shooting is taking place.

It is encouraging that Chinese producers and stars have taken action to respond to the need. Some Europeans too are beginning to recognise the potential. For example, Christos Vlachos, managing partner at Athens-based Silky Finance, has recently switched to invest in the film sector in China. Greece and China, birthplaces of two civilisations, are surely suitable to share in movie production. Many people say that two-way exchanges can be more efficient. When European producers and movie stars think of flocking to Beijing, Xi'an, modern Shanghai or Shenzhen, or even small but historic towns in China to shoot, China and Europe will be tied even closer.

Brussels' tiny Schumann Square, around which European Union institutions and embassies are nestled, may not be as famous as Beijing's Tiananmen Square, New York City's Times Square or Moscow's Red Square. But it has started drawing Chinese tourists, many of whom choose novel ways to reach it.

In mid-August of 2017, I happened to meet some kindergarten and primary school students and their mothers in the square. One of them shouted: "Look, a vehicle from China!"

What they seemed excited about was a "recreational" vehicle passing by slowly. In the vehicle were three painters from China, who were headed to Paris on the next leg of their cultural-exchange journey, after having met their Belgian peers.

Driving from Beijing, they were part of the Silk Road RV (recreational vehicle) cultural-exchange delegation, which was supported by Zhang Guozhong, a businessman-turned-museum curator, on his third journey to Europe. Coincidentally, the kids were also on a painting-themed visit to Belgium, the Netherlands and France.

I have encountered equally inspiring travellers in Brussels in recent years. In February 2015, I met Lai Likun and his companion Zhang Hui, university students from Beijing, who were in the middle of a global cycling tour that they had started in 2009. Now they are preparing for their African adventure.

That year, I also met a group of Chinese and Europeans driving across the Eurasian continent, linking the places where pandas are based. Using pandas as a medium, they aimed to consolidate their friendship and mutual understanding between Chinese and Europeans.

But if you thought only the young would be brave enough to take such odysseys, you'd be wrong. Last year, a retired Chinese couple from Beijing drove about 10,000 kilometers by car for around two months to meet their daughter in the EU capital. They spent six months preparing for the trip and applying for visas.

Home to about 80 countries, Eurasia is massive and has a rugged topography. From Beijing to Brussels, it takes about 10 hours by plane. But many people, such as the artists, the cyclists and the retired couple I met, are passionate enough to cover the distance by car, bicycle or sea, or even on foot.

They are eager to soak in the natural beauty of Eurasia and observe firsthand the diversity of languages and cultures. The retired couple could not speak any foreign language, but still they managed to drive all the way from Beijing to their daughter's house beside the EU headquarters. The artists, too, couldn't speak any language except Chinese, but they say "smiling faces" are the best goodwill sign in all corners of the planet.

Ten years ago, when I met a BBC journalist in Beijing, I was surprised to learn that he had chosen to travel by train from London to Beijing to take up his new posting. In those days, many used to say the difference between China and Europe was reflected in the number of metro lines in Beijing and Shanghai, on the one hand, and London and Paris, even Rome, on the other. It seems that difference no longer exists.

Thanks to China's economic rise, more and more Chinese are travelling to Europe to explore European societies, cultures and lifestyles. And even though most of them prefer to fly, some choose to take the land journey. Europe must be well prepared to receive them. And apart from taking measures to make Europe a safer place, EU leaders should also work with their Asian counterparts to facilitate more people-to-people exchanges, such as by simplifying visa application procedures.

Perhaps a group of a dozen or so countries along the Silk Road should start by considering the possibility of issuing a "Silk Road visa", similar to the EU's Schengen visa, which would be a groundbreaking move to increase travel between Asia and Europe.

The photos below are interviewees in this book and they are identified by their positions they held when interviews were done.

Branislav Djordjevic, Director of the Institute of International Politics and Economics in Belgrade

Dimitris Bourantonis, Deputy Director of Athens University of Economics and Business

Doris Leuthard, Swiss Federation President

Duan Jielong, Chinese ambassador to Hungary

Elena Kountoura, Greek Tourism Minister

Fu Chengqiu, General Manager of Piraeus Port Authority

Harro von Senger, a leading sinologist in Switzerland

Hu Kun, ZTE's Head of Operations in Western Europe

Jean-Pierre Raffarin, former French Prime Minister

Ivona Ladjevac, Coordinator of International Cooperation of the Institute of International Politics and Economics in Belgrade

Jan Kohout, former Minister of Foreign Affairs of the Czech Republic

Jaroslav Tvrdik, former Defense Minister of the Czech Republic

Jean-Pierre Lehmann, professor of International Political Economy of IMD

Ivica Dacic, Serbia's first Deputy Prime Minister and Foreign Minister

Jin Dong, famous Chinese actor

Jiri Paroubek, former Prime Minister of the Czech Republic

Jiri Rusnok, former Prime Minister of the Czech Republic

Jochum Haakma, chairman of the Brussels-based EU-China Business Association

Johann N. Schneider-Ammann, former Swiss Federation president

Jo Leinen, President of the European Parliament's Delegation for Relations with China

Juha Sipila, Prime Minister of Finland

Kyriakos Mitsotakis, honorary president of the New Democracy political party in Greece

Li Manchang, Chinese ambassador to Serbia

Ma Keqing, Chinese ambassador to the Czech Republic

Mark Eyskens, economist and former Belgian Prime Minister

Men Jing, professor of College of Europe in Belgium

Michael Schaefer, former German Ambassador to China

Milos Zeman, President of the Czech Republic

Peter Tamm, Director of the International Maritime Museum in Hamburg

Qu Xing, Chinese ambassador to Belgium

Radosav Pusic, Dean of the Confucius Institute in Belgrade

Romano Prodi, former Italian Prime Minister

Sauli Niinisto, President of Finland

Shi Mingde, Chinese ambassador to Germany

Shirly Karvinen, Miss Finland of Year 2016

Song Sihai, an executive board member of Hesteel Serbia

Stergios Pitsiorlas, Deputy Minister of Economy and Development in the Greek government

Suzana Li, Czech translator

Timo Ritakallio, President of the Finnish Olympic Committee

Vaclav Klaus, former President of the Czech Republic

Vladan Vukosavljevic, Serbian Culture Minister

Vojtech Filip, Deputy Chairman of the Chamber of Deputies of the Parliament of the Czech Republic

Xue Lan, Dean of the School of Public Policy and Management of Tsinghua University

Yang Yanyi, Chinese ambassador to the EU

Zhang Haiyan, Director of Confucius Business Institute of NEOMA Business School in France

Zou Xiaoli, Chinese ambassador to Greece